OCT 1 6 2015

D0779673

Words of Praise

"Bruce Dearstyne brings a fine narrative style and superb story-telling to *The Spirit of New York*. Readers will learn about New York politics, the state's role in racial conflict, recasting the role of women in New York, and far more. The book is about the people of New York responding individually and collectively to the opportunities, problems, and tragedies that have punctuated the history of the Empire State from its beginnings to the present."

— Warren Roberts, author of *A Place in History: Albany in the Age of Revolution, 1775–1825*

"This book offers a fascinating odyssey through New York's past by using examples of its national leadership, ranging from the state's early women's rights movements to Jackie Robinson's historic integration of major league baseball, and from aviation pioneer Glenn Curtis to the construction of a landmark super-highway, the New York State Thruway. Dearstyne presents fresh insight into several salient events that made New York the Empire State. In doing so, he comes as close to a recent general history of the state as currently exists."

— F. Daniel Larkin, State University of New York at Oneonta

The Spirit of New York

The Spirit of New York

Defining Events in the Empire State's History

BRUCE W. DEARSTYNE

Glenview Public Library
1930 Glenview Road
Glenview, Illinois

excelsior editions

State University of New York Press
Albany, New York

Published by State University of New York Press, Albany

© 2015 State University of New York

All rights reserved

Printed in the United States of America

No part of this book may be used or reproduced in any manner whatsoever without written permission. No part of this book may be stored in a retrieval system or transmitted in any form or by any means including electronic, electrostatic, magnetic tape, mechanical, photocopying, recording, or otherwise without the prior permission in writing of the publisher.

Excelsior Editions is an imprint of State University of New York Press

For information, contact State University of New York Press, Albany, NY
www.sunypress.edu

Production, Jenn Bennett
Marketing, Michael Campochiaro

Library of Congress Cataloging-in-Publication Data

Dearstyne, Bruce W. (Bruce William), 1944-
  The spirit of New York : defining events in the Empire State's history
/ Bruce W. Dearstyne.
    pages cm. — (Excelsior editions)
  Includes bibliographical references and index.
  ISBN 978-1-4384-5658-4 (pbk.) — ISBN 978-1-4384-5659-1 (e-book)
  1. New York (State)—History. I. Title.
  F116.D43 2015
  974.7—dc23
                            2014027594

10 9 8 7 6 5 4 3

Contents

ILLUSTRATIONS

Chapter 5. October 1, 1851: Striking a Blow for Freedom   87

Image from Jeremy Wesley Loguen's 1859 autobiography, *The Rev. J. W. Loguen, as a Slave and as a Freeman*, where he recounted his role as a leader in the rescue of fugitive slave William "Jerry" Henry.

Chapter 6. March 30, 1899: Pollution and Politics   109

Theodore Roosevelt and his family hiking near their home at Sagamore Hill, Long Island. Roosevelt enjoyed hiking and hunting and wanted to preserve the natural environment. But his record as governor on the issue of water pollution was mixed, presaging New York's ambivalent and inconsistent water pollution policy over the next half century.

Chapter 7. April 15, 1903: Intervening for the Children   131

Lillian Wald and Florence Kelley, tireless and highly effective advocates for child labor reform in New York.

Chapter 8. May 29, 1910: First in the Air   153

New York aviation pioneer Glenn Curtiss at the controls of his plane the *June Bug*, which made the first publically announced airplane flight on July 4, 1908, in Hammondsport, two years before Curtiss's pioneering flight from Albany to New York City.

Chapter 9. March 25 and 29, 1911: Fires Change History   173

The New York State Factory Investigating Commission, established as a result of the Triangle Fire, documented industrial working conditions through the state. A commission photographer took this portrait of workers outside an International Harvester twine works factory in Auburn in 1912 and two photos inside, where the work was dirty, hot, and heavy and fire a constant menace. The origins of New York's modern labor and industrial code can be traced to the commission's work.

Thomas J. Watson Sr., shown in the photo shortly after being appointed general manager of Computing-Tabulating-Recording Company in 1914, became president of the company the next year and changed the company's name to International Business Machines in 1924. During the next three decades, Watson built IBM into one of the nation's leading corporations.

Jackie Robinson was a model of courage, determination, resilience, and athletic skills.

Governor Thomas E. Dewey on a bulldozer at the groundbreaking for the New York State Thruway at Liverpool, July 1946.

The Unisphere and the New York State Pavilion, shown in this 2006 photo, symbolized the World's Fair's global theme but also New York's leadership.

Lois Gibbs, president of the Love Canal Homeowners Association, discusses the Love Canal health crisis with Governor Hugh Carey in 1978.

New York City firefighters on 9/11 displayed the resilience that characterized their agency throughout its history.

ACKNOWLEDGMENTS

*T*his book could not have been completed without the generous advice and support of many individuals.

My wife Susan identified many of the sources, worked on the research, read drafts of each chapter of the manuscript, and prepared the index. Her patience, wisdom, and insights have inspired and sustained my life and work for more than four decades. Her love of New York State history is, hopefully, represented in the book.

My editor at State University of New York Press, Ms. Amanda Lanne-Camilli, helped shape the original proposal, guided me through the writing and review process, and provided many insightful suggestions along the way. I am very grateful for her guidance and enthusiastic support over the several years that the book was under development.

Ms. Maria Buhl, librarian at the Guilderland Public Library, secured dozens of books through interlibrary loan. Without her tireless work, and the library's outstanding services, this book could not have been completed. Cyra Nealon, my sister in law, carefully read the entire manuscript and identified a number of corrections and changes that significantly improved the final product.

I am grateful to three anonymous reviewers who made very helpful suggestions for strengthening the original manuscript.

Staff at the following institutions were helpful in providing tours of their sites, access to their materials, copies of photographs, or advice:

Fire Department of the City of New York
Glenn H. Curtiss Museum, Hammondsport
IBM Corporate Archives, Somers
National Baseball Hall of Fame and Museum, Cooperstown
New York State Archives, Albany
New York State Historical Association, Cooperstown
New York State Library, Albany
Onondaga Historical Association, Syracuse
Sagamore Hill National Historic Site, National Park Service,
    Oyster Bay
SUNY Buffalo Archives
U.S. Air Force Historical Research Agency, Maxwell Air Force
    Base, Montgomery, Alabama
Women's Rights National Historical Park, National Park
    Service, Seneca Falls

Historical insights and understanding are things that one generation passes on to the next, imparting wisdom that will enrich their lives. A study of New York's past provides a basis for confidence and optimism about its future. In that spirit, I dedicate this book to my four grandchildren, who are a constant delight and inspiration in all of my work: Abigail Gregory, Jack Gregory, Madeline Roberts, and Stella Roberts. Young New Yorkers today, they will hopefully experience all of the best that our state has to offer in years to come.

—Bruce W. Dearstyne
Guilderland, New York

INTRODUCTION

*N*ew York does things on a grand scale. *The Spirit of New York: Defining Events in the Empire State's History*, presents New York history in a novel, unprecedented way, through exploring sixteen dramatic events that altered the course of state history and, because of New York's importance, national history as well. All of the events are exciting, but most are not well known because they are not covered, or covered only in passing, in standard accounts. Each chapter describes what led up to the event, the event itself, and what happened as a consequence. Some of the events are high profile, for example, the Seneca Falls women's rights convention in 1848 and Jackie Robinson's debut as a Brooklyn Dodger in 1947. Others are more symbolic and indicative of broad-scale change, for example, the Albany County farmers' "Declaration of Independence" in July 1839, launching of IBM in February 1924, and dedication and opening of the longest section of the Thruway in June 1954. Two of them, tragic fires, occurred within a few days of each other in 1911. The events illustrate the spirit of New York—the elusive traits that make New York State unique, or at least distinct, among the fifty states—and the complexity of its history.

New York presents a complicated historical mosaic, stretching back over more than four centuries. During most of its history as a state, it has been a leader in the development of business, commerce, agriculture, transportation, culture, education, and other areas. For many years, it was the nation's most populous and influential state, but over the past few decades its leadership and influence have declined. New York has often been on fast-forward, ambitious, eager to advance its prospects, impatient of delay, inclined to go it alone if the rest of the nation did not share its vision. When federal authorities turned down New York's request for aid in building a cross-state canal, DeWitt Clinton, canal advocate and future governor, convinced the state to undertake the enterprise and build the Erie Canal. "It remains for a free state to create a new era in history and to erect a work more stupendous, more magnificent, and more beneficial than has hitherto been achieved by the human race," he declared in 1815.[1]

New Yorkers can sometimes be assertive and inclined to boast about their state's superiority. Writing in 1939, New York City mayor Fiorello LaGuardia confronted critics who asserted that his city is "strictly a money mart... a synonym for Wall Street.... New Yorkers are impolite." The mayor countered that "New York is a warm-hearted and generous community" but so far superior to other cities that "we could afford to stop for the next twenty years and we would still be slightly ahead of the procession."[2]

Capturing New York State's history has never been easy. The state's size, ethnic diversity, cosmopolitan character, and the rapid pace of its historical development all complicate efforts to identify a coherent state history with clear turning points and eras, cause-and-effect patterns, and sharply defined themes. New York City, Long Island, the Hudson Valley, the North Country (roughly the region north of Albany) and Western New York all claim regional historical distinctiveness. Identifying central themes is a challenge. For instance, State Museum staff, planning an exhibit on state history for their new facility in 1976, finally settled on three grand traits: *materialism* ("New Yorkers have fashioned, used, invented, acquired, lusted after, traded for, and aspired to a literally infinite number of material things . . . all bespeak a prodigious productivity and achievement reflecting a people's quest for a material definition of success"); *diversity* (millions of immigrants, ethnic, religious, and cultural mosaic, cities reflecting a cosmopolitan flavor, tolerance); and *change* (rapid transformation and growth driven by transportation facilities such

---

1. Ronald E. Shaw, *Erie Water West: A History of the Erie Canal, 1792–1854* (Lexington: University of Kentucky Press, 1966), 58.
2. Fiorello LaGuardia, "Ten Misconceptions of New York" (1939), in Kenneth T. Jackson and David S. Dunbar, eds., *Empire City: New York through the Centuries* (New York: Columbia University Press, 2002), 647–652.

as the Erie Canal, the New York Central Railroad, and the Thruway and the growth of business and finance).[3]

David M. Ellis, one of the state's most thoughtful historians, asserted that "the New York character" was determined by its geography (distinct regions that complement each other), population diversity (originally settled by the Dutch, in-migration of Yankees from New England after the Revolution, people from all over the world after that), inventiveness, and spirit of fair play and tolerance. New Yorkers formed "a society of infinite variety, complexity and change" and "learned how to balance rival interests, to accommodate change without jettisoning traditional values, to unearth and reward talent, and to take care of those in need."[4]

Novelist and historian Carl Carmer wrote that "York State is a nation," using a diminutive version of the state's name but asserting its expansive claim to elite, near-autonomous status. Writing mostly about "upstate" (north of New York City), Carmer continued that "the knowing Yorker assumes that . . . his country is as separate, as decisively bordered, as any island in the sea." A Yorker might visit neighboring Pennsylvania but is relieved to be "back in the New York State hills." Yorkers are sensible, generous, industrious, easy-going, given to doing things in moderation. "The average Yorker is a hale, humorous fellow." Yorkers are "free and democratic. . . . good-naturedly indifferent to the machinery of their state government." Their state is an easy, satisfying place to live.[5]

Governor Mario Cuomo (1983–1995) saw enlightened, progressive public policies as New York's defining trait. He defined "the New York Idea" as "government using its resources to help create private sector growth, then requiring those who benefit from that growth to share some part of it so that hope and opportunity are extended to those who have not been as fortunate."[6] His son Andrew Cuomo, who became governor in 2011, emphasizes that New Yorkers are exceptionally energetic, innovative, determined, and resilient. "At every difficult moment in our nation's history, New York has emerged as   the progressive leader in

---

3. David Gould, *Forces: Three Themes in the Lives of New Yorkers* (Albany: New York State Museum, 1977), 1–48.

4. David M. Ellis, *New York: State and City* (Ithaca: Cornell University Press, 1979), 1–24.

5. Carl Carmer, "York State Is a Country," in Carmer, *Dark Trees to the Wind* (New York: William Sloane Associates, 1949), 7–46.

6. Mario Cuomo, *The New York Idea: An Experiment in Democracy* (New York: Crown, 1994), 10.

the nation," he explains. "In New York, we may have big problems, but we confront them with big solutions."[7]

To others, the central historical insight has been that New York is a microcosm of the United States, manifesting characteristic American traits such as individualism and courage. It is a place where ideas start and then spread to the rest of the nation, often leading the way or pointing it out through example. New York is "a mirror of the national past. . . . New York was or was always becoming what the rest of the nation turned out to be. As New York changed, so did the country." New York exemplified natural beauty, urban and rural landscapes, and extremes of wealth and poverty. New Yorkers could be thought of as "cosmopolitan Americans: energetic . . . materialistic and brash but also convivial, humane, tolerant, and idealistic. That one state alone should be able to encompass in itself so many of the virtues and limitations of the American people is a measure of New York's unique role in the nation's history."[8]

New York's energy and impatience to get on with things has sometimes inspired a sort of historical heedlessness. Historian Allan Nevins's assessment of New York City history contains insights into the state as a whole:

> [I]t is too protean, too subject to incessant phantasmagoric change . . . its architectural and social record is a palimpsest. Over its skyscrapers hangs some demon forever waving his wand and exclaiming "Presto, Change!" At his command, the change comes—comes through growth, the successive waves of immigration from abroad and migration from within, the passion for rebuilding engendered by high land values, the want of relevance for the past.[9]

"New York gives little time to thinking of its past," another historian observed. "Its concern is with the future."[10]

---

7. Andrew Cuomo, *2011 State of the State Address*, http://www.governor.ny.gov/sl2/ stateofthestate2011transcript, and *2012 State of the State Address*, http://www.governor. ny.gov/assets/documents/Building-a-New-New-York-Book.pdf.
8. Milton M. Klein, "Shaping the American Tradition: The Microcosm of Colonial New York," *New York History* 59 (April 1978), 174–176.
9. Allan Nevins, "The Golden Thread in the History of New York," *New-York Historical Society Quarterly* 39 (January 1955), 7.
10. Bank of Manhattan, *"Mannahatin": The Story of New York* (New York: 1929), 217, quoted in Milton Klein, Introduction, in Milton M. Klein, ed., *New York: The Centennial Years, 1676–1976* (Port Washington: Kenikat Press, 1976), 3.

Telling New York's story is a challenge for historians. "Here is a really interesting story," observed Dixon Ryan Fox, president of the New York State Historical Association, in 1933. "Where is there a history more dramatic, more richly varied, more instructive? In every stage it illustrates the history of the whole United States."[11] Wrote David M. Ellis, "[T]hroughout the past two centuries, New York has been where the action is. . . . Wherever we look, we encounter . . . people who have formed a society of infinite variety, complexity, and change. As America's society grows increasingly pluralistic, it may be able to forecast its future from New York's experiences."[12] The editors of *The Encyclopedia of New York State* observed that "New York State is [not just] diverse; it is radically heterogeneous."[13]

New York, so confident and assertive in some forums, has seemed shy and reticent about its own history. It is one of the few states with a full-time state historian and the only state with officially designated local government historians. It has over five hundred chartered historical societies and some of the most prominent historical programs in the nation. However, these groups work mostly unilaterally, many have limited resources, and there is limited statewide coordination among them. The most recent comprehensive state history was published in 2001, the one prior to that in 1967.[14] The state has held muted commemorations of key events in its history, including its first state constitution in 1777 and its participation in the Civil War, where it contributed more troops, funding, and war materiel than any other state.

"New York State resists tidy conceptualization. . . . the way to view New York State as a unified whole is by embracing its full complexity, not by trying to trim it to a single narrative," advise the editors of *The Encyclopedia of New York State*.[15] *The Spirit of New York* proceeds on that assumption. New York in all its vibrant complexity, creative energy, and puzzling contradictions emerges in these sixteen events and the stories

---

11. Dixon Ryan Fox, Foreword, in Alexander C. Flick, ed., *Wigwam and Bowerie*, Vol. 1 of *History of the State of New York* (New York: Columbia University Press, 1933), vi–vii.
12. Ellis, *New York*, 24.
13. Preface, *The Encyclopedia of New York State*, Peter Eisenstadt, editor-in-chief (Syracuse: Syracuse University Press, 2005), xi–xii.
14. Milton M. Klein, ed., *The Empire State: A History of New York* (Ithaca: Cornell University Press, 2001); David M. Ellis, James A. Frost, Harold C. Syrett, and Henry Carman, *A History of New York State* (Ithaca: Cornell University Press, 1967).
15. Eisenstadt, editor-in-chief, *The Encyclopedia of New York State*, xi, xii.

built around them. The events and the stories built around them were
selected with several criteria in mind:

- The event took place on a particular day and therefore provides focus for vivid, detailed recounting and also for building
  a story illuminating key aspects of history by describing what
  led up to it and what happened afterward or as a consequence.
- It has received insufficient historical attention, for instance, the
  key contributions of New York aviation pioneer Glenn Curtiss; the story of IBM, a company with deep New York roots;
  or the story of the New York State Thruway, one of the greatest public works projects ever undertaken by a state.
- It is an interesting story with lively, engaging New Yorkers at
  the center of it, for instance, innovative novelist James Fenimore Cooper; the incomparable multi-issue reformer Elizabeth Cady Stanton; or the gruff but effective president of the
  1964–1965 World's Fair, New York's master builder Robert
  Moses.
- It has features of drama, excitement, adventure, or courage, for
  instance, a group of rebels writing the first state constitution
  while on the run from British troops or citizens in Syracuse
  rescuing a runaway slave.
- It illustrates something profound and important and is a prelude to other important developments such as the first executive order against stream and lake pollution in 1899 or the
  Department of Health's announcement about the health perils
  of Love Canal, which helped propel Niagara Falls resident
  Lois Gibbs into leadership of the environmental movement.
- It is at heart a "New York" story but has national ramifica-
  tions or demonstrates or foreshadows New York's leadership,
  for instance, child labor protective legislation in 1903 and the
  regulation of working conditions after the 1911 Triangle Fire.
- It reveals and typifies the diversity of New York over its history, for instance, farmers rebelling against a tenant land system
  with roots back to the Dutch colonial period or Jackie Robinson breaking the "color barrier" to play for the Brooklyn
  Dodgers in 1947.

- It illustrates themes of transformation and resilience, for instance, the story of the Fire Department of the City of New York before, during, and after 9/11.

The book is necessarily selective. The events described in it are not evenly distributed across time frames. Other events might have been selected by other historians, for instance, the opening of the Erie Canal on October 26, 1825; the Civil War draft riots on July 13–16, 1863; or the "crash" of the New York Stock Market, October 24, 1929. Some of those events, for example, the Erie Canal, have been covered in detail many times in topical books and textbooks. *The Spirit of New York* tries to elevate lesser-known events and stories, to put new interpretations on ones that are more familiar, and to look at them all as examples of New York's historical distinctiveness.

Chapter 1, "April 22, 1777: New York State Begins," discusses the first state constitution, which boldly proclaimed New York State into existence and gave it a surprisingly durable blueprint for government.

Chapter 2, "February 4, 1826: Fiction Trumps History," analyzes *The Last of the Mohicans*, a novel by a pioneering New York writer that helped establish a new, distinctly American, literary tradition.

Chapter 3, "July 4, 1839: The Farmers' Rebellion," examines a sustained, sometimes violent New York farmer tenant uprising and the political processes and compromises that led to its conclusion.

Chapter 4, "July 20, 1848: A Demand for Equal Rights," describes the Seneca Falls women's rights convention and the career of one of New York's most ardent and steadfast reformers, Elizabeth Cady Stanton.

Chapter 5, "October 1, 1851: Striking a Blow for Freedom," details the rescue of a fugitive slave from a U.S. marshal in Syracuse, revealing the complexity of the abolitionist movement in New York State.

Chapter 6, "March 30, 1899: Pollution and Politics," traces a half century of New York water pollution policy, revealing the scientific theories, political intrigue, and complexity of public health policymaking.

Chapter 7, "April 15, 1903: Intervening for the Children," looks at the process of developing state policy to protect its youngest citizens.

Chapter 8, "May 29, 1910: First in the Air," highlights the career and accomplishments of unsung New York industrial leader, aviation pioneer, and inventor Glenn Curtiss.

Chapter 9, "March 25 and 29, 1911: Fires Change History," presents the story of two extraordinary and tragic fires, one in New York City and the other in Albany, four days apart, both altering the course of history.

Chapter 10, "February 14, 1924: Leading into the Information Age," is the story of IBM, a company that exemplifies New York innovation and commercial success.

Chapter 11, "April 15, 1947: Breaking the Color Line," presents the story of Jackie Robinson, who defied racial prejudice to become the first black major league baseball player with the Brooklyn Dodgers.

Chapter 12, "June 24, 1954: A New Enterprise for Moving around New York," discusses development of the New York State Thruway and the role of its sponsor, Governor Thomas Dewey.

Chapter 13, "April 22, 1964: The World's Fair Opens in New York," presents the story behind the World's Fair and its president, extraordinary New York builder Robert Moses.

Chapter 14, "August 2, 1978: Environmental Crisis and Citizen Activism," describes the campaign of citizen activist Lois Gibbs to secure state action to help people living near the Love Canal toxic dump site in Niagara Falls.

Chapter 15, "September 11, 2001: New York's Resilience," recounts the history of the New York City Fire Department before, during, and immediately after the terrorist attacks on 9/11.

Several themes emerge from the stories. These are worth noting in part because they provide insights into issues and challenges being faced by the state today.

Determined individuals organize around public issues and bring change. New York has produced more than its share of average citizens who became motivated to deal with particular issues, organized others, kept at it, and eventually triumphed in their cause. Love Canal activist Lois Gibbs exemplifies the New York individual citizen activist, driven by motivation connected to the welfare of family and community, organizing other like-minded people who face the same threat, negotiating with other interested groups, and using the news media, political parties, and other tools to magnify their influence and ultimately alter public policy. Elizabeth Cady Stanton made voting rights the centerpiece of her reformist work but insisted that the agenda include other issues including marriage, divorce, and religion. She framed the issues as ones of fairness and fulfillment of the nation's and state's historic commitment to freedom and equality. She led by confounding her critics but also applying a sense of humor. Smith Boughton and the other leaders of the anti-rent movement used a variety of approaches: a rent strike, guerrilla-style tactics, political action, court challenges, and even amending the constitution. Some of the tactics backfired: Attacking lawmen scared and alienated even New Yorkers sympathetic to the cause. Some chipped away at the problem: Legislation levying taxes on landlords and weakening their authority helped undermine the system. Some of it worked indirectly: The rent strike gradually wore down landlords.

Strategies for addressing problems may develop slowly. The growth and development of such a large enterprise as New York State inevitably produces tensions, inequities, imbalances, and injustices. There are lots of examples of the political process being inclined toward delay and compromise. The Hudson Valley landed tenant system was clearly anachronistic by the mid-nineteenth century, but state policy of intermittent investigation, legislation, and court action weakened but did not end it. That finally required hundreds of individual tenants compromising with landlords and buying their farms. Pollution of streams and lakes was well documented by the end of the nineteenth century. But scientific experts differed on solutions, three of the state's most progressive governors—Theodore Roosevelt, Charles Evans Hughes, and Alfred E. Smith—sidestepped the issue, and the first comprehensive antipollution act did not come until 1949. In April 1911, it was easy to see in retrospect that allowing workers to labor in hundreds of high-rise factories lacking fire detection, suppression, and escape provisions was irresponsible from both a business and a public policy perspective. After the Love Canal crisis hit, reasonable New Yorkers wondered aloud how a well-regarded New York company like Hooker Chemical could have dumped deadly wastes inside a city, and how local and state government could have allowed it.

New York's politics are blurred. New York's politics has seldom fit a pattern, for example, rural versus urban, upstate versus New York City, or liberal versus conservative. As the state began, there was the beginning of a division between those who favored strong state government protecting and promoting landowners and business interest and those who felt strong government meant an abridgement of individual freedom. But the sentiments did not crystallize into a liberal versus conservative party. New York's political parties are alliances of factions that shift over time, operating on the basis of compromise and consensus, making it difficult to take and sustain clear-cut policy positions. Whigs and the Democrats both waffled on the anti-rent issue in the pre–Civil War era. Democrats and Republicans avoided taking a clear stand on votes for women and women's rights generally. The Democrats are generally identified with reforms such as legislation protecting individuals' rights, but in New York it was Republicans who enacted child labor reform in 1903. Democrats were mainly responsible for enacting the state's labor and industrial code after the Triangle Fire, but Republicans left it mostly intact when they regained power in 1915. Democrats are often associated with civil rights, environmental reform, and large-scale public works programs. But it was a Republican, Thomas Dewey, who signed the nation's first state civil rights law in 1945, the state's first stream pollution measure in 1949, and the Thruway act in 1950, the greatest New York public works enterprise of the era.

The quest for social justice requires energy and sacrifice. One of the themes in New York's history is the quest for social justice and fair treatment of less fortunate New Yorkers or citizens who cannot speak and fend for themselves, for example, children. Lillian Wald, Florence Kelly, and Frances Perkins saw social evils such as child labor and firetrap factories firsthand, attempted to deal with them through associations and publicity, then moved on to become very successful catalysts for change via the political process. Gerrit Smith, Samuel May, and Jermain Loguen, ardent abolitionists, were tireless in condemning slavery and courageously put themselves at risk for the freedom of fugitive William Henry. It was Henry himself, determined to stay free, who was the foremost hero of the "rescue" story. Branch Rickey courageously hired Jackie Robinson and made him a Brooklyn Dodger. His motives were mixed: hatred of racial discrimination, determination to give free run to athletic talent, making money by winning ballgames. But it was Robinson himself—extremely talented, cool under pressure, an exemplary athlete and citizen—who is the real hero of the story.

Leadership requires innovation and creativity. John Jay led the writing of the first constitution by being knowledgeable about political theory and popular sentiment, an excellent writer and a capable politician who brought others around to his views. He knew when to hold firm to principle and when to compromise for the good of progress. Glenn Curtiss—designer, inventor, tinkerer, aviator, organizer of mass production—exemplified the traits of hard work, cooperation, bringing out the best in others, leading in forming a new industry. Curtiss was the archetypal quiet New Yorker, modest, a deep thinker, always working. Thomas Watson—visionary, organizer, and promoter of both himself and his company, IBM—showed the advantages of building on technology, outdistancing competitors, providing exceptional customer service, and nurturing a positive corporate culture. Joseph Pfeifer, a New York City Fire Department line officer on September 11, 2001, became a leader in the reorganization and transformation of that agency in the following years.

New York produces inconsistent characters. New York State is so large and diverse that sometimes the historian does a double-take because things do not seem to fit any pattern. The behavior of some of the people in these stories likewise seems enigmatic and contradictory. For instance, Revolutionary-era statesman and state constitution architect Gouverneur Morris expressed disrespect or even contempt for New York's common people at the same time he was risking his life and welfare to write a constitution that would keep them safe and free. James Fenimore Cooper, the great chronicler of unfettered living, courage, and loyalty to noble causes, was also a defender of aristocratic Hudson Valley landed estates and a critic of those trying to abolish slavery. Elizabeth Cady Stanton for several years struggled with rivals for leadership of the women's rights movement. Tom Dewey, progressive in many ways, had little use for bipartisanship and political compromise. Governor Hugh Carey could not understand why people living near Love Canal never seemed to be satisfied with the state's remedial action. Robert Moses, New York's great builder, achieved much but applied power relentlessly to do it, ignored critics, and sometimes let his ego trump the public interest.

New York has a special kind of resilience. One of the themes in the stories is resilience, springing back from adversity and continuing forward in progress. Members of the Provincial Congress kept working even as advancing British royal forces scattered continental and New York troops. When the British approached the temporary capital at Kingston, the new government simply dispersed, reassembled later at Poughkeepsie, and kept the fledgling state intact. The new governor, George Clinton, calmly took the oath of office and then hurried off to lead a fight against the enemy. The first chief justice, John Jay, took time to lecture his first jury on the real meaning of the Revolution and New York's new constitution. Setbacks spurred Elizabeth Cady Stanton on to more tenacious campaigning. Mishaps in testing prototypes and patent infringement lawsuits motivated Glenn Curtiss to keep innovating. The New York City Fire Department mourned its dead after 9/11 and then creatively revised its mission, policies, and training to meet the new threat of terrorism.

New York's history is a great experiential treasure trove of wisdom and folly, success and failure, progress and retreat. The stories in *The Spirit of New York* reflect the state's diversity, tenacity, creativity, leadership,

and some of its many successes. Several show a state characteristic of forg-
ing ahead, going around or over obstacles, and using state pride and the
history of its great accomplishments to help sustain the momentum. They
also show the challenges inherent in keeping a large, dynamic state unified
and effecting change and improvement. Some of the stories show a pattern
of drift, hoping problems will go away or resolve themselves. Others document injustice perpetuated too long before being addressed. The New
Yorkers in the stories are vibrant and interesting but activated by complex human motives, blending ego and self-interest with determination
to improve the lot of their community, state, and nation. The stories may
have some loose ends and contradictions but, like New York itself, they
are never dull.

1
April 22, 1777
New York State Begins

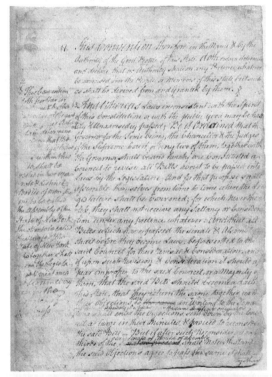

The first state constitution, drafted in haste under wartime conditions, included crossed-out words and interlinear substitutions but launched the new state of New York in 1777. *Photo courtesy of New York State Archives.*

New York State asserted itself into existence as a self-proclaimed geopolitical entity on April 22, 1777. Two days earlier, the Convention of Representatives of the State of New York, an ad hoc revolutionary group elected the previous summer, had completed work on New York's first constitution. The convention had done its work on the fly, scurrying from White Plains to Fishkill to Kingston ahead of advancing British

1

military forces. Delegates voted approval of a final draft that still had strikeouts and marginal corrections; there was no time to waste making a clean copy. The document declared that the convention, acting "in the name and by the authority of the good people of this State, doth ordain, determine and declare that no authority shall on any pretence whatever be exercised over the people or members of this State, but such as shall be derived from and granted by them."[1] In 1777, a document purporting to represent the consensus and will of the people was a startling, radical departure from the past. The men who drafted the constitution tempered their soaring new ideas with pragmatic realism. Given the perils the new state faced, it just wasn't practical to give "the people" a chance to vote on the new document that established "their" government. The convention simply proclaimed it in effect.

New York's birth was a rushed, improbable political miracle. Seldom has a government been established in such forlorn circumstances with such seemingly dim prospects. The previous summer, British army and naval forces had easily conquered Long Island, New York City and the rest of Manhattan Island, and lower Westchester County. As the new constitution was being proclaimed, the British were planning three invasions—south from the British colony of Canada, north from occupied New York City, and west across Lake Ontario from Canada via Oswego and the Mohawk River—to rendezvous at Albany and split and subdue the fledgling state. New York's northeastern boundary was in dispute with separatist Vermonters, uneasy allies against the British who were openly determined to wrest their independence from New York. Even in the areas the newly proclaimed government controlled, there were large numbers of loyalists who resisted calls to join the militia and harbored spies and criminals. Many more people were indifferent or opportunistic, ready to ally with the newly minted state or swing their allegiance back to British colonial authorities, depending on the exigencies of the war.

New York had gradually drifted from proud allegiance to the British Empire to a status of armed rebellion in the late 1760s and early 1770s. British taxes, trade restrictions, and regulations tightened London's control over colonial trade and commerce and violated the colonists' rights as Englishmen. Philip Schuyler, a member of the colonial assembly who held large tracts of land near Albany and in Saratoga County, was typical

1. New York State Constitution, 1777, http://en.wikisource.org/wiki/New_York_Constitution_of_1777.

of the shift in sentiment. In July 1775, he wrote that the British "may be induced to give up their odious claims, and pursue measures tending to reconciliation instead of the nefarious and hostile ones they had adopted." By early 1776, however, enraged by British intransigence, he despaired of reconciliation and accepted an appointment as a major general in the new rebel army. He cautioned about the work ahead: "[I]ndependence and happiness are not synonymous."[2] New Yorkers elected three "provincial congresses" in 1775 and 1776 to deliberate on the growing crisis and what New York should do. The third one met only briefly in the early summer of 1776, its sole accomplishment to arrange for quick election of a fourth provincial congress to take up the issue of independence. By the time the fourth provincial council met at White Plains on July 9, the issue of independence had to be addressed. The Continental Congress had drawn up a declaration of independence on July 2, but New York's delegates, lacking instructions, sent home for direction. The new provincial council quickly took three steps. It changed its name to the Convention of Representatives of the State of New York, as noted previously. This was an audacious leap of faith, since "the State of New York" technically did not exist yet. It instructed New York's delegates to vote for the Declaration of Independence with a resolution that said convention members "will at the risk of our lives and fortunes join with the other Colonies in supporting it." It appointed a committee of fourteen members to draft a constitution for the "state" with the implicit understanding that the constitution itself would call the state into existence.

New York had cast its lot for independence. But the drafting committee seemed unhurried, almost leisurely. The convention was serving as the de facto government of New York, and all its members were busy with other things, including raising money, dealing with loyalists, investigating conspiracies, overseeing the state militia, and supporting continental army forces under General Washington's command. General Philip Schuyler wrote on December 6, 1776, "I am very apprehensive that much Evil will arise if a Government is not soon established for this State. The longer it is delayed, the more difficult it will be to bring the unprincipled and licentious to a proper Sense of their Duty and we have too many such amongst us."[3] Drafting did not begin in earnest until early 1777. Three extraordinarily capable delegates did most of the work: John Jay (1745–1829),

---

2. Don R. Gerlach, *Philip Schuyler and the American Revolution in New York, 1733–1777* (Lincoln: University of Nebraska Press, 1964), 293–294.

Gouverneur Morris (1734–1806), and Robert R. Livingston (1746–1813). They were all among the educated elite, graduates of Kings College, the predecessor of Columbia University. They embodied and reflected traits that would later be associated with the spirit of New York: energetic, tempering idealism with pragmatism and a get-it-done determination, putting the public interest above their own welfare. Relatively young in 1777, they all went on to positions of service and leadership in the state and national governments.

From Reluctant Rebels to Constitutional Statesmen

John Jay, a brilliant, capable, articulate New York City attorney, did most of the actual writing. Jay had been elected a delegate to the first Continental Congress in 1774. He was, in the words of historian Richard B. Morris, a "prudent revolutionary" who at first counseled reconciliation and compromise. He disapproved of parties to the dispute who "observe no medium and are either all flame or all frost." Hoping for a change in British policy, Jay drafted an "Address to the People of Great Britain," which the Continental Congress adopted on September 5, 1774. Americans demanded restoration of their rights as Englishman, he asserted. "No power on earth has the right to take our property from us without our consent. . . . we will never submit to be hewers of wood or drawers of water for any ministry or nation in the world." British intransigence and punitive policies transformed Jay into a revolutionary, and by April 1776 he confided to a friend that "the sword must decide the controversy." Elected to the fourth New York provincial congress, Jay quickly assumed a leadership role, drafting the resolution approving the Declaration of Independence.[4]

The second major constitutional architect was Gouverneur Morris, another astute New York City lawyer. Born in an affluent, well-connected family, Morris built up comfortable wealth through a lucrative law practice and land speculation. He sometimes struck people as arrogant and headstrong, but friends insisted he was a "witty, genteel, polite, sensible,

3. Ibid., 297.
4. Richard B. Morris, *John Jay, the Nation and the Court* (Boston: Boston University Press, 1967), 6; Walter Stahr, *John Jay: Founding Father* (New York: Hambledon and London, 2005), 57; Milton M. Klein, "John Jay and the Revolution," *New York History* 81 (January 2000), 23.

and a judicious young man." As pressure for independence built, Morris at first stood aloof. He referred to the rebel group known as the Sons of Liberty in 1774 as "poor reptiles" and sneered that "the mob begin to think and reason." But his reputation for fairness and his legal abilities led to his election to the first New York provincial congress in 1775 and its successors. Morris was appalled by tyrannical British policies and believed that Americans had the right to control their own internal trade and taxes. He worried that unless men of learning and substance took control of the revolutionary movement, it could fall into the hands of radicals and degenerate into mob rule. On May 24, 1776, he delivered a three-hour "Oration on Necessity for Declaring Independence from Britain" before the third provincial congress. British arrogance and blundering had brought on this crisis, turning back was unthinkable, and now "*an independence is absolutely necessary.*" The British might relent on some coercive measures temporarily but only to buy time to build up their military forces. They were already bringing in ruthless Hessian soldiers ready to brutally subdue the colonists. "Trust Crocodiles, trust the hungry wolf in your flock or a rattlesnake nigh your bosom. . . . But trust the King, his Ministers, his commissioners, it is madness in the extreme! . . . there is no redress but by arms."[5]

The third principal author was Robert R. Livingston, member of a prominent family with extensive real estate holdings along the Hudson River in Columbia County. Livingston was also a lawyer and had been a law partner with John Jay. As a member of an old family, he inherited a prominent social position but also "a certain kind of self-consciousness, at once proud and sensitive, accepting respect as a matter of course. . . . He was a prototype of the Hudson River squires, an individual who did not believe that there could be a better way of life than his own and who borrowed from other ways of life only what happened to suit his fancy."[6] As problems with Britain mounted, Livingston was at first a voice for compromise and reconciliation. Elected to the first Continental Congress, he moved toward the same conclusion that his friends John Jay and Gouverneur Morris reached: Wrongheaded British policies made revolution inevitable. As a member of the second Continental Congress, he served

5. James J. Kirschke, *Gouverneur Morris: Author, Statesman, and Man of the World* (New York: St. Martin's Press, 2005), 40–42.
6. George Dangerfield, *Chancellor Robert R. Livingston of New York, 1746–1813* (New York: Harcourt Brace and Company, 1960), 7, 190.

on the committee to draft the Declaration of Independence but contributed little of substance and left for home before the vote for independence
was taken. Like Morris, he feared mob rule, which might take a particularly menacing form on his manor: rent strikes or land seizures by tenants.
He was elected to the fourth provincial congress and to the committee to
draft the new constitution. But by the fall of 1776, he was already expressing disdain for the new political groups represented among the delegates:
mechanics, small farmers, and country lawyers whom he characterized as
"unimproved by education and unrefined by honor." "I am sick of politics and power," he grumbled on October 10. "I long for more refined
pleasures, conversation and friendship. I am weary of crowds and pine for
solitude nor would in my present humour give one scene of Shakespeare
for one thousand Harringstons, Lockes, Sidneys and Adams to boot."[7]
But Livingston stayed and contributed substantially to the document.

Livingston's list of political philosophers who were making him
weary including three Europeans and one American, the irrepressible
Massachusetts rebel leader John Adams. In April 1776, Adams wrote a
pamphlet entitled *Thoughts on Government*, a concise distillation of the
best thoughts about the purpose and structure of republican government.[8]
John Jay brought back copies from his time as a member of the Continental Congress, used it in his New York constitution drafting work, and
prevailed on other delegates to read it. Republican government requires
"the common people brave and enterprising. . . . sober, industrious, and
frugal," said Adams. A republican government should reflect the people it
represents. The first principle, Adams said, is "to depute power from the
many to a few of the most wise and good." The lawmaking body should
have two houses, to check and balance each other. The larger house, which
Adams called the assembly, "should be in miniature an exact portrait of
the people at large. It should think, feel, reason and act like them." Elections should be frequent. Rotation in office will teach "the great political
virtues of humility, patience, and moderation without which every man
in power becomes a ravenous beast of prey." Executive power should
be vested in a governor, but gubernatorial power should be checked by
annual elections. Many of the ideas distilled in *Thoughts on Government*

---

7. Clare Brandt, *An American Aristocracy: The Livingstons* (Garden City, NY: Doubleday,
   1986), 120; Dangerfield, *Chancellor Robert R. Livingston*, 86.
8. John Adams, *Thoughts on Government*, April 1776, http://www.teachingamericanhis-
   tory.org/library/index.asp?documentprint=37.

can be found in the philosophy, and sometimes in the structure, of New York's constitution.

The New York constitutional statesmen drew on summary writings like Adams's pamphlet, European writers, and their own experience with colonial governors, assemblies, and local governments. Members of the provincial convention divided roughly into four groups. A small number counseled delay, hoping that British concessions would make revolution unnecessary. Another small group wanted to wait until New York and continental army forces controlled more territory. The convention needed to secure the state to govern before devising a means of governing it, they argued. A few delegates hoped to use the constitution-writing process to effect substantial political and social change such as radically broadening the suffrage or breaking up large estates and distributing their lands as individual farms. The majority of delegates wanted to move ahead expeditiously but in a way that did not upset the economic or social order in their new state. They held an unwritten consensus that the constitution should have several features.

A written document. New York leaders had seen firsthand the limitations of the unwritten "British constitution," a hybrid that included the Magna Carta, laws, judicial decisions, and precedents. That "constitution" had proven too vague to protect colonists' rights. The New York constitutional statesmen wanted something concrete.

Clear, readable, and understandable text. The constitution would be read by the literate, read to the illiterate, and broadly discussed by the citizens of the new state. It would help wavering New Yorkers decide which side to support in the great struggle. It needed to be written in language that people could readily understand.

Acknowledgment of derivation from the people. The document would specify that all governmental authority derived from consent of the governed. Everyone understood, though, that over half of "the people" would not actually have political rights. Women were not included in the convention and would not be able to vote; and slavery, which had taken root during Dutch colonial days over a century earlier, would continue.

Suffrage by men with a stake in society. Males of full age who held property or paid taxes should have the vote.

Strong executive, but with limitations. The new state would need a strong governor to win the war, create state government, collect taxes, secure the state's borders, execute the laws, and hold the new state together. At the same time, experience with a tyrannical king and overreaching colonial governors required that the governor's power would be subject to checks.

Two-house legislature. There was a rough consensus on the desirability of a bicameral legislature. One house, with larger membership, elected by a sizeable part of the electorate, would represent all citizens. The second, smaller and elected by men with more substantial property holdings, would be more representative of the upper levels of society.

An independent judiciary. The framers envisioned a tripartite government, with the legal system related to the other two but also insulated from the political considerations that might affect the governor and the legislature.

Protection of citizens' rights. The constitution's architects were determined to protect civil rights, and in fact the drafting committee was given a specific charge to include a bill of rights.

"A Choice of Dishes"

Most of the drafting work fell to the three most capable, educated, and thoughtful members of the drafting committee, Jay, Morris, and Livingston. "We have a government . . . to form and [no one] knows what it will resemble," Jay wrote in July 1776. "Our politicians, like some guests at a feast, are perplexed and undetermined to which dish to prefer."[9] The committee labored through five drafts and finally reported on March 12, 1777. The convention met in a small room above the local jail in Kingston, and its members smoked heavily to dispel the "disagreeable effluvia" in the air from the jail below, overcrowded with loyalist prisoners. The debates sometimes focused on principles, other times on the minutiae of word choices. Some were heated and divisive, and Jay, Morris, and Livingston sometimes had to work behind the scenes to bring people together. The document approved on April 20 represented a blend of principles and pragmatic compromises. It had the following features.

A strong executive but with novel constraints. Morris, apprehensive about radical democratic threats, proposed a strong governor with total power over appointments and a qualified veto as being "necessary for the preservation of society."[10] Livingston and others counseled limiting the

9. Stahr, *John Jay*, 74.
10. Melanie R. Miller, *An Incautious Man: The Life of Gouverneur Morris* (Wilmington, DE: ISI Books, 2008), 29.

governor's veto power. The final version of the constitution declared that "the supreme executive power and authority of this State shall be vested in a governor" who shall "take care that the laws are faithfully executed." The governor, elected to a three-year term, was also made commander of the state militia, assigned power to convene the legislature in extraordinary sessions, and charged to inform the legislature annually about "the condition of the State" and "recommend such matters to their consideration as shall appear to him to concern its good government, welfare and prosperity." Men who held property worth at least one hundred pounds could vote for governors, the same as the requirement for voting for senators, effectively limiting the franchise to the upper middle class and above.

Colonial governors had possessed the power to veto bills passed by colonial assemblies and virtually unlimited power of appointment. They had sometimes used both powers to thwart the popular will. The framers of the New York constitution restricted their governor's prerogatives through creation of two novel, unprecedented review/approval groups to share power with the governor. Jay, Morris, and Livingston were decisive in shaping both of them. Livingston developed the notion of a "Council of Revision" consisting of the governor, chancellor, and judges of the supreme court. This group could veto bills by a majority vote and return them to the originating house with an explanation. But its veto could be overridden by a two-thirds vote of both houses of the legislature. A "Council of Appointment," mostly Jay's handiwork, was established, consisting of the governor and four senators, chosen annually by the assembly. The governor could nominate appointments for state offices, but the council had to approve and the governor could only vote to break a tie. This "allowed indirectly for the interplay of *vox populi* and . . . the evolution of a patronage system." The two councils blurred the boundaries among the executive, legislative, and judicial branches, but they represented a pragmatic compromise between those who favored a strong governor and those who feared too much executive power. "The entire structure comprised an intricate web of powers and functions with something for almost everyone."[11]

A balanced bicameral legislature. The convention wanted to create a two-house legislature, one house broadly representative of the people,

---

11. Richard B. Morris, "New York's First Constitution," in John H. G. Pell, ed., *Essays on the Genesis of the Empire State* (Albany: New York State American Revolution Bicentennial Commission, 1979), 26–27.

the other smaller and more attuned to the interests of business and property. It created an assembly, elected annually; set the number of members at a minimum of seventy; and provided for periodic censuses to keep the number of members growing as the population grew. Voter eligibility was the subject of one of the most complicated compromises of the constitution. Three groups were included: men with freeholds of at least forty pounds, land-renting tenants who paid at least two pounds per year rent, and "freemen" of Albany and New York City (the term "freemen" referred to men who were legally permitted to vote by their municipal governments; by the time of the Revolution, that would have included almost any man who worked or engaged in a trade in the cities). That opened the suffrage broadly among white males. There was a rough model for the new assembly: the previous colonial assembly. But there was no model for the second house, called the senate. The closest approximation was the provincial council, but it had been appointed by the crown on recommendation of the governors. The senate was intended to be smaller, more reflective of the upper class, deliberative, safe from the tumult of the crowd. Senators were to be elected for four years, insulating them from popular clamor and demands. Voting for senators was restricted to men with one hundred pounds or more of property, five times the requirement for the assembly. Four senatorial districts consisting of specified groups of counties were established, and the number of senators to be chosen in each district was specified. The initial number was established at twenty-four. There would be adjustments in the size of delegations and additional members added, as the state's population shifted and the state expanded, as measured by the periodic censuses. Either house could initiate legislation; approval of both was required to enact it into law.[12]

An independent judiciary. The constitution said little about the courts, essentially continuing the colonial system but under the authority of the new state. The local courts of colonial days were adopted with little change but a new "supreme court" was added at the top. The constitution continued a separate court of chancery, which had powers to adjudicate commercial disputes, appoint and supervise trustees of people needing judicial protection such as orphans and widows, foreclose mortgages, and settle disputes where there was no clear legal guidance or common law precedent. The colonial governor had formerly acted as head of the court of

---

12. William A. Polf, *1777: The Political Revolution and New York's First Constitution* (Albany: New York State American Revolution Bicentennial Commission, 1977), 13–20.

chancery; the constitution created a new position, chancellor, to head the court. Over both courts was placed a special appeals court or "court of errors" consisting of the senate, the supreme court justices, and the chancellor, but with the provision that neither the chancellor nor the supreme court justices could vote on appeals from their respective branches. The assembly was given power to impeach, and a special court for the trial of impeachments was established. The constitution also legalized those portions of the common law in effect on April 19, 1775, the date of the battles of Lexington and Concord. That gave the new judicial system a body of precedent and judge-made law to use as a basis for making rulings.

A secret ballot. Balloting in colonial New York had been *viva voce:* Men declared their preferences in an open meeting. The system opened voting to influence and coercion. For instance, landlords knew how their tenants voted, and tenants, not wishing to displease them, might vote as the landlord desired rather than as conscience dictated. The draft included provision for a secret ballot, but Morris spoke against it during the debate as being too great a departure from precedent and he carried the day. Jay happened to be absent for that debate. Just before the final vote, in one of the rare disagreements among the triumvirate, Jay proposed a compromise: Keep voice vote during the war but institute the secret ballot after the war's end. Morris protested, but the convention reversed itself and endorsed Jay's proposal, which was included in the final document.

No bill of rights. The charge to the drafting committee included a provision for a bill of rights but none was included. The constitution included the entire Declaration of Independence as a preamble, but that listed rights violated by the British rather than rights to be protected in New York. The constitution guaranteed the right to trial by jury, but other rights are not mentioned. The most plausible explanation for the absence of a bill of rights is that the framers decided that it might inhibit the new government's flexibility in dealing with loyalists. The legislature enacted a bill of rights in 1787.[13]

Freedom of religion. The document declared that "the free exercise and enjoyment of religious profession and worship, without discrimination or preference, shall forever hereafter be allowed within this State to all mankind." John Jay was suspicious of Catholics because he felt they owed allegiance to the Pope rather than state or nation. He proposed a provision

---

13. Bernard Mason, "New York's First State Constitution," in Pell, ed., *Essays on the Genesis of the Empire State,* 31.

to exclude Catholics from guarantee of religious toleration unless they abjured the authority of the Pope. Few delegates agreed with that. But Jay was persistent, and in the end the constitution included three provisions bearing directly or indirectly on religion. First, after the provision quoted earlier about freedom of religion, the convention added another clause: "provided, that the liberty of conscience, hereby granted, shall not be so construed as to excuse acts of licentiousness, or justify practices inconsistent with the peace or safety of the state." That was a warning against using religion as an excuse to break the law, but it had little impact on New York jurisprudence. Second, a phrase was included barring ministers and priests from holding civil or military offices. Third, naturalized citizens were required to renounce "all allegiance" to "every foreign king, prince, potentate, and state, in all matters, ecclesiastical as well as civil."[14]

The scourge of slavery. The institution of slavery was not compatible with the lofty pronouncements about the sovereignty of the people. John Jay wanted to include a clause to abolish slavery, but most delegates considered that too preemptive. Gouverneur Morris came up with a gradualist approach. He proposed that the constitution should urge "future legislatures" to abolish slavery "so that in future ages, every human being who breathes the air of this state, shall enjoy the privileges of a freeman. . . . The rights of human nature and the principles of our holy religion call upon us to dispense the blessings of freedom to all mankind." But too many New Yorkers owned slaves or were engaged in the slave trade, and Morris's amendment failed. New York did not move to end slavery until 1799, when John Jay, who was by then governor, signed a law that gradually abolished it.[15]

The final version was approved on April 20 by a vote of 33 to 1; Peter Livingston, a distant relative of Robert Livingston, felt it was too radical. The convention declared the constitution to be in effect two days later. Thoughtful observers found it impressive. Alexander Hamilton, General George Washington's military aide and an up-and-coming political leader, pronounced it "happy, regular, and durable." But it showed signs of having been drawn up in haste: "split-the-difference" compromises and, in the councils of revision and appointment, untested mechanisms. No one

---

14. Morris, *John Jay, the Nation, and the Court,* 11–13; Patricia Bonomi, "John Jay, Religion and the State," *New York History* 81 (January 2000), 8–18.
15. Richard Brookhiser, *Gentleman Revolutionary: Gouverneur Morris—The Rake Who Wrote the Constitution* (New York: Free Press, 2003), 34.

was totally satisfied with it. "That there are faults in it is not to be wondered at," wrote Gouverneur Morris, explaining with irritation that the process had necessitated the disagreeable act of compromising with men who did not entirely agree with him.[16]

Jay, Livingston, and Morris, and others who allied with them, had come to see the revolution and independence as inevitable, but they had sought to head off social upheaval. In June 1777, Livingston said he was convinced of "the propriety of Swimming with a Stream which it is impossible to stem" and in fact helping to channel and direct it.[17] George Dangerfield, Livingston's biographer, gives him and his colleagues even more credit. Through skillful leadership, persuasive arguments, and patient consensus-building, "the New York conservatives had managed the radical Revolution so that, while it rid them of Parliament, it did not deprive them of privilege."[18] The document featured many compromises and balances. For instance, the governor was popularly elected and given broad executive power. But the privilege of voting for the governor was restricted to men with a stake in the economy and society, and two of the governor's key powers—veto and appointments—were shared with others. Historian Bernard Mason, emphasizing the property qualifications for voting and the senate as a check for the propertied class on the popular assembly, said the constitution represented a "moderate-conservative consensus."[19]

The New State in Action

New York had proclaimed itself into existence. The convention arranged for election of a governor and legislators in June, to take office in September, but remained the de facto government in the interim. It designated a council of safety from among its membership to handle security and military matters. It set up the judicial branch of the new government on its own authority, building on the basic outline in the new constitution. The convention selected John Jay as chief justice and Robert Livingston as chancellor, thereby placing at the head of the judicial branch two of

---

16. Ibid.
17. Alfred Young, *Democratic Republicans of New York: The Origins, 1763–1797* (Chapel Hill: University of North Carolina Press, 1967), 15.
18. Dangerfield, *Chancellor Robert R. Livingston*, 92.
19. Bernard Mason, *The Road to Independence: The Revolutionary Movement in New York, 1773–1777* (Lexington: University of Kentucky Press, 1966), 248.

the constitution's most influential authors. Jay served for two years, promulgating legal procedures and deciding key cases. He went on to serve as Minister to Spain and Secretary for Foreign Affairs under the Articles of Confederation, first Chief Justice of the U.S. Supreme Court, and governor of New York, 1795–1801. Livingston presided over the court of chancery until 1801. He also served as Secretary of Foreign Affairs under the Articles of Confederation from 1781 to 1783 and as U.S. Minister to France, 1801 to 1804. His work included negotiating the Louisiana Purchase in 1803.

John Jay wrote in July 1777 that "unless the government be committed to proper hands, it will be weak and unstable at home, and contemptible abroad."[20] The conservative-minded revolutionaries who had written the constitution, two of whom had been quickly elevated to the new state's top judicial offices, expected to engineer the election of the governor. Their preferred candidate was General Philip Schuyler, a substantial landholder who could be relied on to protect business and landed interests. He could count on the votes of his tenants in the Albany region, but he was widely regarded as arrogant and overbearing. General George Clinton, an Ulster County native who had built a solid if not stellar military record as commander of rebel forces in the lower Hudson region, was endorsed by local political leaders in his region. He was regarded as reliable, strong, and honest, but he had not been involved in drafting the new constitution and his political views were unknown. Clinton was well liked by just about everyone who knew him. He was popular in the mid-Hudson region, and the sheriff of Dutchess County—a Clinton supporter—allowed any man who showed up to vote, not bothering to check for residency or whether the one hundred pound freeholder qualification imposed by the new constitution was being met. Soldiers were also permitted to vote in the forts where they were stationed with few or no checks on whether they met the qualification. That helped Clinton, who was popular among the troops, but not Schuyler, who was regarded as an overbearing commander. Voter turnout was light. Clinton received 1,828 votes, Schuyler 1,199, other candidates a few hundred each. Schuyler grumbled to Jay that Clinton's "family and Connections do not intitle [sic] him to so distinguished a predominance" but that he had "played his Cards better than Expected." The new legislature included some well-known men who had

---

20. John Jay to Leonard Gansevoort, June 5, 1777, in Henry P. Johnston, ed., *The Correspondence and Public Papers of John Jay*, I, 1763–1781 (New York: Putnam, 1891), 141.

served on the various provincial councils but also many who were new to politics. Like the new governor, they had no affiliation to the prudent revolutionaries who had prevailed at the convention. To men like Jay, Morris, and Livingston, who had dominated the constitution-writing process and the establishment of the judiciary, New York's political future suddenly seemed uncertain.[21]

Military responsibilities prevented the new governor from reporting to Kingston for his inauguration until September 10. In his inaugural speech, Clinton described the state's dire military situation but emphasized the positive. General Nicholas Herkimer and the Tryon County militia had stopped the British invasion from the west at the Battle of Oriskany on August 6. Work was continuing to obstruct the Hudson to prevent the British sailing up to Albany. The state militia law needed revision because many more troops were needed. "The state of our finances likewise claims your serious attention," he told the legislature. "The want of an organized government" had meant that "we have . . . accumulated a debt, which if neglected, will not only prove burthensome [sic] to the state, but [also] strike at the credit of our currency." A government with "vigour and dignity" will also help discourage loyalists and outlaws from making trouble. How did the new governor perceive his own role? He praised the convention for the constitutional provisions that marked "the line between the executive, legislative and judicial powers" and explained, "[I]t shall always be my strenuous endeavor on the one hand to retain and exercise for the advantage of the people the powers with which they have invested me; on the other, carefully to avoid the invasion of those rights which the constitution has placed in other persons." It was a modest and unassuming description of gubernatorial power.

Three days later, the new assembly sent a response to the new governor:

We thoroughly approve your Excellency's intention to retain and exercise all the powers with which you are invested, and we trust that you will exert yourself vigorously to execute the laws, for the restoration of good order and the suppression and punishment of vice and immorality—while as faithful guardians of the rights of our constituents, we are determined neither to encroach upon the privileges of others, nor suffer our own to be invaded; we shall

---

21. Gerlach, *Philip Schuyler*, 303–310; Young, *Democratic Republicans*, 22–23.

heartily concur in all things for the advantage of the people over whom you have been chosen to preside.

Sensing a tone of concern, Clinton realized he might have understated his intention to use executive power. He replied the same day, reassuring the legislature that he would "execute the laws, maintain the peace and freedom, and support the honor, independence, and dignity of the people of this State."[22] The new legislature responded to the governor's plea for funds by levying a tax on real and personal property. Funds began to flow into the state's nearly empty treasury.

Chief Justice John Jay assumed his official duties on September 9, 1777, when he delivered a charge to the first grand jury of the supreme court held at Kingston. He used the occasion to instruct them on the principles upon which the Revolution was being fought and enlighten them about the new constitution. The "charge" took on the status of an important state paper and was reprinted and widely distributed: "[A]ll the calamities incident to this war will be amply compensated by the many blessings flowing from this glorious constitution," said the new chief justice. The constitution came from the people through their elected representatives. "From the people it must receive its spirit, and by them be quickened. Let virtue, honor, the love of liberty and of science be, and remain, the soul of this constitution . . ." The constitution protected "great and equal rights of human nature" including liberty of conscience and equal protection by the laws. It organized the government so "as to promise permanence to the constitution, and give energy and impartiality to the distribution of justice."[23] Jay turned his attention to getting the court system up and running and presiding at cases. "I am now engaged in the most disagreeable part of my duty, trying criminals," he wrote Gouverneur Morris on April 29, 1778. "They multiply exceedingly. Robberies become frequent; the woods afford them shelter, and the tories [give them] food. Punishments must of course become certain, and mercy dormant—a harsh system, repugnant to my feelings, but nevertheless necessary."[24]

---

22. Governor George Clinton, "Opening Speech," September 10, 1777; Assembly Address to the Governor, September 13, 1777; Governor's response, September 13, 1777, in Charles Z. Lincoln, ed., *Messages from the Governors*, II, 1777–1822 (Albany: J. B. Lyon, 1909), 7–12.
23. John Jay, *To the Grand Jury of Ulster County*, September 9, 1777, in Johnston, ed., *The Correspondence and Public Papers of John Jay*, I, 158–163.
24. John Jay to Gouverneur Morris, April 29, 1778, in Johnston, ed., *The Correspondence and Public Papers of John Jay*, I, 179–180.

New York's prospects, dim in 1777, were much brighter by the beginning of the next year. General Horatio Gates continued and intensified the strategies initiated by his predecessor, Philip Schuyler: obstruction of trails and limited attacks that wore down the enemy. On October 17, 1777, British general John Burgoyne, low on supplies, his way forward and retreat backward both blocked, surrendered to Gates near Saratoga in what was arguably the turning point of the war. General Nicholas Herkimer fought the British and Indians invading from the west to a draw at the battle of Oriskany on August 6. A third British invasion force began moving up the Hudson from New York City in October 1777. Washington asked Governor Clinton, who was also still serving as a continental army general, to take charge of defending two forts near West Point that guarded a chain the rebels had strung across the Hudson to impede the British fleet. The new governor of New York could have refused; the Americans had only a few hundred poorly armed defenders in the forts, and the British were expected to assault them with warships and some four thousand troops. Instead, he took personal command of one and his brother, General James Clinton, assumed command of the other one. The British assault on October 6 overwhelmed both forts, but stout resistance organized by the Clintons inflicted unexpected casualties on the enemy. As the British were breaching the front of his fort, Governor Clinton retreated out the back and descended a steep cliff to the Hudson in the darkness. As the British searched, Clinton hailed a boat that had just arrived from the opposite shore to rescue survivors. Seeing that the boat was full to capacity, the governor prepared to swim across the river. The officer in charge, recognizing the governor, insisted on giving up his own spot. Clinton refused. With the British closing in, the new governor made an executive decision: He jumped into the already full boat, and, very slowly, the overloaded vessel was rowed across the Hudson to safety. The new governor had not been able to hold the forts, but he had demonstrated personal courage, a skill in rallying outnumbered forces, and an ability to inflict substantial losses on an overconfident enemy. "The Post [fort] was lost for want of Men to defend it," Gouverneur Morris wrote Robert Livingston after the battle. "The Militia behaved as well as they could do. We shall beat them. We should do so soon if we have as good Officers as our Governor."[25]

25. John P. Kaminski, *George Clinton: Yeoman Politician of the New Republic* (Madison: Madison House, 1993), 25–33

The British proceeded up the river to the New York rebel capital of Kingston. The legislature had plenty of advance warning, delegated its responsibilities temporarily to a committee of safety, and evacuated. They did not meet again until February 1778. Troops led by British general John Vaughn landed on October 15, silenced the shore battery, and marched into town. "Esopus [Kingston] being a nursery for almost every villain in the Country," he wrote, "I judged it to be necessary to proceed to the town. On our approach, [defenders] were drawn up with cannon, which we took and drove them out of the place." Firing continued from the houses, and so "I reduced the place to ashes . . . not leaving a House." A few days later, Vaughn's troops burned Robert Livingston's mansion and other buildings on his land in what seemed like a needlessly vindictive move and one that cost the British among many New Yorkers whose allegiance had been hitherto undecided.[26] By then, Burgoyne had been defeated at Saratoga and was under house arrest at Philip Schuyler's mansion in Albany. The grand plan to link with him at Albany was in shambles. The British sailed back down the river to New York City. It was to be their last major incursion into the territory under the authority of the new state government.

The government reconvened in February 1778, this time in Poughkeepsie, and got down to work in earnest. New York's security was assured after the British defeat at Yorktown; the new state got its biggest city back on November 25, 1783, when the last British troops departed from Manhattan. General George Washington, accompanied by Governor George Clinton, triumphantly led the victorious continental army through the city. Clinton proved to be a popular, effective governor, serving until 1795, returning for another term in 1801–1804, and then serving as vice president under both Thomas Jefferson and James Madison. Morris moved to Pennsylvania, but Jay, Livingston, Hamilton, and Schuyler all stayed in New York and grew apprehensive of Clinton's policies, including taxation of land, harsh treatment of loyalists and sale of their confiscated lands, and issuance of the paper money that promoted inflation. They were alarmed by his ability to appeal directly to the public. In part to counter the growing popular appeal of Clinton—and other popular governors like him in some of the other states who seemed like threats to the established social and economic order—the prudent New York revolutionaries who wrote the state constitution became strong supporters of the movement to create

26. Dangerfield, *Chancellor Robert R. Livingston*, 103–105.

a strong national government. The trio who were most influential in drafting the state constitution in 1777 were soon identified as "federalists," men who supported the proposed U.S. constitution, the move to a strong federal government, and conservative fiscal policies. Morris, a delegate to the constitutional convention from Pennsylvania, drafted much of the document. Livingston was a prominent proponent in New York. Jay was its most important advocate in the state. Along with Alexander Hamilton and James Madison, he wrote *The Federalist Papers*, a comprehensive treatise on the proposed constitution.

New York's first constitution endured without major revisions until 1821, and even then the changes were modest. The Council of Appointment was abolished and state offices were thereafter filled by the legislature, the governor, or the governor with the consent of the senate. The Council of Revision, which had sometimes proved obstructionist and other times seemed overly politicized over the years, was abolished. The governor was given the power to veto bills, subject to reversal by the legislature. Specific civil rights such as freedom of speech and habeas corpus—left out of the 1777 constitution, covered by 1787 legislation, and firmly embedded in the common law and state court decisions—were specifically protected in the 1821 revision.

John Jay noted in his speech to the Ulster County grand jury in September 1777 that "the Americans are the first people whom Heaven has favoured with an opportunity of deliberating upon and choosing the forms of government under which they should live."[27] By just about any measure, the first New York State constitution was a fulfillment of that opportunity.

---

27. John Jay, *To the Grand Jury of Ulster County*, September 9, 1777, in Johnston, ed., *The Correspondence and Public Papers of John Jay*, I, 161.

2
February 4, 1826

Fiction Trumps History

James Fenimore Cooper's novel *The Last of the Mohicans* was widely read and often reprinted. This is an illustration by Frank T. Merrill from the 1896 edition.

An Unlikely Author, a Bestselling Book

*H*istory was made on February 4, 1826, when Carey & Lea, one the nation's most prominent and successful publishers and booksellers, announced the publication of James Fenimore Cooper's *The Last of the Mohicans: A Narrative of 1757.* Cooper was already a best-selling author, widely hailed for presenting nonstop, exciting adventures set in wartime, the wilderness, or other bracing circumstances. He had been honored by being elected to membership in the American Philosophical Society and had been granted an honorary degree from Columbia. Carey & Lea hoped the new book would do as well as his previous ones and paid the author $5,000.

They were not disappointed. The book was an instant best-seller and was reprinted many times. It became one of the most important books in American literary history for the story it conveys and the themes and messages it sets forth about conflict, war, romance, heroism, and values. The book is more famous than the historical event it depicts, the French conquest of Fort William Henry in what is now Lake George, New York, in August 1757 during the colonial wars between England and France. A review in a literary journal in July 1826 described the central character, Natty Bumppo, also known as "Hawkeye" for his forest tracking and scouting skills, as "a bold and original conception . . . [a] creation of genius." The new novel was one nonstop adventure,

> a continuous scene of intense and breathless interest; there is no break, no pause, no abiding place of rest; but we are urged incessantly forward by an irresistible power, hurrying on to the final catastrophe through forests and cataracts, over lakes and mountains, by forts and ambushments, in the midst of bullets and bayonets, tomahawks and scalping knives with the crack of "la longue carabine" [Hawkeye's long rifle] or the yell of a dying Indian, forever ringing in our ears; until we are heartily glad to draw a long breath at the end of the volume.[1]

A few years earlier, not many people would have predicted that James Fenimore Cooper (1789–1851) would become one of America's most famous and widely read authors. His father, William Cooper, was a land speculator and developer who had purchased thousands of acres in what is now Otsego County, sold off building lots, developed a village named after himself (Cooperstown), and held office as a judge and congressman. He died in 1809, probably of natural causes, though family lore had it that it was after a fight with a political opponent in Albany. His son James was a voracious reader with a lively imagination who tramped with his father

---

1. W. H. Gardiner, "Last of the Mohicans: A Narrative of 1757," *North American Review* 23 (July 1826), 158–159.

through the Otsego woods and eagerly took in local folklore about mountain men and Indians. Cooperstown transitioned from a frontier hamlet to a thriving village during Cooper's boyhood years, giving a potential writer ever more hometown material. But Cooper was an indifferent student who disliked writing and even holding a pen. After preliminary schooling in Albany, he was admitted to Yale at the age of thirteen, early but not unheard of in those days. Two years later, though, he was expelled after a number of pranks, including slipping a donkey into a classroom and blowing up another student's door by inserting gunpowder into the keyhole. He worked as a sailor on a merchant vessel that took him to England and Spain, then enlisted in the U.S. Navy, where he spent most of his time relatively close to home, patrolling on lakes Ontario and Erie. Confident of receiving an inheritance from his father the land baron, he married Susan DeLancey, descendant of an old English loyalist family, set up a farm on her family's Westchester estate, and also built a farm cottage and mansion at Cooperstown. He settled into the easy life of a gentleman farmer. James Fenimore Cooper seemed like a young man without any apparent literary interests.[2]

Two factors pushed him out of his leisurely life and toward literary greatness: financial exigencies and a literary vacuum/opportunity. William Cooper's 1809 will made bequests to James and his siblings but mostly in the form of rental properties or bonds and mortgages given by settlers on poor homesteads from Cooper's later, ill-conceived speculations, including hardscrabble farms in St. Lawrence County. James Fenimore Cooper's inheritance soon dwindled, and, by 1820, he was struggling to pay his debts.[3] Friends suggested he try his hand at writing to make money. Books based on the authentic American experience were rare. English literary critic Sydney Smith, writing in the influential *Edinburgh Review* in 1818, had sneered, "Literature the Americans have not—no native literature, we mean. It is all imported. . . . Why should the Americans write books, when a six week's passage brings them [from England] in our own tongue, our sense, science and genius? . . . In the four quarters of the globe, who reads an American book?"[4]

---

2. Wayne Franklin, *James Fenimore Cooper: The Early Years* (New Haven: Yale University Press, 2007), 1–239.
3. Alan Taylor, *William Cooper's Town: Power and Persuasion on the Frontier of the Early American Republic* (New York: Random House, 1995), 372–405.
4. Peter Conn, *Literature in America: An Illustrated History* (New York: Cambridge University Press, 1989), 113.

Cooper was unimpressed by most contemporary English writing, once throwing aside a new English novel in disgust and exclaiming to his wife Susan, "I can write you a better book than that myself!"[5] Susan challenged him to try. Cooper began experimenting with a new genre of literature with fast-moving high adventure set in the American wilderness or countryside and featuring characters motivated by personal courage, self-reliance, and loyalty to family and friends. A few innovative authors on both sides of the Atlantic were showing the way toward the sort of literature that Cooper had in mind. In England, Walter Scott in 1814 had published *Waverly*, a tale of adventure and war set in a rebellion in England in 1745 that is often considered the first "historical novel." Cooper's fellow New Yorker Washington Irving published *A History of New-York from the Beginning of the World to the End of the Dutch Dynasty*, a political satire disguised as a history, in 1809 and *The Sketch Book of Geoffrey Crayon* in 1819, which included the fanciful essays "The Legend of Sleepy Hollow," set in Westchester County, and "Rip Van Winkle" a fictional Catskill mountain character who slept through the Revolution. Cooper's first novel, *Precaution*, published in 1820 and modeled on the sort of English writing so popular at the time but which he was already coming to despise, was a disappointment and confirmed his instincts about the need to strike out in a new direction.

Cooper's imagination began to develop a new model: the forthrightly *American* historical novel with sharply drawn frontier characters, vast and beautiful wilderness, and constant danger and struggle. His 1821 novel, *The Spy*, featured Revolutionary War intrigue and battle in the dangerous, but stunningly beautiful, wilderness of the Westchester area. Two years later, *The Pioneers* presented a fictional version of Cooper's father, William Cooper, personified as Judge Marmaduke Temple of Templeton. The story begins with an argument between Templeton and an independent local hunter, Natty Bumppo, over who killed a deer. It introduces the themes of environmental stewardship, passing of the frontier, wastefulness of modern settlers and civilization, and the tension between order (represented by the judge) and liberty (exemplified by Bumppo). Bumppo became a central character in *The Last of the Mohicans* (represented as a younger man and known as "Hawkeye"), *The Prairie* (1827), *The Pathfinder* (1840), and *The Deerslayer* (1841). In *The Pioneers* he had been

---

5. Susan Fenimore Cooper, *Pages and Pictures from the Writings of James Fenimore Cooper with Notes* (New York: W. A. Townsend and Company, 1861), 17.

called "Leatherstocking" after his buckskin leggings, and this series of five novels became known as the "Leatherstocking Tales."

Cooper produced thirty-five novels and thirteen nonfiction works during his long career. He became the most famous and influential American writer of the early nineteenth century. He could be as contentious as some of his books' characters, for instance, bringing a lawsuit to stop neighbors from picnicking on his Cooperstown land, suing critics of his works for libel, lamenting the excesses of democracy and individualism, defending the prerogatives of landowners over tenants' rights, and criticizing his countrymen's manners and morals. He chastised abolitionist Gerrit Smith for breaking the law by harboring runaway slaves. Cooper was a complex New Yorker, brilliant and enlightened in some ways, closed-minded and a borderline racist in others. Most of his fame rests on the "Leatherstocking Tales" and in particular on *The Last of the Mohicans*.

The Last of the Mohicans and the Historical Record

The novel is set in 1757 during the struggle between the British and the French called the Seven Years' War in Europe and the French and Indian War in North America (1756–1763). The war was the last in a century-long series of conflicts between the two European powers for mastery of North America and preeminence in Europe. When the war began, the French controlled most of what is now eastern Canada and the English held the east coast from Albany south. The war's origins can be traced to a battle in the spring of 1754 between French soldiers asserting their nation's claim to the Ohio Valley and militia from the British province of Virginia commanded by twenty-two-year-old George Washington. A formal declaration of war between the two great European powers followed two years later.[6] New York's geographic location made it of central strategic importance; much of what is now central, western, and northern New York was wild, disputed territory, claimed by both sides and home to thousands of native people. Armies moved slowly overland; they could move faster and more stealthily over water. The Mohawk Valley, the only natural passage through the mountains, and lakes Erie and Ontario were key east-west transportation routes. The Hudson River–Lake George–Lake Champlain

---

6. Fred Anderson, *Crucible of War: The Seven Years' War and the Fate of Empire in British North America, 1754–1766* (New York: Vintage Books, 2000), 11–73.

corridor was essential; with a few overland portages, it constituted an all-water route between New York City and Montreal. Rather symbolically, Lake George, the site of Fort William Henry and much of the action in *The Last of the Mohicans*, is about equidistant from New York City and Montreal. Whichever side controlled New York held the key to mastery of the continent. New York was a British colony but its commitment to the British cause was sometimes lukewarm. The colonial assembly grudgingly appropriated funds to support military action. New Yorkers signed on to colonial regiments for specific campaigns but were restive under the command of haughty British officers and chafed at stiff British military rules, which seemed ill-suited to frontier and wilderness fighting.

In the preface to the first edition of *The Last of the Mohicans*, Cooper asserted that the book was not "an imaginary and romantic picture of things which never had an existence" but instead "a narrative," implying alignment with historical facts. The opening words of the first chapter set the stage: "It was a feature peculiar to the colonial wars of North America that the toils and dangers of the wilderness were to be encountered, before the adverse hosts [Britain and France] could meet. A wide and apparently an impervious boundary of forests severed the possessions of the hostile provinces of France and England."[7] *The Last of the Mohicans* is a mixture of historical fact, accurate and inaccurate historical interpretation, and a good deal of imaginative invention.

Cooper recognized the need to visit the geographical location of his fictional subjects to take in the local flavor. A visiting opportunity appeared fortuitously in August 1824. Four young British sightseeing tourists, including Edward Smith-Stanley, destined to be prime minister decades later, visited New York. Fans of Cooper's *The Pioneers*, they happened to encounter the author at a New York City hotel, and he agreed to join them later as they ventured north of Albany, a region of the state that Cooper had never visited. Cooper caught up with them at Saratoga for a carriage ride north. They stopped at Glens Falls, site of a forty-foot drop in the Hudson, and climbed down to examine a cave that the locals pointed out. Cooper found the setting breathtaking and remarked to his English companions: "I must place one of my old Indians here." Then it was on to Caldwell, as the village of Lake George was then known, where Cooper and his visitors walked around the ruins of Fort William Henry,

---

7. James Fenimore Cooper, *The Last of the Mohicans* (New York: Penguin Books, 1986), 11.

which had been destroyed by the French after they wrested it from the English in 1757. Cooper was fascinated by the village, like his own Cooperstown, at the southern end of a beautiful lake but more secluded and rustic. The group then went by steamer up Lake George and overland to Fort Ticonderoga, famous for its roles in the colonial and Revolutionary wars, and then returned to Ballston Spa, where he parted with his English guests. Like so many visitors to New York historic sites, before and after his time, Cooper took in an exciting sense of the history that had unfolded there. The images of Glens Falls, the cave, the ruins of Fort William Henry, the lake and the forest, settled into Cooper's imagination and would become the setting for his next novel. He probably worked out the outline for *The Last of the Mohicans* before returning home.[8]

Indians are a central part of the novel. Cooper had encountered them in the Otsego area in his youth and, later, arranged meetings with Indians who journeyed to New York City or Washington to become more conversant with their history and culture. But he also relied on historical sources, some of them shaky, leading to inaccurate and misleading characterizations. He used the writings of John Heckewelder, a Moravian missionary to the Indians, whose 1819 book, *Account of the History, Manners, and Customs of the Indian Nations Who Once Inhabited Pennsylvania and the Neighboring States*, conveyed the notion that "Indians are of two sorts, the noble savage and the savage fiend." Heckewelder contended that the Lenni-Lenape, Delawares, Mohicans, and related Algonquian tribes belonged in the former category. He placed Iroquois and Mingos, an independent group in the Iroquois Confederacy, in the second group. In the introduction to the novel, Cooper said that the Lenni-Lenape, Lenope, Delawares, Wapanachki, and Mohicans "all mean the same people or tribes of the same stock." In the novel, he describes them as being mostly neutral or scouts and allies of the British. The introduction says that Iroquois, Mingos, and a few other groups "though not all strictly the same" can be grouped together because they were "politically confederated." In the novel, he makes them mostly allies of the French, and the kidnapper and villain Magua is identified as being a Huron. He explains any potential confusion in names by asserting that Indian tribes called themselves and their enemies by different names, and that European settlers made the situation even more confusing by calling the tribes by still other names. Cooper not only misnames some of the Indian groups.

---

8. Franklin, *James Fenimore Cooper*, 432–439.

He also incorporates and perpetuates a degrading stereotype of Indians as either "good" or "bad," one that has persisted through much of American history.[9]

In fact, as the war began, the Iroquois were apprehensive of both sides and particularly worried about the competition of the two European powers in the Ohio valley where the Iroquois claimed authority over groups of Indians and had trading interests. The Mohawks, one of the Iroquois tribes, joined the British in the early years of the war. The Iroquois as a whole were neutral until 1759 when they became active as British allies. The next year, though, they returned to neutrality but continued to serve the British mostly as negotiators and guides.[10]

The situation on the French side was even more complex. The French commander, Louis-Joseph de Montcalm, had with him over two thousand Indians, from at least thirty-three Indian nations, some as distant as present-day Iowa and Hudson Bay, and others recruited from French missions that extended from the Atlantic to the Great Lakes and included some Iroquois people. Montcalm understood the effectiveness of Indians as wilderness scouts and fighters. He concluded that "in the midst of the woods of America one can no more do without them than without cavalry in open country" but realized they could be independent-minded and difficult to command. At an attack on the English outpost at Oswego in 1756, they had defied French authority and killed some prisoners. Some carried stories back home to the Great Lakes region where they made a deep impression "especially what they have heard tell of everyone there swimming in brandy" as one of Montcalm's aides noted. Equally important was the news that Montcalm had been willing to ransom some English prisoners after the battle at Oswego from their Indian captors. During the summer, encouraged by the French authorities, Indian volunteers flocked to Fort Carillon (the name of the French fort that the English later captured and renamed Ticonderoga). They were promised plunder, trophies, captured weapons, guns, and captives (whom they might adopt, sell into slavery, or ransom). Montcalm knew there was a risk of things getting out of control. He counted on his own authority, flattery, appeasement, and if necessary

9. Cooper, *The Last of the Mohicans*, 1–8; Paul A. W. Wallace, "Cooper's Indians," *New York History* 35 (October 1954), 423–446, http://external.oneonta.edu/cooper/articles/nyhistory/1954nyhistory-wallace.html; John McWilliams, *The Last of the Mohicans: Civil Savagery and Savage Civility* (New York: Twayne, 1995), 89–90.
10. Daniel P. Barr, *Unconquered: The Iroquois League at War in Colonial America* (New York: Praeger, 2006), 117–129.

force, to keep the Indians fighting effectively and not carrying out unrestrained slaughter.[11]

Cooper's description of the military alignment of Indians in the battle is blurry. He may have been deliberately distorting history to appeal to readers who knew the Iroquois had been on the British side in the American Revolution (in the forefront of popular consciousness in the year the novel was published, the fiftieth anniversary of the Declaration of Independence). Or it may be that "Cooper was trying to tease history" by placing his novel in "a deliberately distorted historical and geographical no man's land" where alliances were fluid and Indians changed sides.[12] Furthermore, by making Hawkeye's Indian friend and ally Chingachgook "the last of the Mohicans," Cooper has confounded history ever since 1826. "Contrary to early American literature and Hollywood license, the Last of the Mohicans continue to outlive James Fenimore Cooper's book-ending prediction," says the tribe's current website. "We are alive and thriving in a beautifully forested section of Northern Wisconsin."[13]

The French and Indian War had not gone well for the British and their New York colonial partners in the years before the attack on the fort. In 1755, British forces under William Johnson marched north from Albany and defeated a French and Indian army at Lake George. Johnson constructed a fort there that he called William Henry, after the Prince of Wales, to guard the southern end of the lake, rebuff any invasion from the north, and serve a launch point for future offensives against the French. The fort was constructed of pine logs, not particularly resistant to cannon fire or the rough Lake George climate, but the British built it with two concentric walls, with sand and earth between them. They hoped not to need it for long and were determined to use it as a launch point for expeditions northward to expel the French not only from New York but from all of North America. Johnson built another fort at Fort Edward, about twelve miles south of Lake George, to guard the Hudson. The French countered by constructing a fort at Ticonderoga, which they called Fort Carillon, and at Crown Point, which they called Fort St. Frederic, to cover the portage between lakes George and Champlain.

---

11. Anderson, *Crucible of War*, 186–189.
12. Nicholas Birns, "The Unknown War: *The Last of the Mohicans* and the Effacement of the Seven Years' War in American Historical Myth," paper presented at the 15th Cooper Seminar, July 2005, http://external.oenonta.edu/cooper/articles/suny/2005suny-birns.html.
13. Stockbridge-Munsee Community Band of Mohican Indians, "Welcome to the Stockbridge-Munsee Community," http://www/mohican-nsn.gov/index.htm.

The British northward offensive stalled, and in 1756 General Montcalm led a successful attack on the British outpost at Oswego. In the spring of 1757, he launched a surprise raid on Fort William Henry that the defenders repulsed. But in the summer, Montcalm moved south again with some eight thousand troops, including the Indian forces. Into this tense and dangerous setting Cooper inserts two fictional young women, Cora and Alice Munro, who are determined, for reasons never fully explained, to make the journey from Fort Edward to Fort William Henry, which their father commands, in the company of a fictional gallant English officer, Major Duncan Heyward, despite the obvious danger. (In fact, Colonel George Monro [sic] was in command, and he had three children, but they were all minors and at home in Ireland, not Scotland, where Cooper placed his origins.) The Munro sisters and Heyward are led into an ambush by Magua, an Indian serving as a scout in British service but secretly working for the French. Magua is full of resentment because Colonel Munro had previously had him whipped for drunkenness. He intends to take revenge by kidnapping the colonel's daughters. Cooper makes Magua a model of evil but also makes an opportunity for him to explain that he blames Europeans generally for having introduced alcohol to the Indians and then punishing them for enjoying it. Magua's plans are thwarted by the appearance of Hawkeye (also called Natty Bumppo and Leatherstocking) and his two Mohican companions, father and son, Chingachgook and Uncas. Hawkeye's parentage is unspecified, but the reader learns he grew up with Indians. Cooper also soon lets the reader know of Hawkeye's strengths, resolve, and skills in the forest. Hawkeye, the Mohicans, Heyward, and the Munro sisters hide in a cave at Glens Falls (like the one Cooper and his English friends had visited in 1824). After a fight, Magua abducts the sisters, but Hawkeye and his Mohican friends rescue them and escort them to Fort William Henry.[14]

In fact and in the novel, Montcalm's forces arrived on August 3 and besieged and bombarded the fort. The sand-filled walls mostly held, but French batteries shot over the walls, killed dozens, wounded even more, and destroyed several English cannon. Other cannon exploded from metal

---

14. The action summarized in this paragraph and the next is described in Anderson, *Crucible of War*, 189–198; Ian K. Steele, *Betrayals: Fort William Henry and the "Massacre"* (New York: Oxford University Press, 1990), 78–108; and in Cooper, *The Last of the Mohicans*, 125–174.

fatigue. Monro learned that hoped-for reinforcements from the much larger garrison at Fort Edward would not be coming. The commander there, the timid and ineffective General Daniel Webb, decided to hold all his troops in case Fort William Henry fell and he had to stop Montcalm from marching south to Albany. Montcalm's troops had intercepted a letter from Webb to Monro informing him not to expect help and urging a surrender. Montcalm offered generous surrender terms: Monro's troops could keep their guns (but not ammunition) and go to Fort Edward with a French security guard provided they gave their "parole" not to fight for at least eighteen months. It was a reasonable offer from Montcalm, who was running short of supplies but had enough resources to eventually subdue the fort. It was reasonable for Monro, who had satisfied eighteenth-century standards of military honor by resisting several days, knew the fort would eventually fall, and had faith in Montcalm's promise of safe passage rather than prison. He agreed and surrendered the fort.

Montcalm's Indian allies, informed of the terms after the French general had offered and Monro had accepted, were outraged by what they considered bad faith and betrayal. In the novel, as the surrendered troops and accompanying civilians moved toward Fort Edward, the evil Magua "raised the fatal and appalling whoop" and then

> more than two thousand raging savages broke from the forest at the signal, and threw themselves across the fatal plane with instinctive alacrity. . . . Death was every where, and in his most terrific and disgusting aspects. Resistance only served to inflame the murderers, who inflicted their furious blows long after their victims were beyond the power of their resentment.[15]

The Indians wantonly kill, scalp, and take prisoners, including the Munro sisters. Cooper described the "massacre" in vivid detail, and his account became the one that many people who read the novel accepted as more or less accurate.

In fact, Cooper's research on the attack on the fort and the subsequent atrocities on retreating English who had surrendered shows shaky historical scholarship. Those who escaped told exaggerated tales about the slaughter, some to justify their flight lest they be charged with desertion.

---

15. Cooper, *The Last of the Mohicans*, 176.

One of his sources is David Humphreys's *Life of Israel Putnam* (1788). Putnam was commander of a company of provincial rangers stationed at Fort Edward when the survivors of the "massacre" came straggling in, and he may have visited the destroyed Fort William Henry a few days later. Putnam was not an eyewitness to what happened, but he recorded the horrible tales survivors told as they arrived at Fort Edward, and Humphreys passed them on in the biography. Cooper also used Jonathan Carver's *Travels through the Interior Parts of North America* (1778), which describes the attack on the column in gory detail, including Indians drinking a victim's blood. Carver asserted, without documentation, that as many as 1,500 soldiers and civilians were "killed or made prisoner" in the attack. Carver's book was a standard source in Cooper's day, but later research revealed that much of what Carver represented as being firsthand accounts collected in his travels were actually copied or closely paraphrased the writings of other authors. But he was very influential and was the source for other accounts that Cooper used, including Timothy Dwight's 1821 work *Travels in New England and New York*, which was the first work to refer to the attack as a "massacre." Dwight, president of Yale when Cooper was a student there and widely respected for his writings, had relied on newspaper accounts after the attack, some of them lurid and exaggerated. Like Humphreys, Carver, and Dwight, Cooper mostly blamed treacherous, bloodthirsty Indians for the attack.[16]

The event was tragic, but the loss of life was overstated by many contemporary accounts and by Cooper. Ian Steele, in his 1990 book *Betrayals: Fort William Henry and the "Massacre,"* called the event "a foreseeable collision of attitudes about prisoners of war rather than the drunken or 'homicidal' rage that has been depressingly popular as an explanation among historians." The French were at least partly culpable because they had promised their Indian allies opportunities for trophies, plunder, and captives, but Montcalm had negotiated that away in his safe-conduct agreement with Monro. Many of the Indians wanted guns, money, clothes, and other provisions and killed troops who resisted giving them up. They wanted live captives whom they could ransom or sell into slavery. The total number killed was probably less than two hundred. "It was a limited attack, not a massacre," Steele insists, confronting Cooper and his

16. Thomas Philbrick, "The Sources of Cooper's Knowledge of Fort William Henry," *American Literature* 36 (1964), 209–214; Edward Gaylord Bourne, "The Travels of Jonathan Carver," *American Historical Review* 11 (January 1906), 287–302.

sources. Montcalm was able to secure the release of many prisoners. Many of the other captives were taken to Montreal, where they were ransomed and repatriated through prisoner exchanges negotiated by the governor of New France, who did not want to antagonize France's Indian allies but also would not condone kidnapping and enslavement.[17]

The triumph at William Henry proved to be the high tide of French expansion southward. Montcalm, short of supplies, losing his disillusioned Indian allies, and wary of the strong English garrison at Fort Edward (which was quickly reinforced by colonial New York militia after word of the loss of Fort William Henry got out), destroyed the fort and beat a strategic retreat to Carillon. The loss of Fort William Henry was a rallying point and turning point for the British. Moved by tales of the slaughter at William Henry and seeming French treachery in allowing the slaughter of defenseless people, they vowed retribution. They stepped up changes, already underway to improve their supply and support system, reimburse colonial militia expenses, improve conditions of service for colonial troops, and increase the commitment of regular British troops. In 1759, a capable new commander, Jeffrey Amherst, moved northward with a large, powerful force. He paused near the ruins of Fort William Henry to reflect on the slaughter and build a new fort, called Fort George, after the king. Amherst then moved inexorably northward, destroying Fort Carillon and Fort St. Frederic and replacing them with new English forts, which he called Ticonderoga and Crown Point. The next year the British captured Montreal, and the war ended three years later with a complete British victory.[18]

In the book, in the course of the attack, the Munro sisters are again taken by Magua, who forces them to go with him northward toward Canada. Hawkeye, Heyward, and the Mohicans give chase through the wilds of northern New York for several days all the way to the Canadian border. In the dramatic series of confrontations and struggles to free them, Uncas and Cora are killed and Magua is shot by Hawkeye. Alice and Heyward plan to wed. Hawkeye and Chingachgook, identified as the last of the Mohicans, plan to remain in the wilderness.

17. Steele, *Betrayals*, Preface, 109–185; Steele, "Fort William Henry," in Peter Eisenstadt, editor-in-chief, *The Encyclopedia of New York State* (Syracuse: Syracuse University Press, 2005), 593–594.
18. Anderson, *Crucible of War*, 340–553.

The Historical Hold of *The Last of the Mohicans*

This novel, now nearly two centuries old, has exerted a hold on the imagination and helped shape subsequent literature. Its influence and staying power are attributable to at least six features in the novel.

Vivid, scenic descriptions. The novel abounds with evocative verbal portrayals of primeval nature—forests, lakes, and streams—that let the reader imagine being there. In fact, early readers often commended Cooper for his power to create verbal portraits. Cooper is the literary counterpart to Thomas Cole, a friend and colleague, founder of the Hudson River School of painting known for its detailed representation of the American wilderness and natural landscape. This literary style appealed to readers in the 1820s, a time of growth of towns and cities and westward movement of the American frontier (mostly gone in the eastern part of the country by the time the novel was published), and to readers since then who discern something noble and appealing in nature. It represents a bit of nostalgia for an idealized past. The natural world is presented as wild but ordered, beneficent, and best left inviolate. Cooper has Hawkeye describe "Glenns Falls" where he and his companions hide from the Indians in a cave:

> It falls by no rule at all; sometimes it leaps, sometimes it tumbles; there, it skips; here, it shoots; in one place, 'tis as white as snow, and in another 'tis green as grass; hereabouts, it pitches into deep hollows, that rumble and quake the 'arth; and thereaway, it ripples and sings like a brook, fashioning whirlpools and gullies in the old stone. . . . the river fabricates all sorts of images, as if, having broken loose from order, it would try its hand at every thing.[19]

He describes "Horican" (Lake George) before the battle:

> The mountains looked green and fresh and lovely; tempered with the milder light, or softened in shadow, as thin vapours floated between them and the sun. The numerous islands rested on the bosom of the Horican, some low and sunken, as if imbedded in the waters, and others appearing to hover above the element, in little hillocks of green velvet . . . [20]

19. Cooper, *The Last of the Mohicans*, 55.
20. Ibid., 147.

The description of the scenery turns somber as Hawkeye and his companions view the destroyed fort:

> The wind had fallen and the waves were already rolling on the sandy beach beneath them in a more regular and tempered succession. The clouds, as if tired of their furious chase, were breaking asunder; the heavier volumes, gathering in black masses about the horizon, while the lighter scud still hurried above the water, or eddied among the tops of the mountains, like broken flights of birds hovering around their roosts. . . . Within the bosom of the encircling hills, an impenetrable darkness had already settled, and the plain lay like a vast and deserted charnel-house, without omen or whisper, to disturb the slumbers of its numerous and hapless tenants.[21]

Venture into danger-pursuit-capture-rescue-escape. The novel is essentially two harrowing and suspenseful chase scenes separated by the main characters' short stay at Fort William Henry. In fact, it was originally published as two volumes. The main protagonists, Hawkeye, Uncas, and Chingachgook, constant prowl through the forest, being tracked, attacked, or grappling with their antagonists. The women, Cora and Alice, repeatedly referred to as "the gentle ones," are prototypical damsels in distress, though Cora is more spirited and resistant and Alice more accepting and passive. Cooper makes danger ever-present or just off in the shadows of the woods. This holds the reader's attention, either witnessing exciting action or expecting more to come. Hawkeye, the embodiment of the American hero, served as a model from the popular "dime novels" of the 1870s through the Lone Ranger of the 1950s and even beyond, to James Bond and Indiana Jones. The loner hero, sometimes with a trusted sidekick, ventures into the unknown, lives by his wits and strengths, rescues maidens, and rights wrongs.[22]

Struggles between contending forces. Cooper runs a theme through this work: the struggle between competing titanic forces. It is the English (and their American colonial allies) versus the French at Fort William Henry, a relatively small battle in a century-long contest for mastery of North America. It is Mohicans versus Hurons, the old versus the new,

---

21. Ibid., 191.
22. McWilliams, *The Last of the Mohicans*, 12.

accommodationists versus defiant resisters in the inexorable process of European/American encroachment onto lands occupied by the Indians. "The pale-faces are masters of the earth," laments the old Delaware chief Tamenund at the end of the novel.[23] On an even grander scale, it is humans wrestling a continent from nature, a theme that also runs through the other books in the Leatherstocking series.

Hawkeye's personality and traits. Hawkeye is a prototypical American hero. His character vaguely resembles real-life American icons such as Daniel Boone. He shows enduring strength; he is aloof, upright, trying to live in an ideal way even as the frontier is vanishing. Raised among Indians, he has their instinctive connection to nature and innate sense of right and wrong. Honor and loyalty count above all. Leaving a friend in danger, or a job half done, is never an option. You don't look for a fight, but you never walk away from one, either. Experience and instinct trump formal education: "[Y]our young white [man], who gathers his learning from books, and can measure what he knows by the page, may conceit that his knowledge, like his legs, outruns that of his father; but where experience is the master, the scholar is made to know the value of years, and respects them accordingly."[24] Hawkeye is "the white man of the wilderness whose loyalty to ancient virtues is designed to remind the white settlers and developers of the principles on which a republic dedicated to the preservation of human freedom is based. . . . the foundational truth within the pretensions of civilization."[25] Cooper used this and other novels "to vindicate a mysterious and misunderstood protagonist by ultimately revealing his hidden but true nobility of breeding and spirit, thereby dumbfounding rivals and critics."[26]

Harrowing, hand-to-hand combat. Cooper excels in describing encounters between masculine heroes and villains. Hawkeye, fighting desperately with an Indian who has discovered his hiding place in the cave:

> With ready skill, Hawkeye and his antagonist each grasped that uplifted arm of the other, which held the dangerous knife. For near a minute, they stood looking one another in the eye, and

---

23. Cooper, *The Last of the Mohicans*, 350.
24. Ibid., 213.
25. Richard Hutson, "Cooper's Leatherstocking Tales," in Greil Marcus and Werner Sollors, eds., *The New Literary History of America* (Cambridge: Belknap Press of Harvard University Press, 2009), 185.
26. Taylor, *William Cooper's Town*, 408.

gradually exerting the power of their muscles for the mastery. At length, the toughened sinews of the white man prevailed over the less practiced limbs of the native. The arm of the latter slowly gave way before the increasing force of the scout, who suddenly wresting his armed hand from the grasp of his foe, drove the sharp weapon through his naked bosom to the heart.[27]

In the next paragraph, an Indian with a "grim smile" has Heyward by the throat until Uncas comes up, cuts the Indian's wrist, and hurls him down "the irrevocable precipice" to death. Similar scenes are repeated later in adventure serials, Jack London, John Ford films, westerns, James Bond, *Star Wars* and Indiana Jones's films; *Last of the Mohicans* is the "prototypical source."[28]

Excellent descriptive writing. Cooper can be verbose and roundabout in his use of language. Sometimes, he seems to put overly long narrations into the mouths of usually straight-talking characters like Hawkeye and Magua. Occasionally a character repeats or closely paraphrases something he has already said, perhaps many pages earlier in a slightly different context. On the other hand, Cooper's best writing is a model of selecting just the exact words and not putting in anything extra. For instance, at one point Hawkeye needs to win a competitive shooting contest to confirm his identity:

The scout had shook his priming, and cocked his piece, while speaking; and, as he ended, he threw back a foot and slowly raised the muzzle from the earth. The motion was steady, uniform, and in one direction. When on a perfect level, it remained for a single moment without tremor or variation, as though both man and rifle were carved in stone. During that stationary instant, it poured forth its contents, in a bright, glancing, sheet of flame.[29]

The Last of the Mohicans' Influence on History

By midcentury, both Washington Irving and Herman Melville referred to Cooper as "our national novelist." *The Last of the Mohicans* has gone

---

27. Cooper, *The Last of the Mohicans*, 71.
28. McWilliams, *The Last of the Mohicans*, 34
29. Cooper, *The Last of the Mohicans*, 299.

through at least seventeen editions, has never gone out of print, has been translated into every major language, and has served as the basis for several movies and TV episodes. It was greeted with acclaim in 1826 and has generally stood the test of time. Francis Parkman, renowned nineteenth-century historian and author of the multivolume study *France and England in North America*, criticized Cooper in an 1852 review for taking liberties with history and occasional verbosity. But the book has "a genuine game flavor; it exhales the odors of the pine-woods and the freshness of the mountain wind. Its dark and rugged scenery rises as distinctly on the eye as the images of the painter's canvass . . . they breathe the somber poetry of solitude and danger." Leatherstocking shows "quiet, unostentatious courage. . . . uprightness, kindliness, innate philosophy, and the truest moral perceptions. . . . [along with] wandering instincts and the hatred of restraints."[30]

By midcentury, Cooper had inspired both imitators and parodies, a reliable sign of iconic status. Bret Harte, an author and poet best known for his description of pioneering life in California, composed a parody he titled "Muck-A-Muck: A Modern Indian Novel After Cooper" in 1867. The story is set in California, where Hart, originally from Albany, New York, was living. Strolling through the forest one day, the heroine, Genevra Thompson, suddenly sees a bear, two mountain lions, a wildcat, a buffalo, and a Spanish bull moving menacingly up the trail toward her. Hawkeye suddenly appears, shouts,

> "Dern ye—don't move!" and kills all five with a single shot. The crack of a rifle rang through the woods. Three frightful yells were heard, and two sullen roars. Five animals bounded into the air and five lifeless bodies lay upon the plain. . . . Genevra turned quickly. "My preserver!" she shrieked and fell into the arms of Natty Bumppo, the celebrated Pike Ranger of Donner Lake.[31]

Mark Twain, in a humorous but biting 1895 essay entitled "Fenimore Cooper's Literary Offenses" focused on *The Pioneers* and *The Deerslayer*

---

30. Francis Parkman, "James Fenimore Cooper," *North American Review* (January 1852), reprinted in Allen Thorndike, ed., *Essays from the North American Review* (1879), 358–376, http://books.google.com/books?id=GKoiAAAAMAAJ.
31. Bret Harte, "Muck-A-Muck: A Modern Indian Novel After Cooper," first published in *Condensed Novels*, 1867, in Dekker and McWilliams, *Fenimore Cooper*, 273.

but slammed Cooper's work generally. Twain asserted that "Cooper wrote about the poorest English that exists in our language" and violated eighteen of twenty-two "rules governing literary art in domain of romantic fiction" including "*Say* what he is proposing to say, not merely come near it. Use the right word, not its second cousin. Eschew surplusage. Avoid slovenliness of form."[32] D. H. Lawrence, the twentieth-century English writer, commended Cooper for exploring hard-edged issues of race and individual rebellion and the shaping influences of setting and circumstances. "And Natty, what sort of a white man is he? Why, he is a man with a gun. He is a killer, a slayer. Patient and gentle as he is, he is a slayer. ... The essential American soul is hard, isolate, stoic and a killer."[33]

The novel and subsequent movies based on it have shaped the popular view of history. President Andrew Jackson, rationalizing federal policy in moving Cherokee and other Indian groups out of Georgia in 1829, asserted that the advance of white civilization made continuation of Indian life very difficult. That paralleled a theme in *The Last of the Mohicans*. Jackson's conclusion—that therefore the Indians must leave—was a convenient corollary and justification for pushing the Indians off their lands, one that continued for many years.[34] Four months before publication of *The Last of the Mohicans*, on October 26, 1825, Governor DeWitt Clinton and other state officials boarded a boat with a name also derived from the Indians, *The Seneca Chief*, at Buffalo for a trip to open the newly constructed Erie Canal. The canal, and, later, roads and railroads, facilitated the rapid growth of New York State, which led to coerced treaties and forced land sales that took lands claimed by the Iroquois, forcing Indians onto state-defined "reservations." "Making Indians taxpaying citizens of New York State became the avowed goal of Albany policymakers, one filled with the paternalistic rhetoric of humanely saving tribespeople both from the horrors of removal and, at the same time, from their own alleged 'savagery,'" notes historian Laurence Hauptman. "Indians had to be transformed for their own good through a careful process of 'civilization.'"[35]

---

32. Mark Twain, "Fenimore Cooper's Literary Offenses," *North American* Review 161 (July 1895), http://etext.virginia.edu/railton/projects/rissetto/offense.html.
33. D. H. Lawrence, *Studies in Classic American Literature* (New York: Thomas Selzer, 1923), chap. 5, http://xroads.virginia.edu/~hyper/LAWRENCE/dhltoc.htm.
34. McWilliams, *The Last of the Mohicans*, 106–107.
35. Laurence M. Hauptman, *Conspiracy of Interests: Iroquois Dispossession and the Rise of New York State* (Syracuse: Syracuse University Press, 2001), 219.

In September 1992, a $40 million adaptation of *The Last of the Mohicans* opened in theaters. Director Michael Mann, who prized historical accuracy, considered using the replica of the fort at Lake George but rejected it because it is in a village setting and instead constructed his own replica, using period drawings and plans, in the hills of North Carolina. Mann, who said he was "bored to tears by history when he was a child," found this tale engrossing and exciting. He hired historical experts to get the history right, did a good deal of reading and research himself, and announced that he intended the film to correct misconceptions about eighteenth-century Indian life and culture. Mann and Daniel Day-Lewis, the British-born actor who played Nathaniel Poe (Hawkeye's given name in the film), spent a month in the North Carolina forests, learning wilderness survival skills. Mann hired Indians to play the Indians in the film and the Indian activist-turned-actor Russell Means played Chingachgook. Mann told reporters he felt an "intellectual obligation" to respect history but dismissed the idea that films have to be historically correct in all details, trying for "a middle course between entertainment and history."[36] The 1992 film drew on a 1936 film adaption as well as on the original novel. Hawkeye is more dashing and assertive than Cooper's original. The adventure is nonstop, the "massacre" scene abundantly gory. The evil Magua, motivated mostly by revenge for his earlier punishment by Colonel Munro, kills him and cuts out his heart as well as kidnapping his daughters. By the end of the movie, Chingachgook kills Magua after Magua kills Uncas, and Hawkeye and Cora become a romantic couple.

The film garnered critical acclaim and was a box-office success. A reviewer in the popular journal *American Heritage* said that the movie "gets it right," presenting "a thrilling, romantic adventure" set on the frontier, "a gorgeous, wild, romantic and horribly dangerous place where the seeds of democracy are sown."[37] But historian Ian Steele, whose 1990 book *Betrayals* had presented the most historically accurate account of the episode at the fort, panned the film. The movie, like the book, twisted history too much. Monro and other British officers survived the attack, fewer than two hundred people were killed, and many of the captives were later liberated by French authorities in Canada. Steele faulted Mann for

---

36. Joel Engel, "A Fort, a War and the Last Thousand or So Mohicans," *New York Times*, September 20, 1992.
37. "Editor's Choice: Last of the Mohicans," *American Heritage* 45 (February/March 1994), 109.

perpetuating Magua as "Cooper's fictional bad Indian." He asserted that the Indians "used measured terror to gain booty denied them by the surrender terms." The film endorsed "an ancient lie about Indian savagery."[38]

The Last of the Mohicans maintains a hold on the historical imagination that is at least as strong as historical accounts of the episode it describes. It is flawed in many ways, including Cooper's division of Indians into "good" and "bad," perpetuation of the notion of unprovoked savagery, and implication that Indians were more or less identified with "wilderness" and ill at ease with "civilization." It slights the fact that Indians were a major military force in the colonial wars and that they had a good deal at stake in the outcome. In these areas, Cooper was reflecting the unfortunate sentiments of his times rather than inventing anything new, but because his novels were so popular, the interpretations in *The Last of the Mohicans* and his other works seeped into popular culture.[39] Even today, though, the novel makes for good reading and exciting fictional historical adventuring in colonial New York. Hawkeye is a historical character who has stood the test of time. Cooper, even with all his inaccuracies, exaggerations, interpretations, and anachronistic views on race, war, and civilization, is an extraordinarily skillful writer. He has presented an engaging and enduring tale of danger and adventure.

---

38. Ian K. Steele, "The Last of the Mohicans," *Journal of American History* 80 (December 1993), 1179–1181.
39. See Thomas King, *The Inconvenient Indian: A Curious Account of Native Peoples in North America* (Minneapolis: University of Minnesota Press, 2013), 28–29.

3
July 4, 1839

The Farmers' Rebellion

Rebellious tenant farmers wore disguises in their campaigns to resist collection of rents by estate owners in the two decades after 1839. The July 4, 1839, Berne "Declaration of Independence" was issued by tenant farmers meeting in this Lutheran church. *Photos courtesy of Murray, David, LL.D., ed.,* Delaware County New York: History of the Century, 1797–1897 *(Delhi, NY: William Clark, Publisher, 1898) and Ms. Annmarie Gregory.*

A New Declaration of Independence

On July 4, 1839, angry tenants of Hudson Valley land baron Stephen Van Rensselaer IV gathered at the Lutheran church in Berne (Albany County) to write their own "Declaration of Independence." They were not trying to overthrow the Town of Berne, Albany County, or New York State. Instead, they meant to defy their landlord by demanding lower rent and the right to purchase the hilly farms they were leasing. They threatened a rent strike if he ignored their demands.

Van Rensselaer's estate included most of Albany County. It was one of twenty-four tenanted estates, encompassing about two million acres in sixteen counties in the eastern part of New York. Over 260,000 people, about one-twelfth of the state's population, lived on farms leased from the landlords. The estates originated in Dutch and English colonial land grants and were passed down as inheritances from one generation to the next. They survived the American Revolution, in part because most of the landlords supported the patriots. New York State, established in 1777, had not challenged any of the titles. Minor tenant uprisings in the late eighteenth and early years of the nineteenth century accomplished little. The farmers aligned with the American tradition of citing the Declaration of Independence to justify overthrow of the status quo. Calling Van Rensselaer the "pretended proprietor" and denouncing his uncompromising hold on the land as "an outrage upon the laws of humanity" and the manor system as "wretchedness and unhallowed bondage," the July 4 Berne manifesto asserted:

> We have counted the cost of such a contest, and we find nothing so dreadful as voluntary slavery. Honor, justice, and humanity forbid that we should any longer tamely surrender that freedom which we have so freely inherited from our gallant ancestors, and which our innocent posterity have a right to receive or expect from us. . . . We will take up the ball of the Revolution where our fathers stopped it and roll it up to the final consummation of freedom and independence of the masses.[1]

The Berne protest meeting kicked off the "anti-rent wars," perhaps the most spectacular tenant rebellion in U.S. history.

The Albany County farmers felt they had history on their side. They were asserting the right to the individual liberties that the American Revolution seemed to promise. President Andrew Jackson had dramatically championed the rights of the common man over concentrated financial power and social elites during his term as president, 1829 to 1837, launching the modern Democratic Party. The other major party, the Whigs, also relatively new, were more aligned with commercial interests. But William Seward, New York's young Whig governor, who had taken office in

---

1. Henry Christman, *Tin Horns and Calico: The Thrilling Unsung Story of an American Revolt Against Serfdom* (New York: Henry Holt and Co., 1945), xi.

January 1839, was from Auburn in western New York where the manor system was unknown. Seward regarded government as an agent for change and had little use for an archaic landed aristocracy. The farmers were hopeful that their state government would support their demands.

An Archaic Land System

The Berne declaration confronted a land system that originated two centuries earlier. The Dutch West India Company, which controlled the land in the Dutch colony of New Netherland, had made a large land grant to one of its directors, Amsterdam pearl and diamond merchant Kiliaen Van Rensselaer, in 1629. The bulk of the estate, encompassing most of the land in present-day Albany and Rensselaer counties, passed down through inheritance to Stephen Van Rensselaer III in 1785. The Van Rensselaer land barons were still called by the Dutch term *patroon*, a reminder of how anachronistic the land system was. Van Rensselaer leased long-term rather than sold farms, and the farmers were tenants, not owners, who owed him rent amounting to ten to fourteen bushels of wheat, "four fat fouls," and a day of service with team and wagon to fix roads every year. The owner reserved all water, timber, and mineral rights. The tenant had to pay all land taxes. Not meeting all the requirements could mean eviction. The tenant might sell his contract right, but the landlord could collect a quarter of the sale price or recover full title to the property at three-quarters of market value. Stephen Van Rensselaer advertised to increase settlement in the hilly western parts of Albany County, which he called the West Manor, and eastern parts of Rensselaer County, the East Manor. He added a new inducement: no rent for the first seven years while the new farmers cleared the land, built houses and barns, and began growing crops. Enterprising families who headed into the hills to clear the land and begin subsistence farming found that much of the land was not the fertile soil that Van Rensselaer's agents had advertised. Some tenants joked grimly that rocks were the only dependable crop and that the western Albany County hill towns must have been the last place God created and the dumping ground for all the rock left over from Creation.[2]

Van Rensselaer and the other eastern New York land barons combined wealth with power and claimed a natural right to dominate society

---

2. Ibid., 9.

and politics. Self-interest came first. James Fenimore Cooper, the narrator of ardent frontier adventuring in *The Last of the Mohicans*, was also an eloquent proponent of the ideology of social superiority of the landed gentry. His book *The American Democrat* (1838) extolled the virtues of ownership, contractual rights, social hierarchy, and deference. The innate differences of intellect, talent, and industry, and the head-start advantages of inherited land and wealth, established a natural hierarchy. "Equality of condition is rendered impossible. One man must labor, while another may live luxuriously on his means; one has leisure and opportunities to cultivate his tastes, to increase his information, and to refine his habits, while another is compelled to toil so that he may live." Moreover, the elite were "the natural repository of the manners, tastes, tone and to a certain extent the principles of a country."[3]

Stephen Van Rensselaer III had no doubt of his inherited rights but sometimes was lax in collecting his rents and negotiated for partial payment when tenants claimed hardship. When he died in January 1839, his estate was laden with debt because of rents in arrears of over $400,000. His will specified that his heirs—Stephen IV, who got the West Manor, and William, who inherited the East Manor—were to collect the overdue rents. College educated and aloof, neither brother knew many of the tenants personally and were not interested in their welfare. When greeted by his tenants, Stephen IV did not even shake hands with them, instead extending his forefinger to be grasped. The brothers despised grassroots democracy, feared assertive tenants, and needed money. If the tenants would not pay their rent, they would be evicted from the land and replaced by more willing, deferential tenants. Stephen IV was particularly aggressive, dispatching agents into the hill towns west of Albany with demand for payment in the spring of 1839. The tenants had assumed back rents would be forgiven when Stephen III died. Paying the back debts would confirm their status as perpetual tenants. Farms in neighboring nontenant counties were selling for less than a year's rent on the Van Rensselaer manors. Moreover, many tenants simply did not have the money. Soil depletion or exhaustion was undercutting the land's productivity. The Erie Canal,

---

3. Reeve Huston, *Land and Freedom: Rural Society, Popular Protest, and Party Politics in Antebellum New York* (New York: Oxford University Press, 2000), 73–74, quoting James Fenimore Cooper, *American Democrat*, 39, 84–87, 132–133, 145–146; Martin Bruegel, "Manorial Society and the Market in the Hudson Valley, 1780–1850," *Journal of American History* 82 (March 1996), 1408.

opened in 1825, had exposed them to rising competition from the west for sale of two of their major products, wheat and wool. New York's farm economy was transitioning to dairying, but dairy cows were expensive. Mowing machines, rakes, and other equipment for hay to feed the cows also required cash. But many land barons were also in need of money for another reason. Their investments in western lands, railroad stocks, and state bonds had declined or vanished as a result of the Panic of 1837, a financial crisis that had plunged the nation into a major recession.[4]

In May, 1839, the West Manor tenants elected a delegation of influential working tenant farmers to bargain with their new landlord. Van Rensselaer's land agent scheduled a meeting with the patroon at his mansion in Watervliet near Albany. But when the committee arrived, he refused to meet with them, striding through his front office as they stood waiting in the foyer without even greeting them. The agent informed them that the landlord had decided only to consider written proposals. Undaunted, the group withdrew to a nearby tavern and drew up a document. They requested forgiveness of unpaid rent for those whose debts exceeded the value of their personal property, issuance of new leases in which rents could be paid in cash, abrogation of the "quarter sale" and "reservation" provisions, and the option to purchase their farms for two to two and a half dollars an acre. Van Rensselaer rejected most of their demands. He offered to sell hilly farms but at twice the tenant committee's suggested price. Farms in the more fertile, valley areas were not for sale at any price. All past due rents must be paid. Rents could be paid in cash but at a much higher rate than the committee had requested. The patroon's tone was arrogant and uncompromising. The tenants' July 4 resolution at Berne constituted their defiant response. Taking their cue from the Berne declaration, tenants on other landed estates also began digging in with nonpayment pledges. Like the leaders in Berne, many of the organizers were from the middle strata of rural society. Some owned as well as leased farms. They were respected in their home communities for hard work and personal integrity. They used their reputations as solid local citizens to rally their neighbors to the growing cause.[5]

---

4. Charles McCurdy, *The Anti-Rent Era in New York Law and Politics, 1839–1865* (Chapel Hill: University of North Carolina Press, 2001), 13; David W. Ellis, *Landlords and Farmers in the Hudson-Mohawk Region, 1790–1850* (Ithaca: Cornell University Press, 1946), 184–224; Thomas Summerhill, *Harvest of Dissent: Agrarianism in Nineteenth-Century New York* (Urbana: University of Illinois Press, 2005), 34–50.

5. Huston, *Land and Freedom*, 89–91; Christman, *Tin Horns and Calico*, 15–20.

The Helderberg War

The issue reached a flash point first in the towns of Berne, Knox, Rensse-laerville, and Westerlo in the Helderberg Mountains west of Albany. These independent, enterprising tenant farmers were accustomed to wresting a living from hilly fields and thin, stony soil. The work had made them hearty and resistant. By late summer 1839, Van Rensselaer's agents were reporting sullen attitudes and polite but firm refusals to pay the rent. The patroon called on Albany County sheriff Michael Artcher to begin serving legal writs of ejectment for nonpayment, hoping to make an example of ringleaders. In the ensuing struggles, county sheriffs would constitute the sharp end of landlord legal action against recalcitrant tenants. Often, this would require considerable personal courage in confronting armed resis-tance. On August 20, Deputy Sheriff Amos Adams drove up to the home of Isaac Hungerford in Berne. "I warn you as a friend to go no further," the farmer told the lawman. "You can't go through this country with patroon papers and get home a live man." Adams persisted, Hungerford drew a knife; Adams reconsidered, pocketed the papers, and drove off. He continued to serve papers the rest of the day, spending the night in a Rens-selaerville tavern. But during the night local farmers wrecked his wagon, destroyed his harness, and clipped his horse's mane and tail. Adams scur-ried back to Albany. A few days later, a meeting of tenant farmers issued a public warning to the sheriff to keep his forces out of the Helderbergs.[6]

But on September 15, another deputy, Daniel Leonard, headed into the hills to serve warrants. At his first stop, farmer Paul Vincent warned him, "[I]f you want to get back a whole man, you better git as quick as possible!" Soon, a group of armed men were trailing him. When he paused at a local tavern, a group of fifty men seized him. They warned him to burn the remaining warrants or they would kill him. He complied, and then his tormenters forced him to buy them a round of drinks at a local tavern. Then they loaded him into a wagon and retraced his trip, forcing him to take back all the warrants he had dropped off and burn them. They released him late in the afternoon and he rushed back to the sheriff's office in Albany.[7]

6. McCurdy, *The Anti-Rent Era in New York Law and Politics*, 18–22; Christman, *Tin Horns and Calico*, 20–23.
7. Huston, *Land and Freedom*, 93; Christman, *Tin Horns and Calico*, 23–27.

Sheriff Artcher was not to be cowed by a ragtag army of farmers. On December 2, he summoned a posse in Albany to suppress the rebellion in the Helderbergs. Several of the capitol's most prominent citizens appeared for this civic duty, including bank presidents, former governor William Marcy, President Martin Van Buren's son John, and Stephen Van Rensselaer IV himself, though he dropped out before the posse left Albany. Artcher marched up into the hills at the head of five hundred men to the hamlet of Reidsville on the border between Westerlo and Berne. They were met by an army of 1,500 farmers armed with clubs, knives, and guns. The farmers rushed the posse, which withdrew back down the hill and returned to Albany. Four days later, the sheriff tried again with another posse. The farmers again blocked the way and this time even brought a vintage cannon to intimidate the posse, and the sheriff again retreated.[8]

Artcher appealed to Governor William Seward for help. Seward sympathized with the tenants, but he could not allow an armed mob to block enforcement of the law. New York had no state police in those days—they would not be established until 1917—but Seward ordered the state militia into the mountains to back up the sheriff. "The only security for the preservation of [your] rights consists in the complete ascendancy of the laws," he said in a proclamation to the rebellious farmers. The proper remedy lay in appeal to the legislature and the courts. Seward promised "every facility which the Executive Department can afford in bringing [your] complaints before the legislature."[9] Heartened by the governor's apparent support, the farmers withdrew and the militia marched to Reidsville without incident. Sheriff Artcher served his legal papers without opposition. Action shifted from armed confrontation in the Helderberg mountain passes to political maneuvering in the corridors of the state capitol.

The State Equivocates

Anti-rent leaders busied themselves over the next couple of months with gathering signatures on petitions to the legislature for relief from the landed system. True to his word, Governor Seward, in his January 1840 message to the legislature, said that manors held under ancient grants and oppressive land leases are "unfavorable to agricultural improvements,

---

8. Huston, *Land and Freedom*, 94.
9. Ibid., 94.

inconsistent with the prosperity of the districts where they exist, and opposed to the sound policy and genius of our institutions." New York government "has always recognized its obligation to promote the general welfare and guard individuals against oppression" and has a "bounden duty" to address the tenants' demands.[11]

Both the Democratic and the Whig parties were made up of loose alliances and factions. Coalescing around a policy on an issue as contentious as the rent issue was next to impossible. Both parties temporized, equivocated, and appealed for anti-renters' support. On the other hand, the anti-renters sometimes held the balance of power between the two parties, giving them leverage on issues of concern.[12] Seward's Whig Party controlled the legislature in 1840, and an assembly committee took up the governor's challenge and the farmers' petitions. The committee issued an equivocal report, the first of many on the subject that would emanate from the capitol. The tenants had legitimate grievances, the report said, but the state was powerless to abrogate or modify the leases. The state might, however, seize the lands of the Van Rensselaers and others by eminent domain, compensate the owners, and bestow the lands on the tenants. The legislature endorsed the report, but only in the form of a nonbinding resolution. The action was a political coup for Seward and the Whigs, who could tell voters that they had stood up to the landlords and supported the tenants. But it was really a clever evasion: Seizing land by eminent domain was unlikely to survive legal challenges the patroons were sure to pose against it, and the state, short of money due to overspending on canals and railroads, lacked funds to purchase the lands. The legislature authorized the governor to create a Manor Commission to mediate between the Van Rensselaers and their tenants and estimate the cost if the state were to buy the manors. But the commission could find no middle-ground compromise and was unable to estimate the value of the land. Its report in April 1841 declared that "tenures of the kind existing on the Manor of Rensselaerswyck are in every way unfortunate in their operation upon the tenants individually and upon the general conditions of the country. They are incongruous with the general laws, institutions, customs and habits of the people of this state." But it advanced no action recommendations.

---

10. McCurdy, *The Anti-Rent Era in New York Law and Politics*, 33.
11. Ibid., 42–55; Huston, *Land and Freedom*, 98–100.
12. Summerhill, *Harvest of Dissent*, 42–59.

Seward, beset by other problems including a crisis of rising state debt, took no action on it.[13]

In the fall 1841 elections, Democrats, who at that time favored state government protection of property and contracts, secured control of the legislature. The tenants, growing impatient, began to organize county-by-county committees, and new leaders emerged, including Dr. Smith M. Boughton, a charismatic doctor from Alps in Rensselaer County, who spearheaded the circulation of anti-rent petitions to the legislature. In 1842 the Assembly Judiciary Committee dutifully reported that the patroon system was inconsistent with the American system of land ownership but declared the state had no power to interfere with it. Rather remarkably, it declared that "happily, however, time will cure the evil. Such estates. . . . under the all-prevailing influence of our institutions, will in a few years be gradually worn away."[14]

Unwilling to wait for that unlikely development, Boughton and other leaders held a conference in Rensselaerville on July 4, 1842, and produced a new "Statement of Grievances and Proposed Redress," which condemned the system because the landlords paid no taxes and asserted that their titles to the lands were illegal. The anti-rent forces introduced a bill in the 1843 legislature requiring the Van Rensselaers and others to prove title or give up the land. But that proposal foundered when the U.S. Supreme Court invalidated a law that impaired the ability to enforce contracts, and the state Court of Appeals issued a ruling that eminent domain could not empower government to take one person's property in order to transfer it to another. Undaunted, the next year the anti-renters presented the legislature with petitions with over twenty-five thousand signatures. An assembly select committee reported that the landed system burdened the state and proposed taxing the landlords, court tests for their titles, or use of eminent domain. But the full assembly rejected the report, sent the matter to the Judiciary Committee, which issued a report influenced (and possibly drafted) by Van Rensselaer lawyers. It declared that the alleged hardships were imaginary and remedies were available from the landlords: "[T]he tenants can have all the relief to which they are, in justice and equity, entitled directly from the proprietors of the manor." The legislature endorsed the report and adjourned. The anti-rent forces had been

---

13. McCurdy, *The Anti-Rent Era in New York Law and Politics*, 42–65; Huston, *Land and Freedom*, 98–100.
14. Christman, *Tin Horns and Calico*, 46–72

deceived by both political parties, abandoned by the governor, spurned by the legislature, and undercut by the courts.[15]

Escalating Direct Action

Defeats in Albany made the anti-renters all the more determined. Anti-rent associations in the two Van Rensselaer manors had enrolled over ten thousand members by early 1844. The leaders met at the home of anti-rent leader John Gallup in Berne on May 18 and resolved to organize anti-rent committees in every county where manors existed. They found fertile ground, for anti-landlord feeling was growing throughout eastern New York. Thousands of handbills were posted: "ATTENTION ANTI-RENTERS! AWAKE! AROUSE! A great crisis is approaching. Now is the time to strike!" Soon there were active associations in Albany, Rensselaer, Schoharie, Delaware, Ulster, and other counties. The associations sponsored meetings, held rallies, hosted dances, had liberty pole raisings, and organized massive, festive July 4 celebrations. They endorsed candidates from both parties who pledged to support the anti-rent cause and sometimes fielded their own, independent candidates. In January 1845, representatives of the county associations returned to Berne and formed a statewide committee. Anti-renters soon launched their own newspapers, the *Helderberg Advocate, Guardian of the Soil,* and *The Anti-Renter.* Smith Boughton and other hometown advocates were supplemented by new allies. Horace Greeley, editor of the influential *New-York Tribune,* endorsed the anti-rent cause. Thomas Devyr, a tireless writer, speaker, newspaper editor, and reformer, linked the anti-rent crusade to broader reform campaigns to eliminate land monopolies wherever they existed and to make public lands in the west available free of charge for homesteaders. By mid-1844, the advocates had developed or refined a battery of anti-rent rationales.

- The landlords are aristocrats, incompatible with a free, egalitarian society.
- They prevent productive tillers of the soil from enjoying the fruits of their labor.

---

15. Huston, *Land and Freedom,* 101–102; McCurdy, *The Anti-Rent Era in New York Law and Politics,* 62–70.

- People working farms for many years and making them productive have a greater claim to them than idle landlords whose ancestors were given title to the land because of their connections with Dutch or English colonial officials.
- Tenants are slow to adopt progressive agricultural practices because they do not own the land, and this retards agriculture in New York State.
- Landlords endanger democratic government through influencing tenants how to vote.

The anti-rent leaders also assembled paramilitary groups in the counties with landed manors. Organized in small, networked units with local commanders, the groups consisted of tenants, particularly young men, determined to confront the landlords and their agents. They dressed in masks and calico costumes to preserve anonymity and referred to themselves as "Indians," a tribute to fierce Native American warriors. It was also a patriotic connection to the Boston Tea Party, where rebellious colonists disguised as Indians had dumped tea overboard from a ship to protest arbitrary British taxation.[16] The "Indian" network was a blend of male bonding, vigilantism, and homeland defense by self-proclaimed innocent farmers against oppressive, grasping landlords and the lawmen doing their bidding. By 1845, there were over ten thousand "Indians" commanded by regional "chiefs" with fearsome names like Black Hawk, Red Jacket, and Blue Beard. The county anti-rent committees claimed to be separate from the "Indians" but provided them with financial support and encouragement. In most counties, some committee members also functioned as "Indians."

Smith Boughton, the prominent anti-rent leader, who was also secretly "Big Thunder," the disguised leader of all the "Indians," explained in autobiographical notes,

> Our all was at stake. The law was on their [landlords'] side and we were at their mercy. We resolved to adopt the same kind of protection resorted to by the people of Boston when the tea was thrown into the water of the bay. We raised in the counties a

---

16. See Philip J. Deloria, *Playing Indian* (New Haven: Yale University Press, 1998), for a discussion of groups dressing up as Indians in American history.

large force of men to prevent the landlords from executing their threats. The force was to be on hand to protect the tenants from legal hounds.[17]

The "Indians" trained together and assembled at preassigned points when summoned by blasts from tin horns of the type farmers' wives used to call them to meals. They prevented landlords from collecting rents, blocked deputy sheriffs from evicting tenants for nonpayment or conducting "distress" sales to auction off tenant possessions to pay back rents, and harassed tenants who cooperated with the landlords. The "Indians" were armed with clubs, knives, and guns, which they might brandish but seldom used. Their menacing presence at distress sales was often enough to frighten off potential bidders. When that did not work, they might ambush buyers on their way home and relieve them of their purchases for return to the tenant, or hide behind trees and shoot oxen and cows purchased at the sales.

Their favorite form of humiliation, coercion, and punishment was "tarring and feathering." This involved forcing a victim to remove his shirt, pouring on liquid tar, sprinkling on feathers, and humiliating the victim by parading him up and down the road, threatening him, or forcing him to jump up and down and yell "Down with the Rent!" The tar used was usually pine tar, readily available in the hills, with a relatively low melting point, rather than petroleum tar, which when melted would have been hot enough to sear the victim's skin. Still, tarring and feathering was a harrowing experience. The "Indians" included it in ballads and songs that they composed as part of the mystique of their work. One of the most popular was "Big Bill Snyder," commemorating an attack by Indians on an Albany County deputy sheriff serving papers near Rensselaerville in 1841. The hapless deputy was beaten and forced to hide in the woods for two days. The song began:

The moon was shining silver-bright
The sheriff came in the dead of night,
High on a hill sat an Indian true
And on his horn this blast he blew—

17. Christman, *Tin Horns and Calico*, 74.

Chorus:
Keep out of the way, big Bill Snyder
Tar your coat and feather your hide sir![18]

Schoharie County sheriff John Brown and a deputy, serving eviction notices in the remote Blenheim region of the county in 1845, were captured and menaced by "Indians." Sheriff Brown returned to Schoharie, assembled a five-hundred-man posse, and returned for retribution. His posse galloped up and down rural roads, arrested a dozen men and even some boys (soon released), took potshots at "Indians" in the woods, trampled anti-renters' crops, and generally intimidated the populace.[19] Albany County sheriff Christopher Batterman and deputies were surrounded by "Indians" while serving papers in Berne in 1844. Warned to turn around and go back to Albany, the sheriff refused and said he would hang the "Indians" if he could. They shot his horse, clubbed him in the face, tore his clothes, destroyed his legal papers, and forced his deputies to shout "Down with the Rent!" before chasing them away at gunpoint. On the other hand, the "Indians" believed that some sheriffs were sympathetic to their cause and their actions were only to avoid charges of negligence. When Columbia County sheriff Henry Miller showed up at Copake Falls in 1844 to serve distress warrants, he was met by two hundred "Indians" who escorted him to the accompaniment of a marching band to the farm where he was to serve the first warrant. Brandishing their weapons and threatening violence if he persisted, they convinced him to give up and burn the documents. They marched him back to the local tavern and treated him to brandy and dinner. Toasting the sheriff, the "Indian" chief Big Thunder (Smith Boughton in disguise) told the assembled mob that Miller was "as good an anti-renter as any of them."[20]

Law and Order

Cautious anti-rent leaders and their political allies felt that the Indians' fearsome image and rough behavior was harming their cause. County

---

18. Ibid., 44.
19. Albert Champlin Mayham, *The Anti-Rent War on Blenheim Hill: An Episode of the 1840's* (Stamford, NY: Stonecraft Industries, 2006; reprint of original, published in 1906), 1–57.
20. Huston, *Land and Freedom*, 119–120.

sheriffs demanded state troops to back up their forces. In August 1844, Governor William C. Bouck, an easy-going Democrat elected in 1842 and himself a former Schoharie County sheriff, decided to see the situation for himself. He rode out to West Sand Lake in Rensselaer County to meet with the anti-renters. Several hundred peaceful "Indians" greeted him. The village sported banners of "Down with the Rent!" and "For the Land Is Mine, Sayeth the Lord." The anti-renters made their case to the governor and he mediated a compromise: No state troops would be sent; the sheriff would stop serving legal papers; and the "Indians" would stand down, with the hope that the 1845 legislature would solve the problem.[21]

But the violence continued. In December 1844, at a rally in Columbia County where more than a hundred "Indians" whooped, yelled, and fired pistols into the air, a shot killed William Riffenburg, a young farmhand who had just come to see the show. Some witnesses said it was a stray bullet, others that an "Indian" had shot him for refusing to yell "Down with the Rent!" A few days later, "Indians" in Grafton, Rensselaer County, killed a man hauling away timber for William Van Rensselaer from a tenant's lot. Governor Bouck, in part because he was perceived as being soft on the lawless anti-renters, had not been renominated that fall. He was replaced as the Democratic nominee by former U.S. Senator Silas Wright, who was elected on a promise to enforce the law.

He quickly convinced the 1845 legislature to pass a law making it a felony to appear on the public highways of the state armed and in disguise. Outraged by new anti-rent violence, he declared Delaware, Columbia, and Schoharie counties in a state of rebellion. State troops and sheriffs' posses combed the hills for suspects. In Delaware County alone, almost 250 men were indicted for murder, robbery, riot, or appearing armed and disguised. Wild rumors circulated that hundreds of "Indians" were planning to invade the county seat, Delhi, where the prisoners were being kept. A Delhi woman wrote to a friend:

> The whole village is on duty tonight; poorly armed. It is very certain that we are threatened with attack; whether it will be made tonight or at some future time. . . . A large collection of Indians were seen in Bovina last night and early this morning. In another neighborhood in the western part of the town there was great commotion and persons were seen leaving their homes taking

---

21. Ibid., 3–4; Christman, *Tin Horns and Calico,* 87–88.

small bundles with them. Everything that can be used as a weapon of defense is in demand. . . . my weapon is a long toasting fork.[22]

Governor Wright sent three hundred state troops to guard the village. Trials went ahead and eighty-four men were convicted. Some were fined; others received light prison sentences. Twelve pleaded guilty to manslaughter and received life sentences. Two were convicted of murder and sentenced to hang. Many other men, fearful of being arrested, fled the state. On August 7, 1845, Delaware County deputy sheriff Osman Steele was killed while conducting a "distress" sale of a tenant's cattle to recover overdue rent. Warned that there might be violence, he had quipped, "Lead can't penetrate Steele!" The "Indians" who had assembled to prevent the sale got the blame. The murder of Steele and the other violence discredited the entire "Indian" network, which began to collapse.[23]

In December 1844, Columbia County sheriff Henry Miller had arrested Smith Boughton, identified by eyewitnesses at a number of "Indian" forays as "Big Thunder" despite his disguise. He was charged with manslaughter, theft of legal papers, assault, riot, and conspiracy. Miller testified that he was certain that it was Boughton, disguised as Big Thunder, who had forced him to give up his papers at Copake Falls earlier in the year. Languishing without bail in a jail in Hudson, Boughton became a martyr for the cause. Writing from prison on February 20, 1845, he complained of harsh treatment, asserted that "the aristocratic landlords of this state have long been wishing to make me their victim because I boldly and fearlessly proclaimed that the injured tenantry were deeply aggrieved, and their constitutional rights trampled upon," and signed the letter "Yours till death in the good cause."[24] Boughton was tried in March 1845 but got off due to a hung jury. But he was tried again in September, after the murder of Osman Steele and the attendant rise in anti-Indian hysteria. Governor Wright sent John Van Buren, a member of the posse that had marched into the Helderbergs back in 1839, now state attorney general, to prosecute the case. Boughton was convicted and sentenced to life in prison. He joined the other anti-rent prisoners at the new state prison at Dannemora near Plattsburgh, far from the anti-rent action.[25]

---

22. Christman, *Tin Horns and Calico*, 142.
23. McCurdy, *The Anti-Rent Era in New York Law and Politics*, 163–174, 216–220.
24. Christman, *Tin Horns and Calico*, 150.
25. McCurdy, *The Anti-Rent Era in New York Law and Politics*, 205–233.

Inching toward Resolution

As violence blamed on the "Indians" escalated, the anti-rent committees turned toward mobilization of grassroots support. The movement's leaders established the Anti-Rent Equal Rights Party that nominated its own candidates, but they mostly endorsed Whigs and Democrats who pledged to support the cause. The fall 1844 elections saw the triumph of many independent anti-rent candidates and Whig and Democratic candidates pledged to the tenants' goals. Governor Wright tried to forge a new way forward. In a message to the legislature, he alluded to the manors as "this false system" but also condemned "the violent and criminal conduct" of the anti-renters. He called for legislation to abolish the landlords' "right of distress" (auctioning off tenants' belongings to satisfy back rent), tax landlords' rent income, and give tenants the right to buy their farms when the current proprietor died. The assembly passed Wright's three proposals, but the more conservative senate voted down the third one, bestowing the right of tenants to buy their farms when the landlord died. Wright triumphantly signed the other two bills into law. The taxation bill was a triumph for anti-rent forces. The "distress" law got a mixed reaction; landlords could still evict tenants for nonpayment.[26]

There was more progress the next year, but it was also measured and modest. Anti-renters elected several delegates to the state's constitutional convention that began June 1, 1846. They advocated amending the constitution to extinguish the manorial system, drastic proposals that found little support but did lead to less extreme amendments that were approved. One provision stated that "all feudal tenures of every description, with all their incidents, are declared to be abolished." Leases and land grants were limited to twelve years. Quarter sales were outlawed. However, the amended constitution specified that each of these restrictive propositions applied only to the *future*, not to past or present. Voters approved the new constitution in the fall. The new restrictions were all prospective and did nothing to address the farmers' current grievances. The manorial status quo was not destroyed. But the new amendments were important statements of state antipathy toward the manorial system and determination to contain it. They constituted an important step toward the eventual demise of the system.[27]

---

26. Ibid., 175–176; Huston, *Land and Freedom*, 236–238; Bruegel, "Manorial Society and the Market in the Hudson Valley, 1780–1850," 1422; Summerhill, *Harvest of Dissent*, 70–72.

27. The Third Constitution of New York, 1846, http://www.nycourts.gov/history/pdf/ Library/1846_constitution.pdf.

The Democrats renominated Silas Wright for governor that fall. Disheartened and worn out by the anti-rent struggles, he ran a listless campaign. The state Democratic Party, in the best of times a disputatious and factious entity, was beset by unusually strong internal divisions. Antirent forces detested Wright's law-and-order crackdown; landed interests resented the 1845 laws he had sponsored. Anti-renters endorsed the Whig candidate, Assemblyman John Young. He was silent or evasive on most issues but had said he would pardon the anti-renters still in prison for what he called "offenses quasi-political." Wright, seeing the political tide running against him, commuted the two anti-renters' death sentences to life in prison and pardoned three short-term prisoners. He journeyed to Dannemora prison to meet with Smith Boughton himself, apparently implying or possibly promising a pardon for the doctor if elected, but it did no good. Boughton refused to endorse him. Voters angry with President James K. Polk for plunging the nation into a war with Mexico and slashing the tariff that had helped protect New York manufacturers took their frustration out on his fellow Democrat and ally, Silas Wright. Young, a canny candidate whose reticence and low profile on key issues made him inoffensive to all shades of voters, easily beat the hapless incumbent.[28]

Former governor William Seward, in Albany for Young's inaugural in January 1847, attended a Sunday service at St. Peter's Episcopal Church. Many of New York's political leaders were there. "There was such a jumble of the wrecks of parties in the church that I forgot the sermon and fell to moralizing on the vanity of political life," he wrote his wife. "[H]alf-way down the aisle sat Silas Wright, wrapped in a coat tightly buttoned to the chin, looking philosophy [philosophical], which is hard to affect. . . . On the opposite side sat John Young, the *saved* among the lost politicians. He seemed complacent and satisfied."[29]

The legislature was divided, Whigs the majority in the assembly, Democrats in the senate, and both parties needed anti-renters' votes. Young vacillated. He delivered a message to the legislature that ducked the issue, promised a follow-up message on the topic, but did not prepare one. He said he would pardon the imprisoned anti-renters, procrastinated, and then took action after anti-rent newspapers lambasted him for stalling and petitions with over eleven thousand signatures demanding action landed on his desk. He pardoned Boughton and the other prisoners. The

28. McCurdy, *The Anti-Rent Era in New York Law and Politics*, 260–270.
29. Ibid., 272.

governor hoped the issue would fade and turned to formulating legislation to implement the provisions of the new state constitution and dealing with the state's continuously shaky fiscal situation. Anti-rent assemblymen drafted bills to allow tenants to test landlords' titles, permit them to buy out landlords, and require landlords to pay ejected tenants for improvements. The proposals were referred to an Assembly Select Committee on Leasehold Estates. The committee reported that "large tracts of land in a few hands" were "a public evil" because they made "the cultivators of the soil" into "serfs or slaves" and caused "famine or oppression." The tenants' interests should "preponderate over those of the landlords. . . . the interests of the few must yield to the public interest." But the majority of legislators were tired of the issue, thought it needed to be worked out through tenant-to-landlord negotiations, or had concluded that any state action would be unconstitutional or ineffective. Only one bill, allowing tenants to challenge their landlords' title, made it out for debate and vote and it was defeated.[30]

In January 1848, Governor Young, stung by criticism that he was evading the issue, suddenly returned to the battle. He proposed legislation authorizing the attorney general to challenge the validity of the landlords' leases in the courts, on behalf of the state. Prospects of a court victory were dim; the courts had repeatedly confirmed the validity of the land titles. But it was a politically shrewd move, the majority of both parties supported it, and the governor signed it triumphantly. The attorney general slowly commenced lawsuits for one manor after another from 1848 to 1851. Legal arguments reached back into the feudal era to challenge or affirm the right of colonial authorities to make land grants in the new world. The courts ruled for one landlord after another. A judge in one case conceded that the manors were "antagonistical to free institutions," but the courts could never yield to "the influence of popular convulsion" by undermining ownership laws that ensure "personal protection and security." Ruling for the state in this case would "unsettle and throw into utter confusion and uncertainty all titles to lands." The early decisions were so clear-cut and definite that the attorney general with a sigh of relief dropped the ones still pending.[31]

---

30. Huston, *Land and Freedom*, 177–178; Summerhill, *Harvest of Dissent*, 83–86
31. Huston, *Land and Freedom*, 192–194; David Delaney, "Running with the Land: Legal-Historical Imagination and the Spaces of Modernity," *Journal of Historical Geography* 27 (2001), 498–499.

Rebellion Fizzles, Manorial System Withers

Defeat in the courts was a critical blow to the anti-renters. In the mean-time, conservative Whigs enraged by Governor Young's pardon of the anti-renters dumped him from the ticket and replaced him with his lieu-tenant governor, Hamilton Fish, no friend of law breaking, who was elected in 1848. The organized anti-rent movement began to dissolve. The county committees disbanded, the state executive committee stopped meeting, and the "Indians" faded into memory and folklore. At the local level, newer issues of class and wealth became the topic of political debate; at the state and national level, the focus of debate moved to such things as women's rights, slavery, temperance, and nativism. On the other hand, many of the landlords were tired of defending their titles in court, forcing tenants to pay against their will, and now having their income taxed by the state. The landlords were apprehensive about the possibility of future state action on behalf of the tenants. The landlords were tired of fighting. Over the next two decades, the theme was quiet compromise as tenants and landlords came to terms one by one and the tenants bought their farms or moved on. The basis of farming changed from production for consump-tion to production for sale, particularly of dairy products. Resistance lin-gered in the Albany County hill towns, where the rebellion had begun years earlier, and sheriffs and state militia forces wrestled with recalcitrant tenants as late as 1865. But by the 1880s the issues were resolved, almost all through individuals purchasing farms from weary landlords.[32]

Years of rent boycotts, state lawsuits, and being pilloried as the state's foremost evil land barons took their toll on the Van Rensselaer broth-ers. Stephen sold most of his holdings to a land speculator and retreated into comfortable obscurity, spending his last days in religious study and devotion and service to the church before his death in 1868. William Van Rensselaer sold off his lands, moved to Rye, never returned to his ancestral home, and died in 1872.[33]

The Farmers' Rebellion ended mostly in quiet, begrudging com-promise where farmers bought the farms they occupied from landlords, rather than in a victory that abolished landlords' rights. The system sur-vived criticism by three governors, denunciation by several legislative committees, litigation to kill it, constitutional amendments to contain it,

---

32. Summerhill, *Harvest of Dissent*, 86–88.
33. Huston, *Land and Freedom*, 189–200.

and opposition from both major political parties who appealed for tenant votes when tenants outnumbered landlords by about a thousand to one. Most New Yorkers came to see the system as an anachronism that burdened the state. But most also recoiled from the image of armed, disguised mobs overawing legal authorities by sheer numbers and force of arms. In the long run, violence probably harmed the cause. But the anti-rent movement gradually discredited the notion of huge manors held in perpetuity by families. It infused into the political consensus the notion that the leasehold system was hostile to American traditions and liberties. The 1839 Berne "Declaration of Independence" may not have started a revolution, but it did signal the beginning of a slow, complicated process that resulted in significant change.

4

July 20, 1848

A Demand for Equal Rights

Elizabeth Cady Stanton (*left*) and Susan B. Anthony (*right*) collaborated on women's rights and other reform issues for a half century. *Photo courtesy of Library of Congress Prints and Photographs Division.*

Protesting Second-Class Status

*O*n July 19–20, 1848, three hundred people met in the central New York village of Seneca Falls and issued a manifesto demanding the right to vote and other measures of equality for women. The extraordinary document has been a source of ideas and inspiration since that time.

Elizabeth Cady Stanton (1815–1902), the main organizer of the conference and principal author of the document, launched a remarkable career as a tireless, eloquent leader of the women's rights movement. Her determination, persistence, and resilience helped propel the campaign for women's rights for a half century.

At the time of the conference, women occupied a lower social and legal status than men. They were expected to be devoted wives and mothers, playing domestic and maternal roles. They should marry, reproduce, raise the children, create a comfortable home, and find fulfillment through their families. Women could not vote, hold office, or serve on juries. They could attend church but were not privileged to speak and had to endure sermons exhorting them to be pure, pious, and obedient to their husbands. Pastors often quoted such biblical passages as Genesis 3:16 admonishing, "[T]hy desire [shall be] to thy husband, and he shall rule over thee."[1]

Women's legal status in New York and other states was based mostly on William Blackstone's *Commentaries on the Laws of England*, an eighteenth-century multivolume summary of English common law. Blackstone used the term *feme covert*, or "covered woman," to explain the legal status of married women. "By marriage, the husband and wife are one person in law; that is, the very being or legal existence of a woman is suspended during the marriage, or at least is incorporated and consolidated into that of the husband under whose wing, protection, and *cover* she performs every thing." According to Blackstone, a wife had no legal existence apart from her husband. Husbands had legal rights to wives' possessions and any money they might earn. A wife could not sign contracts in her own name or claim custody of her children in rare instances of legal separation. Adult *single* white women could retain their own property and wages, write contracts, run businesses, and operate independently. Yet few women chose to remain single. Marriage was regarded as part of the natural social order. Women enjoyed few opportunities to earn a decent living. Professional women, except for teachers, were few in number.[2]

A few New Yorkers challenged the repression of women before the Seneca Falls Convention. Central New York, sometimes called the "burned over district" because of the widespread religious revivalism

---

1. Sally G. McMillen, *Seneca Falls and the Origins of the Women's Rights Movement* (New York: Oxford University Press, 2008), 13.
2. Norma Basch, *In the Eyes of the Law: Women, Marriage and Property in Nineteenth-Century New York* (Ithaca: Cornell University Press, 1992), 19–69.

there beginning in the 1820s, included many advocates for women's rights as well as other reforms such as temperance and abolition of slavery. In 1845, influential Syracuse Unitarian minister Samuel May, a leading abolitionist reformer, endorsed equal rights for women. They may be physically weaker than men, he preached, but this should not "consign them to mental, moral, or social dependence. . . . woman is not the creature, the dependent of man, but of God. . . . We have too much power over them." Women understand the true interests of the community, have good judgment "to act wisely in reference to them," and should therefore be accorded voting rights.[3] A delegate to the 1846 state constitutional convention presented a petition from women in Jefferson County citing the Declaration of Independence's principle that government derived its powers from the consent of the governed. That included women, who were also taxpayers, who therefore deserved "equal, and civil and political, rights with men." A proposed amendment to secure those rights was defeated in the convention after several delegates thundered that it would destroy marriage. The idea, however, had been planted and in 1848 it came to fruition. Onondaga County state senator George Geddes, desiring that his own daughter should have the right to inherit and possess property, pushed through the legislature the Married Women's Property Act. It provided that women could keep property they owned when they got married and could receive and possess other property separate from their husbands. "We meant to strike a hard blow" for women's rights, said Geddes.[4]

The law, and the discussions that preceded it, were preludes to the breakthrough at Seneca Falls in July 1848. Elizabeth Cady Stanton, the primary organizer of the conference, was an unlikely revolutionary. Born in Johnstown, daughter of landowner, lawyer, and judge Daniel Cady, Elizabeth grew up in comfortable middle-class circumstances. She was uncommonly inquisitive, widely read, independent-minded, and inclined to rebel against traditional gender roles. At age eleven, when an older brother died, she tried to comfort her father. "Oh my daughter, I wish you were a boy!" lamented her father. "I will try to be all my brother was!" she vowed. At about the same time, she overheard a conversation between her father and a widow who was in danger of losing her home because her husband's

---

3. McMillen, *Seneca Falls and the Origins of the Women's Rights Movement*, 79; Samuel J. May, "The Rights and Condition of Women: A Sermon Preached in Syracuse, November 1845," http://lcweb2.loc.gov/cgi-bin/query/D?naw:3:./temp/~ammem_di7s.
4. Basch, *In the Eyes of the Law*, 136–159.

will left it to someone else. The law gave him that right, Cady explained to the woman. Elizabeth went through her father's law books, marking all the laws that limited women's rights, vowing to cut them out of the books. Her father explained that the only way to change them was to go to Albany and get the legislature to take action. From her cousin, Gerrit Smith, who lived nearby in Peterboro, she derived a hatred of slavery and confidence in political change. She was enraged to find few suitable women's colleges but received a liberal education at the Troy Female Seminary operated by the progressive educator Emma Willard. She fell in love with and married an ardent abolitionist, Henry Stanton, in 1840. (She struck the word "obey" from her marriage vows and insisted on being called Mrs. Elizabeth Cady Stanton rather than Mrs. Henry Stanton as custom dictated.) For their honeymoon, the newlyweds sailed to London for a world antislavery convention. There, women delegates were relegated to the back of the auditorium and required to keep silent. One of the silenced women, American Quaker abolitionist and reformer Lucretia Mott, fired up Elizabeth's interest in women's rights. The Stantons returned to the United States and settled in Boston, where Elizabeth picked up still more reformist ideas. But Boston proved to be a poor place for Henry's abolitionist work, legal career, and political ambitions, and the city's climate seemed to harm his health.[5]

In 1847, they moved to Seneca Falls to a home given to them by Judge Cady. Henry embarked on an ambitious career as an abolitionist speaker, lawyer, and politician, and his travels often took him away from home. Elizabeth settled into the role of homemaker and mother, eventually having seven children. But she was bored by the drudgery of homemaking, found housework "irksome," and reflected more and more on the degraded status of women.

> I suffered with mental hunger, which, like an empty stomach, is very depressing. . . . The general discontent I felt with woman's portion as wife, mother, housekeeper, physical, and spiritual guide, the chaotic conditions into which everything fell without her supervision, and the wearied, anxious look of the majority of women impressed me with a strong feeling that some measures

---

5. Elisabeth Griffith, *In Her Own Right: The Life of Elizabeth Cady Stanton* (New York: Oxford University Press, 1984), 1–46; Lori D. Ginsberg, *Elizabeth Cady Stanton: An American Life* (New York: Hill and Wang, 2009), 15–41.

should be taken to remedy the wrongs of society in general and of women in particular.[6]

On July 9, 1848, a Quaker friend invited her to nearby Waterloo for tea with Lucretia Mott, who happened to be visiting her sister there, and some other friends. Stanton eagerly accepted; she had corresponded with Mott, now a nationally renowned abolitionist and temperance reformer, but had not seen her since the 1840 London convention. Tea, cakes, and small talk soon gave way to angry discussions. "I poured out that day the torrent of my long-accumulating discontent, with such vehemence and indignation that I stirred myself, as well as the rest of the party, to do and dare anything." But what to do? The small group decided on the spot to hold a women's rights convention. It had to be right away because Mott, whose national reputation would guarantee attention and whose organizational experience in conference and public speaking would be essential, could not stay in the area long. So they decided on July 19 and 20. There was no meeting space large enough in Waterloo; Syracuse and Rochester were too far away; so they selected Seneca Falls and secured use of the spacious Wesleyan Methodist chapel on the main street. The group placed an ad in the *Seneca County Courier* on July 14, stating simply that "a convention to discuss the social, civil and religious condition and rights of Woman" would be held at the Wesleyan Chapel in Seneca Falls on July 19 and 20. That was only a few days away, but other local papers picked up the notice and the message spread by word of mouth. Stanton remembered that at first the members of the small organizing group felt "as helpless and hopeless as if [we] had been suddenly asked to construct a steam engine."[7] But they soon settled on a brilliant model for their draft document: the Declaration of Independence. Swelling with revolutionary rhetoric, the document was a source of pride to all Americans and well known to citizens at the time, one whose preamble children were often required to memorize. Its format—a series of grievances followed by justified action steps—was well suited to their intentions. Ironically, the convention assembled seventy-two years after the Declaration was issued, and it would take another seventy-two years, until 1920, to achieve its highest goal, votes for women.

---

6. Elizabeth Cady Stanton, *Eighty Years and More: Reminiscences, 1815–1897* (Boston: Northeastern University Press, 1993; originally published in 1898), 146–148.
7. Elizabeth Cady Stanton, Susan B. Anthony, Matilda Joslyn Gage, and Ida Husted Harper, eds., *History of Woman Suffrage*, 6 vols. (Various publishers, 1881–1922), I, 63–75.

An Elegant Manifesto

The organizers were astonished when three hundred people showed up for the meeting. Most of the attendees were from the region and were linked by preexisting social and advocacy networks. They were affiliated with the new Free Soil Party that opposed the spread of slavery into new territory, were part of local abolitionist or temperance networks, or had been associated with the women's legal rights campaign, which had resulted in the passage of the property act earlier in the year. Others came to Seneca Falls in the company of friends or relatives who were part of those networks.[8]

Only women were allowed the first day, but men were admitted the second day. Lucretia Mott spoke, but the new, rising star of women's rights, Stanton, gave the keynote. "We have met here today to discuss our rights and wrongs, civil and political," and "men's legal and social dominance of women." At the top of the list was the right to vote. All white males have it, including "drunkards, idiots, horse-racing, rum-selling rowdies, ignorant foreigners, and silly boys," she declared. Now, women demanded it: "The right is ours. Have it, we must. Use it, we will."[9]

The final report had two parts. The first was a "Declaration of Sentiments" setting forth issues and problems and a series of resolutions to address them. It began with: "We hold these truths to be self-evident; that all men and women are created equal," paralleling the Declaration but with women introduced as equal to men. The rest of the preamble referred to the need to change abusive governments. But the next paragraph shifted the focus: "The history of mankind is a history of repeated injuries and usurpations on the part of man toward woman, having in direct object the establishment of an absolute tyranny over her." Men in general are substituted for the tyrant King George III and accused of multiple crimes, including:

> He has never permitted her to exercise her inalienable right to the elective franchise.
> He has compelled her to submit to laws, in the formation of which she had no voice.

---

8. Judith Wellman, "The Seneca Falls Women's Rights Convention: A Study of Social Networks," *Journal of Women's History* 3 (Spring 1991), 9–37.
9. The Seneca Falls Convention report is reprinted many places, including http://www.nps. gov/wori/historyculture/Report-of-Convention.htm.

He has made her, if married, in the eye of the law, civilly dead.

He has taken from her all right in property, even to the wages she earns.

He has monopolized nearly all the profitable employments, and from those she is permitted to follow, she receives but a scanty remuneration.

He has usurped the prerogative of Jehovah himself, claiming it as his right to assign for her a sphere of action, when that belongs to her conscience and her God.

The "resolutions" section blended principles, demands, and goals. "Woman is man's equal—was intended to be so by the Creator, and the highest good of the race demands that she should be recognized as such." Men and women should be equal in "the social state" and before the law. Women should abandon complacency and become activists. The document demanded equality in three areas in particular.

In the public arena. Women should be allowed and expected to speak in public meetings and forums. "The objection of indelicacy and impropriety, which is so often brought against woman when she addresses a public audience, comes with a very ill grace from those who encourage, by their attendance, her appearance on the stage, in the concert, or in the feats of the circus." Women should be able to speak up on the great issues of the day, such as temperance and slavery. "It is demonstrably the right and duty of woman, equally with man, to promote every righteous cause, by every righteous means."

In the church. "Woman has too long rested satisfied in the circumscribed limits which corrupt customs and a perverted application of the Scriptures have marked out for her, and that it is time she should move in the enlarged sphere which her great Creator has assigned her." It is men's duty "to encourage her to speak, and teach as she has an opportunity, in all religious assemblies."

Before the law. "All laws which prevent woman from occupying such a station in society as her conscience shall dictate, or which place her in a position inferior to that of man, are contrary to the great precept of nature, and therefore of no force or authority." The right to vote being essential to secure rights, "[I]t is the duty of the women of this country to secure to themselves their sacred right to the elective franchise."

Only the demand for the vote occasioned much debate among the conference's reform-minded attendees, and a spirited endorsement by

Frederick Douglass, a former slave and abolitionist leader who had journeyed to Seneca Falls from his home in nearby Rochester, turned the tide
in its favor. The Declaration concluded with an intention to "use every
instrumentality within our power to effect our object." Sixty-eight men
and thirty-two women signed the final report.

The Seneca Falls declaration had some limitations. Foreshadowing the
later elitism, racism, and nativism that sometimes characterized the woman's rights movement, it expressed anger that man "has withheld from her
rights which are given to the most ignorant and degraded of men—both
natives and foreigners." But it was widely reprinted in the newspapers
and discussed in the press, pulpit, and public forums. Many newspapers
denounced it as shocking, unwomanly, and revolutionary. "The women
folks have just held a convention up in New York and passed a sort of
'Bill of Rights' affirming it their right to vote, to become teachers, legislators, lawyers, divines, and do all and [sundry] the 'lords'. . . now do.
They should have resolved at the same time that it was obligatory [for] the
'lords' aforesaid to wash dishes . . . handle the broom, darn stockings . . .
wear trinkets [and] look beautiful," said the *Lowell* (Massachusetts) *Courier.* "A woman is nobody. A wife is everything," sneered the *Philadelphia
Public Ledger and Daily Transcript.*[10] But the ranting of angry editors and
ministers only served to garner more publicity for the document and the
cause it represented.

Four traits gave the document its powerful influence and staying
power.

- Its origins gave it a measure of gravitas: It was produced by a
  deliberative body of citizens in the heart of the nation's most
  important state, New York. As the first conference of its kind,
  it established the notion that women's rights were important
  and something worth conferring about.
- It was a defiant statement by a subservient class to a dominant
  class and demanded that women be defined in their own right
  as individuals rather than as just mothers, wives, and daughters.
- While many of the sentiments expressed were not new, the document for the first time brought them together and expressed
  them in a concise, systematic, eloquent, easy-to-understand

---

10. Geoffrey C. Ward, *Not for Ourselves Alone: The Story of Elizabeth Cady Stanton and
Susan B. Anthony* (New York: Alfred A. Knopf, 1999), 41–42.

fashion, thanks to the writing skills of Stanton and her colleagues.

- Its kinship to the Declaration of Independence gave it a hybrid character. On the one hand, it was conservative in connecting deeply with U.S. history and its cherished founding document. On the other hand, it was iconoclastic in insisting on changes in law, religion, and the fundamental relations between men and women. It shrewdly aligned the case with the nation's history of equality and rebellion.

Campaigning in New York

Over the next fifty years, much of the women's rights campaign originated or played out in New York, and a great deal of it was propelled by Elizabeth Cady Stanton. A week after the Seneca Falls Conference, she and another organizer wrote an open letter to the *Seneca County Courier*, scolding local ministers who had condemned their meeting. "No reform has ever been started but the Bible, falsely interpreted, has opposed it," they boldly stated. "Wine-drinking was proved to be right by the Bible. Slavery was proved to be an institution of the Bible. War, with its long train of calamities and abominations, is proved to be right by the Bible." People should think for themselves. "Let the people no longer trust to their blind guides," they asserted.[11] Several reform-minded women were so inspired by the Seneca Falls meeting that they organized another conference in Rochester the next month. Stanton, debuting a theme she would often use in the future of expanding the range of issues, spoke on women's economic oppression. The plight of working women was dramatized by two local seamstresses who told the convention that their wages were thirty-one to thirty-eight cents a day but they had to pay $1.50 for weekly board.[12]

Stanton spoke several times to local groups in the fall of 1848 and early 1849, developing something approaching a stock speech on the case

---

11. Elizabeth Cady Stanton and Elizabeth McClintock to the Editors, *Seneca County Courier*, ca. July 23, 1848, in Ann D. Gordon, ed., *The Selected Papers of Elizabeth Cady Stanton and Susan B. Anthony*, 5 vols. (New Brunswick: Rutgers University Press, 1997–2009), I, 88–92.
12. McMillen, *Seneca Falls and the Origins of the Women's Rights Movement*, 93–97.

for women's rights. "Man cannot speak for us—because he has been educated to believe that we differ from him so materially that he cannot judge
of our thoughts, feelings and opinions by [on] his own," she said. Men
have no claim to moral superiority—"not a year passes but we hear of
some sad soul sickening deed perpetrated by some of this class." Men may
be physically stronger but "the power of mind seems to be in no way connected with the size and strength of body." Laws affecting women "violate
every principle of right and justice." It is misreading the Bible to claim a
religious sanction for women's inferiority. Women must "resist the weapons of the enemy, ridicule and holy horror." Better times were coming! "A
new era is dawning upon the world when old might to right must yield
... when woman yielding to the voice of the spirit within her will demand
the recognition of her humanity, when her soul, grown too large for her
chains, will burst the bands around her set and stand redeemed, regener-
ated, and disenthralled."[13]

These speeches marked the emergence of Stanton as an eloquent, logical, systematic advocate, traits she would show in hundreds of letters to
the editor, speeches, tracts, and articles over the next fifty years. By the
early 1850s, she was recognized as the leader of the reform movement. In
1851, she met Susan B. Anthony (1820–1906), a Rochester school teacher
turned temperance and abolition advocate, and they worked together
over the next half century for women's rights, one of the most remarkable
two-person teams in New York's history. Stanton was more widely read,
sociable, open, enthusiastic, persuasive in public forums, witty, and had a
good sense of humor. Anthony was more introspective, serious, driven,
and better at organization, lobbying, and execution. Years later, Stanton
recalled:

> While she is slow and analytical, I am rapid and synthetic. I am
> the better writer [and] she the better critic. She supplied the facts
> and statistics, I the philosophy and rhetoric and together we have
> made arguments that have stood unshaken by the storms of . . .
> long years; arguments that no man has answered. Our speeches
> may be considered the united product of our two brains.[14]

---

13. "Address by Elizabeth Cady Stanton on Woman's Rights," September 1848, in Gordon,
    ed., *The Selected Papers of Elizabeth Cady Stanton and Susan B. Anthony*, I, 94–123.
14. Stanton, *Eighty Years and More*, 186.

Anthony once said that Stanton was superb at giving her audiences "the rankest radical sentiments but all so cushioned that they didn't hurt."[15] Lightening the message with levity, though sometimes with a sharp edge, helped. When a group of "fashionable women" at a convention in tony Newport, Rhode Island, questioned her "immodesty" in speaking from a platform, she responded:

> Really, you ladies surprise me. Our conventions are not as public as the ballroom where I saw you all dancing last night. As to modesty, it may be a question in many minds whether it is less modest to speak words of soberness and truth, plainly dressed with one's person decently covered on a platform, than gorgeously arrayed with bare arms and shoulders, to waltz in the arms of strange gentlemen.[16]

In an article in May 1850, she noted, "Well. . . the Legislature of this state [New York] has at length adjourned. The members have gone to their respective homes with their money and two or three bushels of documents each. The proceedings of the session are now to be published. This whole performance will cost the state about $200,000."[17]

Anthony, who never married and devoted her life single-mindedly to the woman suffrage cause, sometimes became impatient with Stanton's attention to her family. Imploring her friend to draft a speech on coeducation for the New York State Teachers' Association meeting in June 1856, Anthony wrote, "I can't get up a decent document, so for the love of me and for the saving of the reputation of womanhood, I beg you with one baby on your knee and another at your feet and four boys whistling, buzzing, hallooing 'Ma! Ma!' set yourself about the work." Stanton responded, agreeing to do the draft but appealing for understanding. She felt like a "caged lioness . . . imagine me, day in and day out, watching, bathing, dressing, nursing and promenading the precious contents of a little crib in the corner of my room." Henry Stanton told his wife, "[Y]ou stir up Susan and she stirs the world."[18]

---

15. Ginsberg, *Elizabeth Cady Stanton*, 10.
16. Elizabeth Cady Stanton, "Reminiscences," in Stanton et al., eds., *History of Woman Suffrage*, I, 464.
17. Elizabeth Cady Stanton, "Legislative Doings," *Lily* (May 1850), in Gordon, ed., *Selected Papers*, I, 169–170.
18. Susan B. Anthony to Elizabeth Cady Stanton, June 5, 1856, and Stanton to Anthony, June 10, 1856, in Gordon, ed., *Selected Papers*, I, 321–324 and 325; Elizabeth Cady Stanton to Susan B. Anthony, August 20, 1857, in Gordon, ed., *Selected Papers*, I, 351.

The Seneca Falls and Rochester conventions were followed by annual women's rights conventions in Worcester, Massachusetts, in 1850 and 1851 and Syracuse in 1852. The Seneca Falls manifesto was always the starting point. Family responsibilities kept Stanton home, but she sent stirring letters and resolutions that helped frame the issues and propel the discussion each time. She also kept up with a steady stream of essays, speeches, and articles for newspapers and was hailed as the de facto leader of the cause. Stanton's letter to the Syracuse meeting suggested that women owning property should refuse to pay taxes until they had the right to vote, that men and women should be educated together, and that women should stop supporting churches that used religion to degrade them. Women should focus their attention on "the education, elevation, and enfranchisement of their own sex." The letter led to resolutions "of a most radical character" that passed, after a good deal of heated discussion on the religious issue.[19]

The same year, Anthony was denied the right to speak at the annual meeting of the state temperance society that was run by men. Enraged, she enlisted Stanton's aid in forming a new group, the Women's State Temperance Society. Stanton was eager to tie women's rights to temperance. "I am at the boiling point! If I do not find some day the use of my tongue on this question, I shall die of an intellectual repression, a woman's rights convulsion."[20] The new group assembled in Rochester in April and elected Stanton president and Anthony secretary. Stanton, ever eager to expand the agenda, gave one of the most radical speeches of her career. The divorce laws should be broadened to allow a wife to divorce a drunken husband. "Let no woman remain in the relation of wife with a confirmed drunkard. Let no drunkard be the father of her children." Taking another swing at organized religion, she proclaimed that women should withdraw support from churches that were really about "the building up of a theological aristocracy and gorgeous temples to an unknown God" and supporting foreign missions. Instead, they should devote our resources to "the poor and the suffering about us."[21] The convention delegates wanted change, but this was just too radical. The next year, at the behest of conservative members, men were allowed as members. The convention promptly

19. Stanton et al., eds., *History of Woman Suffrage*, I, 518–546.
20. Elizabeth Cady Stanton to Susan B. Anthony, April 2, 1852, in Theodore Stanton and Harriot Stanton Blatch, eds., *Elizabeth Cady Stanton as Revealed in Her Letters, Diary and Reminiscences*, 2 vols. (New York: Harper and Bros., 1922), II, 38–42.
21. Stanton et al., *History of Woman Suffrage*, I, 481–483.

deposed Stanton as president and dropped the religious issue, which the delegates saw as divisive and tangential to the temperance crusade. Anthony resigned in protest.

But the following year the Stanton-Anthony team was very much in evidence once again. In the winter of 1852 to 1853, Anthony traveled throughout the state gathering signatures on petitions demanding votes for women and expansion of the Married Woman's Property Act of 1848. Stanton and Anthony organized a women's rights convention to meet in Albany in February 1854 to coincide with presentation of the petitions to the legislature. Stanton would give the keynote speech to the meeting, but the real audience was the legislature in session at the Capitol just up the street from the convention hotel. Stanton struggled to prepare what she knew had to be a great speech: "[W]hile I am about the house surrounded by my children, washing dishes, baking, sewing, etc., I can think up many points but I cannot search books, for my hands as well as my brains would be necessary for that work. . . . I seldom have one hour undisturbed in which to sit down and write."[22]

The rousing speech began with a reference to women as the daughters of Revolutionary War heroes, "persons, native, free-born citizens, property-holders, tax-payers . . . moral, virtuous and intelligent and in all respects quite equal to the proud white man himself." Making an invidious comparison, she went on to say, "[W]e are classed with idiots, lunatics, and negroes" and in fact lower than any of them "for the negro can be raised to the dignity of a voter if he possesses himself of $250; the lunatic can vote in his moments of sanity, and the idiot, too, if he be a male one and not more than nine-tenths of a fool." Women have "no civil existence, no social freedom. . . . Would to God you could know the burning indignation that fills [women's] souls when she turns over the pages of your statute books and sees there how like feudal barons you freemen hold your women!" Their demands amounted to no more than "justice and equity."[23]

The always well-organized Anthony quickly had copies of Stanton's speech printed, placed a copy on every legislator's desk, and broadcast

---

22. Elizabeth Cady Stanton to Susan B. Anthony, December 1, 1853, in Anthony and Blatch, eds., *Elizabeth Cady Stanton as Revealed in Her Letters, Diary and Reminiscences*, II, 54–55.

23. Elizabeth Cady Stanton, "Address to the Legislature of New-York, adopted by the State Woman's Rights Convention Held at Albany. Feb. 14 and 15, 1854," http://www.nps.gov/wori/historyculture/address-to-the-new-york-legislature-1854.htm.

thousands more to newspapers and individuals around the state. Anthony's petitions were referred to a joint legislative committee established to consider "the legal equality of women with men." The committee reported that "a higher power than that from which emanates legislative enactments has given forth the mandate that man and women shall not be equal." Women do not need to vote for legislators, because they represent all citizens regardless of voting status: "[H]e is the representative of the inhabitants of his district, whether they be voters or not, whether they be men or women, old or young." The committee recommended modest revision of the Married Women's Property Act but did "not deem it wise that a new arrangement of our laws of domestic relations should be attempted." Once again, the legislature took no action.[24]

Stanton, Anthony, and their colleagues faced three obstacles. One was the determined opposition of most men, who saw in their proposals the seeds of marital discord and family strife. Another was the fact that many women, particularly working women and farm wives, were dependent on their husbands and too busy to study the reformers' arguments. Their somewhat lofty demands—the right to vote, easy divorce, defiance of religious authority—seemed less than relevant to most women's daily challenges of housekeeping, cooking, laundry, and child care. They also seemed somewhat risky, pointing to the sort of personal and financial independence that most women did not understand or did not want. A third obstacle was the fact that, very slowly and without fanfare, the status of women began to rise. There were more schools, more colleges (for instance, Vassar College, established in 1861), and a gradual increase in the number of women lawyers, ministers, and doctors. This all represented progress but it removed some of the impetus for key demands such as the right to vote. Sensing no groundswell of support among the electorate to grant women the right to vote, the legislature rejected the suffragists' demands year after year. In March 1857, the Senate Judiciary Committee issued a particularly crude report. Drawing on insights from married life, "the men of the legislature. . . are enabled to state that the ladies always have the best place and the choicest tid-bit at the table. They have the best seats on the carts, carriages, and sleighs. . . . If there is any inequality of oppression in this case, the gentlemen are the sufferers." The committee's only recommendation was that the men who signed the women's petitions

24. *Report of the Select Committee*, March 27, 1854, in Stanton et al., eds., *History of Woman Suffrage*, I, 616–618.

should seek a law allowing them to wear the dresses in their families. The report "set the whole House in roars of laughter."[25]

Stanton, never discouraged, kept up a drumfire of speeches and articles to promote women's rights. In February 1860, after years of deluges of petitions from Anthony and her colleagues, the Senate passed a bill to strengthen the Married Woman's Property Act to provide for women's rights to hold real and personal property without interference from their husbands, to carry on trades and perform services, collect and use their earnings, sue and be sued, share joint custody of children, and other rights. Assembly passage was in doubt. Anthony secured an invitation for Stanton to address the Assembly Judiciary Committee in March and, after some additional behind-the-scenes negotiating, arranged for the speech to be given from the Speaker's podium in the assembly chamber. A large audience assembled to hear one of Stanton's greatest speeches. She called it "A Slave's Appeal," a jarring title at a time when slavery was being intensely debated. "If the object of government is to protect the weak against the strong, how unwise to place the power wholly in the hands of the strong." Women faced a situation of "cruelty and tyranny" worse than slavery, for "woman, from her social position, refinement, and education is on a more equal ground with the oppressor." Women were tired of being patronized by the claim that they were too delicate for the rough world of politics. They were all too accustomed to dealing with "the drunkard, the gambler, the licentious man, the rogue, and the villain." Women were weary of "[the] kind of protection . . . which leaves us everything to do, to dare, and to suffer, and strips us of all means for its accomplishment." Women demand equality, full citizenship, the same rights and privileges as men.[26] The eloquent speech, replete with soaring arguments, helped speed assembly passage of the bill.

On May 8, Stanton spoke at Cooper Union in New York City before the American Anti-Slavery Society. It was another high-energy, provocative performance before a large audience with plenty of press coverage. "This is generally known as the platform of one idea—that is negro slavery," she began. White men might be able to eloquently describe the degradation and horrors of slavery, "but a privileged class can never conceive the feelings of those who are born to contempt, to inferiority, to

25. Gordon, ed., *Selected Papers*, I, 318n2; Ward, *Not for Ourselves Alone*, 75.
26. Elizabeth Cady Stanton, "Address to the New York State Legislature, 1860," in Stanton et al., eds., *History of Woman Suffrage*, I, 679–685.

degradation. Herein is woman more fully identified with the slave than man can possibly be, for she can take the subjective view. She learns the misfortune of being born an heir to the crown of thorns, to martyrdom, to womanhood. For while man is born to do whatever he can, for the woman and the negro there is no such privilege." Turning to another favorite theme, she blamed religion for the degradation of both women and slaves. "Thank you, oh Christian priests, meekly I will take your insults, taunts, and sneers. To you my gratitude is due for all the *peculiar blessings* of slavery, for you have had the morals of the nation in your keeping." Women have known "human wretchedness and woe" but would rise to "clouds of dazzling radiance."[27] It was another militant, upbraiding speech that got Stanton plenty of attention but won her few friends in the convention, which wanted to focus on slavery in a critical presidential election year.

Two days later, on May 10, she was back at Cooper Union for another bombshell speech, this time on marriage and divorce, before the National Women's Rights Convention. New York, like most states, made divorce very difficult, allowing it only for adultery and, under very narrow circumstances, permitting annulments. But divorces and annulments were very hard to get, and divorced women were often shunned. The New York legislature in its 1860 session had defeated a bill to slightly liberalize divorce laws. Stanton proposed several resolutions, some deliberately shocking: Men who showed "mental or moral or spiritual imbecility" were unfit to be husbands; marriage should be considered a contract that could be abrogated by either party; children born in "unhappy and unhallowed connections are, in the most solemn sense, of *unlawful birth*"; either party should be free to end a marriage in case of drunkenness, desertion, or cruelty. She shocked the audience by going further: Marriage is "nothing more than legalized prostitution. . . . There is one kind of marriage that has not been tried, and that is a contract made by equal parties to lead an equal life, with equal restraints and privileges on either side. Thus far, we have had man marriage and nothing more."[28]

The convention erupted in bitter debate. Wendell Phillips, the renowned abolitionist leader and woman's rights advocate, argued that Stanton's radical sentiments would discredit the cause. In the end, the convention adjourned without voting on them. But the resolutions were

27. Elizabeth Cady Stanton, "Address to the American Anti-Slavery Society," May 8, 1860, in Gordon, ed., *Selected Papers*, I, 409–418.
28. Elizabeth Cady Stanton, Speech at Tenth National Woman's Rights Convention, May 11, 1860 in Gordon, ed., *Selected Papers*, I, 418–431.

highlighted in the public press and in public discussions for several weeks before being upstaged by the presidential campaign. Horace Greeley editorialized in the *Tribune* that Stanton's speech was "simply shocking." The *New-York Evening Post* warned that even Stanton's friends "will be disgusted with this new dogma" that equates marriage with a business contract. This "exceedingly loose view" would enable women to seek divorce whenever their marriages became "distasteful," essentially "abolishing marriage." Stanton welcomed the controversy. To a close friend she exulted, "[W]e have thrown our bombshell into the center of woman's degradation and of course we have raised a rumpus." Stanton was a champion provocateur, but once again she was way ahead of her time. New York did not substantially expand the grounds for divorce until the Divorce Reform Law of 1966.[29]

The Long Road to the Twentieth Century

The rather radical 1860 speeches might have been the end of Stanton's career, but they proved to be only the end of the beginning. In 1862, she accompanied her husband Henry, now a leader of the state Republican Party who had been appointed Assistant Collector of the Port of New York, to a new home in that city. She, Anthony, and other reformers decided to suspend the woman's rights campaign during the war and push for emancipation of the slaves in the belief that emancipation would be accompanied by granting of rights to women. Stanton and Anthony led the establishment of the Woman's Loyal National League in 1863 to support the war effort and emancipation. They spearheaded a campaign that garnered over 400,000 signatures on petitions to Congress for freedom for slaves. But they were dismayed by congressional approval of the Fourteenth (ratified 1868) and Fifteenth (ratified 1870) amendments to the Constitution intended to guarantee the rights of *male* voters. The amendments were proposed to protect and enfranchise newly freed black men. Wendell Phillips, speaking in May 1865 just after the war ended, expressed sympathy to the woman's cause but said, "[H]owever . . . we must take up but one question at a time, and this is the negro's hour."

---

29. Ibid., I, 431; Ginsberg, *Elizabeth Cady Stanton*, 100; Elizabeth Cady Stanton to Martha Coffin Wright, May 28, 1860, in Stanton and Blatch, eds., *Elizabeth Cady Stanton as Revealed in Her Letters, Diary and Reminiscences*, 2, 80–81.

Women would have to wait. Stanton wrote a bitter essay with racist over-tones for the *National Antislavery Standard*. Women had campaigned for black freedom for a generation, but now "it becomes a serious question whether we had better stand aside and see 'Sambo' walk into the kingdom first." Women should be given "the rights, privileges and immunities of citizens."[30]

Petitions to Congress to broaden the amendments to grant woman suffrage had no effect. Stanton, increasingly frustrated, ran as an indepen-dent candidate for Congress in the eighth congressional district in New York where she lived in 1866. She could not vote, but there was no law barring her from running and holding office if elected. Her "campaign" consisted of a series of public notices in the press. "Belonging to a dis-enfranchised class," one notice began, "I have no political antecedents to recommend me to your support but my creed is *free speech, free press, free men* and *free trade*—the cardinal points of democracy." But her main plank was the demand for woman suffrage. "If the [Republican] party. . . . makes its demand for 'Negro Suffrage' in good faith, on the ground of natural right, and because the highest good of the State demands that the republican idea be vindicated, on no principle of justice or safety can the women of the nation be ignored." She received only twenty-four votes.[31]

"Some tell us that this is not the time for woman to make the demand; that this is the negro's hour," she told a Brooklyn audience in February 1867. "No, my friends . . . this is the Nation's hour. This is the hour to settle what are the rights of a citizen of the Republic; and upon the right settle-ment of that question depends the life of this nation."[32] Her impatient, militant stance and the racist cast to her rhetoric alienated former sup-porters. Frederick Douglass, her ally since he had spoken out for woman suffrage at Seneca Falls in 1848, asserted that the votes for women would be "deserved and desirable," but for blacks it was an absolute necessity to protect basic rights. Woman suffrage, a much lower priority, now "meets nothing but ridicule" he insisted.[33]

---

30. Elizabeth Cady Stanton to the Editor, *National Anti-Slavery Standard*, December 26, 1865, in Gordon, ed., *Selected Papers*, I, 564–565.
31. Ginsberg, *Elizabeth Cady Stanton*, 120–121.
32. Elizabeth Cady Stanton lecture "Reconstruction" in Brooklyn, NY, February 19, 1867, in Gordon, ed., *Selected Papers*, II, 25–41.
33. Stanton et al., eds., *History of Woman Suffrage*, II, 311; Elisabeth Griffith, *In Her Own Eight: The Life of Elizabeth Cady Stanton* (New York: Oxford University Press, 1984), 134; Ginsberg, *Elizabeth Cady Stanton*, 124.

Stifled in their campaign to broaden constitutional protection, Stanton and Anthony turned their attention back to New York and secured petitions with twenty-eight thousand names demanding votes for women for presentation to the 1867 New York State constitutional convention. The convention's ad hoc committee on woman suffrage happened to be chaired by *New-York Tribune* editor Horace Greeley, a sometime friend of women's causes. Stanton testified, making her usual eloquent case for women suffrage. Greeley interrupted to ask why the women should have the ballot when they could not defend it by the bullet; they could not join the armed forces. Stanton replied facetiously, "We are ready to fight, sir, just as you did in the late war, by sending our substitutes," a reference to men who had paid to have others fight and had not gone themselves. Greeley was not amused. He was angered even more when Stanton revealed in her talk that his wife had signed one of the petitions without telling him. His committee recommended universal manhood suffrage but dismissed the women's rights appeals. "[P]ublic sentiment does not demand and would not sustain an innovation so revolutionary and sweeping, so openly at war with a distribution of duties and functions between the sexes . . . and involving transformations so radical in social and domestic life," said the committee report.[34]

Stanton and Anthony traveled to Kansas in the fall to lecture in support of constitutional amendments there for woman suffrage and black suffrage; both lost. In 1868, she bought a house in Tenafly, New Jersey, where she lived until 1887 when she moved back to New York City to live with her children. She seldom saw her husband Henry, who stayed behind in their New York home. In 1866 Stanton cooperated on formation of the American Equal Rights Association to push for voting rights for women and blacks. Feminist leader Lucy Stone, formerly a friend and ally, led the formation of a new organization, the American Woman Suffrage Association in 1869, and Stanton and Anthony led formation of their own new group, the National Woman Suffrage Association, the same year. The two groups became rivals, dividing on whether to concentrate on the federal or state levels and whether to focus only on suffrage or a broader agenda, including easier divorce laws and other economic and social issues. The rivalry dissipated the energy of the movement until 1890 when, after a good deal of shuttle diplomacy by Anthony, they merged as the National

---

34. Ginsberg, *Elizabeth Cady Stanton*, 127; Stanton et al., eds., *History of Woman Suffrage*, II, 285.

American Woman Suffrage Association and elected Stanton president. Stanton and Anthony launched a newspaper, *The Revolution*, in 1868 with a slogan on its masthead of "Men, Their Rights and Nothing More— Women, Their Rights and Nothing Less." It gave Stanton and Anthony a platform to write not only about women's issues but also economic, labor, and social issues, but limited circulation put it out of business in 1872. Stanton lectured widely, including on the lyceum circuit, speaking on women's issues. Anthony continued her crusade, including defying the law by voting in Rochester in the 1872 election. She was arrested, tried in a federal court, convicted, and fined in a highly publicized trial. She used the trial to assert her right to vote and refused to pay the fine. The court, determined not to give her a platform for more advocacy, did not pursue the penalty.[35]

A Long, Grand Finale

In 1880, Stanton and Anthony, along with another feminist leader Matilda Gage, began work on a multivolume history of the woman suffrage movement. They were documenting their struggles for the next generation and also securing their place in history. Stanton did most of the writing. They relied on personal papers and clippings, elicited reminiscences and documents from other leaders in the movement, searched through legislative proceedings and newspapers, and retrieved women's conference proceedings from dusty files. Stanton's daughter Margaret described the process:

> Susan is punctilious on dates, mother on philosophy, but each contends stoutly in the other's domain. . . . Sometimes these disputes run so high that down go the pens and one sails out of one door and one out of the other and just as I have made up my mind that this beautiful friendship of 40 years has at last terminated, I see them, arm in arm, walking down the hill . . . when they return they go straight to work where they left off as if nothing had happened.[36]

35. Ginsberg, *Elizabeth Cady Stanton*, 133–152; Kathleen Barry, *Susan B. Anthony: A Biography* (New York: New York University Press, 1988), 195–305.
36. Griffith, *In Her Own Right*, 177.

The first volume appeared in 1881, the second in 1883, the third in 1886, bringing the story down to that year. (Anthony collaborated with another author later on a fourth volume covering the period up to 1900 and, after her death in 1906, other authors added two final volumes, taking the story through the adoption of the woman suffrage amendment in 1920.) Their goal, Stanton, Anthony, and Gage declared in the preface to the first volume, was to assemble "an arsenal of facts for those who are beginning to inquire into the demands and arguments of the leaders of this reform. . . . the impelling motives to action; the struggle in the face of the opposition; the vexation under ridicule; and the despair in success too long deferred."[37] The *History* is a magnificent documentary, the source for much of our understanding of the movement.

In 1892, Stanton gave her last speech to Congress, entitled "The Solitude of Self." It is introspective, brooding, and bleak. Her emphasis was on the struggles individuals, men and women, face in life, personal isolation and "the individuality of each human soul." Women need rights and empowerment to deal with the "awful solitude" they necessarily face.[38]

In the early 1890s she assembled a committee of twenty-six women to produce a work challenging the traditional religious orthodoxy that woman should be subservient to men. The committee identified passages in the Bible that referred to women or that had implications for them and showed that most of the passages had been misinterpreted, taken out of context, or were written by men with the clear intention of suppressing women. Most of her committee members were feminist activists rather than Bible scholars, and Stanton did most of the writing. The first volume, entitled *The Woman's Bible*, covering the first part of the Old Testament, appeared in 1895; the second volume, covering the rest of the Bible, in 1898. Volume 1 was an instant best-seller, going through seven printings in six months and being translated into seven languages. The introduction begins with the statement that "from the inauguration of the movement for woman's emancipation the Bible has been used to hold her in the 'divinely ordained sphere,' prescribed in the Old and New Testaments." In her commentary on the creation story in Genesis, Stanton insisted that the text "plainly shows the simultaneous creation of man and woman, and

---

37. Stanton et al., eds., *History of Woman Suffrage*, I, Preface.
38. Elizabeth Cady Stanton, "The Solitude of Self," January 18, 1892, in Gordon, ed., *Selected Papers*, IV, 423–435; Karlyn Kohrs Campbell, "Stanton's 'The Solitude of Self': A Rationale for Feminism," *The Quarterly Journal of Speech* 66 (1980), 304–312.

their equal importance in the development of the race. All those theories based on the assumption that man was prior in the creation, have no foundation in Scripture. . . . not one word is said giving man dominion over woman." Dismissing the assertion that woman was eternally punished because Eve caused Adam to sin, she wrote, "It is evident that some wily writer, seeing the perfect equality of man and woman in the first chapter, felt it important for the dignity and dominion of man to effect woman's subordination in some way."[39]

The Woman's Bible received a mostly hostile reaction. Even Anthony did not like it, and the National American Woman Suffrage Association, of which Stanton was by now a past-president, passed a resolution disavowing it, fearing it would taint the woman suffrage movement. Stanton, frustrated with the seeming stalemate on woman suffrage, was pleased at the reaction it engendered from churchmen. "Our politicians are calm and complacent under our fire but the clergy jump around . . . like parched peas on a hot shovel," she wrote. In the second edition, ever defiant of critics, she included the association's disavowal resolution and other critical reviews as an appendix.[40]

In 1898, she published her autobiography, *Eighty Years and More: Reminiscences, 1815–1897*. It is both an account of her life and a personal history of the women's rights movement over more than fifty years. It is written in an informal style with many personal insights and touches of humor. It is highly laudatory of friends and supporters (the book was dedicated to Susan B. Anthony) and critical of opponents, who are portrayed as uninformed or simply wrong in their opinions. Much of it is excellent eyewitness history: accounts of meetings, reasoning with open-minded people, facing down angry critics, appealing again and again to legislators. Her strong views on voting, marriage, divorce, and religion receive a good deal of coverage. Her husband Henry makes only a few cameo appearances and little space is devoted to her children or other family members.[40]

Stanton died at her daughter's home in New York City in 1902. The day before she died, she finished work on two more articles. Her last work was a draft of a letter to President Theodore Roosevelt. Lincoln immortalized himself by emancipating four million slaves; Roosevelt should

---

39. Elizabeth Cady Stanton, *The Woman's Bible. Part I. Comments on Genesis, Exodus, Leviticus, Numbers and Deuteronomy. Part II. Comments on the Old and New Testaments from Joshua to Revelation* (New York: European Publishing Company, 1895 and 1898), I, Introduction and 1–10.
40. Stanton, *Eighty Years and More.*

"immortalize [himself] by bringing about the complete emancipation of thirty-six million women."[41]

In her obituary, the *New York Times* paid tribute to her accomplishments and influence but noted that woman suffrage had not really taken root except in a few western states. "The chief obstacle to its progress has been the indifference or hostility of the women as a class," it claimed.[42] A new generation, including her daughter Harriot Stanton Blatch, had already taken up the cause, pursuing new strategies that led to New York granting women the right to vote in 1917 and the approval of the Nineteenth Amendment to the U.S. Constitution, conferring the right nationally, in 1920. Leaders of the generation that achieved that milestone sometimes slighted Stanton's leadership and influence or feared that her controversial stands on marriage, divorce, and religion would taint their movement. They highlighted Susan B. Anthony because of her single-minded focus on suffrage and managed to have the Nineteenth Amendment named informally the Susan B. Anthony Amendment.

More recently, Stanton's historical reputation has received well-deserved elevation. She and Anthony should be seen the way they regarded themselves, as more or less equal partners, but Stanton's reformist interests were much broader. The Seneca Falls declaration is a masterpiece of social and political writing that kicked off a long process resulting in woman suffrage many years later but achieved many other things for women along the way. Stanton framed issues, provided ideas, and crafted the concepts that made their way into the public debate for five decades, an impressive track record for both influence and longevity. She was far from perfect, stubborn, and sometimes seemed to harbor racist views. But many of her ideas about equality, individualism, and the process of political change, still reverberate in the twenty-first century. Strong willed, eloquent, resilient, and sometimes prickly and provocative, she typifies those New Yorkers who are determined to change and improve the status quo.

41. Elizabeth Cady Stanton to Theodore Roosevelt, October 25, 1902, in Stanton and Blatch, eds., *Elizabeth Cady Stanton as Revealed in Her Letters, Diary and Reminiscences*, 2, 368–369.
42. *New York Times*, October 27, 1902.

5

October 1, 1851

Striking a Blow for Freedom

Image from the title page of Jeremy Wesley Loguen's 1859 autobiography, *The Rev. J. W. Loguen, as a Slave and as a Freeman*, where he recounted his role as a leader in the rescue of fugitive slave William "Jerry" Henry. *Photo Courtesy of Onondaga Historical Association, Syracuse, New York.*

The Crusading Spirit in Central New York

On October 1, 1851, a mob of over two thousand citizens broke down the doors of a Syracuse police station to liberate William "Jerry" Henry, who had been arrested by a deputy U.S. marshal under the federal Fugitive Slave law. The "Jerry Rescue" was one of the most dramatic acts of public defiance of federal authority in U.S. history. It was part of the New York tradition of crusading for social justice, defending the rights of the oppressed, and occasionally resorting to violent confrontation with the law when that was the only way to defeat oppression. The city where it took place was in the heart of the central region of the state, distinguished in that era for its ardent support of temperance, women's rights, and other social reform causes. The organizers of the rescue were men of deep religious faith who believed that human slavery contravened Christian teaching and offended American values of equality and human dignity. The "rescue" was a milestone that revealed the divisiveness of the slavery issue, the failure of compromise, and the inevitability of the armed conflict that engulfed the nation a decade later.

The spirit of individual liberty ran deep in Syracuse. It was a rapidly growing, vibrant metropolis with about 22,000 white inhabitants and 370 blacks in 1850. The Erie Canal, completed in 1825, went right through the center of the city, and the first railroad, eventually linked to the New York Central, reached the city in 1839. The canal and the railroad were well suited to bringing in people and ideas; transporting the city's bulky main product, salt; and generally connecting the city with the rest of the state and nation. The region had been settled mostly by "Yankees," people from New England who tired of the social stratification, small farms, and thin soil that predominated in their region. Land in central New York was abundant, relatively inexpensive, and the soil was rich. The Revolutionary War had led to the removal of most of the Indian population to the western part of the state or Canada. New Englanders started emigrating there after the Revolution and sent back home for extended families. They laid out new villages in a "town green" pattern with a shared central meadow bordered by churches, stores, and homes. The vast majority were Protestants, many descended from New England Puritans. Their culture and outlook on life was subtly different from their "Yorker" neighbors, many of Dutch and German descent, in the older, eastern part of the state. They believed firmly in individual responsibility, personal thrift, and education. They tended to be moralistic, independent-minded, hard-working, and inclined to interpret good fortune as God's blessing for uprightness and enterprise.[1]

The in-migrating New Englanders and their descendants developed a fervent interest in participating in intense spiritual experiences and

---

1. Kathryn Clippinger Kosto, "Yankee Migration," in Peter Eisenstadt, editor-in-chief, *The Encyclopedia of New York State* (Syracuse: Syracuse University Press, 2005), 1734–1735.

exploring new religious direction. The rapid settlement of the area; the rise of a new influential class of merchants, manufacturers, and bankers; and the general upheaval and transformation wrought by the Erie Canal all intensified an earnest search for religious anchoring. Central and western New York became known as the "burned-over district" for the many religious revivals and movements in the region in the three decades after 1820. Chief among the incendiaries was Charles G. Finney, a Presbyterian minister possessed of a powerful preaching voice and a dramatic technique of calling people who attended his revivalist rallies to come forward, accept Christianity, and be saved from sin. Finney preached the doctrines of human free will, individual responsibility, and the need to do good works by taking action against the evils of the world. He held over 1,300 rallies and camp meetings in New York from 1825 to 1835, mostly in the central region of the state, converting thousands of people, and he inspired other ministers in mainline Protestant denominations to copy his style and message. Finney was in good company. A diverse lot of evangelists, reformers, radicals, and a few eccentrics made central New York an exciting place in the years before the Syracuse mob liberated William Henry: Shakers with their distinct form of worship; discovery of religious tablets near Palmyra, leading to founding of the Mormon church; millennialists who predicted the second coming of Christ in 1843 or 1844; spiritualists with claimed power to communicate with the dead; and communal experiments in Oneida, Skaneateles, and elsewhere. Three years before the Jerry Rescue, a convention at Seneca Falls founded the modern woman's suffrage movement. Constant religious meetings, revivals, discussions, and exhortations to do good work to achieve salvation after death naturally inspired and reinforced a hatred of human slavery. Nearly 70 percent of the leaders in the abolitionist movement in New York were ministers, deacons, church elders, or people otherwise engaged in evangelical activity. Many others were lawyers, merchants, and other men of standing and influence in their communities. They were intensely religious and imbued with the idea that salvation demands not only faith and grace but also initiative and good works.[2] These individuals endorsed the values of evangelical piety, family stability, republican government, and the diffusion of secular knowledge. They recoiled at the notion that one person should have the right to subject another to the moral and physical degradation of

2. Gerald Sorin, *The New York Abolitionists: A Case Study of Political Radicalism* (Westport, CT: Greenwood Press, 1970), 101–120.

slavery. They worried about the power of slaveholders in the south and their influence in Washington.[3]

By the mid-1830s, New York State was a center of the abolition movement, and central New York in particular was a hotbed of abolitionist activity. "Half the moral power of the nation lies within 24 hours easy ride (mostly steam boat) of New York City," declared Henry Stanton, then secretary of the American Anti-Slavery Society, founded in 1833 by Massachusetts abolitionist leader William Lloyd Garrison and New York City businessman and abolitionist Arthur Tappan. "There the fulcrum must be placed by which we are to overturn the nation."[4] By 1835, there were approximately three hundred abolitionist organizations scattered from Long Island to the Niagara Frontier, with many concentrated in the area from Utica to Buffalo. Syracuse was a center of antislavery activity. Its residents had few personal ties to the South, though its business community had some commercial ties to the cotton industry there. It was a natural stop on the route north to Canada, then part of the British colonial system, where slavery had been abolished in 1833. From Syracuse, a fugitive could go north to Oswego and over Lake Ontario to freedom or west to Buffalo and cross into Canada from there. But even in this "burned-over district," there was lack of unanimity. People were glad to see New York free of the scourge of slavery (1827), opposed its expansion beyond where it existed in the South, and hoped it would gradually be discredited and die out. They listened to antislavery advocates from their own communities. But they were apprehensive about rabble-rousing abolitionists from the outside who seemed too condemnatory of the South's sinful ways and who demanded confrontation and immediate emancipation. Moreover, New York's economy was intertwined with the "Cotton Kingdom" in the South. New York City merchants who purchased upstaters' raw materials and goods derived much of their income from the cotton trade. Like so much of New York's history, the campaign against slavery is complex and sometimes seems to exhibit internal contradictions.

For instance, in 1838, when Methodist pastor Luther Lee, an itinerant speaker for the New York State Anti-Slavery Society, spoke near Corning, a drunken mob invaded the meeting, intent on attacking him. A

3. James Brewer Stewart, *Holy Warriors: The Abolitionists and American Slavery* (New York: Hill and Wang, 1996), 38, 80.
4. Fergus M. Bordewich, *Bound for Canaan: The Epic Story of the Underground Railroad, America's First Civil Rights Movement* (New York: Armistad, 2006), 158.

burly blacksmith came to his defense, though insisting he was "an opposer of abolition in an honest way." Lee shouted defiantly: "Back, you cowardly miscreants! Do you come to disturb me in the exercise my right of free speech? I am the son of a Revolutionary soldier, who fought through seven bloody years to win this right for me, and do you think I will resign at the clamor of a mob? No, never!"

The crowd quieted down and Lee finished, but as he was leaving he discovered that the anti-abolitionists had hidden a quantity of gunpowder beneath the platform and had hoped to blow him up. When he tried to speak at a Methodist church in Litchfield (Herkimer County), someone shouted, "Shoot him right in his eyes!" Another man came forward and threw a mixture of whiskey and soot in his face. His face covered with the foul concoction, Lee nonetheless finished his speech. His courage impressed even people who were indifferent to his message. "The devil often overdoes his plans and defeats them," Lee observed philosophically.[5] In July 1843, when abolitionist Frederick Douglass, at that time living in Massachusetts, came to Syracuse to preach the gospel of antislavery, he could not find a church that would host him or a building he could rent. Undaunted, he made his stand under a tree in what is now Fayette Park. He began in the morning with only five listeners, but by evening, the number had grown to over five hundred. Syracuse's First Congregational Church, which had been organized in 1831 by abolitionists, stepped in and agreed to let him use an old building that the congregation had once used. Douglass preached to sizeable crowds for three more days.[6]

In 1850, the majority of Syracuse's citizens were tolerant rather than idealistic on race issues and law-abiding gradualists rather than law-defying revolutionaries. They hoped "moral suasion" would eventually lead slaveholders to see the error of their ways. Most did not favor racial equality, espouse integration, or advocate attacking the South to eradicate slavery. On the other hand, they cheered the courage of runaway slaves and welcomed those who decided to settle in their city. It was a source of pride that Syracuse was a refuge for the oppressed. In October 1851, many were incensed that outsiders acting under cover of federal law would presume to violate Syracuse's peaceful, tolerant consensus on racial issues by seizing one of their citizens to return him to bondage.

---

5. Milton C. Sernett, *North Star Country: Upstate New York and the Crusade for African American Freedom* (Syracuse: Syracuse University Press, 2002), 57–58.
6. Ibid., 75–76.

Four New Yorkers Head for a Rendezvous with History

Many citizens were involved in the Jerry Rescue in 1851 but four stand out: fugitive slave William Henry, called "Jerry" (ca. 1815–1853); Reverend Jermain Loguen (1813–1872), pastor of Syracuse's African Methodist Episcopal Zion Church, and also a runaway slave; Reverend Samuel May (1797–1871), minister at the United Church of the Messiah, probably the city's most public abolitionist; and Gerrit Smith (1797–1874), one of New York's wealthiest citizens, reformer, philanthropist, and tireless crusader against slavery.

William "Jerry" Henry, the central character in the drama, had been borne to a slave mother and a white father (probably her master) in Buncombe County, North Carolina, around 1815. He was described as a "mulatto," slender, and distinguished by a striking head of red hair. He moved around the South, winding up as an adult in Marion County, Missouri, where he learned to work as a farmer, mechanic, and carpenter. Henry struck out for freedom in Canada 1843, stopping in Syracuse on his way north. But he liked the city's racial tolerance and job opportunities and decided to stay. Soon he had a job in a cooperage and cabinet shop. He lived a quiet, productive, low-profile life as a law-abiding citizen except for some minor run-ins with local police over alleged larceny. Feeling comfortable in Syracuse, he had stopped being wary about apprehension as a fugitive. After all, Syracuse had a small but active and vigilant abolitionist community pledged to protect runaways who took refuge in the city.[7] At noon on October 1, 1851, Henry was working alone making a barrel in the shop where he worked. His fellow workers had left for lunch. His life was about to undergo a cataclysmic change that would rocket him into historical fame.

One of the lead "rescuers" was Reverend Jermain Loguen, born into slavery as Jarm Logue in Davidson County, Tennessee, in 1813, the son of a white man, David Logue, and his slave, a woman named Cherry. He was about the same age as William Henry and the circumstances of their births were similar. Loguen's friend Reverend Samuel May described Loguen's father as "an ignorant, intemperate and brutal slaveholder" whose beatings left the young man "bleeding and senseless." One day in 1834, Jarm stole his master's horse and began the arduous trek to freedom in Canada.

---

7. Earl R. Sperry, *The Jerry Rescue* (Syracuse: Onondaga Historical Society, 1924), 22–23; Sernett, *North Star Country*, 136.

A few years later, he moved down to Rochester and worked as a waiter. Determined never to return to slavery, he changed his name to Jermain Loguen. He attended a school established by abolitionist Beriah Green at Whitesboro but did not graduate. Seized by a determination to free and uplift blacks, he started a Sunday school for black children in Utica. He married and had six children, one of whom (Amelia) married Lewis Douglass, son of famed abolitionist Frederick Douglass. The Loguens moved to Syracuse in 1841 where Jermain became a teacher and then a minister with the church. A gifted and eloquent speaker, he used his sermons and public presentations to advocate abolition and resistance to slaveholders and to urge slaves to escape from their masters. Loguen had a special apartment in his Syracuse home on East Genesee Street for runaway slaves. He advertised his address and his "underground railroad" work in the local newspapers and identified himself on business cards as "Underground Railroad Agent." Loguen assisted more than 1,500 blacks to freedom, earning the title "King of the Underground Railroad" in Syracuse.[8] At midday on October 1, 1851, he sat quietly at home, thinking about material for his next Sunday sermon.

Reverend Samuel May had been born into a wealthy Boston family, graduated from Harvard College and Harvard Divinity School, and entered the ministry. He moved from concern about slavery to activism in 1830 after hearing an eloquent speech by the nation's leading abolitionist, William Lloyd Garrison, who denounced slavery as a sin. That resonated with May, who stressed moral purity and personal responsibility in individuals' lives. May began preaching about the need for immediate emancipation. His ardent antislavery sermons were too much for churches where he ministered in Connecticut and Massachusetts, and the congregations forced him out. But his message was a good fit for the Unitarian Church of the Messiah in Syracuse, which invited him to serve as its minister in 1845. May supported women's rights, temperance, education reform, peace, and ending capital punishment, but he soon became the city's foremost proponent of abolishing slavery.[9]

May asserted that because slaves had been degraded and kept in ignorance for centuries, whites automatically assumed they were inferior.

---

8. Samuel J. May, *Some Recollections of Our Antislavery Conflict* (Boston: Fields, Osgood & Company, 1869), 292; Bordewich, *Bound for Canaan*, 410–411.

9. Donald Yacavone, *Samuel Joseph May and the Dilemmas of the Liberal Persuasion, 1797–1871* (Philadelphia: Temple University Press, 1991), 27–41.

Given an education and a chance to prove themselves, they often excelled. May cited his colleague and friend, Reverend Jermain Loguen, as a good example. He raised money to aid runaway slaves, and his home in Syracuse was a popular stop on the Underground Railroad. Some fugitives told him tales of beatings and savage, degrading treatment. But May later recalled a conversation with one runaway who admitted he had been well treated in bondage. Then why try to escape, May asked? "Oh, sir, slavery at best is a bitter draught. Under the most favored circumstances, it is bondage and degradation still. I often writhed in my chains, though they sat so lightly on me compared with most others." May welcomed blacks into his church in Syracuse and ended the traditional practice of segregation at Sunday services. When a prominent white parishioner protested May's inviting a black family to sit in a front pew, May told him that if he did anything to hurt the family's feelings, "'the first time you afterwards appear in the congregation, I will state the facts of the case exactly as they are and administer to you as severe a reproof as I may be able to frame in words.' This had the desired effect. My colored [sic] friends retained their new seats."[10]

May was committed to his church but campaigned unsuccessfully to get national Unitarian conferences to condemn slavery. He fulminated that the ingrained, conservative attitude of the clergy was "the most serious obstacle to the progress of the antislavery cause." Confronted with historical evidence that the Constitution protected slavery, he called out the hypocritical Founding Fathers for their "brave words and cowardly deeds." Looking to history for evidence to refute slavery, he cited the Declaration of Independence with its ringing endorsement of equality and the Mayflower Compact of the first Pilgrim settlers in his native New England with their commitment to liberty and self-government. Frustrated that "moral suasion" did not seem to be weakening slavery, he nevertheless cautioned against violent confrontation. "Are muskets spiritual weapons?" he asked colleagues who favored armed force to eradicate slavery.[11] Samuel May sat down to a quiet lunch at home on October 1, 1851. Like Reverend Loguen, he was thinking about his next sermon. His principle of peaceful resistance to slavery was about to be tested.

Gerrit Smith's father amassed a fortune as a fur trader and landowner, and Smith became one of the state's largest landholders when he took

---

10. May, *Some Recollections of Our Antislavery Conflict*, 270–271, 299–301.
11. Ibid., 329–344.

over his father's business in 1819. Operating from his ancestral home in Peterboro (Madison County), Smith became one of the most influential reformers and philanthropists of the era. Over the years, he supported women's rights, the temperance movement, prison reform, international peace, and progressive education. He set up an orphanage in Peterboro and provided funding for educational institutions, churches, and individuals. He also became one of the most prominent abolitionists in New York and the nation. His conversion to that cause came in 1835 when, partly out of curiosity, he attended a meeting in Utica called by regional antislavery groups to organize a state society. A mob organized and, encouraged by the mayor and the local congressman who condemned the organizers as fanatics, invaded the church where the meeting was being held. Smith, appalled at the blatant attack on free speech, invited the delegates to adjourn to his estate at nearby Peterboro. The delegates gathered at Smith's estate, then adjourned to the local Presbyterian church to continue their deliberations and formally establish the New York Anti-Slavery Society. Smith later called the Utica riot "an instructive providence" for him. Slaveholders and their sympathizers wanted to "strangle free discussion . . . the question is not merely nor mainly whether the blacks of the South shall remain slaves but whether the whites of the north shall become slaves also."[12]

Smith regarded slavery as "an unendurable defiance of the moral sense of the civilized world." In 1836, he was elected to the first of four terms as president of the New York Anti-Slavery Society. Smith poured sizeable sums of money into antislavery activities and purchased the freedom of dozens of slaves. He spoke widely and paid for the printing and distribution of his speeches. He wrote letters articulating his views and also published them as tracts. He shipped antislavery literature into the South. He supported abolitionists, particularly in New York, including providing funds to Frederick Douglass to help underwrite the costs of his newspaper *The North Star.* Speaking to the New York State Abolition Convention in 1842, he said, "We call on every slave who has the reasonable prospect of being able to run away from slavery to make the experiment." Peterboro became a busy stop on the Underground Railroad, and many escapees settled in the area. "There are two places where slavers cannot come," an appreciative abolitionist wrote in 1849, "heaven and Peterboro."[13]

---

12. Sernett, *North Star Country*, 49–50; Bordewich, *Bound for Canaan*, 146–153.
13. Norman K. Dann, *Practical Dreamer: Gerrit Smith and the Crusade for Social Reform* (Hamilton, NY: Log Cabin Books, 2009), 383–387, 466–468.

But "moral suasion" and aiding slaves to escape to freedom did not seem to put a dent in slavery. Smith tried other strategies. One was empowering and uplifting northern blacks, including demonstrating that they could be enterprising, productive citizens if given the opportunity. To this end, he launched a grand scheme in 1846 to give 120,000 acres of land he owned in Essex and Franklin counties to approximately 3,000 poor blacks. The experiment failed; few blacks were interested in trying their hand at subsistence farming in New York's North Country with its short growing season and thin soil.[14] Smith and others saw the need for political action. Smith believed that both the Whigs and the Democrats were "stone blind, both morally and politically" on the issue of slavery. He was a founding member of the antislavery Liberty Party in 1840 and supported its candidate for president, James G. Birney, in 1840 and 1844. The party sputtered out with its remnants mostly absorbed by a new "Free Soil" Party, which fielded its own presidential candidate, former New York governor and president Martin Van Buren in 1848. The Free Soilers called for exclusion of slavery from the territories. Van Buren polled more than a quarter of the votes cast in New York State but only about 10 percent nationwide. Smith himself ran for president on the diminished Liberty Party ticket that same year but received few votes. He kept up his vigorous speaking, writing, and publishing regimen.[15] On October 1, 1851, Smith happened to be attending a conference of the state Liberty Party in Syracuse.

Buildup to the Rescue

Slavery per se was not the precipitating cause of the Jerry Rescue. Rather, it was the Fugitive Slave law of 1850. The law was one of five statutes approved by Congress in 1850 to settle a confrontation between Northern and Southern states over the status of territories acquired as a result of the Mexican-American War, 1846–1848. It replaced a weak federal fugitive slave law on the books since 1793 and was a major victory for the South, which demanded the federal government stop the fleeing of slaves via the Underground Railroad, the very sort of work at which Loguen, May, and Smith excelled. The new law, approved in August, made it much easier for slave owners to reclaim runaways, provided fines or imprisonment for

---

14. John Stauffer, *The Black Hearts of Men: Radical Abolitionists and the Transformation of Race* (Cambridge: Harvard University Press, 2002), 136–158.
15. Dann, *Practical Dreamer*, 405–443.

anyone aiding a fugitive, appointed special commissioners to settle fugitive slave cases, and provided that these commissioners could summon bystanders to aid in capture and transportation of runaways. In what abolitionists called an obvious built-in bribe, a commissioner would receive $10 for each slave remanded to the claimant but only $5 if he found in favor of the accused runaway. All law enforcement officials had a duty to arrest anyone accused of being a fugitive slave on no more evidence than a claimant's sworn testimony of ownership. Officers making such arrests were entitled to compensation for their work. Testimony by an accused slave was forbidden, and there was no provision for trial by jury.[16]

Even before it passed Congress, many people in the North, including the men who would rescue Jerry Henry the next year, were condemning it and planning how to obstruct its enforcement. Smith, May, and Frederick Douglass organized a protest meeting in Cazenovia on August 21, 1850. Nearly two thousand men and women convened, too many for the small church reserved for the meeting, and they adjourned to a nearby apple orchard. Douglass arranged for about fifty former slaves to attend and speak against the proposed law. Smith drafted and the meeting endorsed a militant appeal to slaves: "You are prisoners, in an enemy's country . . . and therefore by the rules of war, you have the fullest duty to plunder, burn, kill as you have occasion to do to promote your escape." People in the North stood ready to nullify efforts to enforce the pending Fugitive Slave law. "We can assure you that, as to the State of New York and the New England states, such efforts must prove fruitless. . . . Live! Live to escape from slavery!"[17]

President Millard Fillmore signed the Fugitive Slave law on September 18, 1850. A drumfire of defiant protest erupted from central New York. Smith arranged for a Liberty Party convention meeting in Syracuse in October to pass a resolution vowing to "defend them [fugitive slaves] even as we would defend ourselves, however imminent the danger of the dungeon or death" and to "resist the execution of this diabolical law, cost what the resistance may of property, or liberty or life."[18] Jermain Loguen

---

16. Fergus M. Bordewich, *America's Great Debate: Henry Clay, Stephen A. Douglas and the Compromise That Preserved the Union* (New York: Simon & Schuster, 2012), 319–392.
17. Sernett, *North Star Country*, 129–132; Dann, *Practical Dreamer*, 478–485; "Letter to the American Slaves from Those Who Have Fled from American Slavery," http://national-humanitiescenter.org/pds/maai/community/text7/ltramerslaves1850.pdf.
18. Dann, *Practical Dreamer*, 482.

was the star speaker at another large protest meeting in Syracuse the same month. Calling the law a "hellish enactment," he asserted that fugitives "will have their liberties or die in their defense. . . . I don't respect this law—I don't fear it—I won't obey it! It outlaws me and I outlaw it and the men who attempt to enforce it on me." He urged his fellow Syracuse citizens to "smite to earth the villains who may interfere to enslave any man in Syracuse."[19] Later in October, Samuel May, in a Sunday sermon and several public speeches, told his audiences,

> [Y]ou have the highest obligation to disobey this law. . . . which offends every feeling of humanity, sets at naught every precept of the Christian religion, outrages our highest sense of right. . . . If we yield to it, all will be lost. Our country will be given up to oppressors. . . . I will not help to uphold our nation in its iniquity. . . . if it cannot be reclaimed, let it [the union] be dissolved.[20]

A few days after that, yet another protest meeting in Syracuse resolved that the law "is nothing less than a license for kidnapping under the protection and at the expense of our Federal Government." Now is the time to "take our stand for liberty and humanity" against "the tyrants who aspire to absolute power in our republic."[21] In March, May appeared before another antislavery rally with five fugitive slaves who had taken refuge in his church before moving on to Canada. "Shall these fugitives be taken from Syracuse?" he asked rhetorically. "No!" roared the crowd. "Will you defend them with your lives?" "Yes!" the crowd responded.[22] The Syracuse antislavery forces established a vigilance committee to be on the lookout for slave catchers.

Public defiance of the law by the citizens of Syracuse did not escape the attention of federal authorities. President Fillmore, a former congressman whose hometown was Buffalo, was embarrassed by the fierce opposition to the Fugitive Slave law from his home state. Daniel Webster, the Massachusetts senator who had helped broker the Compromise of 1850, resigned under a cloud due to the public criticism it brought him. Fillmore

---

19. Jermain Wesley Loguen and Elymas Payson Rogers, *The Rev. J. W. Loguen, as a Slave and as a Freeman* (Syracuse, NY: J. G. K. Truair, 1859), 391–394.
20. May, *Some Recollections of Our Antislavery Conflict*, 356–362.
21. Sperry, *Jerry Rescue*, 20.
22. Jayme A. Sokolow, "The Jerry McHenry Rescue and the Growth of Northern Antislavery Sentiment During the 1850s," *American Studies* 16 (1982), 431.

appointed him secretary of state, and Webster took to the speaking circuit to defend his handiwork. In May 1851 the Syracuse City Council invited him to give a public speech on "the present condition of public affairs." Webster devoted most of his speech to noncontroversial public issues. But suddenly growing agitated near the end, the famed orator defended the Fugitive Slave law and warned that the full weight of the Fillmore administration was behind it. "If men get together and declare a law of Congress shall not be executed in any case, and assemble in numbers to prevent the execution of such law, they are traitors and guilty of Treason. It is treason, *treason*, TREASON and nothing else." Well aware of the city's fondness for antislavery meetings, and knowing that the Liberty Party had scheduled another convention in the city in the fall, Webster declared that "the law will be executed in all the great cities; here in Syracuse; in the midst of the next Anti-Slavery Convention if the occasion shall arise!" The crowd reacted with sullen silence. "Indignation flashed from many eyes in that assembly," Samuel May recalled. "One might almost hear the gritting of teeth in defiance of the threat."[23]

The Rescue

Just about the time Daniel Webster was chastising Syracuse, William Henry's former owner, having despaired of getting him back, sold him in absentia to one James McReynolds, a Missouri neighbor. McReynolds determined to recover his newly purchased "property." Acting under the new Fugitive Slave law, McReynolds obtained a warrant for Henry's arrest and return. He hired James Lear, who worked as a slave catcher, and he, in turn, convinced Marion County, Missouri, sheriff Samuel Smith to accompany him to Syracuse. They arrived late in September 1851 and went to the office of the U.S. commissioner appointed under the Fugitive Slave Act, Joseph Sabine. Sabine was a weak embodiment of federal power and authority. He was sympathetic to runaway slaves and privately admitted he hoped not to have to enforce the Fugitive Slave Law in his home city. His wife Margaret had many abolitionist friends and in fact may have tipped them off to the Missourians' arrival. This was Sabine's first case. He

---

23. Monique Patenaude Roach, "The Rescue of William 'Jerry' Henry: Antislavery and Racism in the Burned-Over District," *New York History* 82 (2001), 135–136; May, *Some Recollections of Our Antislavery Conflict*, 374.

delayed issuing the arrest warrant for William Henry until the Missouri authorities produced all the required paperwork to meet the requirements of the law. The paperwork arrived, the warrant was issued on September 30, and the slave catchers enlisted the aid of the local deputy U.S. marshal, Henry Allen, to arrest Henry the next day, October 1. Because of the delay in the paperwork, the arrest would come just as the Liberty Party was starting a convention in the city. The abolitionists, however, saw the timing as a deliberate attempt to fulfill Daniel Webster's threat.[24]

The arresting party waited until noon on October 1, when Henry's fellow workers had left for lunch. Suddenly, three marshals and a Syracuse policeman barged into the shop where he was working and seized him from behind. They told him they had a warrant accusing him of theft and handcuffed him. But instead of taking him to the local courthouse or jail, they took him instead to Commissioner Sabine's office and informed him that he had been arrested as a fugitive slave. Charles Wheaton, a hardware store owner and a member of the vigilance committee, witnessed the prisoner being led away or may have been tipped off by Margaret Sabine. He ran to the convention of the Liberty Party, which had just convened at the Congregational church, announcing, "A slave has been arrested!" The convention, at the direction of Gerrit Smith, adjourned and its members headed for Sabine's office. Another member of the vigilance committee rang the bell at the Presbyterian church, a prearranged signal that slave catchers were at work, and soon the bells of the city's other churches joined in. It happened that another conference, the Onondaga County Agricultural Society, was also in town, adding to the crowd, black and white, that now surged toward Sabine's office. Jermain Loguen also got the news and ran to Sabine's office, arriving at about the same time as Smith and his colleagues. Samuel May heard of the arrest, went to Sabine's office a few minutes later, and was astonished to see a crowd that had grown to over a thousand jeering people outside.[25]

Under the law, an accused runaway was not allowed to give evidence on his own behalf. The arrest and extradition paperwork was in order.

---

24. Sokolow, "The Jerry McHenry Rescue," 424–455.
25. This paragraph and the rest of this section describing the rescue are based on Sperry, *Jerry Rescue*, 23–42; Bordewich, *Bound for Canaan*, 334–339; and Angelia Murphy, "'It Outlaws Me and I Outlaw It: Resistance to the Fugitive Slave Law in Syracuse, New York," *Afro-Americans in New York Life and History* 28 (January 2004), 43–73; and Roach, "The Rescue of William 'Jerry' Henry," 134–154.

Sabine expected the proceedings would be expeditious. Federal attorneys began their proceedings. But suddenly Gerrit Smith and another Liberty Party attendee, Leonard Gibb, stepped to the front of the room and asserted that they would act as Henry's counsel. Henry, reeling from the unfolding events, at first did not believe that the famed Gerrit Smith had suddenly appeared to defend him. "I will never go back into slavery," the prisoner whispered to his new counsel. "I will have every bone in my body broken first." James Lear, the Missouri slave catcher who wore a pair of pistols prominently around his waist, tried to speak several times, but the crowd overrode him with hisses and jeers. Smith and Gibbs raised objections and asked for an adjournment to prepare their case. Sabine waved their objections aside but, frustrated and alarmed, announced an adjournment for half an hour to find a larger room. Taking advantage of the lull and encouraged by the crowd, Henry suddenly bolted for the door. "Jerry, with eyes flashing fire, and the strength and agility of a tiger, threw himself across the table, scattering papers and pistols, Marshal and constables," Jermain Loguen recalled.[26] The crowd delayed his pursuers, but the manacles slowed his progress. Two constables overtook him on a bridge over the canal, knocked him down, and put shackles on his feet. They brutally threw him into a wagon, one policeman sat on him, and he was transported to the city jail in Clinton Square, a much sturdier and more secure building than Sabine's office. Sabine announced another adjournment, this time until 5:30 in the afternoon.

To Deputy Marshal Allen and his officers, Henry was now a dangerous black man resisting arrest. But hundreds of Syracuse residents had seen his dash for freedom, his brutal subjugation, and the sneeringly triumphant forces of the law carting him off to jail. The sight of a peaceful runaway being so brutally treated enraged many citizens of Syracuse who might have looked the other way if there had been a quiet arrest, hearing, and extradition. "I have just witnessed a scene (Heaven save me from a repetition) that has frozen my heart's blood," an eyewitness recorded the next day. "I have seen the perdition of slavery enacted in Syracuse, in the heart of New York. Oh such a look! Oh such a wail!"[27]

By late afternoon, an angry crowd of around two thousand people was milling around the prison building. Speakers who had orated at the Liberty Party meeting a few hours before now exhorted them to resist this

---

26. Loguen and Rogers, *The Rev. J. W. Loguen, as a Slave and as a Freeman*, 403.
27. Ibid., 403; Bordewich, *Bound for Canaan*, 334–335; Dann, *Practical Dreamer*, 469.

outrageous display of federal authority in their city. Samuel May urged calm. Seeing him in the crowd, the Syracuse police chief asked him to come in and calm Henry, who was described as being "in a perfect rage, a fury of passion." May reassured the agitated prisoner, whispering, "Jerry, we are going to rescue you. Do be more quiet!"[28] He then went off to meet with the vigilance committee, which was already deliberating what to do. Some men counseled delay; there were rumors that Sabine would free Henry on the excuse that the paperwork was still defective. Gerrit Smith joined the vigilance committee meeting and argued that an acquittal and release would not have enough dramatic impact. "A forceful rescue will demonstrate the strength of public opinion against the possible legality of slavery and this fugitive slave law in particular. It will honor Syracuse and be a powerful example everywhere." Loguen went even further, upbraiding his white colleagues like May who seemed inclined to talk rather than act. "Now is the time to try the spunk of white men. I want to see whether they have courage only to make speeches and resolutions when there is no danger."[29]

The vigilance committee hatched a simple plan. The mob would scream for the authorities to release their prisoner. If not, they would storm the jail, seize Henry, drive him around the city in a wagon that they would arrange to have just outside the jail to shake off any pursuers, then hide him until they could spirit him out of the city and to freedom in Canada. May, still hesitant about the use of force, insisted on a condition that the police guards would not be intentionally injured. As the meeting broke up and the attendees headed into the night, he said a short prayer aloud: "If anyone is to be injured in this fray, I hope it may be one of our own party."[30] May, fearing that the melee that was about to unfold would turn violent, went home. Smith's exact role—probably as an observer rather than a participant—was never revealed. Loguen undoubtedly was part of the mob and possibly at its head, though he later denied it.

Meanwhile, Deputy Marshal Allen anticipated needing reinforcements for his small posse if the mob should charge the jail. The Syracuse chief of police was not eager to take on a mob of his city's citizens. The Onondaga county sheriff, William Gardner, also declined to have his deputies confront the mob. Allen asked him to summon the local contingent of the

28. Sokolow, "The Jerry McHenry Rescue," 234.
29. Loguen and Rogers, *The Rev. J. W. Loguen, as a Slave and as a Freeman*, 402, 409.
30. May, *Some Recollections of Our Antislavery Conflict*, 377.

state militia from the state armory down the street. Gardner reluctantly agreed and conveyed the request to the local lieutenant at the armory, who ordered his troops to muster. But vigilance committee members got wind of it and convinced the local commander, Origen Vandenburgh, who was an abolitionist sympathizer, that the sheriff had no authority to call out the militia and that he could be court marshaled for putting state forces behind slave catchers. "My soldiers will never be kidnappers with my consent," Vandenburgh declared, ordering the troops to stand down.[31]

Commissioner Sabine resumed the hearing at 5:30. The crowd, now grown to over 2,500, roared outside. It included whites, blacks, and a few whites with blackened faces to make them harder to identify later. The sheriff tried to quiet the crowd, but that seemed to incite them all the more. He tried to stop one speaker who was haranguing the crowd, but the speaker roared, "As you command me to stop, I shall begin again, to test the liberty of speech!" The crowd shouted, "Let him go! Bring him out!" Soon, rocks were hitting the building and shattering the windows. Sabine adjourned the proceedings until the next day and left by the back door. James Lear and Deputy Marshal Allen also left through the back, leaving one of Allen's deputies, Henry Fitch, in charge. Sheriff Gardner had managed to secure the support of a local military artillery group, the Washington Artillery, who suddenly appeared on the scene. But they only looked menacing. Their commander, not at all interested in firing on his fellow citizens, had ordered the cannon loaded with blanks. The artillery fired, away from the crowd, and it was only noise rather than cannon balls. In fact, the noise may have added to the din and confusion and actually encouraged the mob. The resourceful Charles Wheaton had placed clubs, axes, and iron rods outside the door of his hardware store. The vigilance committee had arranged for a large beam to be brought up to be used as a battering ram. At around 8:30 someone shouted, "Now!" and the mob surged ahead and attacked the building. They smashed windows, chopped away the casings, and began removing the bricks from the structure. The battering ram was brought up to smash down the doors. The mob entered, splintering furniture. Fitch fired into the crowd but did not hit anyone, and a member of the crowd smashed his arm with a club, breaking it. The terrified deputy ran to the back of the building, jumped out the widow, and ran away. He turned out to be the only casualty of the day. The other guards retreated, and the crowd carried Henry out the

---

31. Bordewich, *Bound for Canaan*, 336–337.

front of the building. They put him in a wagon that had been brought to the scene, and the driver drove him around the streets of the city for the next couple of hours in case anyone tried to recapture him. No one did.

Aftermath

Henry was taken to the home of a local black family where a blacksmith removed his shackles (the vigilance committee later sent them to President Fillmore as a defiant symbol of the city's determination to resist the law). After a couple of days, he was moved to a hiding place in the home of Caleb Davis, a local butcher, a Democrat, and someone known as a proslavery man and a vocal critic of Reverend Samuel May. But Davis was outraged by the Fugitive Slave law and the slave catchers' violation of his city. During the next few days, he was out in the streets, denouncing abolitionists and the rescue as expected, while at the same time joining others in secret plans to get Henry out of the city. A few days later, Davis secreted the fugitive beneath blankets in a freight wagon, then headed out into the countryside to buy beef from local farmers, which he did routinely. Henry was passed off to antislavery activists in Mexico, New York, where he hid in a barn for a few days, and a few days later put on a steamer to Kingston, Canada, and freedom.[32]

Gerrit Smith kept the Liberty Party convention going and, a few days after the rescue, got them to pass a resolution that "our beloved and glorious city of Syracuse still remains undisgraced by the fulfillment of the satanic prediction of the satanic Daniel Webster."[33] May addressed one of several public meetings organized to endorse the rescue on October 15. "We have not come here to array against the government of our country but to denounce a most tyrannous act of our government," he began. But "nothing can sanction or legalize injustice . . . no law subversive of natural rights has any binding obligation. . . . We are bound by our obligations to God and man to set this law at naught." Not everyone agreed. There were a number of "law and order" rallies that denounced the mob action. The *Syracuse Daily Star* condemned "pulpit abolitionists" like May and Loguen and warned that "to make war against the laws is to make war against the government or country." Newspapers in the South were

---

32. Ibid., 338–339.
33. "The Jerry Rescue," http://www.nyhistory.com/gerritsmith/jerry.htm.

uniformly critical. There were calls in Congress for retaliation, including a special federal tax on salt, Syracuse's most important product, but no action was taken.[34]

Federal authorities fumed that they would make an example of the Syracuse attackers. There were cries in Washington to indict them for treason, but everyone knew that would not stick. They could not be prosecuted for violation of the Fugitive Slave Act because technically Henry was not the property of McReynolds, having been sold in absentia. That left only the lesser charge of resisting a federal officer. Eventually twenty-six men, including fourteen whites and twelve blacks, were indicted. Legal proceedings dragged on for over a year. It was difficult to empanel jurors who could swear they had no preconceived notions about the case. Witnesses were scarce or, when the time came to testify, suddenly could not seem to recall for sure just what they had seen. Some of the rioters had been disguised, and it had been nighttime. The legal authorities decided not to try Samuel May and Gerrit Smith, who took out ads in the local papers admitting they had assisted in planning the rescue and threatened to rest their defense on the unconstitutionality of the law if arrested. Some of the blacks involved fled to safety in Canada. Samuel Loguen, a fugitive slave himself and almost certainly present at the rescue, also went to Canada. But he felt uncomfortable. "Has it come to this? Is slavery so mighty that I must quit my country? Shall the battle of slavery be fought and I not suffered to engage in it? And who shall engage in that battle if I may not?" Loguen returned quietly to Syracuse in the spring of 1852. Marshal Henry Allen served an arrest warrant but did not actually arrest him. As Loguen put it, "it would have been like throwing a fire brand into a powder house . . . enflame Syracuse to madness." Loguen was never tried. Several trials ended in hung juries. In the end, only one rioter, a black named Enoch Reed, was convicted, and he died while his case was on appeal.[35]

William Henry stayed safe in Kingston, Ontario, Canada, working as a cooper, until his death in 1853 from tuberculosis.

---

34. Yacavone, *Samuel Joseph May and the Dilemmas of the Liberal Persuasion*, 147–150; Samuel J. May, "Speech of Rev. Samuel J. May to the Convention of Citizens of Onondaga County in Syracuse on the 14th Day of October, 1851," http://ebooks.library. cornell.edu/cgi/t/text/pageviewer-idx?c=mayantislavery;idno=19869201;view=image; seq=1.

35. Loguen and Rogers, *The Rev. J. W. Loguen, as a Slave and as a Freeman*, 428–442; Sperry, *Jerry Rescue*, 25–28; Sernett, *North Star Country*, 138–161.

Jermain Loguen resumed his role as a lead conductor on the Underground Railroad, aiding more than 1,500 freedom seekers in total but otherwise playing a quiet role after the Jerry Rescue. After the Civil War, he was promoted to the rank of bishop in the African Methodist Episcopal Zion church and worked for the welfare of newly freed blacks.

Samuel May organized Jerry Rescue Days for October 1 of each year, continued his work in aiding fugitives, and raised money for the cause. Because of the work of May and his colleagues, fugitives continued to feel safe in Syracuse and slave catchers avoided the city. But May was increasingly torn between his commitment to peaceful resolution of the issue and his growing belief that only armed force could destroy slavery. When the antislavery fanatic John Brown led a violent raid into Virginia to free slaves in October 1859, he was stopped and captured at Harpers Ferry. Soon he was tried and sentenced to death. May, and other moderates, condemned the raid but also protested the death sentence. Slavery "defiles everything it touches," he lamented in February 1860. "We cannot get over it, nor under it, nor around it, nor through it; and we certainly cannot get along with it." He despaired of a peaceful solution and, disillusioned with the nation's political leadership, did not vote in 1860. He condemned secession by the Southern states early in 1861 but, in another turnabout of sometimes seemingly mercurial public opinion as the crisis deepened, was threatened by a mob and burned in effigy in Syracuse by citizens who blamed abolitionists for the crisis. After the firing on Fort Sumter in April 1861, Syracuse rallied to the union cause, and May was once again recognized as a respected public figure. He saw the Civil War as the terrible price the nation had to pay for the sin of slavery. Following the war, he continued his work for racial equality and women's rights and developed an interest in education, serving as president of the Syracuse public school district.[36]

Gerrit Smith remained one of the nation's foremost abolitionists. He prevailed on the Onondaga County district attorney to indict James Lear and Deputy Marshal Henry Allen for kidnapping and arranged to be appointed an adjunct prosecutor. Lear had returned to Missouri and was never tried, but Allen was tried in Syracuse in June 1852. Smith used the trial to attack the constitutionality of the Fugitive Slave law. "Our fathers, who created the American Government, created it 'to establish justice and secure the blessings of liberty,' and not to be a gigantic slave-catcher, and

---

36. Yacavone, *Samuel Joseph May and the Dilemmas of the Liberal Persuasion*, 149–244.

to expend in slave-catching the contributions which honest toil is compelled to make to the national treasury. . . . Slavery is a war upon nature, and is the devourer of the rights of nature . . ." [37] The judge directed a verdict of not guilty, holding the marshal was enforcing a valid federal law. Smith was elected to Congress in 1852 by a coalition of abolitionists and reformers but, frustrated with federal policy and congressional inaction, resigned after only one term. Smith supported and encouraged John Brown's violent confrontation of slave forces in Kansas in 1856 and knew that Brown planned a violent incursion into the South to free the slaves. But he was shocked by Brown's raid in Virginia in October 1859 and claimed not to have known about Brown's specific plans. However, a letter found in Brown's possession exposed Smith as one of his backers. He feared being indicted as a coconspirator and lapsed into a state of fear, remorse, depression, and anxiety. "I am going to be indicted, sir, indicted!" he blurted out to a *New York Herald* reporter who traveled to Peterboro to interview him in late October 1859. Smith was so distressed that he suffered a nervous breakdown and was confined in the State Insane Asylum in Utica for several weeks with "acute mania." Smith screamed that people were going to kill him, had to be restrained and strapped into bed, and was given a concoction of marijuana, brandy, and morphine to calm and sedate him. But after a few weeks, he achieved a miraculous return to good mental and physical health, was released, and returned to Peterboro. He was not indicted but blamed his close call on being overly ardent for abolition and stopped being a vocal champion of the cause. When the Civil War came, he supported it, but when it was over, he advocated a mild policy toward the former Confederacy, arguing that the North had been partially guilty for the war by tolerating slavery for so long.[38]

The Jerry Rescue was soon upstaged by other dramatic events, including John Brown's raid and Southern secession, leading up to the Civil War in 1861. The liberation of William Henry seemingly represented New York at its best, standing up for the oppressed. But the record, like so much of New York history, is complex and nuanced. Part of the motivation was supporting social justice and fair play. Part was a deeply held religious and moral obligation to do the right thing. Some of the motivation was an instantaneous reaction to seeing a man who had committed

---

37. Gerrit Smith speech in "Trial of Henry Allen, Deputy U.S. Marshal, for Kidnapping," 1852, http://library.syr.edu/digital/collections/g/GerritSmith/478.htm.
38. Stauffer, *The Black Hearts of Men*, 238–261; Dann, *Practical Dreamer*, 487–521.

no crime other than lunging for his own freedom being dragged through the streets in chains. Part was resentment against the reactionary South dominating the federal government. A disproportionate number of the participants were professional and commercial people, and the episode was in part "a community demonstration against a distant enemy and its local law enforcers."[39] The rescue demonstrated New Yorkers' resolve when principle was at stake but also the complexity of their perceptions, motivations, and goals.

---

39. Sokolow, "The Jerry McHenry Rescue," 438.

6

March 30, 1899

Pollution and Politics

Theodore Roosevelt and his family hiking near their home at Sagamore Hill, Long Island. Roosevelt enjoyed hiking and hunting and wanted to preserve the natural environment. But his record as governor on the issue of water pollution was mixed, presaging New York's ambivalent and inconsistent water pollution policy over the next half century. *Photo Courtesy of Sagamore Hill National Historic Site, National Park Service, Oyster Bay, New York.*

The Governor and the Polluters

On March 30, 1899, Governor Theodore Roosevelt issued a dramatic order mandating abatement of pollution in Kayaderosseras Creek in Saratoga County. That modest stream begins near Ballston Spa, passes Saratoga Springs, and empties into Saratoga Lake. By the time of TR's order, its banks were lined with tanneries and paper pulp and bag manufacturing mills (including the Union Bag and Paper Company, owned by wealthy local resident George West, known as the "Paper Bag King"). The mills drained manufacturing residue into the stream. The villages of Ballston Spa and Saratoga Springs, tourist hotels, and private residents also emptied their sewage there. In 1898, thirty-one Saratoga Springs residents, tired of the stench, petitioned Governor Frank Black to curtail this "public nuisance. . . . filthy and noxious material, offensive to the eye and giving out offensive odors." Black ordered the State Board of Health to investigate. That board had a small administrative staff but little technical expertise and contracted with Olin H. Landreth, an engineering professor at Union College, as a consulting engineer to carry out a field investigation. Landreth walked the shores of the creek and the lake in December, found the water brackish and foul-smelling, and reported that "a public nuisance exists." Reflecting the caution of the agency that employed him, however, the investigator did not publicly identify the sources.[1]

Governor Black's administration was tarnished by a scandal involving overpayments for Erie Canal repairs, and he was not renominated in the fall. Instead, the Republicans put up Theodore Roosevelt, a former assemblyman, New York City police commissioner, assistant secretary of the navy, and a hero famous for daring leadership of troops in the just-completed Spanish American War. After elected, TR promised an activist, reformist administration. The Saratoga petitioners quickly appealed to the new governor for action. He asked the Board of Health for a report and recommendation. The board sent Landreth back in March 1899 with an order to identify the sources. He reported that "lime-water neutralized by lactic acid and the tanning liquors" from the tanneries, "large quantities of chloride of lime and other chemicals" from the paper mills, and sewage from thousands of people in the two villages, resorts, and households were fouling the stream and the lake, producing "odors which are offensive, often producing nausea." The pollution should be forbidden, Landreth wrote in his report, which the Board of Health forwarded to the governor. Roosevelt seized on the report and cited and quoted it in his order, noting that the creek "is practically an open sewer from Ballston Spa to the lake." His order specified that the companies, villages, and individuals were to cease dumping in the stream or else ensure that the effluent materials "have been treated in a sanitary manner" approved by the Board of Health "so as to render the same innocuous."[2]

The governor's widely publicized order noted that in fact many New York streams had become "little more than open sewers, transmitting disease germs from one place to another [and] emanating offensive and disagreeable odors." That seemed like the prelude to bold action. But the story turned out to be nuanced and complex, something very common in New York history. The villages installed sewage treatment systems that

---

1. "Saratoga Lake," *Nineteenth Annual Report of the State Board of Health of New York*, 1898 (Albany: Wynkoop Hallenbeck Crawford, 1899), 107–112 and 485–491.
2. "Public Health—Order Directing Abatement of Nuisances in Saratoga Lake," March 30, 1899. *Public Papers of Theodore Roosevelt, Governor*, 1899 (Albany: Brandow, 1900), 58–64.

were approved by the Board of Health, but its standards were vague, its measurements for pollution imprecise, and its inspection and enforcement staff small. The companies procrastinated, offered the excuse that they were experimenting with treatments to neutralize their effluents, and threatened to leave the state if pressed too hard. Health authorities vacillated and compromised. In 1907, a delegation of Saratoga citizens met with Governor Charles Evans Hughes to complain that TR's order was being ignored. Hughes declined to intervene. Six years after that, a farmer along the stream sued the Union Bag company for polluting it so badly that he could not use it to water his cows or grow vegetables. The Court of Appeals fined the company and issued an injunction against further pollution.[3]

Roosevelt is remembered for his great achievements in the area of conservation and parks as president, but his conservation record as governor was actually a modest one. His reformist zeal upon taking office was quickly tempered by Albany's political realities, particularly the need to compromise with Senator Thomas Platt, the conservative, pro-business head of the state Republican Party. TR pushed through a tax on public utility franchises and a few other regulatory reforms, but Platt thwarted him on others. In his January 1900 annual message to the legislature, he called for protecting and developing state forests "along scientific principles," banning dyes and effluents from leather tanning from being discharged into streams in the Adirondacks and Catskills, and building dams and reservoirs in those areas, but only after "careful and scientific study of the water resources of the region." But he did not press any of those issues. He increased the size of state forests, got legislation passed to outlaw the use of bird skins or feathers for ornaments or wearing apparel, and initiated planning for the Palisades Interstate Park, all easy wins. Constantly cautioned by Platt not to antagonize business interests, he abandoned any plans he might have had for pursuit of water polluters. In 1900 the governor had to decide on a bill to permit the City of Gloversville to discharge sewage into Cayadutta Creek. Acknowledging privately the strength of the arguments against it, he nevertheless signed the bill because a political ally, Lucius Littauer, a glove manufacturer known as the Republican "Boss of Gloversville," wanted it.[4] Politics and pollution trumped reform and sanitation, a pattern that continued for many years.

---

3. "Hughes Is Told of River Pollution," *New York Times*, March 16, 1907; *Whalen v. Union Bag and Paper Company*, March 25, 1913, 208 NY 1.

4. Paul Grondahl, *"I Rose Like a Rocket": The Political Education of Theodore Roosevelt*

The Problem and the Experts

By 1900, many of New York's fifty-one thousand miles of streams and dozens of lakes were laden with municipal refuse and chemical pollutants. Public concern and understanding of requirements for clean drinking water, and for treating sewage, were slowly evolving. In years past, people had associated disease with "miasmas": decaying matter, foul smells, and "bad air." By the turn of the century, the "germ theory" that infectious diseases are caused by microorganisms too small to be seen without magnification and that enter the body was becoming popular. Municipal water systems developed as villages and cities grew, with sand or mechanical filters to remove impurities, but their effectiveness varied widely. Chemical treatment, for example, the addition of chlorine, was still uncommon. Municipal waterworks led to more flush toilets, escalating water use and construction of sewers to carry away wastes. But often, the sewers emptied directly, or with minimum filtering or other treatment, into the nearest large body of water. A river might carry one city's sewage downstream to where another city drew its drinking water. Industry also contributed pollution. For instance, processes for extracting pulp from spruce and other trees that were abundant in New York led to rapid construction of paper mills to produce paper for newspapers, magazines, insulation, and other products. But the process produced a high-acid effluent that was piped into the same streams that were used to float logs to mills and also used as sources of drinking water. Industrial pollution was regarded more as a nuisance than a threat to human health. In fact, some medical experts asserted that industrial waste was something of a germicide that would kill the dangerous organisms in domestic waste.[5]

How to balance municipalities' need to get rid of waste, industry's desire to discard liquid by-products of manufacturing, and the public's right to clean, healthy water? Professionals in an emerging field called sanitary engineering began offering their expertise at the intersection of

---

(New York: Free Press, 2004), 322–323; Douglas Brinkley, *The Wilderness Warrior: Theodore Roosevelt and the Crusade for America* (New York: Harper Collins, 2009), 338–367; Marvin W. Kranz, Pioneering in Conservation: A History of the Conservation Movement in New York State, 1865–1903 (Dissertation, Syracuse University, 1961), 490–495; G. Wallace Chessman, *Governor Theodore Roosevelt: The Albany Apprenticeship, 1898–1900* (Cambridge: Harvard University Press, 1965), 244.

5. Martin V. Melosi, *The Sanitary City: Environmental Services in Urban America from Colonial Times to the Present* (Pittsburgh: University of Pittsburgh Press, 2008), 103–148; Martin V. Melosi, *Precious Commodity: Providing Water for America's Cities* (Pittsburgh: University of Pittsburgh Press, 2011), 37–77

pollution, public health policies, and public education in the early twentieth century. They were widely quoted in the press, gave public lectures, and wrote books that were frequently cited as authoritative. They were often hired as consultants by municipalities planning water or sewage treatment facilities. They cautioned that the alarms expressed by the medical community, and often echoed by state health departments headed by doctors, about the threat of waterborne disease needed to be balanced by pragmatic understanding about what municipalities could afford to do in treating sewage. The sanitary engineers were inclined to play down the toxicity of factory waste and to endorse the business community's argument that available treatments were impractical and expensive. The experts lacked a consensus and sometimes testified against each other in public hearings on water quality issues. Their bland views on tolerable levels of pollution seem alarming today. But their ideas were influential as New York, and other states, struggled to find a policy for clean water.[6]

For instance, Allen Hazen, a mechanical engineer, helped develop the "slow sand filter" method of treating incoming water. In 1897, he designed the system for Albany, which drew its drinking water from the polluted Hudson River, and the rate of typhoid and other waterborne diseases plummeted. Hazen established a practice as a consulting engineer in New York City and joined with another expert, George Whipple, discussed later, to create the firm of Hazen and Whipple in 1904. In 1907, Hazen published *Clean Water and How to Get It*, which soon became a must-read book in the public health community. The book emphasized the efficacy of sand and mechanical filters in taking out dirt to which typhoid and other disease microbes might cling. "Sand filtration alone, without preliminary treatment, is able to remove nearly all of the objectionable bacteria, as well as other organisms, from many waters, at the same time purifying them in other ways," Hazen assured readers. Effective filters can remove the effects of sewage pollution "without difficulty." These processes would yield "a purification that was reasonably satisfactory and that could be reached at a cost that was not burdensome." Adding disinfectants to the water could provide added assurance but would usually not be necessary.[7]

6. Joel A. Tarr, James F. Yosie, and James McCurley III, "Disputes over Water Quality Policy: Professional Cultures in Conflict, 1900–1917," *American Journal of Public Health* 70 (April 1980), 427–435.

7. Allen Hazen, *Clean Water and How to Get It*, revised edition (New York: John Wiley & Sons, 1914), 78–85, 94–131.

George C. Whipple, a sanitary engineer and microbiologist, published *The Microscopy of Drinking Water* in 1899, identifying the microscopic aquatic organisms that could cause problems in drinking water and setting forth measures of the transparency and turbidity of water. Regarded as highly authoritative, Whipple was frequently employed as a consultant and was cofounder of a school of public health created jointly by MIT and Harvard in 1913, which evolved into the Harvard School of Public Health in 1922. His influential 1907 book *The Value of Pure Water* asserted that "the purification of a polluted water is a sort of life insurance for people" and relatively easy to accomplish through filtration. Whipple was also an early advocate of chlorination of drinking water, designing a pioneering system for Jersey City, New Jersey, in 1908, but that practice was slow to spread. In discussing sewage pollution, Whipple reminded readers that "sewage treatment" was a better term than "sewage purification," because sewage could never be fully purified. Treatment systems would not only reduce "the foul, putrescible matter with its accompanying offensive smell" but also eliminate "living, disease-producing mechanisms." Like his consulting partner Allen Hazen, Whipple put his faith in filters for drinking water: "[W]hen public health authorities in this country compel large cities to construct sewage treatment plants for the avowed purpose of protecting water supplies taken from rivers below them," he said, "they are attempting to accomplish the impracticable and are compelling the expenditure of money without adequate returns."[8]

The Search for Policy

The public interpreted the work of sanitary engineers such as Hazen and Whipple to mean that water pollution was not an urgent issue so long as municipalities had water filtration systems. Moreover, responsibility was divided at the state level. The legislature created the Fisheries, Game and Forest Commission in 1895, changed its name to the Forest, Fish and Game Commission in 1900, and to the Conservation Commission in 1911. It had broad powers to regulate state forests, protect game, regulate hunting, and propagate fish, including banning pollution that was strong enough to harm fish. As early as 1894, fishermen responding to a

---

8. George C. Whipple, *The Value of Pure Water* (New York: John Wiley & Sons, 1907), 42–52; "Sewage Treatment vs. Sewage Purification," *American Journal of Public Health* 3 (June 1913), 513–518.

commission survey said pollution in the Hudson River was killing fish and giving those fish that were caught a bad taste. The commission found it hard to pinpoint a specific culprit when fish died, however, and seldom targeted polluters. But it repeatedly updated the legislature on the problem. In 1911, for instance, it reported, "[P]ollution of our public waters by the untreated sewage of municipalities and the waste of manufacturing plants" was jeopardizing public health as well as killing fish and destroying oyster beds in Long Island Sound and Raritan Bay where "slimy ooze" was visible in the water. It continued:

> [L]arge manufacturing concerns, in utter disregard of the rights of our citizens and the State, further pollute our waters with waste. . . . these commercial plants have no more right in law or equity to deposit upon the properties of the State than upon the farms or grounds of their neighbors.

The commission asked the legislature to bestow more funding for inspection and penalties for pollution.[9]

The second agency, much more centrally involved in the pollution issue, was the State Board of Health, created in 1880, with a broad mandate to promote public health, discover and prevent adulteration of food and drugs, and carry out research and report on prevention of diseases. The board could make regulations to protect "public supplies of potable waters" from contamination. It could review plans for local government water and sewer systems when asked to do so by local authorities. It could issue an order when it found that a proposed sewer system might pollute a public water supply, but seldom did so. It could also investigate "nuisances" on its own initiative, on the request of local governments or health officials, or when requested to do so by the governor, as Black and Roosevelt did for Saratoga. The board's enforcement power was weak; it depended mostly on education and on the power of local public opinion to secure compliance by local government officials. Governor Benjamin Odell, TR's successor, pushed through legislation that transformed the board into the Department of Health with a single head in 1901 with broadened powers to inspect public water and treatment facilities and a larger staff. Local boards of health could formulate rules for the protection

---

9. "Fish Commissions Work," *New York Times*, December 3, 1894; *First Annual Report of the Conservation Commission*, 1911 (Albany: Argus, 1912), 19–20, 106–108.

of water supplies, petition the department to approve them, and the department would then issue the rule. But local boards often lacked the expertise to investigate and analyze sources of pollution and found it politically uncomfortable to accuse their own municipalities or local businesses of fouling waterways. It was difficult to secure the cooperation of several jurisdictions when there were multiple municipalities or pollution along a lengthy stream. The state board sometimes intervened in such situations but still lacked strong enforcement power. Headed by a doctor, the department emphasized the "germ theory" of disease and established one of the nation's first research laboratories to explore infectious diseases. Its staff sometimes asserted that the sanitary engineers took too casual an attitude toward waterborne pollution.

Its main strategy in the area of pollution was to investigate, report, and generally raise awareness. In 1898, summarizing its investigations and surveys dating back a decade, the Board of Health reported widespread pollution of streams by sewage disposal and "manufacturing refuse." More authority was needed to restrict pollution to prevent transmission of waterborne diseases and "to improve general unsanitary conditions arising from noxious emanations [and] miasmic or malarial influences."[10] Specific examples were described in subsequent annual reports. In 1901, for instance, the department investigated a complaint about pollution of Eighteen Mile Creek near Lockport, which was lined with paper, aluminum, and steel mills. The creek below the mills was "loaded with suspended matter" and "decomposting organic material," and the banks were coated with "deposits of a slimy, leathery character resembling curd" making the whole stream "foul in character." But the department did not issue abatement orders.[11] In 1902, it issued a report on the pollution of major New York streams noting, for instance, that the Hudson River at Troy was receiving the output of "the entire sewer system, city of Troy, population 72,000" and "manufacturing, refuse and chemicals from 24 mills, factories, breweries, packing establishments [and] laundries aggregating 7000 employees." Professor Landreth was dispatched to investigate paper mill pollution of the Ausable River and Lake Champlain the next year. A large

10. "Brief in Support of the Passage of a Bill for the Protection and Improvement of the Water of the State," *Nineteenth Annual Report of the State Board of Health of New York*, 1898 (Albany: Wynkoop Hallenbeck Crawford, 1899), 485–491.

11. "Town of Lockport. Eighteen Mile Creek," *Twenty Second Annual Report of the State Department of Health for the Year Ended Dec. 31, 1901* (Albany: J. B. Lyon, 1902), 172–201.

party of local citizens turned out to walk with him on his inspection. "The Ausable water looked like coffee and has such a fetid odor that it made one of the women in the party ill," the leader of the local group told a news reporter. "A dog we had with us refused to drink the water."[12] Landreth wrote his report describing the pollution, but the Health Department issued no decisive orders. Pollution of the lake eventually abated, but it took many years and combined pressure by New York, Vermont, and federal authorities.

Typhoid fever outbreaks in Ithaca and Rochester in 1903 convinced the legislature to increase the department's authority. A law passed that year declared that "no person, corporation, or municipality" shall discharge "sewage, garbage . . . or any decomposable or putrescible matter of any kind or any substance, chemical or otherwise . . . in quantities injurious to the public health" into any public waters of the state without the approval of the commissioner of health. But the law applied only to *future* installations; systems existing at the time of the law's passage were exempted. Moreover, the appropriation for enforcement was small, the penalties for violation modest.[13]

The 1903 law nevertheless made the Department of Health the state's leading agency in the area of water pollution. The department took up its new responsibilities cautiously, working with local public health boards and cooperating with municipalities and companies seeking permits. But Dr. Eugene Porter, a leading proponent of the germ theory of disease, who was appointed commissioner in 1905 by Governor Frank Higgins, dramatically escalated the issue. Porter was determined to stamp out typhoid fever, a deadly disease that was often waterborne. He was impatient with Albany's slow-moving political responses to health issues and began an appeal to the public to raise awareness of pollution and its impact on public health. At a conference of local sanitary officials in October 1905, he said that there had been more than sixty thousand typhoid cases in the state that year. "For a series of years, an increasing volume of sewage has been poured into our streams until practically all are contaminated and many of them are little better than open sewers. . . . The continued pollution of our streams and lakes must stop."[14]

12. "Refuse Kills Fish," *New York Times*, October 4, 1903.
13. *Twenty-Fourth Annual Report of the State Department of Health for the Year Ended Dec. 31, 1903* (Albany: Oliver A. Quayle, 1904), 1–19, 735–749; *Laws of New York*, 1903, Ch. 468.
14. "Typhoid Fever in New York," *New York Times*, October 9, 1905.

The next year, the department's report to the legislature said bluntly, "[P]ollution of our lakes, rivers and streams is a sin against the public health, a crime that strikes a deadly blow at the comfort and lives of our fellow citizens. . . . inexcusable, shameful." The report recommended more education of the public, who would demand local action; more power for the department, including the power to order municipalities to cease pumping sewage into any waters; and more money for research. But the call for action was diluted with caution about the magnitude and complexity of the task. "The work of the purification of our streams must proceed along broad and comprehensive lines," including where possible study of an entire watershed—water sources, character of the soil, population of each municipality, "condition of sewage," and other factors—before deciding on a given application. Of course, work of such magnitude would require a significantly increased budgetary appropriation for the department. Furthermore, people would have to be patient. Citizens who demanded that pollution cease immediately should be disregarded. "Half-baked enthusiasts, rendered dangerous by the possession of a little knowledge, should be gently but firmly led to the rear."[15] Porter's condescending tone did not help his cause.

The next year, Porter noted that there were limits to how much pollution a stream could handle and, "[M]any, if not most, of our larger streams have reached this limit and in many cases have even passed it." The department should be given power to order municipalities to install effective sewage filtering systems. But again the recommendation was offset by an insistence on the complexity of the issue. Industrial wastes "vary greatly in composition, strength, and volume and in very many cases no scientific methods of practical and economical purification are known." More research was needed, and of course that required more money. Using accusatory language unlikely to win him friends in the governor's office or legislature, the commissioner declared that "the state has spent far more money for the protection of the health of cattle than it has for its citizens."[16]

Under Porter's direction, the department could be heavy-handed when deciding on applications from municipalities for new sewage treatment plants. This made the legislature cautious about increasing its regulatory

15. *Twenty-Seventh Annual Report of the State Department of Health for the Year Ended Dec. 31, 1906* (Albany: J. B. Lyon, 1907), 10–16.

16. *Twenty-Ninth Annual Report of the State Department of Health for the Year Ended Dec. 31, 1909* (Albany: J. B. Lyon, 1909), 1–27; "Urges Aid for Health Work," *New York Times*, February 20, 1909.

and oversight power. Dr. Palmer Ricketts, president of RPI, located in Troy, described that city's exasperation in trying to get approval to build a new sewage treatment system in 1905. Troy was a well-known polluter of the Hudson at that time. When the city applied to extend its sewers and improve treatment, the department's rejection began with a menacing reference to possibly ordering "the stopping of the increase of population" of the city until it got its sewage under control. The department's initial requirements would have required a treatment plant so expensive that city taxes would have doubled to pay for it. The city and the department reached a more economical compromise, but the incident showed the department's alarming inclination to overreach, said Ricketts. "A large river in a thickly populated district is a sewer," he added, even if sewage is treated, because there will be runoff from city streets. "No sewage treatment will make it other than a sewer." Citing sanitary engineer Allen Hazen, Ricketts said that even polluted water "can be and is made safe for drinking purposes when filtered." Communities downstream on the Hudson should filter their drinking water rather than expecting state health officers to force upstream communities like Troy to purify their sewage. The department too often listened to "ignorant popular clamor" for impossible sewage purification.[17] The RPI president's views on pollution are certainly dated by today's standards, but his skepticism about allowing the Health Department too much authority was widespread.

On the other hand, there was occasionally public clamor for action. The press, particularly in New York City, took up the campaign for pollution abatement in the Hudson. The Merchants' Association of New York, a business group that acted as a watchdog on water issues relating to New York City, in 1907 petitioned newly elected Republican governor Charles Evans Hughes to act to clean up the Hudson. Hughes, a progressive reformer, had limited understanding of pollution issues and lots of other things on his agenda, including public utility, banking, and insurance reforms and enactment of a direct primary law. He asked Porter to investigate. It was a good opportunity for a vocal commissioner to advance concrete recommendations to an activist governor. But the report was surprisingly inconclusive. It described the polluted river but emphasized the diluting effects of the dispersal of municipal sewage. It let industrial polluters off easy:

---

17. Palmer C. Ricketts, "Some of the Reasons Why Stream-Pollution Legislation in New York State Has Been Defeated," *Engineering News* 64 (October 13, 1910), 396–397.

When we consider that the industrial wastes when discharged into the streams do not carry with them the germs of disease and probably very few bacteria at all, and that many of the chemicals discharged with them will have germicidal properties, the effect of these wastes upon health must be very slight.[18]

Disappointed, Hughes realized a wholesale executive order mandating cleanup of the river was unrealistic. In his 1909 annual message, the governor said, "[W]e can no longer afford to permit the sewage of our cities and our industrial waste to be poured into our water courses." But he warned there could be negative consequences if industries were compelled to institute special waste treatments and called for "proper experimentation under state authority in order that as soon as possible means may be devised for complete protection of our streams from pollution without industrial dislocation."[19] He endorsed a bill expanding the Health Department's authority but his support was lukewarm, and legislation stalled in 1909 and 1910. The next year, with Democrats now in charge of both the legislature and the governor's office, Governor John A. Dix proposed legislation that was quickly approved. It gave the department authority to review and approve new sewage systems and industrial discharges, but enforcement required an order approved by both the governor and the attorney general.[20] That constituted a very modest step forward in the campaign against pollution.

The department took up its expanded duties, emphasizing education and guidance rather than coercion through orders that would require gubernatorial and attorney general approval. Once again, politics intervened to change the conversation. In 1913, William Sulzer, a flashy maverick Democratic congressman from New York City, replaced Dix as governor. Sulzer surprised even Albany political veterans by declaring that the state's death rate from infectious diseases was too high and placing much of the blame on the Health Department. The governor appointed a blue ribbon public health commission that studied major diseases and

---

18. "Report on the Pollution of the Upper Hudson by Industrial Wastes," *Twenty-Eighth Annual Report of the State Department of Health for the Year Ended Dec. 31, 1907* (Albany: J.B. Lyon, 1908), 454.
19. Robert F. Wesser, *Charles Evans Hughes: Politics and Reform in New York, 1905–1910* (Ithaca: Cornell University Press, 1967), 336.
20. Charles A. Holmquist, "Status of Sewage Treatment in New York State," *Sewage Works Journal* 2 (January 1930), 82–87.

recommended a public health council attached to the Health Department to promulgate a comprehensive sanitary code. Clean water issues were slighted. "The better protection of water supplies" was listed as one of the "Important Subjects Not Covered" in the appendix of the report.[21] Sulzer offered the post of commissioner to the doctor who had headed the commission, Hermann M. Biggs, the commissioner of health in New York City. But Biggs refused, doubting that the legislature would provide the resources needed to carry out the new responsibilities. Porter stayed on through the end of 1913. By then, Sulzer himself was gone. Headstrong and defiant, he alienated Democratic Party bosses who plotted to get rid of him. He was impeached and removed from office for misuse of campaign funds in October 1913. His successor, Martin Glynn, convinced Biggs to accept the post of commissioner in 1914. Biggs turned out to be a distinguished leader in public health and served until 1923. But he concentrated on fighting tuberculosis and infectious diseases. Water pollution was not a priority.

The Health Department and the Conservation Commission dealt with pollution on a case-by-case basis, but population increased, industries grew, and major streams got dirtier by the year. Republican governor Charles Whitman (1915–1919) was not much concerned about the issue except for the Mohansic controversy, discussed later. But his successor, Democrat Alfred E. Smith (1919–1921 and 1923–1929), a reformer who consolidated and reorganized state government and instituted the modern budget system, and his Democratic colleagues in the legislature, realized New York needed a comprehensive, effective water pollution policy. Smith decided to bypass the Health Department, whose priorities were elsewhere, and instead signed a bill in 1919 calling on the Conservation Commission to study the issue and advance policy recommendations. Press reports predicted that at last there would be a concrete solution.

But the commission dithered. Preliminary reports in 1919 and 1920 identified issues; reported on pollution in a number of streams, including the Hudson, where it was already well documented; cited the need for more study; and asked for more funding from the legislature. When Smith was defeated by a Republican in 1920, the issue faded; when he was reelected in 1922, it suddenly became a priority again. The commission's report, finally issued in 1923, aligned with the community of sanitary

---

21. *Governor Sulzer's Message on Public Health with Report of Special Public Health Commission* (Albany: J. B. Lyon, 1913), 40.

engineers in recommending caution and limited state intervention. "There is a popular tendency to exaggerate the destructive effects of stream pollution and to impute to it many ill effects for which it may be only in a minor measure responsible," the report asserted. Many streams were polluted by municipal sewage, but disposing of human waste is a natural use for a stream. Manufacturers were willing to deal with industrial pollution, but the technical solutions were not yet available to neutralize industrial wastes. Moreover, there was usually little harm a short distance downstream from where chemicals enter the stream. Using a stream to "dispose of the wastes of life and human activity" is in fact "the most natural use of a stream" and should be considered "a riparian right." Harmful bacteria die quickly in water and industrial wastes are diluted to harmlessness. In addition, fish, one of the commission's statutory responsibilities, can actually benefit when "organic pollution"—meaning sewage—supports the growth of worms and insects, which fish eat. If industrial pollution threatens them, there should be "careful consideration . . . whether the fish or the industries are more important." The report recommended establishment of a new "Conservancy Commission" to regulate and control pollution. That recommendation was politically naïve and also too late. Smith's governmental consolidation and reorganization plans were well along, and they included continuation of the Health Department and a new Conservation Department to supersede the Conservation Commission. Creating a new agency was out of the question. The report, expected to be a trumpet call for clear state action, instead contributed to the pattern of drift.[22]

Counting on Dilution: The Rochester Sewage Disposal Project

Lack of clear state policy often led to a process of accommodation and compromise among Health Department officers, local officials, and sanitary engineers. One of the most prominent examples was the Rochester sewage disposal project. Rochester, a growing industrial city of about 163,000 people in 1900, drew its drinking water from a pristine source, Hemlock Lake, south of the city. It had developed a sewer system, but it discharged sewage directly into the Genesee River, which ran through the city and emptied into Lake Ontario a few miles to the north. The sewage pollution produced a sharp odor and discoloration in the summer, when

---

22. State of New York Conservation Commission, *Report on the Pollution of Streams* (Albany: J. B. Lyon, 1923), 10–21, 33–49.

the river was low. Several damage suits to force the city to stop dumping sewage were filed after 1900, most were dropped, but one resulted in a monetary settlement by the city. Clearly, something had to be done.

In 1904, the city hired New York City–based sanitary engineer Emil Kuichling to come up with a solution. Kuichling, like most of his colleagues in the emerging sanitary engineering community, believed in extensively treating drinking water while also taking a more relaxed view of sewage: screening, filtering, allowing settling, and discharging the effluent into a large body of water. After three years of study, in 1907 he proposed a dramatic solution: Filter and treat the sewage and pump the effluent through a new pipeline north to Lake Ontario and out seven thousand feet into the lake, discharging it about fifty feet below the surface. Getting rid of the treated sewage was no small job—Rochester was consuming over fifteen million gallons of water per day—but Lake Ontario was huge and, with the Niagara River emptying into it on the west and the St. Lawrence draining it on the east, the current would keep the discharged sewage effluent moving. "There will be no tendency for the screened sewage to rise to the surface of the lake, and a rapid sedimentation of the suspended matter will take place," Kuichling wrote, reassuringly. "Putrefactive processes will also be greatly retarded and the dissolved organic matter will be thoroughly diffused in the vast amount of water by the action of the wind and currents." Other methods, including intense chemical treatment, were discussed and dismissed as too expensive or impractical. Two other prominent sanitary engineers and the Rochester city engineer endorsed the plan. Kuichling's proposal was debated locally for the next two years. In 1910, he produced another report reassuringly documenting how the "natural power of self-purification of the fresh water" in Lake Ontario would easily accommodate and nullify the pollution. Reassured, the city submitted its proposal to the State Health Department for approval.[23]

Commissioner Porter saw the Rochester application as a challenge. Coming from one of the state's largest cities, it attracted statewide attention. New York City clean water advocates, particularly those who had been campaigning against pollution in the Hudson, urged rejection or at least significant modification. On the other hand, sanitary engineers endorsed the Rochester proposal and their journal, *Engineering News*,

---

23. "Report of E. Kuichling, Consulting Engineer, Feb. 1, 1907" and "Supplementary Report of E. Kuichling, Consulting Engineer," March 1910, in Edwin A. Fisher (Rochester City Engineer), *Report on the Sewage Disposal System of Rochester, N.Y.* (Rochester: John B. Smith, 1913), 4–42, 47–73.

followed the review process closely. Porter had another audience, Albany lawmakers. Letting Rochester off too easily would show weakness; rejecting the application outright and requiring much more stringent, and expensive, measures might sidetrack pending legislation to increase the department's pollution regulatory powers. Porter ordered the department's engineers and health experts to review the plans. He held a hearing in Rochester. The only significant opposition came from representatives of Oswego, about seventy miles to the east, which drew its water from the lake. They urged disapproval of the plan to pollute the lake with "partially purified sewage."[24]

Porter decided on a bold move: He hired three outside sanitary engineers to review and advise him on the plans. The most prominent was nationally renowned expert Allen Hazen, a sometime critic of the department for being too demanding in its sewage abatement requirements. Hazen endorsed the Rochester proposal without reservation. The solution was practical and effective; alternatives such as totally disinfecting the sewage were deemed impractical or prohibitively expensive. Lake Ontario with its estimated 410 cubic miles of water—Hazen converted that figure to 450 trillion gallons to dramatize the magnitude—could easily absorb what came out the pipe from Rochester. Any "organic material remaining in the sewage will undoubtedly be ultimately oxidized or else reduced to an unappreciable and absolutely harmless residuum of stable material," and "extreme dilution . . . would be effective in rendering the matter harmless."[25] The other outside consulting engineers also endorsed the Rochester plan, with recommendations for minor modifications. The Health Department's chief engineer, Theodore Horton, however, recommended more restrictions. At the end of July 1910, based mostly on Horton's recommendations, Porter rejected the Rochester application in a public announcement. But he also made clear he would approve if the application were modified in relatively minor ways, including modification of the outlet in the lake. Rochester quickly agreed, submitted revised plans, and Porter approved them.[26]

---

24. "Notes of the Hearing Held by the New York State Commissioner of Health at Rochester," in Fisher, *Report on the Sewage Disposal System of Rochester, N.Y.*, 76–78.
25. Allen Hazen to Eugene H. Porter, June 17, 1910, in Fisher, *Report on the Sewage Disposal System of Rochester, N.Y.*, 81–88.
26. "Plans Returned for Alteration," July 26, 1910, "Submission of Amended Plans," August 19, 1910, and "Permit Issued," September 22, 1910, in Fisher, *Report on the Sewage Disposal System of Rochester, N.Y.*, 78–80, 112–113, 120–123.

Porter's handling of the Rochester application demonstrated the art of early twentieth-century water sanitation politics in New York State. He went through a highly visible and very deliberative process, sought public input, and involved objective outside experts. Porter appeared resolute in increasing pollution abatement requirements, a nod to the principle of clean water. But at the same time he did not increase it by much, an acknowledgment that he understood the limitations on municipal fiscal resources. Political reality was an unstated but always present consideration. His decision was hailed as a victory for enlightened sanitary engineering principles and the notion of management of sewage by dispersal and dilution.[27] Porter's willingness to compromise with municipal authorities while rendering a scientifically defensible decision helped convince the 1911 legislature to modestly increase the department's pollution oversight powers, as noted previously.

Erring on the Side of Caution: The Mohansic State Hospital Project

A second example of the interplay of politics and pollution involved the Croton Reservoir in northern Westchester County, completed in 1842 and expanded in 1905 and 1911, New York City's principle water supply. The water was filtered and treated, but city authorities were vigilant in opposing anything that might pollute their water source. In 1910, the State Commission in Lunacy (the state's mental health agency) purchased land in the Yorktown Heights area several miles from the aqueduct to construct a mental hospital to be called the Mohansic State Hospital. The site was adjacent to a small state "training school" for boys (essentially, a minimum-security facility for "incorrigibles," as first-offender juvenile delinquents were then called), which the state also planned to expand. The hospital was projected to house as many as six thousand patients. New York City authorities, including John P. Mitchell who became mayor in 1914, initially supported it because it would serve people from his city.

Sewage from the hospital would be filtered and treated, the effluent flushed into Mohansic Lake, which connected via a creek to a small body of water known as Crom Pond, which in turn connected via another small steam to the reservoir, a total distance of about fourteen miles. The stream

---

27. "The Rochester Sewage Disposal Case: Sewage Disposal by Dilution Strongly Endorsed," *Engineering News* 64 (August 11, 1910), 154–155.

would empty into the reservoir about seven miles from the water intake for New York City. Moreover, the city's water was thoroughly treated. But State Health Commissioner Eugene Porter, discerning a very slight risk of pollution to the city's water supply, vetoed the state's application in 1913. The next year, however, his successor, Commissioner Hermann Biggs, appointed a panel of experts, mostly sanitary engineers and including George Whipple, to reexamine the plans. They found the state's sewage treatment plans more than adequate. Biggs then reversed Porter and approved the plans. Democrats in the legislature raised an alarm about potential pollution of the Croton and rushed through a bill to kill the hospital project. But Governor Martin H. Glynn vetoed it after receiving reassurance from Biggs that the sewage treatment plans were adequate.[28]

The issue seemed to have its own momentum. In 1915, the *New York Times* and other city papers carried stories that the mental hospital would pour sewage into Croton Lake. The Merchants' Association of New York sounded the alarm that the Croton was at risk. In September, Mayor Mitchell withdrew his support and requested Glynn's successor, Republican Charles Whitman, to kill the project. Quoting Porter's 1913 rejection rather than Biggs's 1914 approval, Mitchell asserted that no sewage treatment process was completely safe and that, in any case, human error in operating the system might allow contaminated sewage to reach the Croton. New York City must oppose anything that might "permit its citizens to drink polluted water," said the mayor. The treated sewage should be pumped to the Hudson River, about seven miles away, rather than flushed toward the Croton, an option Biggs had considered but had deemed impractical and unnecessary.[29] Mitchell's position was ironic because it came at a time when many New York City residents and businesses were growing increasingly concerned with pollution of the Hudson.

Mitchell had been elected mayor as a "fusion" candidate in 1913, but Whitman sensed the hidden hand of the New York City Democratic organization behind the mayor's newfound concern for the Croton. Responding that Mitchell's letter was "far from expressing the real facts," the governor recalled the history of the project, including Mitchell's own support, and lectured the mayor on the fundamentals of sewage treatment:

28. *Report of the Joint Committee of the Legislature to Investigate What Disposition Should Be Made as to the Sites at Yorktown, Westchester County* (Albany: J.B. Lyon, 1918), 1–15.
29. Mayor John Purroy Mitchell to Governor Charles S. Whitman, September 16, 1915, in *Public Papers of Charles Seymour Whitman, Governor,* 1915 (Albany: J.B. Lyon, 1916), 515–518.

[T]he sewage from these institutions [will be] first subjected to screening, sedimentation, filtration, and disinfection; and the effluent then a clear, colorless, sterile fluid, is discharged beneath the surface of Mohansic lake, where a further purifying effect and an emergency safeguard is furnished by sedimentation in both Mohansic lake and Crom pond. To this is added the purifying effect of the steam flow of some twelve miles, and the subsequent sedimentation in Croton lake before any trace of this effluent can reach the intake of the New York city water supply, which is still further protected by sterilization.

The hospital was needed, as New York City had insisted for years. Whitman promised to pursue the Hudson discharge alternative, though it would be costly, and implement it if possible. But temporarily, at least, the plans for treatment and eventual discharge into the Croton would stand.[30]

Mitchell condemned Whitman's response and threatened to seek a court order to halt construction of the facility. The press escalated the protest. "New York City has no desire to include in its water supply the sewage of a great hospital, no matter how sterile such an effluent can be made by modern sanitary methods," said the popular magazine *Outlook*. New York City residents would resist "the privilege of drinking such sewage," said the Merchants' Association. Commissioner Biggs reiterated that the plans were safe. A rising tide of New York City critics not only disputed the commissioner but also said that even the alternative of piping the effluent to the Hudson might not be safe, since the pipe might spring a leak and the pollution eventually seep into the Croton water supply. Sensing the quickly growing opposition, Whitman retreated, shut down the project, and asked the legislature for guidance on what to do next.[31]

The legislature wrestled with the Mohansic sanitation issue for nearly three years featuring unusually heated debate and dilatory tactics. Early in the 1916 session, Senator Robert F. Wagner, a progressive New York City Democrat who was at that time minority leader and also had a strong affiliation with the Tammany Hall organization, introduced a bill to stop

---

30. Governor Charles S. Whitman to Mayor John Purroy Mitchell, September 20, 1915, in ibid., 519–525.
31. "Sewage and Water Supply," *Outlook*, September 29, 1915, 247; Letter from the Merchants' Association of New York to Mayor Mitchell, September 22, 1915, 526–529; Whitman to Mitchell, November 11, 1915; Whitman to the Merchants' Association of New York, November 16, 1915, ibid., 526–558; "Whitman Willing to Save Watershed," *New York Times*, November 17, 1915.

the Mohansic project and also ban future state correctional or educational institutions in the Croton watershed. Republicans controlled the legislature, and Westchester Republicans denounced Wagner's bill as an attempt by New York City to deny jobs in Westchester. Legislative hearings brought in dueling sanitary and health experts, some of whom claimed the plans were safe, while others described a potential threat to the Croton. Westchester Republican senator George Slater called the pollution threat a "bugbear" and taunted New York City legislators that even the Croton had some impurities and city residents were drinking polluted water now "and growing fat on it." The legislature killed Wagner's proposal and passed a bill to set up a study commission. Whitman, who had by now sided with Wagner, vetoed that bill on the reasoning that such a group might just endorse existing plans, which he now said he firmly opposed.[32]

Early in 1917, Whitman, in an alarmist and pandering communication to the legislature, asserted that polluted water from the hospital could "become commingled" with New York City water. The "constant and dangerous menace" of "a large population of defectives, particularly liable to many virulent diseases" might lead to "an epidemic of disease" in New York City. The legislature must kill the project once and for all.[33] Senator Wagner in a long letter to the *New York Times* said that permitting any "impurities and filth" into the city's water supply would constitute "governmental madness."[34] After more contentious debate, the legislature established a joint legislative committee to find a solution.

The committee held hearings and its members walked around the site in the fall to get a better understanding of the topography. It called multiple expert witnesses. Some testified that the plans would be safe but others that there might still be some risk, even if remote. In its report, issued in 1918, the committee cited Allen Hazen's book *Clean Water and How to Get It* in support of the idea that filtration systems would remove most objectionable sewage and water filtration systems would take care

---

32. "Urges Bills to Kill Peril to Croton," *New York Times*, February 25, 1916; " Can Buy Mohansic Safety," *New York Times*, March 16, 1916; "Kills Bill to Keep Watershed Safe," *New York Times*, March 22, 1916; "Pass Mohansic Bill After Senate Fight," *New York Times*, April 16, 1916; "Governor Whitman Acts on Many Measures," *New York Times*, May 20, 1916.

33. "Recommending Legislation for Protection of Water Supply of the City of New York and the Abandonment of the Proposed Mohansic State Hospital, also the Abandonment of the Training School for Boys at Yorktown Heights," March 16, 1917, in *Public Papers of Charles Seymour Whitman, Governor,* 1917 (Albany: J. B. Lyon, 1919), 75–77.

34. Robert F. Wagner, letter to the editor, *New York Times*, March 4, 1917.

of the rest. But it also acknowledged that "sanitary science is fallible" and sometimes treatment plants failed. The committee recommended a compromise, which the legislature adopted and the governor approved. The Mohansic hospital project was terminated. Instead, the Middletown state mental hospital, several miles north on the opposite side of the Hudson from the Croton watershed, would be expanded. The boys' school would be expanded, but still kept small. The rest of the Mohansic site should become a public park, something the Merchants' Association had suggested during the hearings.[35] Mohansic Park was created in 1922, transferred to Westchester County, deeded back to the state in 1957, and renamed Franklin D. Roosevelt State Park in 1982.

Pollution and Politics: The Continuing Challenge

The quarter-century from the complaint about the Kayaderosseras pollution in 1898 to the Conservation Commission's comprehensive report in 1924 demonstrated the complexity of the issue. Developing precise standards for clean water was elusive, particularly when medical experts in health departments stressed the threat of terms but sanitary engineers tended to minimize the threat and expressed confidence in available solutions. State regulatory policy attempted to balance public health, on the one hand, and the need not to burden industry with overly restrictive regulations and municipalities with overly expensive requirements, on the other. Gubernatorial leadership was essential but none of the governors in this period made clean water a priority. Political considerations played a major role.

Progress continued in subsequent years with advances in water purification and sewage treatment. But overall, New York's water policy continued to be fractured and inadequate.[36] Pollution increased, new programs were instituted to diminish it, and pollution waned for a while but never went away. In 1949, after an alarming legislative report on water

---

35. *Report of the Joint Committee of the Legislature to Investigate What Disposition Should Be Made as to the Sites at Yorktown, Westchester County*, 1918, 20–30, 227–228.
36. Melosi, *The Sanitary City*, 235–260, 494–501; Roscoe C. Martin, *Water for New York: A Study in State Administration of Water Resources* (Syracuse: Syracuse University Press, 1960), 24–66.

pollution, Governor Thomas Dewey signed the Water Pollution Control Act, defined pure water as public policy, and created the Water Pollution Control Board to enforce it. But pollution continued, particularly in the Hudson River. By 1960, notes Tom Lewis in his history of the river, companies all along the river were dumping toxic wastes daily and "industries and most people regarded the Hudson as an open trough of toxic water that they could use as they saw fit."[37]

In the 1960s, citizen activism led to a long campaign to clean up the Hudson. The State Department of Environmental Conservation, successor to the Conservation Commission and the Conservation Department, created in 1970, developed and enforced stricter standards throughout the state. The federal Clean Water Act of 1972 brought tougher federal standards, oversight, and resources. Industrial and municipal pollution have significantly diminished. The long saga illustrates the interplay of science, politics, and public health policy in New York. The story is one of marking time, gradual progress, occasional setbacks, and lots of compromises along the way, that sort of complex pattern that often characterizes major issues in New York history.

37. Tom Lewis, *The Hudson: A History* (New Haven: Yale University Press, 2005), 262; Robert H. Boyle, *The Hudson River: A Natural and Unnatural History* (New York: Norton, 1969), 88–104, 245–281.

7
April 15, 1903

Intervening for the Children

Lillian Wald (*left*) and Florence Kelley (*right*), tireless and highly effective advocates for child labor reform in New York. *Photos courtesy of the Library of Congress Prints and Photographs Online Catalog.*

New York State Moves to Protect Its Youngest Citizens

On April 15, 1903, Governor Benjamin B. Odell signed what came to be known as the Finch-Hill Factory Act, banning children under fourteen from working in factories. It was one of a series of five important child labor bills passed that year by a legislature mostly remembered by historians for its deference to political bosses and its inclination toward laissez-faire, probusiness industrial policy. It was signed by a moderately progressive governor overshadowed in history by his colorful predecessor,

131

Theodore Roosevelt, and his successor a few years later, prominent progressive governor Charles Evans Hughes. It was mostly the handiwork of the New York Child Labor Committee (NYCLC), organized only a year earlier, one of the most effective coalition and lobbying groups in New York history. The Factory Act and its companion bills represented the triumph of an against-the-odds campaign to put New York State government into action to rid the state of the scourge of child labor.

Children at Work

By the late nineteenth century, thousands of children under age sixteen were at work in factories, canneries, stores, and shops throughout New York State. Three concurrent waves of historical change thrust them into the labor force: industrialization, with its immense appetite for labor; immigration, which brought thousands of families, including children, especially from central, eastern, and southern Europe; and urbanization, which concentrated millions of people in urban areas, especially New York City, including thousands of children, within walking distance of factories. The demand for finished goods such as readymade clothing led to hundreds of textile mills that employed child workers to spin thread and sew and assemble clothes. Canneries and food processing plants needed workers to process fruits and vegetables on their way from farms to growing urban markets. The growth of modern urban newspapers gave rise to newsboys or "newsies," who sold papers on street corners, streetcars, and subways. The 1880 federal census revealed that about 6 percent of the nation's children between ten and fifteen years old worked in some kind of industry. By 1900, New York State had over seventy-nine thousand factories employing around seventy-five thousand children and over two hundred thousand more in tenement homework and street trades. They worked at many trades, including making clothing, laying bricks, packing fish, and tanning leather and as machinists, glassworkers, and in vegetable fields and canning factories.[1]

Children workers experienced traumatic injuries such as broken bones or losing fingers that got caught in machinery. They risked stunted growth, damage to their health through inhaling dirt and fumes, and debilitating injuries such as repetitive stress syndrome. Some even died on the

---

1. Jeremy P. Felt, *Hostages of Fortune: Child Labor Reform in New York State* (Syracuse: Syracuse University Press, 1965), 17–18, 39.

job. The public and the complacent government acquiesced at children as young as twelve laboring in factories, shops, and stores. Social theories of the era regarded children as miniature adults, fully capable of working. Poor or destitute families needed, or at least said they needed, the extra income a young worker could bring in for the family. Child workers usually just turned their pay envelopes over to their parents, contributing to the upkeep of the household. Pauline Newman began working in a hairbrush factory in 1901 at the age of ten, two years later moved on to the Triangle Shirtwaist Factory, and later became a labor union organizer. Later she penned descriptions of the shops where children worked when she was young, evoking the sense of gloom that many children must have experienced:

> Most of the so-called factories were located in old wooden walk-ups with rickety stairs, splintered and sagging floors. The few windows were never washed and their broken panes were mended with cardboard. . . . In the winter, a stove stood in the middle of the floor, a concession to the need for heat, but its warmth seldom reached the workers seated near the windows. . . . During the summer months the constant burning of gas jets added their unwelcome heat and smell to an atmosphere already humid and oppressive. . . . There was no drinking water available. . . . Dirt, smells and vermin were as much a part of the surroundings as were the machines and the workers.[2]

The damaging effects on physical and intellectual development were ignored, misunderstood, or just dismissed. Public sentiment mostly condoned child labor and was slow to accept the notion of compulsory education to enable children to develop work and citizenship skills.

Beginning around 1800, three groups began to coalesce around the issue of state labor policy: labor unions, children's aid groups, and settlement house directors. For most of the next two decades, the first two took the lead. Labor unions, such as the American Federation of Labor, founded in 1881, saw child labor as competition to adult laborers that contributed to low adult wages. In the unions' view, employers reasoned:

---

2. Annelise Orleck, *Common Sense and a Little Fire: Women and Working-Class Politics in the United States, 1900–1965* (Chapel Hill: University of North Carolina Press, 1995), 32.

"Why hire an adult for a dollar when you can hire a kid for a dime?"[3] Side-stepping accusations of self-interest, the unions began pushing for compulsory school attendance laws to achieve their goals of moving children out of the workforce.

Private groups formed to aid children directly also gradually shifted to advocating state government action. The Children's Aid Society, founded in 1853 in New York City, established shelters for runaway and homeless children, an industrial school for boys, an agricultural training school, dental and medical clinics for needy children, and a system of social workers, nutritionists, and nurses to aid children and their mothers in the slums. It began the "Orphan Train" movement, taking orphans and abandoned or neglected children and placing them with families on farms in upstate New York and the Midwest. Some stayed for a few weeks for "fresh air" vacations. Many became foster children or were adopted by country families.[4] The Children's Aid Society's intervention sometimes fractured families. Critics pointed to instances of children being neglected or abandoned by their new guardians and the potential for exploitation of child labor in their new homes. But in the absence of government programs for children or systematic, regulated adoption programs, the Children's Aid Society's interventionist work was regarded by contemporaries as mostly positive.

The New York Society for the Prevention of Cruelty to Children (NYSPCC), established in 1875, dealt with the maltreatment of children. "The object of the Society is to prevent not punish cruelty to children," declared its founder, Elbridge Gerry. The NYSPCC's directors and supporters over the years included such prominent New Yorkers as Cornelius Vanderbilt, August Belmont, John D. Rockefeller, and J. P. Morgan. The NYSPCC stressed prevention, education, and counseling and operated shelters for lost and runaway children. But it also arranged with the state and county district attorneys in New York City to act on behalf of their offices in legal proceedings against negligent and abusive parents and guardians. In one of its first prosecutions, a NYSPCC officer caught a man publicly beating his son over the head with a heavy whip. Police were summoned and the man was arrested, tried, convicted, and sentenced to thirty days in prison. The NYSPCC had started its crusade against people

---

3. New York Child Labor Legacy Project, *From Forge to Fast Food: A History of Child Labor in New York State: Vol. II, Civil War to the Present* (Albany: New York State Education Department, n.d.), 5.

4. *The Children's Aid Society: The First 100 Years*, http://www.childrensaidsociety.org/about/history/history-firsts.

who abused children. By the end of the century, the NYSPCC had investigated 130,000 complaints, prosecuted 50,000 cases with a 94 percent conviction rate, aided 370,000 children, and provided temporary shelter to 84,000 others. It also helped reform the juvenile justice system and helped secure the establishment of a children's court in New York City in 1901.[5]

Unions and child welfare organizations gradually concluded that a state compulsory education law was needed to keep children out of the factories and ensure they grew up to be productive, responsible citizens. An 1874 law, amended and slightly strengthened in 1876, required that all children ages eight to fourteen must attend school at least fourteen weeks each year. Employment of children under fourteen was forbidden unless they had met this attendance requirement and could present a certificate from the school proving it. Local school officers were charged to enforce the law, including inspecting local establishments where children might be employed. In fact, the law was seldom enforced except in areas of the state where it was moot because there was little demand for child labor. Many parents ignored it, asserting their right to send their children to work rather than to school. School officers lacked the resources (and often the interest) to make inspections. Some school administrators complained that enforcement would just force unruly boys to attend school against their will, creating a discipline problem in classrooms. Owners of factories and shops conveniently forgot to ask for the required certificates. The public and state government seemed indifferent.[6] An 1881 law initiated by the child welfare organizations made it a crime for anyone having "care or custody" of a child to "cause or permit" the child's "life to be endangered, or its health to be injured, or its morals to become depraved" or to permit a child to engage in an occupation where these things might happen.[7] It seemed like a clear threat to child labor. But there was no real provision for enforcement, and the law remained practically a dead letter.

Reformers tried a different tact in attacking cigar manufacturing in tenement houses, mostly in New York City. At that time, most smokers were men, and cigars were almost as popular as cigarettes. It was a profitable business. Tobacco could be purchased inexpensively in the South.

---

5. *The New York Society for the Prevention of Cruelty to Children, 125th Anniversary, 1875–2000,* http://www.nyspcc.org/nyspcc/history/attachment:en-us.pdf.

6. *Laws of New York,*1876, Ch. 372; Frederick R. Fairchild, *The Factory Legislation of the State of New York,* Publications of the American Economic Association, 3rd Series, 6, 4 (November 1905), 7–9.

7. *Laws of New York,* 1881, Ch. 676.

Manufacturers bought New York City tenements—multi-unit residential buildings with small, cramped, poorly ventilated rooms—and rented apartments to cigar makers who lived there with their families. Often the entire family worked; the manufacturer paid them very low piecework wages and profited twice, once from the apartment rent and again from the sale of cigars. The cigar makers' union condemned it, in part because it was next to impossible to unionize tenement house workers. Public health officials cited its harmful effects on the health of women and children.

Bills to outlaw tenement tobacco manufacturing went down to defeat in the legislature in 1881 and 1882 due to business opposition. But in 1883 the legislature passed a law with what seemed like an ironclad prohibition: "The manufacture of cigars or preparation of tobacco in any form, in any room or apartments which, in the city of New York, are used as dwellings, for the purpose of living, sleeping, or doing any housework therein, is hereby prohibited."[8] But seemingly rock-solid public policy once again soon crumbled. The City Board of Health backed away from enforcement, citing lack of specific authority in the law to do so. The Court of Appeals invalidated the law due to a technicality: The title, which referred to tenement houses, was out of sync with the text, which referenced all dwellings. Undaunted, the union and its allies prevailed on the legislature to correct the flaw in the title and repass it in 1884. Two days after it passed, a tobacco manufacturer named Peter Jacobs was arrested for deliberately violating the law to create a test court case. With the support and encouragement of his fellow manufacturers, Jacobs asserted a defense that the law was unconstitutional because it was an unwarranted interference with personal freedom and private property in violation of the U.S. and state constitutions. The Court of Appeals agreed. The law was held to be an interference with personal property, not a legitimate exercise of state authority since it did not really concern public health, and a violation of the U.S. Constitution because it impaired the obligation of contracts (in this case, between the manufacturer and individual cigar makers).[9] The law's champions, discouraged, gave up. The court's attitude also discouraged reformers from trying to outlaw other types of tenement house piecework. Tenement house cigar manufacturing eventually died out because it could not compete with factories using automated machinery in the early twentieth century. A 1901 statute required construction of

8. *Laws of New York*, 1883, Ch. 93.
9. *Laws of New York*, 1884, Ch. 272; *In Re. Jacobs*, 1885, 98 NY 98.

future tenement buildings to meet new, higher standards of light, space, ventilation, and fire protection. But tenement house manufacturing persisted for years.

Labor reformers in the meantime turned to a new tact: gathering and assembling facts on laboring conditions, including those of children. The Workingmen's Assembly of New York State, a coalition of labor leaders whose power was gradually increasing, was instrumental in persuading the state legislature to create a State Bureau of Labor Statistics in 1883 to collect and present annually to the legislature statistics "relating to all departments of labor in the state, especially in relation to the commercial, industrial, social, and sanitary conditions of workmen and to the productive industries of the state." It got off to a modest start—the first commissioner, Charles Peck, was not a workingman or labor expert but instead a friend of lieutenant governor David B. Hill. The office produced reports with difficult-to-interpret statistical tables that few people read and provided little that the legislature could use for policy guidance.[10]

Child labor reform advocates read Peck's reports and produced their own analyses pointing to the need for state action. But a series of narrative reports on Harmony Cotton Mills in Cohoes, near Albany, provided more dramatic evidence of need. Harmony was a notorious employer of children. Commissioner Peck traveled to Cohoes to observe for himself. Standing in the street on a cold winter day in 1883, he observed "hundreds of thin and scantily clad boys and girls ranging from eight to fifteen years of age, hurrying home with dinner pail in hand." He observed that "their sallow, parchment-like complexion, dwarfed bodies, pinched and care-worn faces spoke more eloquently than words." Peck checked back three years later. He found 3,200 workers including 1,200 under the age of sixteen and 200 under thirteen. Peck interviewed some of the young workers who could not tell him the name of the country or the state in which they lived, the state capital, or the name of the president of the United States. The mayor of Cohoes told him he was doing nothing to enforce the compulsory education law of 1874. Why compound the misery of parents who were already poor and needed the income, though very small, that their children brought home?[11]

---

10. *Laws of New York*, 1883, Ch. 356; Fairchild, *The Factory Legislation of the State of New York*, 24–27.

11. Felt, *Hostages of Fortune*, 15–16.

Unions and child protective groups, particularly the NYSPCC, whose officers took the time to interpret Peck's statistics and publicize his narrative reports, pushed for more state action. Bills to restrict child labor in 1883 and 1884 were sunk by opposition from manufacturers through their lobbyists and friendly legislators. Restricting child labor would reduce their profits, businesses declared, force them to move their businesses to other states that were more lenient on the issue, and harm poor families dependent on the earnings of young children. This last argument was transparently self-contradictory: As the unions pointed out, the availability of cheap child labor depressed adult wages and hurt poor families. In 1885, Democrat and lieutenant governor David B. Hill became governor upon the election of Grover Cleveland to the presidency. Hill, a shrewd politician who needed labor's support in his run for election as governor that fall, supported the demand for regulatory legislation in a message to the legislature. With Hill's strong support, both houses passed the Factory Act of 1886. It forbade the employment of children under thirteen in manufacturing establishments, required all children thirteen or older to produce notarized affidavits signed by their parents confirming their age, and set a maximum work week of sixty hours for minors under eighteen and women under twenty-one.[12]

The 1886 law was New York's first real child labor legislation. But like its predecessors, it proved less than effective. There was a loophole that enabled overtime for making "necessary repairs" and repairs seemed to be needed in surprisingly large numbers in the next few years. It provided for only two inspectors (increased to ten in 1887, twenty-nine in 1896) to cover thousands of factories. State inspectors came in through the front door of factories and went first to the manager's office, leaving supervisors plenty of time to usher young workers out the back door. Managers told inspectors that young people who happened to be on the factory floor were visiting or had just "wandered in." Children who were supposed to be in school were taught by their parents to lie about their age. Inspectors who found violations in a factory might not be able to return for months or years to see if they had been corrected. If pressed by the inspectors, factories might fire their young employees and rehire them the next week. In the few court cases that were brought for violation of the law, it was hard to find witnesses to testify (particularly given the fact that testimony

---

12. *Laws of New York*, 1886, Ch. 409.

against the company could result in dismissal from one's job). Fines for violations were light.[13]

The law was amended over the years to add more inspectors, require sanitary bathroom facilities, prescribe time for a noontime meal, and tighten the restriction on numbers of hours. Requirements for fire escapes were added in 1887, but the requirement was so vague that many factories met it by nailing a straight ladder extending from the ground to the roof beside the windows but without any balconies or connections of any kind to the windows. The age limit was raised from thirteen to fourteen in 1889. The "necessary repairs" loophole in the law was stricken out in 1890. An 1896 amendment required certificates from local health officers for children between fourteen and sixteen years of age. Health officials, however, had to rely primarily on what the parents told them. An 1896 act extended restrictions on women and children's hours to stores but with certain exceptions (e.g., suspended during the Christmas holiday shopping season). Enforcement was placed in the hands of local boards of health rather than the state factory inspector. Stores resisted and openly violated the law; boards of health lacked staff and willpower to enforce it in most cities. It became another element in New York's regulatory quilt, impressive on the statute books, something to cite to voters when a legislator or gubernatorial candidate ran for office, but with limited impact in actual practice.[14]

Political New York seemed indifferent. Governor Hill lost interest after making the first factory inspector appointment. The next three governors, Roswell P. Flower, a Democrat, and Levi P. Morton and Frank S. Black, both Republicans, were not concerned. U.S. Senator Thomas C. Platt, leader of the state Republican Party in the waning years of the nineteenth century and the opening ones of the twentieth, was opposed to reforms that would upset business. Governor Theodore Roosevelt (1899–1901), a Republican, defied Platt on a few issues, compromised on others, and deferred to him on many more. TR got the legislature to increase the number of inspectors and to expand their authority to enter and investigate sweatshops. But he appointed a Platt political ally as commissioner of labor statistics, turning aside protests that he was unqualified. Roosevelt was skeptical about unions, which he associated with violent strikes and

---

13. Fairchild, *The Factory Legislation of the State of New York*, 75.
14. Ibid., 47–70.

incipient radicalism. His record on child labor—in fact, on labor policy generally—was modest.[15]

A New Coalition of Determined Advocates

By the opening of the twentieth century, New York's child labor policy was sketchy and lightly enforced. The new campaign for the children that sprang up in the early years of the new century did not originate with politicians, unions, or even the child welfare organizations long dedicated to helping children. It came primarily from New York City settlement houses and consumer activist groups. The settlement house movement began in Britain and spread to the United States beginning in the 1880s. They provided (some are still in business and still do provide) social, medical, educational, and other services for the poor in urban areas. Educated, cultured, and sometimes wealthy individuals took up residence in settlement houses out of a desire to teach and uplift people in destitute conditions. Many were staffed by university-educated women who found professions restricted or closed because of their gender and saw settlement work as a socially acceptable way to apply their skills. There were eighteen settlement houses in New York City by 1897; eighty-nine by 1911. Programs included meeting rooms for clubs, recreation and summer programs, health clinics, dramatic presentations, concerts, exhibits, milk stations for infants, and classes in housekeeping, English, citizenship, carpentry, needlework, and other trades.[16]

Two in particular, University Settlement and the Henry Street Settlement House, became launch points for the renewed child labor campaign. University Settlement was founded on the Lower East Side of New York City in 1886. It aimed to be a force for ameliorating poverty and helping immigrants, particularly those from Eastern Europe, adjust to their new life. University Settlement's trustees included some of New York's most prominent and influential citizens, including Seth Low (president of Columbia University and a reform mayor of New York, 1902–1903) and industrialist Andrew Carnegie. University Settlement ran a kindergarten, clubs for children, educational offerings for adults, and even a library. It

---

15. G. Wallace Chessman, *Governor Theodore Roosevelt: The Albany Apprenticeship, 1898–1900* (Boston: Harvard University Press, 1965), 200–225.

16. "Settlement Houses," in Kenneth T. Jackson, ed., *The Encyclopedia of New York City* (New Haven: Yale University Press, 2010), 1170–1172.

worked for city parks, higher standards for tenements, and improved sanitation. It took initiatives to improve working conditions and in particular to combat child labor.[17]

The Henry Street Settlement House on the Lower East Side of Manhattan, established in 1893 by Lillian Wald, was also central to the growing child labor reform movement. Wald grew up in Rochester and graduated from the New York Hospital Training School for nurses. She volunteered for nursing work in an orphanage and taught health care to poor immigrant families on the Lower East Side. One day a weeping child begged her to look in on her mother in an apartment on Ludlow Street. The child led her over "broken roadways . . . between tall, reeking houses . . . over dirty mattresses and heaps of refuse." Wald entered the squalid, cramped apartment to find a woman who had just given birth, and she was shocked to learn that the two small rooms housed a family of seven and sometimes also additional tenants needed to pay the rent. The father, who had a crippling condition, begged on street corners. Wald tended to the mother and the infant. It was one of many heartrending experiences that turned her to the path of social reform.[18]

She began caring for sick residents as a visiting nurse and then opened a small facility for her patients. In 1893 she coined the term "public health nurse" to describe nurses who made home visits and whose work was integrated into the community. The Henry Street Settlement began as a headquarters for these mobile nurses. Soon, it attracted the attention of Jacob Schiff, a wealthy Jewish leader, financier, and philanthropist and senior partner in the international investment banking firm of Kuhn, Loeb & Company. Schiff agreed to provide funding for Henry Street and to prevail on his wealthy, influential friends to provide additional support. Buoyed by his support and encouragement, Wald took on more nurses, who in turn made more visits and sent back reports of children, as well as adults, living in squalid conditions and sometimes working at home in cigar manufacturing or clothing trades.

Lillian Wald saw hundreds of children playing in the streets, living in crowded homes, afflicted by hunger and disease, and working at dangerous, demanding jobs that would exhaust adults. It offended her sense of social justice and seemed totally unnecessary in a great city like New York

---

17. "University Settlement of New York City," http://www.socialwelfarehistory.com/organizations/university-settlement-of-new-york-city.
18. Lillian Wald, *The House on Henry Street* (New York: Henry Holt, 1915), 1–6; Beatrice Siegel, *Lillian Wald of Henry Street* (New York: Macmillan, 1983), 36–37.

in the progressive and enlightened Empire State. What could be done? Wald opened a playground in Henry Street's small backyard; helped form the Outdoor Recreation League, which obtained land from the city for a neighborhood park; got wealthy uptown supporters to open their country homes to poor children; and convinced the school district to hire the first public school nurses. But she was increasingly outraged at the sight of children put to work at home and in factories at a young age.

The settlement house officers, backed by influential and affluent New Yorkers, became social activists and a campaign force for good. Gradually, they learned how to work with the political bosses whose concern for people might parallel the concern of the settlement houses but whose tactics, including voting fraud, kickbacks from public contractors, and other practices, they disliked. They worked to get good nominees for both parties. Sometimes they endorsed candidates and handed out literature. They got behind the campaign to elect reformer Seth Low mayor in 1901.[19] Their most politically savvy leaders insisted that state government action would be needed to deal with the working conditions, particularly those of children.

The most extraordinary of these new-style activist leaders was Florence Kelley. Like so many of the Progressive Era reformers, she came from a comfortable middle-class background. Her father was a congressman and she graduated from Cornell University, went on to study at the University of Zurich, and became interested in socialism. Her social justice goals led her to become a passionate reformer. In the 1890s she lived in Hull House, the famous settlement in Chicago founded by Jane Addams. Appalled at urban working conditions, she lobbied the state government for reform and was appointed Illinois State factory investigator in 1893, fought for improved working conditions, and got the legislature to pass a law establishing an eight-hour workday for women. In 1899, she was appointed director of the new National Consumers League, founded in New York City on the principle that "the working conditions we accept for our fellow citizens should be reflected by our purchases, and that consumers should demand safety and reliability from the goods and services they buy."[20] She would hold that position for thirty-four years and build the league into a formidable organization, starting with the issuance of a

---

19. Allen F. Davis, "Settlement Workers in Politics, 1890–1914," *The Review of Politics* 26 (October 1964), 505–517.
20. National Consumers League, "History," http://www.nclnet.org/about-ncl/history.

White Label designating products made under "clean and healthful working conditions." Planning her move to New York, Kelley needed a place to live. She chose the Henry Street Settlement, already home to like-minded reformers and activists such as Lillian Wald, where she resided until 1926. In addition to administering the league, she became an organizer and catalyst for change in New York City and New York State. Kelley and Wald became tireless allies for civic betterment. "Miss Wald and I are getting a park for our ward and a street widened," she wrote on a warm day in July 1903. "It's more fun than any ordinary vacation!"[21] She mentored many reformers, including Frances Perkins, who later became FDR's secretary of labor. Perkins recalled the force of her personality: "Explosive, hot-tempered, determined, she was no gentle saint. She spoke accusingly and passionately when moved by the sight of what she thought of as social injustice or callous unconcern."[22]

Kelley made child labor reform a personal priority. She galvanized reformers to work together. She framed the issue clearly: As a matter of moral principle and public policy, children should not be exploited, and their health, welfare, education, and future were all being jeopardized by child labor. Child labor must be outlawed. But "the best child labor law," she repeatedly asserted, "is a compulsory education law" that is effective and enforced. This would diminish child labor and produce informed, capable adults who would contribute to the social and civic life of the community.[23] Wald, Kelley, and an informal group of settlement house representatives formed a temporary "Child Labor Committee" early in 1902. It began raising funds and awareness among the influential supporters of the various settlement houses. Informal discussions led to the realization that a more formal group would be needed to break through New York's history of indifference and lukewarm child labor legislation. The result was the New York Child Labor Committee (NYCLC). Years later, the committee claimed that it originated in

> a fireside conversation among five prominent New Yorkers. . . .
> in 1902. One told about the tiny cash boy whom she had found

21. Florence Kelley to Nicholas Kelley, July 5, 1903 in Kathryn Kish Sklar and Beverly Wilson Palmer, *The Selected Letters of Florence Kelley, 1869–1931* (Urbana: University of Illinois Press, 2009), 118.
22. Frances Perkins, "My Recollections of Florence Kelley," *Social Services Review* 28 (March 1954), 12–19.
23. Florence Kelley, "An Effective Child-Labor Law: A Program for the Current Decade," *Annals of the American Academy of Political and Social Science* 21 (May 1903), 96–103.

standing with his head against the counter—sound asleep—too tired to bring back her change and too little to be noticed. Other flagrant abuses of childhood were then recalled. *That night* the New York Child Labor Committee was born.[24]

The committee set forth three purposes: Secure stronger child labor laws, encourage and assist the authorities in their enforcement, and educate the public to support curtailment of child labor.[25]

The Great Breakthrough of 1903

The New York Child Labor Committee was mostly comprised of well-off, socially prominent New Yorkers, including Jacob Schiff; William Baldwin, president of the Long Island Railroad; Felix Adler, a professor at Columbia; William Maxwell, the New York City superintendent of schools; Lyman Abbott, editor of the influential magazine *Outlook*; and other civic, religious, and labor leaders. The campaign was mostly a New York City initiative but the committee soon had branches in upstate cities where there was also a child labor problem but on a much smaller scale.

These accomplished people, in turn, networked with peers to raise money for the campaign and exert influence in the legislature. Both houses of that body were solidly in control of the Republicans in 1903, who in the past had taken their cue from "Boss" Platt, seldom a friend of reform. But the political winds shifted in 1903. Governor Benjamin B. Odell, elected in 1900 and reelected in 1902 (governors were elected every two years at that time), was a former state Republican Party chairman and had been a longtime Platt lieutenant. But Odell grew more independent in his first term as governor, challenging his former boss. In 1901, he recommended, and the legislature approved, creation of a State Labor Department to consolidate the state factory inspector, the Bureau of Labor Statistics, and the Board of Mediation and Arbitration, a small office that occasionally intervened to settle strikes. It was the first state labor department in the nation. Odell's main justification was that consolidation would save money, but it brought new visibility to state labor policy and bolstered his leadership status.

---

24. Felt, *Hostages of Fortune*, 45.
25. *Reports from State and Local Child Labor Committees and Consumers' Leagues—New York*, in *Annals of the American Academy of Political and Social Science* 29 (July 1907), 142, http://ann.sagepub.com/content/29/1/142.extract.

Odell fought a hard reelection campaign in 1902 based on economy in government and a claim that he had brought "prosperity and happiness" to New York.[26] He won without much help from Platt. The senator was aging, and Republicans were beginning to resent his opposition to even moderate reform and blamed him for the allegations of "bossism" that Democrats hurled at their party. Odell used patronage appointments to build up his support and convinced reform-inclined legislators that it was time for the party to change. The governor had a behind-the-scenes ally in Theodore Roosevelt, now a reform-minded president who had been unable to best Platt when he was governor. But he now quietly urged Republican legislators to fall in behind Odell. In a message to the legislature in January 1903, the governor asserted that "the laws relative to the employment of children are in such an unsatisfactory condition that their enforcement is almost impossible." The compulsory education law and the child labor law were incompatible, he noted. The 1900 census documented that illiteracy was on the rise among New York's young, a trend the governor found intolerable. Evincing a desire to "guard against physical and mental degeneracy" in youth, the governor called for effective child labor laws.[27] It was an unusually clear summons for action from an increasingly assertive governor. Encouraged by the governor's leadership, the reformers set to work drafting legislation and finding sponsors.

The NYCLC's main work in the closing months of 1902 and the opening ones of 1903 was dramatic publicity of the problem. It was one of the most sophisticated public information programs in the history of the state up to that time. Investigations, studies, and surveys were written up and distributed by advocates like Florence Kelley and Robert Hunter of University Settlement. New York City was reported to have more children at work than in the entire South. The NYSPCC pointed to gaps in the law, false age affidavits by parents, and lackadaisical enforcement by local education and health officials. The reports were summarized in the press, which emphasized actual examples:

Giuseppe is ten years old . . . . His average earnings [from peddling newspapers] are about 20 cents [per day]. . . . In school he lacks almost wholly concentration and attention and he is consequently very unruly and uninterested in school work. . . . On

---

26. "Governor Odell Opens His State Campaign," *New York Times*, October 14, 1902.
27. "Text of Governor's Message," *New-York Tribune*, January 8, 1903.

hard luck nights, he sleeps where he can. Twice he has been caught stealing led [sic] pipe when he was not able to make enough to take home. His father is able-bodied and makes from $8 to $10 a week.

A local express company employs children of eleven and upward. Their work begins at 11 AM and they make their last trip between 9 and 10 o'clock at night. On Friday and Saturday they work until midnight. If the packages are not all delivered by midnight on Saturday, they must return on Sunday morning to finish the task. There are children who deliver milk from 4 AM until school time.

Bridget Brennan is now fourteen. She commenced working in the box factory when she was ten. When she left school she was in the third [grade]. She measures at fourteen only four feet. She works from 7:30 in the morning until 7 at night with one half hour off for luncheon.

Mary Force was employed for rush work [in a paper box factory]. For over six weeks she worked from 7:30 AM to 8:30 PM daily with one half hour intermission for lunch. . . . She received six cents an hour for overtime. She had secured a regular certificate for the work on the representation that she had reached the legal age. She was an undeveloped child of twelve.[28]

The NYSPCC also refuted myths that work was good for young children. New Yorkers had long been fond of the image of self-reliant, independent newsboys who grew up to be successful businessmen. A NYSPCC report showed that 40 percent of the boys confined in the New York Juvenile Asylum had been newsboys.[29] Florence Kelley reminded an audience of women that the making of "every article of a woman's apparel . . . is participated in by children. Every woman here is clothed largely by child labor. Children of nine and ten work in the hosiery mills. . . . silk, beaded trimmings, buttons and cheap jewelry are all objects of their work."[30]

---

28. "The City's Child Labor," New-York Tribune, January 12, 1903; "Child Labor Investigators Collect Facts for Crusade," New York Times, February 1, 1903; "Little Wage Earners," New-York Tribune, February 13, 1903.
29. "Regulate Child Labor," New-York Tribune, March 4, 1903.
30. "Clothes and Child Labor," New-York Tribune, January 27, 1903.

The legislative campaign proceeded with equal fervor. Committee members consulted quietly with Governor Odell as they shaped the final legislation. They selected two particularly effective legislative sponsors. New York City assemblyman Edward R. Finch, a member of an old New York family, was an attorney with a law degree from Yale and was a colleague of reform mayor Seth Low. Senator Henry W. Hill of Buffalo was an attorney and scholar with a strong progressive background in educational reform and administration. Five separate bills were introduced and eventually passed, with even very conservative legislators feeling the force of public opinion behind them. Every member of the legislature received literature about the evils of child labor. Citizens read and acted on newspaper editorials urging them to write their legislators in favor of the bills. Unions passed literature to their members who added their voices. Key legislators were lobbied directly by the influential trustees of the committee. Newspapers were mostly in support. Business opposition was muted. Who wanted to be seen as favoring the sort of cruel exploitation that the NYCLC was exposing every day? A few businessmen grumbled about increased production costs and losing a competitive edge to other states. Owners of large department stores begged for loosening the restrictions so they could stay open longer (for shoppers' convenience, of course). All five bills passed. Taken together, they escalated New York's child labor protections to a new level.[31]

Four of the bills had relatively smooth sailing through the legislature:

> The *Finch-Hill Factory Act* provided that no child under 14 could be "employed, permitted, or suffered to work in a factory" or in connection with a factory or business. The law would take away the excuse sometimes offered by employers in the past that underage workers had just "wandered in" on the day a factory inspector found them. The law was written broadly to include office boys and delivery boys. It established a maximum nine hour day for children under 16. It significantly tightened the proof or age requirement.
>
> The *Finch-Hill Commercial Establishments Act* brought department stores, telegraph offices, restaurants, hotels, and apartment houses under the child labor law for the first time.

---

31. Felt, *Hostages of Fortune*, 51–58.

The Finch-Hill amendment to the state penal law imposed fines and imprisonment on any person found guilty of making a false statement to secure the certificates and documents that the law required a child to have. This was intended to penalize false documents created by parents and guardians.

A bill sponsored by Senator Merton E. Lewis of Rochester amended the state's compulsory education law to require children to stay in school up to age 14. The bill met resistance in the Assembly, where rural interests dominated and constituents included many farmers who asserted a need for children to leave school and work on the farm. School superintendents and the NYCLC lobbied hard for it. Governor Odell turned the tide with a demand for passage, and it was approved.[32]

The fifth measure had a harder journey. The Hill Street Trades Bill applied only to first-class cities (New York City and Buffalo). It provided that children under twelve would be prohibited from working as newsboys, bootblacks, peddlers, or street vendors. Those aged thirteen and fourteen had to obtain a permit from school authorities with documentation similar to that required for factory work. All street work for those under sixteen would be banned after 9:00 p.m. Parents who permitted their children to contravene the law could be fined. While Buffalo was included, this act was aimed squarely at the situation in New York City. Newspapers, though mostly supportive of the law, tried to get it amended to give them more leeway with newsboys, who delivered and sold their papers in the streets. Newspaper resistance had been expected, but opposition from two other sources was a surprise to the NYCLC and the bill's supporters. A number of justices of the Court of Special Sessions, which handled child labor abuse cases, objected to the provisions regarding peddlers, shoeshine boys, and newsboys. The proposed law would leave the judges little leeway to take extenuating circumstances into account when violations were reported. "The husky boy of thirteen who is helping a respected widowed mother is placed on the same footing with the undersized cigarette-smoking street arab [sic] who runs away from home and peddles newspapers in a dive in some notoriously bad neighborhood," one judge wrote to the Senate Judiciary Committee. This "vicious" legislation would "take from the Judge his power of inquiry and discretion and

---

32. Fairchild, *The Factory Legislation of the State of New York*, 70–88.

substitute therefor laws as immutable as those of the Medes and Persians," lamented another jurist.[33]

The New York Society for the Prevention of Cruelty to Children, a friend to abused children since 1875, shocked the bills' proponents by announcing its opposition. Elbridge Gerry, its highly respected leader, saw the proposed law as a threat to the work of his organization. Street trades were comparatively healthful and preferable to young people being shut up in dirty, airless tenement buildings, he asserted. He testified that the NYSPCC had the situation in hand and often "rescued" young people exploited as street workers. Gerry objected particularly to including newsboys in the bill. NYCLC leaders patiently explained the dangers confronting children engaged in delivering newspapers and other work in the streets and cited decisions by lenient judges who based their decisions on the assumption that parents had the right to deal with their children as they pleased.[34] But opposition by the NYSPCC and the judges hurt. The final bill, substantially weakened, focused on newspaper sellers only; other forms of street trade were left unregulated. It was not a strong law but, in concert with the other four, represented a breakthrough.

Making the Laws Work

The new laws were hailed by organizations like the NYCLC but also by political leaders, civic organizations, and the press. "No longer could Annie, the cobbler's daughter, by unchallenged perjury obtain the state sanction to her premature employment," wrote Lillian Wald. "Gone are the easy days when Francesca's father, defying school mandates, openly offered his little ones in the labor market."[35] President Theodore Roosevelt, a silent partner in easing the laws through the legislative passage, now became a very public cheerleader. "I heartily congratulate you upon the fact that we now have in New York State child labor laws which I believe can be enforced," he telegraphed the head of the Child Labor Committee. He added, in a bit of a lecture mode, "It is of utmost importance that these laws shall not be left idle on the statute books."[36] Reformers agreed. As

---

33. "Justices Oppose Child Labor Bill," *New York Times*, March 10, 1903.
34. "Child Labor Bills, "*New York Times*, March 12, 1903; Felt, *Hostages of Fortune*, 58–62.
35. Wald, *The House on Henry Street*, 135–136.
36. "Child Labor Laws in Effect," *New-York Tribune*, October 1, 1903.

the bills were going through the legislature, Florence Kelley, never one to mince words, told a meeting of the National Consumers League that "the widespread, habitual violation of the law has for years been notorious" and enforcement "deplorably insufficient and incompetent." In the previous year, there had been only three convictions for violation of the law, resulting in fines of $30 each.[37] The reformers' confidence sagged when the state factory inspector in the Labor Department announced that a major tactic would be to print posters with the text of the laws for distribution to factories with a request that they display them (he did not mention a requirement for factory managers to read them). Sensing limited enthusiasm, the reformers began a public campaign to oust the commissioner of labor and succeeded in replacing him with P. Tecumseh Sherman in 1905. Sherman, an independent Republican who had gotten his political education serving for several years on the New York City Board of Aldermen and brought the same energy to enforcement of the law that his father, General William T. Sherman, had brought to leading Union troops in the Civil War. Sherman's inspectors vigorously enforced the law. In 1907, his office prosecuted 443 violators and got 294 convictions. He also widely publicized violations, adding public exposure to legal penalties.[38]

In the meantime, the committee itself also took action to get the new law enforced. The Chelsea Jute Mills, where fiber from jute plants was spun into thread, had long been a notorious violator of the child labor laws. The committee called on the New York City Board of Education to enforce the new compulsory attendance law. The school inspectors saw obvious violations and selected one child, Annie Ventre, to test the law in municipal court. Annie was eleven years old when she went to work in 1903, but an affidavit, sworn by her father, declared that she was sixteen. School was in session while she was at work. The violation of the law was apparent. But the company said it has just relied on the father's affidavit of her age. It also said that the law was unconstitutional and "an unwarranted, illegal and unconstitutional deprivation of their liberties." But her father admitted on the stand that he had lied about her age. The NYCLC and the school officials called the girl to the stand, and the judge observed for himself that she was "a living picture of the results of child labor in a factory at a delicate age." Affirming the constitutionality of the law, he

---

37. "Factory Inspection," *New-York Tribune*, May 19, 1903.
38. "McMackin Out, Sherman In," *New York Times*, May 4, 1905; Felt, *Hostages of Fortune*, 71.

declared, "[C]hildren are the wards of the state and the state is particularly interested in their well-being as future members of the body politic and has an inherent right to protect itself and them against the baneful effects of ignorance, infirmity, or danger to life and limb." He found the company guilty and fined them $50. They decided not to appeal and offered to cooperate with the committee and educational authorities in dismissing other illegally employed children. It was only a municipal court decision, but it was so well reasoned that further challenges to the law were discouraged.[39]

Many companies decided that it was simply better to hire adult employees, who might cost more but could do more work, than violate or skirt the law by hiring underage workers. Moreover, as Florence Kelley noted in 1905, continued massive immigration into New York State, particularly New York City, meant that New York had an inflowing abundance of labor. "No employers in the world can better afford to acquiesce in the retention of all children in school . . . than the employers in New York." Keeping young people in school would make them better workers and citizens as adults.[40]

Reformers kept pushing for vigorous enforcement. The 1920 U.S. Census reported that the percentage of New York State's ten- to fourteen-year-olds working in nonagricultural work had decreased by more than two-thirds compared to 1900.[41] The work of the Factory Investigating Commission, set up after the Triangle Fire in 1911, revealed some remaining abuses, which were addressed in another round of legislation. In the meantime, success in New York encouraged action on the national stage. A meeting of child labor reformers including Florence Kelley and Lillian Wald met in New York's Carnegie Hall to form the National Child Labor Committee to eradicate child labor across the nation. The committee, working with Kelley's National Consumers League and other groups, pressured Congress to pass the first federal child labor law in 1916. It was declared unconstitutional two years later on the grounds that it violated a child's rights to contract to sell his or her own labor. The reformers

39. "Compulsory School Law Held Valid," *New York Times*, March 25, 1904; Fairchild, *The Factory Legislation of the State of New York*, 100–103; Felt, *Hostages of Fortune*, 68–69.
40. Florence Kelley, "Child Labor Legislation and Enforcement in New England and the Middle States," *Annals of the American Academy of Political and Social Science* 25 (May 1905), 72, http://www.jstor.org/stable/1010930.
41. "Child Labor," in Peter Eisenstadt, editor-in-chief, *The Encyclopedia of New York State* (Syracuse: Syracuse University Press, 2005), 322.

then began a multiyear crusade for a constitutional amendment that would authorize such a law, without success. During the Great Depression, child labor diminished because so many adults were out of work. The federal Fair Labor Standards Act, passed in 1938, finally placed federal limits on child labor. It was signed by another New Yorker, President Franklin D. Roosevelt.

The 1903 child labor laws constituted a milestone in New York's social and educational policy. Child labor in New York State was not fully eradicated by the statutes, and there were still instances of children working in violation of the law. But the laws put the full force of the law and state government behind stamping out child labor and increasing educational requirements and opportunities. They made New York a model and inspiration for other states and action at the national level. Their passage reflects the power of organized coalitions of concerned citizens to frame issues, galvanize public opinion, alter the course of the political debate, and help sway the policies of political parties. The story of child labor reform also shows, however, how strong the status quo and resistance to change can be and how long, therefore, it can take to effect significant, positive change.

8

May 29, 1910

First in the Air

New York aviation pioneer Glenn Curtiss at the controls of his plane the *June Bug*, which made the first publically announced airplane flight on July 4, 1908, in Hammondsport, two years before Curtiss's pioneering flight from Albany to New York City. *Photo courtesy of the Air Force Historical Research Agency.*

A New Yorker Helps Launch the Aviation Industry

On the last Sunday in May 1910, Glenn Curtiss (1878–1930), a pioneering aviator from Hammondsport, New York, made the first flight from Albany to New York City in a small biplane he called the *Albany Flyer*. Curtiss was a leader in the race to design, fly, and manufacture a manned flying machine, a contest played out in inventors' labs, in the air, and in the courts in the first two decades of the twentieth century. He is credited with over five hundred inventions, including several types of wing designs, controls, throttles, brakes, retractable landing gear, pontoons, and amphibious airplanes. Some of his seminal contributions are still used in modified applications in airplanes today. He established the first airplane factory in the nation, at Hammondsport, New York, in 1909. Unlike his contemporaries (and rivals), the famed Wright brothers,

153

Curtiss was inclined to share his inventions rather than keeping them proprietary and locking them up with patents. His designs endured while many of the Wrights' engineering innovations were obsolete within a decade of their famous pioneering flight at Kitty Hawk, North Carolina, in December 1903.[1]

Glenn Curtiss was a modest, publicity-shy New Yorker, given to understating his personal accomplishments and crediting others for applying his ideas and putting them to work. *Time* magazine, reporting on an international air show to honor the Wrights in 1924, noted that at least half of the planes there were powered by Curtiss engines and that there was "not one plane but bore some evidence of the contributions he has made to mankind's knowledge of the air" through "ingenuity, mechanical skill, persistence, enterprise [and] daring." Citing a long list of inventions, *Time* put Glenn Curtiss on its cover.[2]

The Route to Albany

Glenn Curtiss's career before his takeoff from Albany on that fateful morning in May 1910 was a blend of experimentation, tinkering, and invention. He led and contributed to progressively higher levels of mobility technology: bicycle/motorbike/motorcycle/dirigible/airplane. Mostly self-taught, he left school after eighth grade but showed a marvelous ability to develop and apply mechanical solutions, test, tinker, improve, and move on. "I used to resent being called an inventor," he noted in 1927. "An inventor, as people in country towns thought of him, was a wild-eyed impractical person with ideas that wouldn't work. . . . I'm more or less reconciled now to being called one though I've always felt that I was a developer rather than an inventor."[3] In his first job at Eastman Dry Plate and Film Company (later Eastman Kodak) in Rochester, he invented a machine to stencil frame numbers on film. Returning to Hammondsport, he worked as a bicycle messenger for Western Union, took up bicycle racing, moved on to selling bicycles, and then opened his own shop to manufacture them under the brand name "Hercules," later changed to

1. Seth Shulman, *Unlocking the Sky: Glenn Hammond Curtiss and the Race to Invent the Airplane* (New York: HarperCollins Perennial, 2002), 29, 231–233.
2. "AERONAUTICS: At Dayton," *Time*, October 23, 1924, 26–27.
3. Frank Parker Stockbridge, "Glenn Curtiss—Air Pilot No. 1," *Popular Science Magazine*, April 1927, 21–22, 130.

"Curtiss." He developed a passion for speed, building sleek bikes with gear ratios that maximized the number of pedaling cycles to turns of the bikes' wheels.

His next step was moving from human pedal power to gasoline engine power. In 1901, he tried bolting an early gasoline engine he had purchased onto a bicycle, but the engine failed. Curtiss began to experiment with making engines himself, mounting them on bikes, then building bigger bikes and larger engines, creating motorized bikes and later motorcycles. On an early engine, "the carburetor consisted of a tomato can filled with gasoline, containing a gauze screen which drew up the liquid by capillary attraction, when it vaporized and was taken to the cylinder by a pipe from the top of the can."[4] Through experimentation, primitive engines gave way to smooth-running, powerful ones. Curtiss was soon producing engines that were masterpieces, known for their low weight-to-horsepower ratios and high performance. He tested his motorized bikes at high speeds on the narrow roads in the hills above Hammondsport, often startling local residents out for a ride in horse-drawn carriages. He expanded his Hammondsport "shop" (as he always called his factories, no matter how large) to keep up with expanding demand for both engines and Curtiss motorcycles. Curtiss tested his motorcycles himself by riding them as fast as they would go in public competitions. In 1907, he set an unofficial world record of 136.36 mph on a 40 hp motorcycle of his own design and was hailed as "the fastest man on earth," until his record was beaten by an early auto in 1911. The motorcycle record stood until 1930.[5]

"Experimenting is never work—it is just plain fun," he once explained to a reporter. A navy aviation officer who worked with him later described him as "a mechanical wizard" who "would speak little as he attacked a problem with logic and at-hands materials, cutting and trying until it worked." Curtiss developed mental pictures of the devices he wanted but, rather than spend time on elaborate drawings and designs, he went to work building models and refining as he went along. He tried fifty different pontoon designs for the "hydro-aeroplane" (what we now call a seaplane) that he developed in 1911. As his enterprises expanded, he drew in other like-minded, hands-on, get-it-done, entrepreneurial partners and

---

4. Augustus Post, "The Evolution of a Flying Man," *Century Magazine* 79 (November 1910/April 1911), 14.

5. Cecil R. Roseberry, *Glenn Curtiss: Pioneer of Flight* (Syracuse: Syracuse University Press, 1991), 18–34.

developed a cooperative style. Theodore Ellyson, who collaborated with Curtiss for many years, described him as "a comrade and a chum, who made us feel that we were all working together and that our ideas and advice were really of some value."[6] Curtiss was a model of the inventor-turned-businessman, encouraging and pushing others, inspiring, always sharing credit, and constantly pushing the technological edge outward.

Motorcycles led indirectly to the next phase in his work, dirigibles. In the summer of 1904, Thomas Baldwin, a pioneer California dirigible maker, purchased a Curtiss engine, mounted it on his aircraft, and used it to win a race at the St. Louis Louisiana Purchase Exposition in October, 1904. "[T]he Curtiss motor is absolutely perfect," he told reporters and ordered more engines, including one that he installed in the first dirigible purchased by the army in 1908. Another dirigible pioneer and daredevil, Lincoln Beachey, made headlines in 1906 when he landed a dirigible on the White House lawn, talked with Edith Roosevelt (her husband, President Theodore Roosevelt, was out of town), took off again, circled the Capitol, and then landed and talked with astonished congressmen. Beachey's fame soared, and he told newspaper reporters that he used Curtiss engines "exclusively." Watching dirigible flying became a form of popular entertainment, and Curtiss engines powered the best of them. "I get twice as much money for my motors from those aviation [dirigible] cranks" than from other buyers, he confided to a friend.[7]

In 1906, Curtiss exhibited his engines at a show in New York City sponsored by the Automobile Club of America and a new offshoot organization, the Aero Club of America. The keynote speaker, Alexander Graham Bell, the eminent inventor of the telephone, extolled the potential of flying. Bell had become interested in heavier-than-air flying devices and had developed huge flying machines that were a hybrid of gliders and kites. He needed powerful engines to make the awkward machines fly. He purchased an engine from Curtiss and was pleased when it lifted one of his contraptions and propelled it through the air. Bell invited Curtiss and several other aeronautical pioneers to join him in a new organization, called the Aerial Experiment Association (AEA) in 1907. After a few experiments with Bell's ponderous machines near his Nova Scotia estate, the group moved its operations to Hammondsport and switched to

---

6. Shulman, *Unlocking the Sky*, 33, 208.
7. Roseberry, *Glenn Curtiss*, 33–49; Schulman, *Unlocking the Sky*, 93; "Lincoln Beachey," http://www.centennialofflight.gov/essay/Dictionary/BEACHEY/DI191.htm.

experimenting with fixed-wing biplanes in 1908. Curtiss transitioned from engine maker to airplane designer and test pilot. The team's first biplane crashed on its second flight. "In scientific experiments," Bell reminded them, "there are no unsuccessful experiments. Every experiment contains a lesson. If we stop right here, it is the man that is unsuccessful, not the experiment." Bell suggested installing hinged flaps, soon to be called "ailerons," to the trailing edge of each wing that the pilot could maneuver to aid with horizontal stability and control. The concept was not new, but Bell and Curtiss refined it, and it helped the AEA's next plane, the *White Wing* (white cotton cloth covered its wings), to achieve four successful short flights in May 1908 before crashing on a fifth attempt.[8]

Curtiss assumed primary responsibility for designing the next plane, another fixed-wing biplane, which he called the "June Bug" after insects of the same name that were chirping during the warm evenings around Keuka Lake where Hammondsport was located. He built and installed a more powerful engine, made the aileron system more responsive, and mounted the plane on three bicycle wheels from his shop. Evidencing a growing passion for winning, Curtiss decided to fly the *June Bug* himself and compete for the trophy and cash prize offered the previous year by the prestigious journal *Scientific American* for the first publicly witnessed manned flight of over a kilometer. Members of the press, curiosity seekers, and a delegation from the Aero Club of America—which would observe and certify the results—assembled in Hammondsport at the beginning of July. Curtiss gave interviews to newsmen and arranged for use of a racetrack near a local winery for takeoff and landing (the winery's owner generously provided free samples, grateful for the free publicity). He flew a number of test flights, one of which ended abruptly when the engine failed. The aviator announced that the historic flight for the prize would take place on Independence Day. Hundreds of people converged on the village. Rain delayed the flight for several hours. Toward evening, the *June Bug* taxied and rose from the race track, then settled right back down because of a tail wing malfunction. Never daunted, Curtiss tried again and effected a flawless flight of 1 minute and 40 seconds, traveling 1.6 kilometers. An eyewitness reported: "Hemmed in by bars and wires, with a 40 HP engine exploding behind him leaving a trail of smoke, and with

---

8. Charlotte Gray, *Reluctant Genius: Alexander Graham Bell and the Passion for Invention* (New York: Arcade Publishing, 2006), 364–373.

a whirling propeller cutting the air 1200 times a minute, he sailed with 40 feet of outstretched wings 20 feet above our heads." Curtiss won the trophy, the $25,000 prize that went with it, and instant fame. It was, as the Curtiss Museum's website proclaims, "the first pre-announced flight in America of a heavier-than-air flying machine," unlike the Wright Brothers' earlier flights, which had not been public affairs.[9]

After one more successful flight, Bell's AEA disbanded. Curtiss, now committed to aviation, established his own airplane manufacturing company at Hammondsport in 1909, in partnership with Augustus Herring, another flying pioneer. Curtiss designed larger, faster, more rugged planes with better controls, particularly through creative use of ailerons, which he continued to refine and which gradually became standard control devices on planes. He continued to prove himself "less a research man than a developer . . . a great *ad hoc* engineer whose genius was in his ability to improvise, synthesize, and simplify promising ideas and devices at hand, and to transform them into something immediately useful—and marketeable."[10]

The Aeronautic Society of New York, formed in 1908 to promote aggressive development of airplanes, ordered a new biplane from Curtiss, named it the *Golden Flyer*, leased a former racetrack at Morris Park in the Bronx for flying, and asked Curtiss himself to make the initial flight. In July 1909, Curtiss piloted the *Golden Flyer* at a speed of 45 mph to win the *Scientific American* prize for a second time. The society then sponsored him in the first international air show in August in Rheims, France. Unfortunately, the *Golden Flyer* crashed during a test flight just as Curtiss was planning to leave. The Hammondsport plant scurried to produce a replacement, but there was no time to test it. Curtiss made last-minute modifications to what he named on the spot the *Rheims Racer* just before the competition. The most important prize was a trophy and cash award for the best speed record, established by James Gordon Bennett, publisher of the *New York Herald*. Curtiss got some breaks: The *Rheims Racer* performed exceptionally well, and an English rival dropped out after crashing into a haystack. Curtiss won the main contest, beating the time of French flying ace Louis Blériot, who a month earlier had been the first pilot to fly

9. Roseberry, *Glenn Curtiss*, 102–118; "Flight of the June Bug," http://www.glennhcurtiss-museum.org/museum/flight_of_the_june_bug.html.
10. Richard K. Smith, *First Across! The U.S. Navy's Transatlantic Flight of 1919* (Annapolis: Naval Institute Press, 1986), 19.

across the English Channel, by six seconds. He won another contest the next day and three more prizes in Italy before leaving for home.[11]

Curtiss received worldwide press acclaim and was hailed as a hero. Wanamaker's department store, which quickly secured the *Rheims Racer* plane for display in the lobby of its New York City and Philadelphia stores, issued a celebratory booklet: "And here [Rheims], where all the kings of France have been crowned. . . . there was placed upon the head of a simple, modest American boy the international crown of the 'King of the Air.'"[12] Curtiss was uncomfortable in the limelight, and modesty tempered his natural pride in victory. Feted at a luncheon by the Aero Club of America upon his return, where a speaker toasted "the greatest victory in the history of aerial effort," Curtiss responded simply: "Gentlemen, I managed to get the cup and win the race in France without any serious blunders and with your kind indulgence I will leave it to others to interest you, so far as the talking goes."[13] Addressing a crowd of people who greeted him at the Hammondsport train station, he said: "Ladies and gentlemen, I'm back from France. Had a very nice time. Had a whole lot of luck and a little success. As you know, I had just a common school education. I didn't learn any words big enough to show you my appreciation of this welcome home."[14]

Suddenly, the taciturn Glenn Curtiss was much in demand for flying demonstrations. Joseph Pulitzer, wealthy publisher of the *New York World*, a newspaper well known for its investigative journalism, sometimes sensational news, and popular entertainment, saw pioneer aviation as a potential promotional venue. Pulitzer offered a prize of $10,000 for anyone who could fly from New York City to Albany, as part of the Hudson-Fulton Celebration in 1909. Curtiss made an attempt then, but his engine failed. But Curtiss's daredevil flying was soon to become almost legendary. After several demonstration flights in Los Angeles, "his propeller splintered—just a trifle—but enough to cause the machine to wobble slightly and Curtiss shut off his engine and sailed to the ground unharmed."[15] He was quickly becoming a celebrated flying ace.

---

11. Richard P. Hallion, *Taking Flight: Inventing the Aerial Age from Antiquity through the First World War* (New York: Oxford University Press, 2003), 257–267.
12. Wanamaker's Department Store, *The Wonderful Story of the Conquest of Air* (pamphlet, 1909).
13. Roseberry, *Glenn Curtiss*, 211–212.
14. Shulman, *Unlocking the Sky*, 170.
15. "Glenn Curtiss Flies Over Aviation Park," *Los Angeles Times*, January 10, 1910.

The Historic Flight

By 1910, several aviators, including Curtiss, had flown planes in exhibitions and competitions, demonstrating the primitive aircrafts' airworthiness. Publicity stunts where newspapers and businesses offered prizes for record flights were becoming more common public events. Pulitzer extended his Hudson-Fulton offer to 1910 and broadened it to include a flight either from New York to Albany or vice versa within a twenty-four-hour time period, with two stops permitted. Curtiss determined to win the prize. He needed the money for a patent fight against the Wrights (discussed later), knew victory would show the competitive abilities of his airplane, and reasoned that such a sensational event would give a boost to the public's (and possibly the military's) interest in flying. He built another single-engine biplane based on models he had already flown. Like the earlier ones, and most other planes of the day, it was a bi-wing "pusher"; the propeller mounted in the rear pushed rather than pulled it through the air. Curtiss tested it several times in Hammondsport in the early spring, disassembled it, and sent it overland to Albany in May, an optimal time for flying. He reassembled it, tested the engine, and told reporters its name, the *Albany Flyer*. Van Rensselaer Island, just outside Albany, would be the launch point; the army agreed to let flyers land at Governor's Island military base in New York City. Curtiss scouted out the route by taking a steamship from Albany to New York City and returning by rail, stopping at several places near Poughkeepsie, the approximate midpoint of the projected flight, to identify a landing site for refueling. Weight restrictions on the mostly wooden craft limited the plane's gas tank to ten gallons, so a nonstop flight was impossible. The superintendent of the State Hospital for the Insane in Poughkeepsie offered to let him land there, joking that almost all the flying machine inventors wound up there anyway![16] Curtiss thanked him but chose another spot and made arrangements with a local resident to meet him there with gas for refueling.

Twenty years later, the pioneering aviator recalled:

> The machine . . . looked very much like a box kite. It was a biplane, thirty feet long and thirty feet wide. The elevator was set in front

---

16. Glenn H. Curtiss and Augustus Post, *The Curtiss Aviation Book* (New York: Frederick A. Stokes Company, 1912), 94; http://www.archive.org/stream/curtissaviationb00curtrich/curtissaviationb00curtrich_djvu.txt; Albany Flyer, 1910, http://www.glennhcurtissmuseum.org/educational/articles/albany_flyer.

of the pilot's seat, which was completely open. The wings were arched but rigid. Instead of warping the wings to balance, I had ailerons on either side of the machine. It was of course a home-made machine. The fittings were sheet iron. The wire was twisted cable and the turnbuckles were made of bicycle spokes.[17]

Just in case he had to ditch in the Hudson, Curtiss installed airtight metal pontoons under both wings and attached an elongated bag filled with champagne corks to the undercarriage.

A local farmer with a meadow on Van Rensselaer Island was approached and demanded $100 for letting Curtiss use his field as a launch point, but Curtiss, claiming (accurately) that he was nearly broke, got him to accept $5. After several delays, Curtiss took off in his "aeroplane" just after 7:00 a.m. on May 29. "The air was calm. . . . The motor sounded like music and the machine handled perfectly."[18] Excitement abounded. More than a hundred people saw him off at Albany, hundreds looked up in amazement along the route, and thousands scanned the sky from rooftops in New York City. The *New York Times*, trying to upstage its rival the *World*, chartered a special train to carry Mrs. Curtiss, reporters, and officials from the Aero Club of America, which monitored the event and certified the results. The plane flew over the train for much of the flight, providing an opportunity for people on board to wave at the aviator. Running low on fuel, Curtiss landed at the designated refueling spot near Poughkeepsie, but the man who had agreed to rendezvous there with gasoline was late. "Automobilists," as early car drivers were called, excitedly pulled up near the plane. In those days, with gas stations scarce, auto drivers carried gasoline with them, and two New Jersey drivers enthusiastically offered theirs to Curtiss.

After checking the plane, Curtiss took off again. Near Storm King Mountain, where the Hudson narrows, Curtiss encountered what he later described as a "hole in the air," a falling air current that nearly dunked him in the river. The plane began to "toss and eddy about almost beyond control. My heart was in my throat. I thought it was all over."[19] Continuing south, he ran out of oil, which he had to inject into the engine via a

17. Glenn H. Curtiss, "Down the Hudson in a Box-Kite Plane," *New York Times*, May 25, 1930.
18. Curtiss and Post, *The Curtiss Aviation Book*, 98.
19. Curtiss, "Down the Hudson in a Box-Kite Plane," *New York Times*, May 25, 1930.

hand pump.[20] He landed on an estate at 214th Street, where the astonished owner looked up from reading the Sunday paper to see the plane descend on his front lawn. The estate's owner and another group of passing motorists gave the aviator more gas and oil. His landing spot was within the boundaries of New York City, satisfying Pulitzer's condition, but Curtiss was determined to fly further south. Taking off again, he circled the Statue of Liberty and landed at Governor's Island just after noon. This last leg of the trip gave thousands of New Yorkers an exciting chance to see a plane in the air for the first time. The official record showed he had flown 150 miles at an average speed of 54 mph, as the press noted, "one mile every 1 minute 6 seconds."[21]

"Man has now conquered the air," said the *New York Times*, putting Curtiss's lengthy flight in a higher category of accomplishment than previous flights by the Wrights and others. "[T]he development of the airship practically and commercially, and the growth of its usefulness as a carrier, are only matters of time."[22] European aviators had set multiple speed and distance records, but "by his daring feat, Curtiss . . . has made a record never before approached in the United States. . . . has demonstrated that the world must reckon with Americans in the development of aviation."[23] This was "one of the handful of flights to change the world. . . . the airplane, once a novelty, suddenly and all at once presented itself as a useful and practical technology," says aviation historian Seth Shulman.[24] The aviator himself was as usual more modest. "Curtiss appeared to be the calmest man in New York at the end of his great flight," noted the *New York Times*. He answered reporters' questions simply and directly and gave a very short speech at a black-tie dinner in his honor at the swank Astor House hotel. For aviation to succeed, he said, there would need to be more places to land, what we now call runways and airfields. Presaging the next step in his career, he predicted, "Some day soon aeroplanes will have to start from the decks of battleships and from the water, and I am not sure but what they could be launched from a battleship going at top speed even now."[25]

---

20. Curtiss and Post, *The Curtiss Aviation Book*, 101–102.
21. "Curtiss' Career in Aeronautics," *New York Times*, May 30, 1910.
22. "Curtiss Flies Albany to New York at the Speed of 54 Miles an Hour," *New York Times*, May 30, 1910; "Flight of Curtiss," *New York Times*," May 30, 1910.
23. "Curtiss' Great Flight," *Washington Post*, May 30, 1910.
24. Shulman, *Unlocking the Sky*, 203.
25. "Curtiss' Own Story of the Long Flight," *New York Times*, May 30, 1910.

Curtiss carried a letter from Albany mayor James B. McEwan to New York City mayor William J. Gaynor, which hailed the flight as "historic . . . but the forerunner of what may be in no long while a commonplace occurrence." Curtiss was a bit overwhelmed by the hoopla in New York City, observing later, "New York can turn out a million people probably quicker than any other place on earth."[26] Curtiss was adjusting to his newly elevated status as a hero, someone to be celebrated. On the other hand, Mayor Gaynor did not know quite what to make of the quiet, unassuming upstate New Yorker who had landed in his city. He told reporters that Curtiss came from a tranquil rural village where "people have time to think" and "sit around and talk about two thirds of the time."[27]

Fighting the Wrights

Much of Curtiss's flying took place during a bitter contest with the Wright Brothers over their allegations that his planes infringed on their patents, particularly the one they obtained in 1906 for "A Flying Machine." The Wrights sought a broad patent and intended to sell licensing rights; they did not even set up a manufacturing company until 1909, six years after Kitty Hawk and a few months later than Curtiss. Their subsequent patents built on the first one. Their original patent did not actually cover their plane but, instead, their system for in-the-air control, in the words of the patent: "The objects of our invention are to provide means for maintaining or restoring the equilibrium or lateral balance of the apparatus, to provide means for guiding the machine both vertically and horizontally, and to provide a structure combining lightness, strength, convenience of construction and certain other advantages . . ." The patent also included such open-ended statements as "our invention is not limited to this particular construction. . . . we do not wish to be understood as limiting ourselves strictly to the precise details of construction hereinbefore described."[28]

The wording was supplied by the Wrights' patent lawyers and was intended to be so broad and all-encompassing that anyone trying to build an airplane would have to pay them for a license. Their main control

---

26. Shulman, *Unlocking the Sky*, 201.
27. "Gaynor Puts Faith in Country Youth," *New York Times*, June 12, 1910.
28. Orville and Wilbur Wright, Flying-Machine, Patent no. 821,393, May 22, 1906, http://www.google.com/patents?vid=821393.

method was "wing warping," a system of cables and pulleys to twist the trailing edges of a plane's wings in opposite directions, causing it to veer right or left and also tilt up or down. The "wing warping" technology was clumsy even for the time and was soon displaced by the aileron wing-flap technology pioneered by Bell, Curtiss, and others. But the patent also protected a "combination" of wing warping and a movable vertical rudder, and Curtiss and other aviation pioneers all relied on a rudder of one sort or another. Curtiss had met the Wrights, corresponded with them, and even offered to cooperate with them but developed his own aileron-based system through his work with Bell and the AEA. Curtiss believed he was not infringing on the Wrights and got his own share of patents, including one in 1916 for a "Hydroaeroplane" (flying boat). But he showed little interest in using patents to block others and competed mostly by building better engines and planes than his competitors. The Wrights, by contrast, became obsessed with enforcing their patent rights in U.S. and European courts. They asserted that it was their inventive work that made flying possible. Aviation experts joked that if you jumped up in the air and flapped your arms, the Wrights would sue for patent infringement. Many upstart airplane makers paid them licensing fees rather than fight, and the Wrights waged dozens of legal battles against those who refused. Curtiss ignored their warnings of legal action. The 1908 public *June Bug* flight angered them; the *Rheims Racer* the next year put them over the top. They served legal papers on Curtiss's company while he was in France.[29]

The expansive wording of the Wrights' patent gave them an advantage. It was also regarded as a "pioneering invention" and as such, under the patent rules and court decisions of the era, entitled to be broadly construed in favor of the inventor.[30] The intention was to encourage and protect original inventions, but the result, in the case of an emerging field like aviation, was to block experimenters and innovators like Curtiss. In January 1910 the Wrights' case against Curtiss was decided by U.S. district judge John R. Hazel in Buffalo. Hazel in 1900 had upheld a patent for Rochester inventor George Selden's "Road Engine," which presented

---

29. Tom Crouch, *The Bishop's Boys: A Life of Wilbur and Orville Wright* (New York: W.W. Norton, 1989), 410–423. Crouch presents the competition from the Wright Brothers' perspective. A useful, objective account is the U.S. Centennial of Flight Commission, "Glenn Curtiss and the Wright Patent Battles," http://www.centennialofflight.gov/essay/Wright_Bros/Patent_Battles/WR12.htm.
30. Herbert A. Johnson, "The Wright Patent Wars and Early American Aviation," *Journal of Air Law and Commerce* 69 (2004), 21–60.

the general features of an early automobile. Selden's patent—almost as broad and open-ended as the Wrights—made Selden one of the wealthiest men in Rochester. Selden's monopoly was legally challenged and broken by pioneering automaker Henry Ford, but not until 1912. It was no surprise when Judge Hazel issued an injunction against Curtiss in 1910. The Wrights were entitled to broad "pioneering" status, said the judge, and "the claims of the patent in suit should be broadly construed." Curtiss appealed and posted bond to go on flying while the appeal was being considered, enabling him to take the *Albany Flyer* into history in May 1910. Fighting the Wrights had drained his finances; the cash prize from Pulitzer replenished his bank account for more litigation. In June 1910, an appeals court, considering additional information submitted by Curtiss, lifted the injunction. In the meantime, his business partner, August Herring, proved incompetent and deceptive and their company went out of business. Curtiss started a new company. His quality planes outpaced the Wrights, who increasingly focused their energies on engines.[31]

Wilbur Wright died in 1912. Orville publicly asserted that the stress of the Curtiss litigation hastened his brother's death and intensified legal action. Curtiss tried negotiating, but the Wrights' terms for licensing "their" technology were exorbitant. In 1913, Hazel ruled again in favor of the Wrights, and this time the appeals court upheld him in 1914. Curtiss seemed finished. But Henry Ford unexpectedly approached him at a dinner in New York City and later visited him at Hammondsport to examine a flying boat for possible purchase. Ford maintained that patents like those held by Selden and the Wrights "don't . . . stimulate invention . . . but they do exploit the customer and place a heavy burden on productive industry." Ford made available to Curtiss the services of his chief patent lawyer, W. Benton Crisp, who had won the fight against the Selden patent in 1912. Crisp noted that the Wright patent said the wings must be twisted simultaneously and suggested Curtiss refine his design so that the ailerons on each wing could operate independently of each other. It was something of a technical dodge, but it was enough to serve as a basis for an appeal. Curtiss was given permission to keep flying while the litigation went forward.[32]

Curtiss tried one other tactic in 1914, a blend of publicity stunt and appeal to public opinion. A week before the Wright Brothers' flight at

31. Roseberry, *Glenn Curtiss*, 237–260, 335–336.
32. Hallion, *Taking Flight*, 290–294.

Kitty Hawk in December 1903, another aviation pioneer, Samuel P. Langley, secretary of the Smithsonian Institution, had launched an ungainly motorized aircraft by catapult off a boat on the Potomac. Developed over several years with funding from the army, the awkward "Aerodrome" nosedived into the Potomac, the pilot barely escaped, and Langley was widely derided. "The only thing he made to fly was government money," said one congressman.[33] Langley packed up his wrecked machine and stored it at the Smithsonian. In 1914, Curtiss arranged to borrow it in the hopes that he could restore it and make it fly, faulting the catapult and launch mechanism for the 1903 failure. If the reassembled "Aerodrome" with a new launch mechanism got off the ground, it would mean, at least in Curtiss's view, that Langley had beaten the Wrights with manned flight by a week. That would weaken them in the patent fight. Curtiss and his staff unpacked the wreck, repaired the damage, made some minor changes including a new carburetor, and added pontoons for a water launch from Keuka Lake. Curtiss was able to get the restored machine into the air on May 23, 1914, with dozens of witnesses observing. Subsequent upgrades, including substituting a more powerful Curtiss engine, resulted in longer flights. A Wright supporter derided the restoration effort in letters to the *New York Times*, contending the Langley flyer was defective in 1903, Curtiss's "restoration" was actually an upgrade, and that tests by "the person who had been found guilty of infringement of the Wright patent" lacked credibility.[34] Curtiss announced that his tests substantiated Langley's claim, and the Smithsonian displayed the restored Aerodrome after Curtiss's flights, claiming it was the first heavier-than-air manned powered aircraft capable of flight. That was a shaky assertion at best and one the Smithsonian finally recanted in 1942. The whole episode tarnished both the Smithsonian and Glenn Curtiss and did nothing to resolve the patent dispute.

Wilbur Wright sold out to a group of investors in 1915 and retired. But the litigation continued to exhaust both Curtiss and the Wright companies, discouraged new startups, and made raising capital difficult. In 1917, with the United States entering World War I, the U.S. government, following the recommendation of a committee formed by Assistant Secretary of the Navy Franklin D. Roosevelt, convinced the industry to form a cross-licensing organization. All aircraft manufacturers were required

---

33. Shulman, *Unlocking the Sky*, 15.
34. Griffith Brewer, "Langley Flier Tests," *New York Times*, June 22, 1914.

to join and pay a modest per-plane fee for the use of aviation patents, and the proceeds were divided by a formula among Wright, Curtiss, and a few other companies with patents, with the Wright and Curtiss companies getting the largest shares. The litigation was not renewed after the war. Eventually several of the contentious patents expired or were rendered moot by advancing technology. But the agreement, with modifications, survived until 1972. It was then invalidated by the Department of Justice, whose review contended it had long hampered competition, research, and development.[35]

The Airman Takes to the Water

Curtiss was fascinated by water-based flight. Much of his testing of early planes took place on Keuka Lake near his factory rather than at a Hammondsport airfield. He eventually sold planes to the army, but the Wrights had gotten there first and began conducting tests and training army pilots. Curtiss moved toward work with the navy. Curtiss disassembled the *Albany Flyer* after its triumphant flight down the Hudson, sent it home to Hammondsport by rail, and reassembled it. In June, with invited naval officials present, he dropped lengths of lead pipe from a thousand feet up into a section of Keuka Lake marked by buoyed flags to approximate the deck of a battleship. It was one of the earliest recorded "aerial bombardments" in history. In another demonstration in July, he dropped oranges as "bombs" within three feet of a yacht (carefully avoiding the deck to keep from injuring officials and spectators gathered there).[36] In July, he achieved a new speed record along the coast at Atlantic City; in August 1911, he set a new overwater navigation record by flying sixty miles over Lake Erie.[37] That same month, he described "the ultimate possibilities of this new force in warfare," including reconnaissance, mapmaking, aerial bombardment, and other capacities.[38]

The navy equivocated. In 1898, Assistant Secretary of the Navy Theodore Roosevelt had appointed a committee of officers to look into the

---

35. George Bittlingmayer, "Property Rights, Progress, and the Aircraft Patent Agreement," *Journal of Law and Economics* 31 (April 1988), 227–248.
36. Roseberry, *Glenn Curtiss*, 283; "Mock 'Bombs' Rained on Yacht from an Airship," *Atlanta Constitution*, July 13, 1910.
37. "$55,000 in Prizes in Aero Flights," *New York Sun*, September 1, 1910.
38. Glenn H. Curtiss, "The Aeroplane for the Navy," *St. Louis Post-Dispatch*, August 27, 1910.

wartime potential of aviation, but the conservative naval establishment was only interested in dirigibles and balloons. The navy considered early airplanes fragile, difficult to maneuver, and vulnerable to rifle fire from the decks of warships.[39] Curtiss demonstrated that planes were fast, maneuverable, and capable of carrying a modest payload of bombs. In September 1910, the navy designated Captain Washington I. Chambers as liaison for naval aviation. Chambers first approached the Wright Brothers, who were dismissive of the notion of water-based or ship-based flying, and then talked with Curtiss, whom he encountered at a flying meet in the fall.[40] Curtiss excitedly accepted Chambers's challenge to prove the feasibility of naval aviation and built special heavy-duty Curtiss demonstration "fliers." Curtiss proved the potential for use in naval combat in three highly publicized, spectacular flights.

November 14, 1910. Curtiss test pilot Eugene Ely took off in a 50-hp Curtiss plane from a wooden platform built on the cruiser *Birmingham,* anchored off Hampton Roads, Virginia. Ely dropped fast, his plane actually touched the waves, but he rose majestically and landed near Norfolk a few minutes later.

January 18, 1911. Ely took off in another Curtiss plane from a spot near San Bruno, California, and flew to the cruiser *Pennsylvania,* anchored in San Francisco Bay. Ely was feted by the ship's captain, got back in his plane, and flew back to shore. The press covered his flight, and a crowd estimated at seventy-five thousand gathered along the waterfront to see him return. It was, Ely claimed when he landed, "a conclusive demonstration of the adaptability of the aeroplane to military purposes."[41]

February 17, 1911. The November 14 and January 18 flights were impressive, but not enough for Chambers to persuade Secretary of the Navy George Meyer to purchase test planes and begin training naval aviators. The secretary set a new standard: A plane must fly from shore, land in the water beside a ship, be hoisted aboard, let down again, and fly back to shore. Curtiss modified one of his planes to equip it with both pontoons and wheels, and on February 17, 1911, flew it himself out to the *Pennsylvania,* was hoisted aboard, saluted by the crew, lowered back into

39. Roy A. Grossnick and William J. Armstrong, *United States Naval Aviation, 1910–1995,* 4th ed. (Washington, DC: Naval Historical Center, Department of the Navy, 1997), 1–2.
40. William F. Trimble, *Hero of the Air: Glenn Curtiss and the Birth of Naval Aviation* (Annapolis: Naval Institute Press, 2010), 98–99.
41. Daniel J. Demers, "What Goes Up . . ." *Naval History Magazine,* February 2011, http://www.usni.org/magazines/navalhistory/2011-01/what-goes.

the water, and returned triumphantly to base. "The trip to the cruiser was without incident, the hoisting aboard was made without a hitch and the rest of the program was equally as easy," Curtiss told reporters.[42]

That was enough for Secretary Meyer. On May 8, 1911, the navy ordered two Curtiss biplanes and contracted with him to train pilots. The navy considers this date the birthday of naval aviation; Chambers and Curtiss, successful collaborators in the pioneering effort, contend in history for the title "father of naval aviation." Curtiss began building plans for the navy and established training schools for naval pilots at Hammondsport and San Diego.[43] Naval aviation was barely three years old when it had its first hostile encounter, over Mexico in April 1914. U.S. forces invaded and occupied the city of Vera Cruz after a diplomatic incident during the tumultuous Mexican revolution. The Mexicans deployed water mines and snipers. The naval commander ordered two shipboard planes aloft for reconnaissance. The first flights were not auspicious: The pilots failed to spot the mines or the snipers and an engine problem forced a landing in rough seas. On a subsequent flight, one plane came under fire. "I wanted to return the favor but we were under orders not to use our revolvers offensively," the pilot wrote later. As he was suiting up for the next flight, a mechanic handed him a bar of soap. Aloft over enemy lines, he threw it at the Mexicans, apparently the first object dropped from a U.S. plane on an enemy.[44]

As the navy made more and more use of his planes, Curtiss's vision expanded. Aviation was restricted to where there were landing strips, he wrote, but "rivers, lakes, bays and oceans are the world's greatest highways," and he developed the "flying boat," a bi-wing plane with a large buoyant hull that permitted it to land, float, and take off from water. In 1912, he predicted people would soon be able to fly across the Atlantic Ocean.[45] He cooperated with Elmer Sperry on development of a "gyro-stabilizer" to control the ever-larger planes. In 1914, with financial backing from department store magnate Rodman Wanamaker, the Curtiss shop

42. Grossnick et al., *United States Naval Aviation, 1910–1995*, 3; Glenn Curtiss, "Curtiss Tells of Alighting on Sea in Test Flight," *St. Louis Post Dispatch*, February 18, 1911.

43. Centennial of Naval Aviation, http://www.public.navy.mil/airfor/centennial/Pages/welcome.aspx.

44. Mark L. Evans, "'Performed All Their Duties Well,'" *Naval History Magazine*, October 2009, http://www.usni.org/magazines/navalhistory/2009-10/performed-all-their-duties-well.

45. Glenn Curtiss, "Man Gull of the Sea," *St. Louis Post Dispatch*, December 9, 1912.

produced the *America*, a biplane with a seventy-two-foot wingspan and a hull thirty-two feet long, the largest plane built to that time and intended for a transatlantic flight. The outbreak of World War I in August put plans for flying across the Atlantic on hold. But the British placed an order for several of the big planes, which they used primarily for antisubmarine patrol.[46] Curtiss built larger, more powerful flying boats for the navy during the war, including three-engine biplanes called NC Flying Boats—the NC standing for Navy-Curtiss. On May 8, 1919, NC-1, NC-3, and NC-4 took off from Rockaway on Long Island for a transatlantic journey. The first two dropped out from mechanical problems and other mishaps, but NC-4 flew to Newfoundland, then to the Azores, from there to Portugal, and finally to Britain. The journey, carefully organized by the navy to provide for aircraft refueling and maintenance and crew rest, including a series of naval ships along the route to give the pilots navigating points, took twenty-three days.[47] The segmented flight by the navy and Glenn Curtiss beat Charles Lindbergh across the Atlantic by eight years.

Flying into History

During the years preceding U.S. entry into World War I, Curtiss made great progress with the navy, less with the army. General John J. Pershing used Curtiss JN-4s, commonly known as "Jennies," for reconnaissance in his punitive expedition into Mexico in search of revolutionary leader Pancho Villa in 1916 to 1917. The planes helped, but operating problems led to the loss of all of them. By the time of the declaration of war in April 1917, the army had only fifty-five planes, mostly obsolete, and the navy fifty-four, all trainers. The new Aircraft Production Board called for 4,500 new planes in a year. Curtiss, Wright, and others ramped up production, and the cross-licensing agreement described earlier cleared the patent competition out of the way. But in this unprecedented situation, the military often changed their priorities and specifications, complicating production.[48] Curtiss's needs outgrew Hammondsport and he expanded production to Buffalo, rented a factory there, and built another one. Curtiss Aeroplane and Motor Corporation became, for a couple of years, the

---

46. Roseberry, *Glenn Curtiss*, 363–380.
47. Navy-Curtiss NC-4 Flying Boat, http://www.aviation-history.com/navy/nc4.html.
48. Hallion, *Taking Flight*, 388–390.

largest aircraft company in the world and one of the largest companies in New York State, employing eighteen thousand workers in Buffalo and turning out over ten thousand planes by the end of the war.[49] But because the military could not seem to settle on plans for armed aircraft, most of the American planes were for training and reconnaissance. Most American combat pilots wound up flying British or French aircraft. As soon as the war ended in November 1918, the army and navy immediately cancelled contracts, including for aircraft already in production, adding up to a $75 million loss for Curtiss. Ironically, Curtiss had to compete for sales with surplus military "Jennies" sold at bargain-basement prices by the government. The used planes were so well built and durable that they significantly decreased sales for new ones. New enterprises, such as the Glenn Martin Company, made the scene even more competitive. Lack of landing fields continued to be a problem.[50] Curtiss, ever the optimist and experimenter, pushed flying boats and planes for air taxi services and tried to expand foreign sales, but to little avail. In 1920, he cashed out his stock in the company, retaining a connection as a consultant, and retired to Florida.

The Buffalo Curtiss plants were downsized after the war. Prospects brightened in the late 1920s after the creation of the Army Air Corps, but a new aggressive competitor, Boeing, leapfrogged Curtiss's company and got most of the contracts. The Curtiss and Wright companies merged in 1929, and the company remained strong in aircraft engines but gradually lost its edge in aircraft design. Production increased during World War II, and Buffalo facilities were ramped up. But cancelled military contracts forced curtailment of Buffalo operations in August 1945 and termination the next year, with production shifted to Columbus, Ohio. Thereafter, Curtiss-Wright fades from the story of New York.[51]

After leaving the company in 1920, Curtiss and his family moved to Florida and an entirely new set of opportunities, though he kept a summer home in Hammondsport. Curtiss became a Florida land developer. He partnered in the development of the cities of Hialeah, Opa-Locka (a planned community that featured Moorish architecture), and Miami Springs, where he built a family home. He grew wealthy in the Florida

49. Roseberry, *Glenn Curtiss*, 402–404.
50. John B. Rae, "Financial Problems of the American Aircraft Industry, 1906–1940," *Business History Review* 39 (Spring 1965), 99–114.
51. Louis R. Eltscher and Edward M. Young, *Curtiss-Wright: Greatness and Decline* (New York: Twayne, 1998), 1–163.

land boom of the early 1920s but lost most of it when the bubble burst
in the late years of the decade. But his Florida accomplishments are dramatic: Curtiss invented the airboat for better transportation in the Everglades; established Miami's first aviation school; built several golf courses;
donated land for road construction and railroad expansion; built the Miami
Jockey Club, later Hialeah Race Track; opened the first state-chartered
bank in Dade County; and was a founding donor of the University of
Miami, where he received an honorary doctorate for his civic work.[52] His
frequent hunting trips to the Everglades led to his final invention, which
he called the "Aerocar," a forerunner of the modern RV trailer. Even in
the late 1920s, he still dabbled with aeronautics and worked on developing
the technology of skywriting. In June 1930, he flew in a modern Curtiss
Condor aircraft from Albany to New York City in a commemoration of
his famous flight two decades earlier. But he was stricken by appendicitis
and died suddenly on July 23, 1930, at the age of fifty-two. "[A]lthough
the Wright brothers gave the airplane to the world, to Glenn Curtiss must
go much of the credit for perfecting it and making it the commonplace
vehicle that it is today," said an editorial in the *Washington Post* noting
his death.[53]

Curtiss was a tireless innovator, passionate about his work, but personally modest, disdainful of self-promotion, and not much concerned
about his place in history. "He was a visionary but not a wild-eyed one,"
notes his biographer Seth Shulman. "He was a businessman too. He was
that perfect kind of visionary who didn't look too far off into the future
but just to the next thing."[54] Just a couple of months before his death, he
speculated about the future of aviation. With more airports, flying could
become almost as common as traveling by automobile. "Saving time is the
equivalent of increasing the duration of life," he noted. "[T]ime used in
traveling from point to point is largely wasted. That is where the airplane
comes in." Looking ahead, he projected a vision of growth. "There is certainly a wonderfully wide-open field for improvement and expansion in
the manufacture and operation of planes."[55] That was an understatement
by a modest New Yorker of high achievement.

52. The Historic Glenn Curtiss Mansion, http://www.miamisprings-fl.gov/sites/default/
files/fileattachments/Curtiss%20Mansion%20Brochure.pdf.
53. "Glenn Curtiss," *Washington Post*, July 25, 1930.
54. Mark Woverton, "Talking with Seth Shulman," *American History* (February 2003), 58.
55. "Future of Air Transport," *New York Times*, May 4, 1930.

9
March 25 and 29, 1911

Fires Change History

The New York State Factory Investigating Commission, established as a result of the Triangle Fire, documented industrial working conditions through the state. A commission photographer took this portrait of workers outside an International Harvester twine works factory in Auburn in 1912 and two photos inside, where the work was dirty, hot, and heavy and fire a constant menace. The origins of New York's modern labor and industrial code can be traced to the Commission's work. *Photos courtesy of New York State Archives.*

Two Fires Destroy and Transform

*M*ajor fires are tragedies, killing people and destroying property, but they can also have significant impact on the course of history. Two destructive fires four days apart in March 1911 changed New York.

A fire on March 25, 1911, at the Triangle Shirtwaist Factory in Manhattan was relatively small, burning itself out in a half hour, destroying three floors in a ten-story factory building, one of hundreds of such facilities in New York City. But it killed 146 employees and kindled public outrage that led to state legislation mandating protection for its citizens working in factories, mills, and canneries. Because of the fire, New York's leadership in manufacturing and commerce was matched by a commensurate industrial code, one of the strongest in the nation. Another fire four days later, at the State Capitol in Albany, killed a night watchman, burned up much of the documentation of New York's early history, and altered state politics. The capitol fire lacks the outsized dimensions of human tragedy and historic transformation associated with the Triangle fire. It has significance, however, for insight into politics and documentation and study of New York's history. The fires helped launch the careers of four outstanding New Yorkers: Frances Perkins, Alfred E. Smith, Robert Wagner, and Franklin D. Roosevelt.

Saturday, March 25: Tragedy in New York City

The New York City garment industry was flourishing in the opening years of the twentieth century, bolstering city prosperity. The Triangle Shirtwaist Factory was the largest of about five hundred companies in the city that manufactured shirtwaists, the fashionable women's blouses of the day. It was located on the top three floors of the ten-story Asch Building on Washington Place in lower Manhattan. Constructed in 1901, that building was one of about eight hundred new factory loft buildings erected in the city in the first decade of the twentieth century. Built of steel and mortar, with access via two narrow stairways, an elevator, and one flimsy fire escape, and with no fire alarms or sprinklers, it met the minimal fire codes of the day and was considered "fireproof." "They are fireproof, yes, when the builders get through and before the tenants move in," said City Fire Chief Edward Croker in 1910. "But after the tenants are in, they are only slow-burning buildings. They are safe so far as [structural] damage is concerned, but not so far as human life is concerned." His department's tallest rescue ladders were too short to reach their upper floors. Croker's plea for requiring sprinklers in high-rise factories, more fire escapes, and expanded inspection authority for his department went unheeded. City government, under control of the New York Democratic Party organization known as Tammany Hall, scorned industrial regulations as unnecessary burdens that might drive manufacturers out of the city.[1]

The Triangle's owners, Max Blanck and Isaac Harris, known as "The Shirtwaist Kings," were among the city's business elite. They had started their own careers years earlier as laborers in garment sweatshops where workers made clothing by hand. Entrepreneurial and energetic, they had helped transition the industry to a new system where hundreds of workers in large factories sat at cutting and sewing machines in long rows and powered by electricity. As their sales expanded, they opened other highly profitable shirtwaist factories in New Jersey and Pennsylvania, expanding the Triangle facility to about five hundred workers, many young immigrant women from Eastern Europe and Italy. The Triangle factory hummed efficiently. The work was hard, monotonous, and fast paced. Women employees often worked as much as eighty hours per week for as little as $7.00. Women across the nation proudly wore blouses with the Triangle label. Blanck and Harris believed their employees should be appreciative of their jobs and grateful for working in a modern factory rather than the bleak sweatshops of the past.[2]

Oppressive working conditions and low wages led to the "shirtwaist uprising" of 1909–1910. It was a genuine grassroots protest, organized and led by the women who worked at the Triangle and other factories. Clara Lemlich, one of the 1909 strike's organizers, rallied support at a mass meeting of workers in November as the strike gathered momentum: "I have no further patience for talk! I am a working girl, one of those striking against intolerable conditions!" Fledgling unions such as the Women's Trade Union League and socially prominent women reformers supported the strike, but the workers themselves were the force behind it. Young women strikers were shoved around and bullied by police and strikebreakers hired by the companies. Public opinion shifted in their favor because of their tenacity and press coverage of their brutal treatment. The companies grudgingly made modest concessions of better pay and shorter hours, and the strike ended early in 1910. Triangle was one of the last holdouts. Harris and Blanck "recognized" the workers' union but only in the sense that they no longer prohibited membership. The workers returned

---

1. Terry Golway, *So Others Might Live: A History of New York's Bravest—the FDNY from 1700 to the Present* (New York: Basic Books, 2002), 168–169.
2. David Von Drehle, *Triangle: The Fire That Changed America* (New York: Grove Press, 2004), 35–48.

to their cutting and sewing machines. But working conditions and safety provisions were not improved.[3]

Owners and workers in the Triangle regarded each other with wariness. Doors were often locked to keep union organizers out. Women workers' handbags were searched as they left at quitting time to prevent theft of fabric or blouses. March 25 was a Saturday, and only about 250 people, about half the normal workweek number, were present. A fire began on the eighth floor around 4:40 p.m., as workers were beginning to wind down their day's work and preparing to leave. The fire was probably the result of a match or cigarette carelessly thrown into a bundle of scrap cloth. Scraps of fabric, tissue paper, and oil from the sewing machines caused it to move quickly. Throwing buckets of water on the fire, which had worked for small fires in the past, was futile this time. The fire quickly spread to the ninth and tenth floors. "The smoke and flames seemed to be coming from all sides," recalled one survivor. There was "fire coming in all around us." One survivor described it as "a mass of traveling fire along the floors." Soon women were stampeding toward the exits. Many workers on the eighth floor streamed down the stairs, and most on the tenth floor escaped to the roof, where they were later rescued, some by climbing onto a roof of an adjacent New York University building. On the ninth floor, where the greatest loss of life occurred, a door leading to one of the stairwells could not be opened. It was probably locked, but that was hard to prove afterward. Soon the fire escape collapsed, the elevator was put out of service by the fire, and the stairwells filled with smoke and flames. Workers died by being burned, suffocating from smoke, or being trampled. Many decided in an instant to jump to their deaths rather than die from the fire.[4]

A reporter for United Press, a news service of that era, happened to be walking by the building when he saw a "puff of smoke" from an upper story. His widely reprinted eyewitness account said:

> I learned a new sound—a more horrible sound than description can picture. It was the thud of a speeding, living body on a stone

---

3. Annelise Orleck, *Common Sense and a Little Fire: Women and Working-Class Politics in the United States, 1900–1965* (Chapel Hill: University of North Carolina Press, 1995), 53–63.

4. Von Drehle, *Triangle*, 116–166; Leon Stein, *The Triangle Fire* (Ithaca: Cornell University Press, 1962), 46–59.

sidewalk. Thud-dead, thud-dead, thud-dead. Sixty-two thud-deads . . . I even watched one girl falling. Waving her arms, trying to keep her body upright, until the very instant she struck the sidewalk, she was trying to balance herself. Then came the thud.[5]

New York City firemen, some aboard the department's first motorized units, arrived within six minutes after receiving the alarm from the factory, hooked up their hoses to nearby hydrants, and began shooting water through the factory's shattered windows. But ladders reached only up to the sixth floor, not nearly high enough. People jumping crashed right through the department's safety nets, and soon firemen put them away because they seemed to be encouraging more jumpers. Firemen rushed up the stairs to the burning floors. They had the fire under control in about eighteen minutes and fully extinguished in a half hour. But by then 146 people had died.

Consequences

Who was to blame? The city coroner's report was inconclusive about responsibility, the fire commissioner blamed the Buildings Department for lax inspection and enforcement, the buildings commissioner said the Fire Department should have smashed down doors and extinguished the fire faster. The state Labor Department claimed it had no authority to take action. New York City had endured tragic fires before, followed by public apathy and government indifference. This time, it would be different. People recalled the recent bitter shirtwaist-makers' strike. The fire seemed to confirm the image of greedy, wealthy businessmen who forced workers to labor in deathtraps. Eyewitness accounts and press reports of young people jumping to their deaths and photographs of broken bodies laid out in coffins on a city pier that served as a makeshift morgue deepened public shock. The largest public funeral march in the city's history, over one hundred thousand people, with four hundred thousand more looking on, was held to honor the victims. Socialite and reformer Martha Bruere watched the procession go by her window.

---

5. William G. Shepherd, "Eyewitness at the Triangle," March 27, 1911, http://www.ilr.cornell.edu/trianglefire/primary/testimonials/ootss_williamshepherd.html.

Well, the fire is over, the girls are dead, and as I write, the procession in honor of the unidentified dead is moving by under my windows. . . . thousands of working men and women carrying the banners of their trades through the long three-mile tramp in the rain. Never have I seen a military pageant or triumphant ovation so impressive . . . it is dawning on these thousands on thousands that such things do not have to be![6]

The fire quickly came to symbolize exploitation of and disregard for the poor and the innocent. Labor unions demanded action and began to murmur about staging a general strike. At a large public protest meeting at the Metropolitan Opera House a few days after the fire, union activist Rose Schneiderman shouted, "I would be a traitor to these poor burned bodies if I came here to talk about good fellowship. . . . Every time the workers come out in the only way they know to protest against conditions which are unbearable, the strong hand of the law is allowed to press down heavy upon us. . . . Too much blood has been spilled." Socially prominent men and women, including Anne Morgan, daughter of renowned financier J. P. Morgan and a supporter of the 1909–1910 strike, echoed the call for action. The city's influential newspapers joined the public outcry.[7]

Republican New York County district attorney Charles S. Whitman, an ambitious politician with gubernatorial aspirations, decided to bring Harris and Blanck to justice. Rather than trying them on multiple charges, which might be hard to prove, he secured a grand jury indictment on a single charge of manslaughter of Margaret Schwartz, one of many women who had died in the fire. The owners were accused of having locked a critical escape door on the ninth floor in violation of city and state codes, preventing workers from escaping the fire. The highly publicized trial in December 1911 lasted 18 days and featured 155 witnesses, including many survivors. "Gentlemen of the jury, that door was locked," said Assistant District Attorney Charles Bostwick in his opening statement. "That locked door barred their escape." The DA's witnesses testified that the door could not be opened, but they were inconsistent on whether it was locked, jammed, or, because it opened inward, just could not be opened

6. Martha Bruere, "What Is to Be Done?" *Life and Labor* (May 1911), http://www.ilr.cornell.edu/trianglefire/primary/testimonials/ootss_MarthaBensleyBruere.html.

7. Richard A. Greenwald, *The Triangle Fire, the Protocols of Peace, and Industrial Democracy in Progressive New York* (Philadelphia: Temple University Press, 2005), 141.

because frantic workers pressed up against it. Kate Alterman, a key prosecution witness, testified in vivid terms, with tears streaming down her face,
that Margaret Schwartz tried to open the door but could not. "I pushed
her aside. I tried to open the door—and I couldn't. . . . And then a big
smoke came and Margaret Schwartz I saw bending down on her knees. . . .
And she screamed at the top of her voice *Open the door! Fire! I am lost!
There is fire!*" Alterman described a "red curtain of fire" that engulfed her
coworker and recounted her own harrowing dash out another exit. Whitman's case seemed persuasive.[8]

Harris and Blanck had hired Max D. Steuer, one of the city's most
prominent and politically well-connected defense attorneys. He was well
known for his work in defending—and getting acquittals for—Tammany
Hall politicians accused of bribery and other crimes. The capable and
crafty defense attorney set out to prove that the owners, though they were
in the factory that day and escaped, could not have known if the door was
locked. He recalled Kate Alterman to the stand, asked her to describe what
she saw that day, and when she repeated her earlier testimony almost word-
for-word, he accused her of cooking it up with the DA's staff and memo-
rizing it. Steuer brought in employees who assured the jury that the doors
were usually unlocked and salesmen who said they saw them open during
visits. The real problem was hysterical employees jamming up against the
door, making it impossible to open, said Steuer. The fire "was the kind
that creates panic, deprives people of their reason and makes them insane,"
he said in his summary. "You ask these girls, pursued by these flames at
that time to use reason. It is impossible. The panic drove them. The panic
kept them at the door; the panic prevented it being opened." The DA's
staff had coached some of the witnesses and others exaggerated or recited
rehearsed fabrications, he insisted. The judge, a Democrat affiliated with
Tammany Hall, instructed the jury that they could convict only if there
was no reasonable doubt that the door was locked *and* the owners knew
it. Steuer had introduced enough doubt to make meeting those two goals
impossible. The jury acquitted the defendants.[9]

---

8. "Opening Statement by Mr. Bostwick for the People (prosecution), Outlining Theory of
the Case," *People of the State of New York v. Isaac Harris and Max Blanck*, Volume 1,
Section 1, 10, http://digitalcommons.ilr.cornell.edu/cgi/viewcontent.cgi?article=1000&c
ontext=triangletrans; Von Drehle, *Triangle*, 239–244.

9. "Summation by Attorney for Defendants (Mr. Steuer)," *People of the State of New York
v. Isaac Harris and Max Blanck*, Volume 4, 2080, 2240, http://digitalcommons.ilr.cornell.
edu/triangletrans/14; Von Drehle, *Triangle*, 245–258.

"The monstrous conclusion of the law is that the slaughter was no one's fault," said a popular magazine, *Literary Digest.* "There are no guilty. There are only the dead." An editorial in the journal *Outlook* noted that "morally, at least, the people of New York are convinced that these men . . . were guilty of carrying on their work (whether through greed or indifference) in such a way that their employees' lives were in constant danger." The DA reindicted Harris and Blanck, Counsel Steuer argued double jeopardy, and the jury voted them innocent. Three years later, the owners settled twenty-three civil suits against them by the victims' families for $75 each.[10]

The courts may have failed to deliver justice, but city and state government were pushed into action. Mayor William Gaynor, a Democrat elected in 1909 with Tammany support but increasingly independent since then, quickly pushed new regulations though the city council. New York City made sprinklers mandatory in factory buildings, tightened its fire code, and created a Bureau of Fire Prevention that immediately began a campaign of fire inspections. But everyone knew that enforcement would depend on who controlled city government and that vigilance might be relaxed as time went by. Besides, there were fire risks in factories throughout the state. Action was needed in Albany. Frances Perkins, director of the New York Consumers League, an organization that lobbied for better working conditions, happened to be visiting a friend near the scene of the fire. Rushing to the sidewalk near the building, she was appalled to see people jumping to their deaths. The needless, tragic deaths of so many young people demanded action. She later recalled, "I can't begin to tell you how disturbed the people were everywhere. It was as though we had all done something wrong."[11] Collective anguish, guilt, and deep-seated realization that the nation's leading state had an obligation to protect its workers from senseless death by fire led to action. A few days after the fire, a group of social reformers like Perkins, labor activists, and many of New York's leading citizens got together and established a "Committee on Safety." It was a broad coalition that transcended class boundaries, representing a spectrum of New Yorkers ranging from workers to the

10. "147 Dead, Nobody Guilty," *Literary Digest* (January 6, 1912), http://www.ilr.cornell.edu/trianglefire/primary/newspapersmagazines/ld_010612.html; "The Acquittal in the Triangle Case," *Outlook* (January 6, 1912), 100; Greenwald, *The Triangle Fire*, 150–153.
11. Frances Perkins lecture, September 30, 1964, Cornell University, http://www.ilr.cornell.edu/trianglefire/primary/lectures/FrancesPerkinsLecture.html?CFID=20799021&CFTOKEN=97224350&jsessionid=84306023694f8301d3cd3b5f364d60443b1b.

social elite. A delegation including Perkins took the train to Albany early in April to demand action.

Democrats had swept into office in 1910 after scandals tarnished Republicans who had been in charge for many years. That meant that Tammany Hall effectively controlled the legislature. The new governor, John A. Dix, vacillated between independence and subservience to Tammany boss Charles Murphy. Murphy, in charge of Tammany since 1902, was a big, taciturn man who had built political support by doling out favors while leaning against a lamppost in front of his saloon, Charlie's Place, on Second Avenue. The "Quiet Boss" seldom spoke in public and was a master at making political deals in smoke-filled rooms. He was devoted to traditional grassroots politics of patronage, pro-business in part because of the campaign contributions that businessmen made to his party, and averse to meddling by social reformers.

Charles Murphy, however, was also attuned to popular sentiment and opportunistic. His New York City base was shifting from traditional Irish immigrants to a more diverse mix, including immigrant Italians and Eastern European Jews who demanded that government protect workers. The strikes of the past few years demonstrated the growing strength and demands of organized labor. Maverick Democrat William Randolph Hearst, publisher of the sensationalistic *New York Journal*, had run for mayor in 1905 and governor in 1906, alternately feuding with Tammany and courting its support. Murphy distrusted him but recognized that his attacks on business and his radical agenda had a growing following. Republican reform governors Theodore Roosevelt and Charles Evans Hughes had demonstrated the popularity of social and economic reform and the potential of progressive Republicans to lure away Democratic voters.

In January 1911, Murphy bypassed senior party legislators to select Robert F. Wagner as president pro tem of the senate and Alfred E. Smith as majority leader, the number two post in the assembly. Wagner, a skilled New York City attorney and impressive speaker, had worked hard for Tammany-endorsed candidates but recognized the rising public demand for social justice. Smith, also from New York City, pragmatic and gregarious, was known for his attention to detail and legislative procedures. He studied every bill and was said to be one of the few legislators in Albany who actually read the massive annual appropriations bill.[12] Reporters

12. Robert F. Wesser, *A Response to Progressivism: The Democratic Party and New York Politics, 1902–1908* (New York: New York University Press, 1986), 43–67.

smiled when, in response to a question about Murphy's behind-the-scenes power at the Capitol, Senator Wagner replied: "Adhering closely to his long-established policy, Mr. Murphy has not attempted to influence the legislature in any way."[13] But that quiet but potent influence was gradually swinging behind reform, and Smith and Wagner were about to become reform leaders.

The Committee on Safety first tried Governor Dix, who disclaimed any authority to act and sent them upstairs to the legislature. Wagner was interested in taking action; Smith, positively eager to act. Some of the Triangle victims lived in his district. He had accompanied family members to the morgue to identify bodies and visited their homes afterward. Don't bother trying to get a blue-ribbon commission appointed by the governor, Smith advised Perkins and her allies. The legislature would not pay attention to it. The Committee on Safety agreed. Working with Wagner, Smith quickly drafted a bill to create a "Factory Investigating Commission" with unprecedented sweeping powers to investigate factory working conditions, safety, hours of labor, and issues related to employment of women and children. Wagner appointed himself chair with Smith as vice chair. The other members were all influential and well connected, including Samuel Gompers, president of the American Federation of Labor. Frances Perkins and Pauline Newman, an organizer for the International Ladies Garment Workers Union (ILGWU) and former Triangle employee, were appointed as advisers and investigators.[14]

Smith and Wagner devoted a good deal of time to commission work, and Perkins and Newman engaged experts, lined up witnesses, arranged inspection visits, and kept pushing commission members to take an expansive view of this unprecedented opportunity. The commission held an average of one public hearing per week from July to December 1911, calling two hundred witnesses. The press closely followed their work, reporting on the risky working conditions documented in the testimony. By the end of the year, Smith and Wagner had drafted fifteen new laws covering fire safety, factory inspection, restrictions on women and child labor, and other areas. The commission's initial report, published early in 1912, was practically a manifesto for state intervention and protection of workers.

13. J. Joseph Huthmacher, *Senator Robert F. Wagner and the Rise of Urban Liberalism* (New York: Atheneum, 1968), 24.
14. Alfred E. Smith, *Up to Now: An Autobiography* (Garden City: Garden City, 1929), 91–95; George Martin, *Madam Secretary: Frances Perkins* (New York: Houghton Mifflin, 1976), 76–90; Orleck, *Common Sense and a Little Fire*, 131–132.

"A great awakening has taken place throughout the state," said the report. "The state is bound to do everything in its power to preserve the health of the workers who contribute so materially to its economic wealth and its industrial prosperity. Aside from the humanitarian aspect of the situation, economic considerations demand from the state the careful supervision and protection of its workers."[15]

Endorsed by Smith and Wagner, most of the proposed bills sailed through the legislature. The commission had originally been authorized for only a year, but the legislative leaders extended it. The investigatory pace in 1912 was even greater, with multiple visits by the commissioners to document working conditions. Perkins noted that at one factory Senator Wagner "personally crawled through the tiny hole in the wall that gave exit to a step ladder covered with ice and ending twelve feet from the ground, which was euphemistically labeled 'Fire Escape.'" In another factory, "[W]e made sure they saw the machinery that would scalp a girl or cut off a man's arm." They visited a Buffalo candy factory where chocolate boiled over into open gas flames and a single narrow stairway served as the only escape route from the upper floors of the wooden building. On the steps leading down from the third floor was a jumble of mops, pails, and brooms. "Ah," murmured Wagner, in the new terminology he was assimilating. "An 'obstructed exit.'"[16]

The commission's work continued through 1914. It issued thirteen volumes of reports, including long transcripts from public hearings documenting working conditions and special reports on fire safety, building construction, heating, lighting, ventilation, machine safety, and other topics. It cultivated the support of New York's growing unions, which, in turn, cited commission reports to buttress their demands for better conditions and higher wages. It worked closely with progressive organizations such as the Consumers League, the New York Child Labor Committee, and the New York section of the American Association for Labor Legislation. It cited with praise in its reports employers who operated factories that were exemplary models of safety and sanitation. It cooperated with the insurance industry, which stepped up efforts to have policyholders focus on fire prevention and workplace safety. The terrible fire led to other developments that dovetailed with the commission's work, for example,

---

15. New York Factory Investigating Commission, *Preliminary Report of the Factory Investigating Commission, 1912*, 3 vols. (Albany: Argus, 1912), I, 13–20.
16. Frances Perkins, *The Roosevelt I Knew* (New York: Viking Press, 1946), 22; Martin, *Frances Perkins*, 103–107.

support for organized labor, especially the ILGWU, whose recruitment efforts accelerated after the Triangle fire.

With growing public support, under the continuing direction of Smith and Wagner, the legislature passed laws requiring fire alarms and sprinklers, improved building access and egress, fireproofing requirements, better lighting and ventilation, and reorganizing and expanding the State Labor Department to oversee implementation. The legislature also created the Workmen's Compensation Fund in 1914 to insure employees against on-the-job occupational injury and disease.

Sometimes, proposals encountered rough political waters. Frances Perkins and the Consumers League pushed a bill in 1912 to restrict working hours for women in factories to fifty-four hours per week. Canning companies, substantial contributors to Democratic candidates, claimed that it would mean vegetables and fruits would spoil before they could be processed. Charles Murphy was not supportive. Undaunted, Perkins went to another influential Tammany legislator, Senator "Big Tim" Sullivan. He represented the Bowery area of Manhattan and was a self-declared champion of working people. He usually followed Murphy's lead but occasionally exhibited a streak of stubborn independence. "Me sister was a poor girl," he told Perkins, "and she went to work when she was young. I kinda feel sorry for them poor girls that work the way you say they work. I'd like to do them a good turn. I'd like to do you a good turn. You don't know much about this parliamentary stuff, do you?" Perkins admitted she had some things to learn. Sullivan convinced her to accept a compromise bill with the canneries excluded, which passed. The Democratic leadership took credit for it. "That bill made us many votes," Murphy admitted to Perkins years later. The next year, 1913, the legislature considered a bill to limit cannery hours to a ten-hour day and a six-day week and exclude children under fourteen. The canners, predictably, opposed. This time Al Smith, who had moved up from majority leader to Speaker, weighed in with his shortest speech: "I have read carefully the commandment 'Remember the Sabbath Day, to keep it holy.' But I am unable to find in it any language that says 'except in the canneries.'" The bill passed.[17]

Democrats triumphed in the 1912 elections, but then their political fortunes waned. Dix's successor as governor, the impetuous and arrogant

---

17. Perkins, *The Roosevelt I Knew*, 12–14; Martin, *Frances Perkins*, 91–113; Richard F. Welch, *King of the Bowery: Big Tim Sullivan, Tammany Hall, and New York City from the Gilded Age to the Progressive Era* (Albany: State University of New York Press, 2009), 157–162; Smith, *Up to Now*, 96.

William Sulzer, was impeached and removed from office in 1913 for violation of campaign finance laws. His successor, the bland lieutenant governor Martin Glynn, a former newspaper editor, tried to revive the party's progressive image, including supporting a direct primary bill, something reformers had endorsed for years, but the Democrats' political infighting had worn out the public's patience. Republicans triumphed in the 1914 elections, and Charles Whitman was elected governor. He had featured his indictment of the Triangle owners prominently in his campaign.

Conservative business leaders had already begun a drumbeat for repeal of some of the new factory regulations, which they called burdensome and expensive. "You can no longer distinguish the real estate owner by the smile of prosperity," complained the counsel of the Real Estate Board of New York, "because his property is now a burden and a liability instead of a comfort and source of income. To own a factory building in New York is now a calamity."[18] The Republican-dominated legislature began passing repeal measures in 1915. Whitman had promised "competency, efficiency, and economy" in his inaugural address and was no friend of overreaching government regulation. But he had concluded reluctantly that industrial reform was an idea whose time had come. New York's new industrial code was safe. A bill to give the Labor Department power to suspend enforcement of any provision of the labor law deemed to be an "unnecessary hardship" was vetoed because it would "repeal, temporarily at least, the provisions of a legislative statute." A bill to exempt salt refineries from a requirement for a six-day workweek was disapproved as "another instance of a specific industry seeking exemption, and if the measure should be approved, then other exemptions will be sought by other industries."[19]

Opponents also went to court. The courts of the era often overturned industrial regulations on the grounds that they violated workers' rights to contract as they pleased, a right protected by the Fourteenth Amendment to the U.S. Constitution. In 1907, for instance, the court of appeals had struck down a state law forbidding night work for women. The legislature enacted a new version of the law based on the recommendation of the Factory Investigating Commission. Businesses challenged it in court. The court of appeals upheld it in 1915. The court noted that little evidence had

---

18. Huthmacher, *Senator Robert F. Wagner*, 9.
19. *Public Papers of Charles Seymour Whitman, Governor*, 1915 (Albany: J. B. Lyon, 1916), 10, 100, 115.

been presented in 1907 about why the law was needed. This time, though, the state had presented extensive data and reports from the commission. "[T]he present legislation is based upon and sustained by an investigation by the legislature deliberately and carefully made through an agency of its own creation, the present factory investigating commission," the court noted. It was impressed by "investigation of actual conditions and the study of scientific and medical opinion that night work by women in factories is generally injurious, and ought to be prohibited."[20] Evidence from commission investigations helped sustain other factory regulating laws in state and federal courts. State protection of workers, the enduring legacy of the Triangle tragedy, would stay, embedded in statute and ratified by the courts.

Thursday, March 29: Tragedy in Albany

Four days after the Triangle fire, an early-morning blaze in the New York State Capitol building had a lesser, but still important, impact on state history. The fire broke out on the third floor in an assembly meeting room near the State Library, which was then located in the Capitol. That building, completed in 1899 after nearly three decades of intermittent construction work, changes in design, and massive cost overruns and contract scandals was, like the Asch building, regarded as "fireproof." The massive stone structure would not burn, but it housed the legislature and most state offices that had a good deal of files other flammable material. The library was jammed with books and historical records.

The legislature was deadlocked that spring over election of a U.S. senator to succeed Republican Chauncey M. Depew, whose term expired later in 1911. In those days, before the Seventeenth Amendment to the Constitution, legislatures elected senators. Democrats were wrangling over a choice. They had been caucusing until 1:00 a.m. in the room where the fire started, leading to speculation that a cigarette or cigar, not fully extinguished, had started the fire. The Albany Fire Department arrived quickly on the scene after receiving the alarm and poured on water from seven different lines. They extinguished the fire, but not before it had

---

20. *People v. Charles Schweinler Press*, 214 NY 395; Louis D. Brandeis, "The Living Law," speech, January 3, 1916, http://www.law.louisville.edu/library/collections/brandeis/node/223.

destroyed most of the contents of the State Library—some 450,000 books and 270,000 manuscripts—and water had soaked much of what survived. A night watchman, Samuel Abbott, perished in the flames. The assembly chamber was "a watery wreck . . . the center of the well-shaped room was a good-sized pond." Librarians entering the burned-out library stack area reported that "the sight was appalling . . . nothing but an empty shell with four feet of smoldering debris on the floor. Fires were starting up in various places, a stream of water played on the ruins, and water poured down from the floor above." Burned scraps of historical documents were blown by the March winds as far away as East Greenbush across the Hudson River. A librarian familiar with the historical records exclaimed that "the very basis of early history of the state has been wiped out."[21] The governor's office was unharmed, but several other state offices and the legislative chambers, particularly the assembly, were badly damaged. Albany mayor James B. McEwan invited the beleaguered legislature to meet in Albany City Hall while restoration work was carried out.

Consequences

The fire had three major impacts. First, it highlighted the weak leadership of Governor Dix. He had campaigned on a platform of fiscal austerity, but the $4 million needed to clean up and restore the Capitol upset his budget plans. He backed off a promise to investigate the fire after the State Architect, who was responsible for the building, reported that faulty wiring was the probable culprit, without citing any solid evidence. Dix realized that a thorough investigation might have highlighted careless smoking by assembly Democrats, a potential embarrassment. The governor made a point of ordering new electrical wiring for the entire building but did not ban smoking. Newspapers exposed the fact that much of the lumber for the restoration work was purchased on a noncompetitive bid basis from a firm partially owned by Dix's former business partner. As noted earlier, he sidestepped responsibility for action after the Triangle fire. His waffling on the U.S. Senate seat impasse, described later, earned him a citation for "distinguished gallantry on both sides of the fight" during the

---

21. Paul Mercer and Vicki Weiss, *The New York State Capitol and the Great Fire of 1911* (Charleston SC: Arcadia, 2011), 1–90; Cecil R. Roseberry, *Capitol Story* (Albany: State of New York, 1964), 119–123; "Old Papers Escaped Flames in Capitol Fire," *New York Times*, March 31, 1911.

annual lampoon of politicians at the Legislative Correspondents' Association dinner in April 1911.[22] He sent a direct primary bill to the legislature but seemed indifferent as Smith and Wagner, not yet ready for something so unsettling, conducted it to a quiet death in committee. The pattern of weakness and evasion continued, and he was not renominated in 1912. As noted previously, his successor, William Sulzer, proved to be the Democrats' undoing.

A second impact was on the selection of a new U.S. senator. Charles Murphy, like other citizens of New York, wanted his state well represented in the Senate, but he was also keenly aware of a senator's influence over federal patronage and contracts. His choice was William F. Sheehan, a former lieutenant governor and speaker of the assembly. Sheehan was honest and capable but also firmly aligned with Tammany Hall. Democrats in the legislature, led by Smith and Wagner, were expected to comply with Murphy's choice. But the same reformist spirit that was pushing the legislature toward reform after the Triangle fire also broke through in the choice of a senator. A minority of Democrats wanted someone more independent than Sheehan. An unlikely leader emerged: freshman senator Franklin D. Roosevelt from Dutchess County. FDR, distant cousin of the famous and popular New York Republican Theodore Roosevelt, had just been elected after a spirited campaign in a district that had not sent a Democrat to Albany since the Civil War. A new state senator, a newsman wrote, was usually "of an importance somewhere between that of a janitor and a committee clerk." But FDR was confident and assertive. "You know," he later told Frances Perkins, "I was an awfully mean cuss when I first went into politics." Roosevelt rocketed to celebrity status as he took charge of the insurgents who dug in against Sheehan. Without the insurgents' votes, Sheehan could not be elected. Accused of opposing Sheehan because he was Catholic and Irish, FDR responded, "This is absolutely untrue! All we ask is that he be a fit man for United States Senator." The insurgents stuck together. The impasse continued. The deadlock lasted for seventy-three days and sixty-two ballots, with over three dozen names being floated.[23]

The Democratic caucus meeting the night before the fire, which FDR and his allies had boycotted, had wrestled with the issue once again. Cynics

22. "Gov. Dix Lampooned at Albany Dinner," *New York Times*, April 28, 1911.
23. Geoffrey C. Ward, *A First-Class Temperament: The Emergence of Franklin Roosevelt* (New York: Harper & Row, 1989), 124–149.

joked that the Democrats, unable to elect a senator or steal the Capitol, had tried to burn it down. Patience vanished as the legislature reconvened in cramped quarters at City Hall. The fire had forced them out of the Capitol and, indirectly, pushed them toward a compromise that would end the impasse. Moreover, there was pressing work to be done, including dealing with the aftermath of the Triangle fire and appropriating money to rebuild the Capitol. Murphy, counseled by Wagner and Smith that Sheehan could not be elected, convinced him to withdraw. Murphy then quietly substituted the name of New York City judge James A. O'Gorman. He had been one of the Tammany "Sachems," the group of insiders that ran the organization under Murphy's direction. But as a judge he had displayed a degree of independence from the political machine while on the bench. Roosevelt and his band of insurgents, worn down and condemned for needlessly prolonging the legislative session, gave in. The legislature quickly elected O'Gorman. The insurgents had "won" in the sense that Murphy's initial public choice had been defeated. FDR and his allies could claim that the process showed that their party was more independent and responsive to the public will. O'Gorman proved to be a lackluster senator and served only one term. The whole episode helped swing New York's support behind the Seventeenth Amendment to the Constitution, providing for direct election of senators, which was approved and took effect in 1913.[24]

The Capitol fire had helped sidetrack a governor, elect a senator, and resolve a legislative impasse that had been led by a future governor and president. It also resulted in a confrontation between the state historian and the commissioner of education and enactment of new archival policies. The post of state historian had been created in 1895 to "collect, collate, edit, and prepare for publication" official records pertaining to New York's participation in past wars and its relation with other states and the federal government. The first state historian, Hugh Hastings, resigned in 1907. Governor Charles Evans Hughes, on the recommendation of several academics, appointed as his successor Victor Hugo Paltsits, a librarian and recognized expert in American colonial history. Utterly self-assured, impatient with Albany politics, he soon exhibited traits of an uncompromising crusader on a sacred quest. His painstaking editorial work was

---

24. "Review of the Contest," *New-York Tribune*, April 26, 1911; Wesser, *A Response to Progressivism*, 43–52; Ward, *A First-Class Temperament*, 149–154.

meticulous, but this slowed the output of publications. That earned him criticism from legislators who liked to show their love of state history by sending state historical volumes to their constituents. He was also ambitious and drafted a bill to expand his office to become "state records commissioner" with authority to inspect records in state and local government offices. Hughes refused to endorse it and it died in committee in 1908.[25]

An 1892 statute authorized state agencies to transfer "books, papers, maps [and] manuscripts" with historical value to the State Library. Under this vague, permissive statute, the library had accepted official government records, mostly dating from the colonial and early statehood periods. When the State Education Department was created in 1904, the library was made part of it. The first commissioner, Andrew S. Draper, expressed alarm over the overcrowding and fire risk and transferred a few of the most precious documents, including the original state constitution and a draft of Lincoln's Emancipation Proclamation that the state had purchased years earlier, to a safe in his own office.

In 1909, Paltsits's Republican friends introduced another bill to expand the office. This time, it encountered the opposition of Commissioner Draper, who had developed a bill of his own to move the state historian's office into the Education Department. That department already included the library, which held many of the records that the state historian was publishing, and the state museum. It chartered local historical societies and supervised teaching of history and social studies in the schools. Draper also believed that the historian's office should publicize New York's historical achievements to inspire a sense of pride and accomplishment in the state's young people. Draper invited Paltsits to his office and got right to the point: "I think it would be better to put your office under the State Education Department. You could do there all you need to do, and get all the money you need, without the present difficulties of obtaining appropriations every year." Paltsits angrily declined, writing Governor Hughes, "I would never agree to being an employee of the State Education Department." Draper's bill was defeated.[26]

---

25. Bruce W. Dearstyne, "Archival Politics in New York State: 1892–1915, *New York History* 66 (April 1985), 165–173. This article is the source for the discussion in this paragraph and the next four paragraphs.
26. Victor H. Paltsits, "The Executive Relation of New York State to Historical Scholarship," *Proceedings of the New York State Historical Association* IX (Albany, 1910), 223, quoted in Dearstyne, "Archival Politics in New York State, 1892–1915," 176.

After the Capitol fire, Paltsits called in newsmen to suggest that the Education Department had been negligent in not protecting the records in the State Library. A few days later, walking near the Capitol, Paltsits noticed two partially burned manuscripts among the debris. The singed documents had a strange irony: They were a 1760 request from the governor of Massachusetts for assistance for sufferers from a recent Boston fire and New York governor James DeLancey's reply. Paltsits took them to the press with the claim that he had rescued them "virtually from the gutter" and that other historical documents were "blowing about the streets" due to the careless indifference of the library salvage team. The accusation was particularly unfair to library staff, who had been working day and night to save what they could from the fire- and water-damaged records. Even Paltsits's friends were appalled by his unfair accusations and shabby tactics.[27]

Draper appealed to Al Smith to sponsor his consolidation bill, and Smith, who saw the connection between history and education, agreed. Paltsits, sidelined by his own reckless tactics, protested in vain and then resigned. The legislature quickly enacted Smith's proposal. It moved the state historian's office to the Education Department, created a Division of Public Records with power to inspect local government records, forbade disposition of local government records without the consent of the commissioner of education, and provided that local governments could transfer archival records to the State Library for safekeeping. The law was expanded in 1913 to cover disposition of state government records but it gave the commissioner of education limited enforcement authority in that area. The state library resumed its collection of historical records and protected them in a fire-resistant facility in the new State Education Building, which opened in 1912. New York did not establish a formal state archives program until 1971.[28]

Fires and Political Transformation

The fires of 1911 had a broad and lasting impact. The destruction of historical records in the State Library undermined the study of New York's

27. "May Save One Third of Library Records," *New-York Tribune* April 4, 1911, quoted in Dearstyne, "Archival Politics in New York State, 1892–1915," 180.
28. Dearstyne, "Archival Politics in New York State, 1892–1915," 181–184.

colonial and early statehood years. The fire gave both Charles Murphy and Franklin Roosevelt a way out of their intraparty confrontation. To Murphy it was further evidence that the era of "boss rule" was over, and he began shifting toward more of a consensus-making style. To FDR it was evidence that a determined, reform-minded minority could serve as a catalyst in changing his party, but that confrontation had its limits and that conciliation, negotiation, and compromise were essential to get things done. He applied these lessons later as governor and president. Al Smith's work on labor legislation and the Factory Investigating Commission helped him prepare for tenure as one of New York's most successful governors in the 1920s. He learned to blend idealism, dedication to the public good, pragmatism, and politics. As governor, he streamlined state government, instituted the modern budget system, and enacted pioneering housing, health care, and parks legislation. Robert F. Wagner went on to become one of New York's most distinguished U.S. senators. He was the sponsor of the National Labor Relations Act, also known as the Wagner Act, which guaranteed the right of labor to organize and bargain collectively. He was a principal author of the Social Security Act and architect of other key New Deal policies. Wagner's service on the commission, his biographer noted, helped develop his reformist leanings and "made him, and the political organization he represented, essential links in the chain of reform that spanned the Progressive Era and marked the emergence of modern, urban liberalism on the American scene."[29]

In May 1913, Frances Perkins gave the keynote address at the National Fire Protection Association's annual meeting in New York City. The association, established in 1896, was an advocate of sprinklers and fireproof construction. Perkins described the Triangle fire's lasting impact on its victims and proudly described New York's new industrial regulations. She called on the conference participants to go home and initiate similar efforts. Perkins's stirring message received a standing ovation, and her speech helped broaden the association's focus to include more public education and business' accountability for human life. A month after her speech, the association's leaders formulated a broad fire safety code that was embraced nationally. It was a good example of New York's leadership and role as a model for the rest of the nation. In her memoirs, Perkins recalled: "The extent to which this legislation in New York marked a

---

29. Huthmacher, *Senator Robert F. Wagner*, 10–11.

change in American political attitudes and polices toward social responsibility can scarcely be overrated."[30]

Perkins herself was perhaps the best example of the spirit of New York and the change in attitudes and policies in the two decades after the fire. In 1933, she became the first woman to serve in the cabinet when Franklin Roosevelt appointed her secretary of labor. She oversaw New Deal relief and employment agencies, helped implement Social Security, crafted federal laws against child labor, formulated the first minimum wage and overtime laws, and defined the standard forty-hour workweek. Her career and achievements are one more example of how fires can change the course of history.

---

30. Kirsten Downey, *The Woman behind the New Deal: The Life of Frances Perkins, FDR's Secretary of Labor and His Moral Conscience* (New York: Doubleday, 2009), 51; Casey Cavanaugh Grant, "Triangle Fire Stirs Outrage and Reform," *NFPA Journal* (May/June 1993), 73–82, http://www.nfpa.org/assets/files/PDF/Research/triangle.pdf; Frances Perkins lecture, September 30, 1964, Cornell University, http://www.ilr.cornell.edu/trianglefire/primary/lectures/FrancesPerkinsLecture.html?CFID=20799021&CFTOKEN=97224350&jsessionid=84306023694f8301d3cd3b5f364d60443b1b; Perkins, *The Roosevelt I Knew*, 23.

10
February 14, 1924

Leading into the Information Age

Thomas J. Watson Sr., shown in the photo shortly after being appointed general manager of Computing-Tabulating-Recording Company in 1914, became president of the company the next year and changed the company's name to International Business Machines in 1924. During the next three decades, Watson built IBM into one of the nation's leading corporations. *Photo courtesy of IBM Corporate Archives.*

A New York Company with High Aspirations

New York State has always been a leader in invention, development, and application of technology. For instance, Robert Fulton developed the commercially successful steamboat in the early nineteenth century. Eastern New York, particularly the Albany-Saratoga region, has often been referred to as "tech valley" in the early twenty-first century because of its leadership in cutting-edge nanotechnology. But in the early twentieth century, the modest village of Endicott near Binghamton could claim to be the location of the leading edge of transformational technology. It was the main office of the Computing-Tabulating-Recording (CTR) Company, a hybrid enterprise that made calculating and timekeeping machines and commercial scales. On February 14, 1924, the company shed its awkward and overly long name and announced that it had become

International Business Machines (IBM). It was "a very euphonious and suitable name," the company's dynamic president, Thomas J. Watson, told the press. The new company had a grand vision for leadership in data and information processing. "Our machines are aids to business big and little, ranging from the accounting departments of railroads to the ordinary transactions of retail stores," said the announcement. "Everywhere, there will be IBM machines in use. The sun never sets on IBM."[1] Watson would make good on that prediction through his dynamic leadership of the company for another three decades. IBM became one of the most innovative and successful companies in history, leading and shaping the fields of data processing and information management, serving as a model for customer service, and pioneering in enlightened employee practices.

Machines to Control Enterprise Information

IBM capitalized on a critical, long-standing management need: In order to control and manage a large company or other enterprise, you have to control and manage the *data* and *information* on production, employees, and customers. "Control of any purposive system can be no better than its most generalized and distributed processor of information. . . . its ability to process information," notes historian of technology James Beniger.[2] As railroads, factories, banks, and insurance companies had expanded in the late nineteenth century, the traditional means of control through oral communication and handwritten ledgers and other documents could not keep pace. New forms of organization (bureaucracy, standardized processes, assembly lines) and new technologies (telegraph, telephone, typewriters, adding machines, vertical filing systems) helped managers cope. But more expansive and robust systems for creating, recording, storing, processing, and manipulating information were needed for the increasingly complex commercial enterprises and government programs that were making their debut in the closing years of the nineteenth century.

Herman Hollerith (1860–1929), born in Buffalo to German immigrant parents and educated as an engineer at Columbia University, invented the equipment in the 1880s that first provided this capacity: mechanical card punch, automatic card-feed mechanism, and electromechanical tabulator.

1. Martin Campbell-Kelly and William Aspray, *Computer: A History of the Information Machine* (New York: Basic Books, 2004), 24.
2. James R. Beniger, *The Control Revolution: Technological and Economic Origins of the Information Society* (Boston: Harvard University Press, 1986), 390–393.

Hollerith opened a factory in New York City, leased his equipment to the federal government for use in the 1890 and 1900 censuses, and formed the Tabulating Machine Company to reach commercial customers. Soon, the New York Central Railroad, General Electric, Eastman Kodak, and dozens of other companies were using Hollerith machines, and several foreign governments adopted them for census work. By the turn of the century, they were indispensable in many large enterprises. A Hollerith sales manual from approximately 1910 described the system succinctly:

> Data appearing on order blanks, bills, time cards, or forms of any kind, are transferred by means of punching machines to cards. These cards are then sorted by automatic electronic sorting machines into the desired classifications, and are then passed through the electronic tabulating machine, which automatically adds the amounts or value of these classes upon one or more counters.[3]

But Hollerith the brilliant inventor did not translate into Hollerith the astute manager. He declined to hire salesmen, asserting that "if the machines are any good, they will sell themselves." He fretted over small details, lost his temper too easily, and was too detached and hesitant when problems arose. He promised to deliver machines faster than his factory could make them, then frantically searched for new suppliers and chased down spare parts to meet deadlines. The new director of the 1910 census thought Hollerith had charged too much in 1890 and 1900 and set to work to develop his own equipment. As the Census Bureau's historic account on its website delicately puts it, "[B]arely skirting patent restrictions, Census Bureau employees were able to create their own tabulating machines, more advanced than Hollerith's, in time for the 1910 census." Hollerith sued the bureau for violating his patents but lost. The patent fight was exhausting, the company's management challenges overwhelming, and years of overindulging in cigars, wine, and rich food had taken a physical toll. By 1911, depressed and discouraged, Hollerith was ready to sell the company.[4]

---

3. James W. Cortada, *Before the Computer: IBM, NCR, Burroughs, Remington Rand, and the Industry They Created, 1865–1956* (Princeton: Princeton University Press, 1993), 46.

4. U.S. Census Bureau, "Herman Hollerith," http://www.census.gov/history/www/census_then_now/notable_alumni/herman_hollerith.html; Geoffrey D. Austrian, *Herman Hollerith: Forgotten Giant of Information Processing* (New York: Columbia University Press, 1982), 241.

An extraordinary New York City adventurer, businessman, and international trader, Charles R. Flint (1850–1934) put together a deal in 1911 to combine Hollerith's company with two other "high-tech" firms: the Computing Scale Company of America, based in Dayton, and the International Time Recording Company of Endicott, New York. The scale company made scales that weighed produce and toted up prices; the recording company was a pioneer in machines to keep track of employee working hours. The new entity, actually a holding company for control and direction of all three, was named the Computing-Tabulating-Recording Company (CTR). Flint had made a fortune in negotiating international trade deals and furnishing arms and munitions to South American governments and to rebel groups. A fan of mechanical technologies, Flint as early as 1902 could be seen tearing through New York City streets and Long Island roads in his Locomobile. He helped found the Auto Club of America and sold airplanes for the Wright Brothers in Europe. Flint was also outstanding at assembling large industrial organizations, including the U.S. Rubber Company and the American Chicle Company (dubbed "the Chewing Gum Trust" by the press). "A combination of labor is a trades union, a combination of intelligence is a university, a combination of money a bank, and a combination of labor, intelligence and money is an industrial combination—Work, Brains, and Money," he declared in 1900.[5] But the new CTR enterprise staggered from the outset with too much debt and limited integration of its three constituent divisions. Flint needed an effective leader to take charge of his foundering creation.

Flint knew just the man he wanted: Thomas J. Watson (1874–1956), until recently the well-known sales manager for National Cash Register Company in Dayton. Watson had been born and raised near Painted Post, New York, and educated at a one-room schoolhouse and then the Miller School of Commerce in Elmira. He moved to Buffalo and took a job selling sewing machines door to door from the back of a wagon. He developed a lifelong aversion to alcohol after his horse, wagon, and goods were stolen while he was in a tavern one day drinking to celebrate a sale. He then worked for a man selling bank stock that turned out to be worthless and was left penniless when the man skipped town. Watson had bought a cash register for another venture he hoped to pursue, a butcher shop.

---

5. Charles Ranlett Flint, *Memories of an Active Life: Men, and Ships, and Sealing Wax* (New York: G.P. Putnam's Sons, 1923), 286.

Broke, he had to return the machine to the Buffalo office of the National Cash Register (NCR) Company, but he talked himself into a sales job for the company. He learned the art of persuasive salesmanship and closing the deal. One day, he told his boss that he had "some good business in sight." "Don't come and talk to me about business in sight!" the supervisor said. "You bring in the orders so I can see the signature. That is what I want."[6]

Watson settled down and excelled. Soon he was appointed to manage the Rochester office, where he set sales records. His next stop was a promotion to a supervisor's job at the company's Dayton headquarters and soon promotion to national director of sales. There, he learned from NCR's eccentric but effective president, John Patterson, who built a sales school for his salesmen, developed a sales manual and script for them to follow, and established incentives for sales associates who met their quotas. But Patterson was a ruthless competitor and an unpredictable boss, feared for his tirades berating salesmen who fell short of expectations. In 1912, NCR was found guilty of violating the federal Sherman Antitrust Act through its anticompetitive sales practices. Patterson, Watson, and several other NCR executives were convicted and sentenced to a year in prison. The conviction was overturned on a technicality. A few days later, the always unpredictable Patterson fired Watson, whose success and popularity among the sales force Patterson was beginning to see as a threat to his own leadership. But in a final odd twist, Patterson gave Watson a $50,000 severance bonus.[7]

Being fired by the eccentric Patterson was no deterrent to new employment. Watson traveled to New York City, where his organizational and sales prowess was well known, to seek work. Flint sent for Watson and was impressed by his organizational instincts and inclination toward aggressive salesmanship. "I want a gentleman's salary and part of the profits when I am able to make the company a success," he told Flint and the CTR board. He was hired as general manager in 1914 and promoted to president the next year.[8]

---

6. Kevin Maney, *The Maverick and His Machine: Thomas Watson, Sr., and the Making of IBM* (New York: Wiley, 2004), 18.

7. Ibid., 1–47.

8. Emerson W. Pugh, *Building IBM: Shaping an Industry and Its Technology* (History of Computing) (Boston: MIT Press, 2009), 30.

A New Yorker Ahead of His Time

Tom Watson got off to a fast start. He quickly secured a business expansion loan from a New York City bank by explaining away the company's shaky financial history and emphasizing its exciting prospects, arguing, "[B]alance sheets reveal the past; this loan is for the future."[9] He consolidated administration of CTR's three disparate units. Watson invested heavily in research and development of cardpunch and tabulating equipment, helped popularize the term "data processing" to describe the work, and scaled back the time clock and scales operations (both of which were later sold by IBM). Watson repeatedly insisted, "[W]e must all pull together in this business . . . this business has a great future and everybody has a bearing on the future of the business." Supervisors should not direct employees too closely and in fact should support their staff members. "Every supervisor must look upon himself as an assistant to the men below him, instead of looking at himself as the boss," he admonished at an early meeting with CTR executives.[10] Watson was decisive, sometimes verging on autocratic, but he encouraged employees to challenge him and generate new ideas. He insisted that people working for him have up-to-date knowledge. "In a business like ours where there are so many things to take into consideration, it behooves every man to analyze every report that comes out."[11] CTR's profits continually increased except for a dip in the post–World War I recession. In 1924, Watson easily convinced the board of directors—by now almost all Watson fans who deferred to him on all major decisions—to focus on information processing, rename the company International Business Machines, expand its operations, and take the enterprise to a much higher level.

IBM, with its administrative offices in New York City and its main production facility in Endicott, was very much a *New York* company. New York was the nation's leading industrial, commercial, and financial state. By 1914, New York led the nation in manufacturing, with New York City alone accounting for one-tenth of the nation's output. Eastman Kodak in Rochester was the leading maker of cameras and film; General Electric in Schenectady was surging in lamps, motors, and power generation hardware; American Locomotive Company in Schenectady was an

---

9. Ibid., 37.
10. Maney, *The Maverick and His Machine*, 54–55.
11. Ibid., 73.

industry leader; the New York Central Railroad a leading carrier of freight and passengers. New York City's banks, insurance companies, and other financial establishments held a high percentage of the nation's capital and offered assets and financial services. Watson made multiple connections with New York City people and institutions. IBM's headquarters was in New York City, first at 50 Broad Street and after 1938 at a much grander setting at 590 Madison Avenue in the heart of the business district. Here, Watson proudly held widely covered press conferences, sometimes put IBM's newest computing equipment on display in the lobby, and hosted meetings with bankers and other businessmen. Watson and his wife Jeannette moved from a home in Short Hills, New Jersey, to New York City in 1933. As their son Thomas Watson Jr. described it,

> [T]hey joined the city's elite. During the social season, from October to May, their lives became a regular round-robin: Monday night at the opera with a few other couples, maybe two dinner parties and a charity banquet during the week, and then, every few weeks, an IBM dinner. Father wanted to know everyone important in New York, and eventually succeeded.[12]

Watson became head of the Merchants Association of New York, a powerful trade group that included the city's largest and most influential companies. He socialized with people like John D. Rockefeller Jr., newspaper magnate Frank Gannett (whose papers often carried favorable stories about Watson and IBM), Henry Luce (publisher of *Time* magazine), and Governor (and later president) Franklin D. Roosevelt. He was a benefactor and trustee of Columbia University and established and supported a research lab there.

Watson loved New York City but made Endicott the place where most of IBM's engineering, training, and manufacturing was done. It was a business-friendly town, also home to Endicott-Johnson Shoe Company, a progressive and very profitable enterprise. Endicott's pastoral setting encouraged happy workers, Watson believed. The Endicott labs produced most of IBM's breakthrough technology in the 1924–1960 period. Many of the nation's foremost information system scientists and inventors did their work there. The "IBM Schoolhouse," built by Watson at Endicott in

---

12. Thomas J. Watson, Jr., and Peter Petre, *Father, Son & Co.: My Life at IBM and Beyond* (New York: Bantam, 2000), 43.

1932, trained thousands of professionals and technicians. The IBM Country Club, just outside the village, which IBM employees could join for a dollar a year, boasted a golf course and other amenities and served as a social hub for IBM families. Adjacent to the country club was another area with soaring pine trees and, in the center, a magnificent country lodge, which Watson called the Homestead. It became a meeting place for IBM customers and IBM even hosted, over the years, a number of U.S. senators, chief executive officers from other major companies, and foreign government leaders. Watson visited Endicott often, strolled around the country club in contemplative silence, had the biggest suite at the Homestead, lectured to trainees in the Schoolhouse, conferred with scientists in the lab, and gave inspirational talks to employees in the manufacturing shops. After 1949, he used the country club to host the yearly meeting of the IBM "Hundred Percent Club," whose members were sales people who had attained their annual quotas. Attendees were housed in hundreds of individual sleeping tents and met under one large "main tent" for uplifting (and often long) speeches by Watson.[13]

If IBM was a *New York* company, its president was very much a *New York*–style leader: confident, visionary, proud, constantly promoting his company, and envisioning something more and better for the future; but also sometimes arrogant, condescending, impatient, and contemptuous of rivals. Thomas Watson came to personify IBM, and the public identified one with the other. His vision, values, and work styles were models for IBM employees. Watson was a masterful showman and cheerleader. His speeches, while seldom short and rarely spellbinding, conveyed dedication and pride in company and product. He demanded that IBM salesmen dress like the people to whom they were hoping to sell products—mostly executives—so that meant a dark suit, white shirt, and conservative tie, which became something akin to an IBM salesman dress code. Watson emphasized salesmanship that matched quality equipment with real needs and service, including making sure that IBM equipment worked well and was repaired quickly when needed. The equipment was almost always leased rather than being sold outright, which meant customers could constantly upgrade to newer systems, but the practice also maximized IBM's profits.

---

13. Maney, *The Maverick and His Machine*, 242–251; Endicott Chronology, http://www-03. ibm.com/ibm/history/exhibits/endicott/endicott_chronology.html.

His working philosophy—respect for employees, service to the customer, excellence in all things—permeated the culture and was embodied in themes from his talks and writings:

Yesterday, we pioneered for today; today, we are pioneering for tomorrow.

Our aim is higher every year and we always reach our mark.

It is better to aim at perfection and miss it than to aim at imperfection and hit it.

Whenever an individual or a business decides that success has been attained, progress stops.

Too many people are waiting for someone else to give them a push. We have tried to develop self-starters at IBM.

A manager should regard his position as one that gives him a splendid opportunity to render assistance.[14]

He brought the iconic term "THINK" from his work at NCR; made it the company's informal slogan; put it on signs, letterhead, and brochures; and used it as the title for an IBM periodical that carried news of the day, Watson editorials, and IBM ads. *THINK* magazine was used as a tool by salesmen to interest clients and was often seen in corporate boardrooms and university libraries. Watson commissioned inspirational songs that were sung at employee picnics, meetings, rallies, and conferences, the most famous entitled "Ever Onward!":[15]

EVER ONWARD—EVER ONWARD!
That's the spirit that has brought us fame!
We're big, but bigger we will be
We can't fail for all can see
That to serve humanity has been our aim!
Our products are known, in every zone,
Our reputation sparkles like a gem!
We've fought our way through—and new
Fields we're sure to conquer too
For the EVER ONWARD I.B.M.

14. Quintessential Quotes—Thomas J. Watson, http://www-03.ibm.com/ibm/history/documents/pdf/quotes.pdf.
15. IBM Rally Song: Ever Onward, http://www-03.ibm.com/ibm/history/multimedia/everonward_trans.html.

Watson's views on business and economic issues were often quoted in the press, magnifying his influence and the company's reputation. He arranged for an "IBM Day" at the 1939 World's Fair in New York City, invited four thousand guests, and hired conductor Eugene Ormandy and the Philadelphia Orchestra to play "The IBM Symphony." In a soaring piece of oration at a dinner at a swank New York hotel in the evening, Watson declared, "We do not consider the IBM as a business or a corporation but as a great world institution."[16] The company paid for nearly ten thousand employees to attend a second "IBM Day" at the fair in 1940, and Watson arranged for Metropolitan Opera diva Lily Pons to sing. He was a friend and informal advisor to Franklin D. Roosevelt, publicly defended New Deal economic policies when most businessmen condemned them, and with his wife often traveled to Hyde Park for lunch with the president and Eleanor Roosevelt. "The average businessman's opinion of what is right for the country is almost always wrong," he remarked to his son Tom Watson Jr. FDR counted on him to welcome and host visiting dignitaries, once remarking, "I handle 'em in Washington and Tom handles 'em in New York."[17] As president of the International Chamber of Commerce in the 1930s, he coined the slogan "World Peace through World Trade," traveled several times to Europe, and held press conferences to share his views on the international situation after returning home from the trips. Adolf Hitler awarded him a medal for his peace efforts in 1937; Watson very publically returned it in 1940 after Hitler dragged Europe into war.[18] Watson's long list of accomplishments, titles, awards, honorary chairmanships, and other recognitions gave him the longest entry in Who's Who in the early 1950s.[19]

Get to know customer needs and offer real solutions, he repeatedly counseled salesmen: "We're selling service, not machines." Salesmen were

---

16. "Watson to Dedicate Exhibit to Peace," New York Times, May 4, 1939; Maney, The Maverick and His Machine, 234.

17. Thomas J. Watson Jr. and Peter Petre, Father, Son & Co.: My Life at IBM and Beyond (New York: Bantam, 2000), 44–45.

18. A 2001 book by investigative journalist Edwin Black, IBM and the Holocaust, asserted that the use of tabulating equipment produced by IBM's German subsidiary facilitated Nazi genocide policies. The book raised a controversy but failed to make a convincing case. IBM pointed out that its German subsidiary "came under the control of Nazi authorities prior to and during World War II." IBM Statement on Nazi Era Book and Lawsuit, February 24, 2001, http://www-03.ibm.com/press/us/en/pressrelease/1388. wss.

19. Maney, The Maverick and His Machine, 380.

paid mostly on commission, so their livelihoods depended on what they sold or leased. But carrying out Watson's desires was easy because IBM usually offered superior machines and unequalled service. He held periodic meetings to sift through customer comments and review complaints. At one 1941 meeting with top executives, he reviewed recent complaints and said, "This doesn't discourage me. . . . In fact, it encourages me because I know when those things are resolved, we'll save a lot of money and do a better job."[20]

Keeping on the Move

By the late 1920s, IBM was describing its offerings as "systems" rather than just equipment and punch cards. Watson held numerous meetings with sales staff to discuss what customers wanted and used this input to integrate product development, manufacture, and marketing. Watson knew that keeping on the move made all the difference in the data equipment field, the high-tech arena of his time. He was similar to later entrepreneurs like Bill Gates and Steve Jobs, investing in imaginative people and new technologies and constantly bringing out new machines and systems. Watson nurtured and mentored promising inventors and engineers, but he particularly cultivated people who could invent things themselves and also motivate and supervise others in the same process. For instance, James Bryce, an engineer who was already with CTR when Watson took over, was a prodigious inventor (he would amass over five hundred patents in his lifetime) but also an astute manager whom Watson promoted to chief engineer and charged with developing what became some of the company's most outstanding products.[21]

Sometimes, he badgered teams to accelerate work and frustrated his executive staff by giving orders directly to junior engineers. Other times, he set competing teams loose on the same problem, sometimes informing them of the fact, sometimes trying to keep it secret. Watson managed to keep the internal competition within bounds, however; winning teams got bonuses (or IBM stock), but losing teams got recognition and the president's good will, which in IBM counted for a lot. Competition often produced notable results. In 1927, Watson organized two competing teams

---

20. Ibid., 254.
21. James W. Bryce, http://www-03.ibm.com/ibm/history/exhibits/markI/2413JB01.html.

to redesign the punched card, little changed since Hollerith's time. The winning design, turned in by a team headed by senior Endicott engineer Clair D. Lake, proposed a new size with eighty columns, nearly twice the number of the older cards. The new "IBM Card" (as Watson insisted it be called) was quickly patented by the company. It recorded more data than competitors' cards and would only operate on IBM equipment. IBM Cards became "the most commonly used method of data storage for nearly a half century."[22]

IBM was an enlightened enterprise, a good place to work by the standards of the day. It had no union in Watson's time; organizers couldn't get a foothold of dissatisfaction. Employees were relatively well paid and for the most part worked in clean, safe, appealing working conditions. The educational programs were industry leaders. Amenities like free membership in the IBM Country Club built loyalty and satisfaction. An in-house newspaper, *Business Machines*, kept everyone up to date. Watson's themes of loyalty, enthusiasm, and all IBM employees pulling together trickled down through the organization.[23] In 1935, IBM hired its first professional women, twenty-five specially recruited college seniors who went through training at Endicott and then into customer contact positions traditionally filled by men. Watson established a women's division to coordinate recruitment, education, and placement, He pushed sometimes reluctant regional offices to accept and support the new women professionals. Enlightenment had its limits, though. Watson could be condescending to women employees. For years there was an informal policy that women would leave the ranks when they married, to be supported by their husbands and be replaced by unmarried women. IBM pioneered in other ways. It offered group life insurance in 1934, pay for holidays and vacation in 1937, a hospitalization plan in 1946, and a disability plan in 1947. It pioneered in hiring minorities and adopted an equal opportunities policy in 1953.[24]

IBM in Depression, War, and Beyond

IBM's business began to slide after the "crash" of the stock market in 1929. As the Depression deepened, however, Watson counseled optimism,

---

22. The IBM Punched Card, http://www.ibm.com/ibm100/us/en/icons/punchcard.
23. Maney, *The Maverick and His Machine*, 55.
24. A Selective Chronology of IBM Women in Technology, http://www-03.ibm.com/ibm/history/witexhibit/pdf/wit_timeline.pdf; IBM Highlights, 1885–1969, http://www-03.ibm.com/ibm/history/documents/pdf/1885-1969.pdf.

realizing that a good deal of the economy's future depended on what business leaders said and how they acted. "There are unmistakable indications of business improvement," he said in April 1931. Hard work and the natural "inventive genius" of the American people were propelling the economy upward, he said in February 1932.[25] Rather than cutting back production, as most companies were doing, Watson *expanded* on the assumption that sooner or later returning prosperity and pent-up demand would result in more business. In January 1932, he announced that IBM would spend $1 million—nearly 6 percent of its annual revenue—to build a new research lab in Endicott. The lab, opened the next year, featured rich wood paneling, an elegant black-and-white tiled floor, state-of-the-art labs, and a research library. He moved the company's New York City headquarters from a modest building on Broad Street to a much larger and more expensive setting at 590 Madison Avenue in the busiest part of Manhattan in 1938. Watson loved to preside over new product announcements even as the economy sank.

But IBM sales and leases continued to dip. Then came a sudden turnaround: On August 14, 1935, FDR signed the Social Security Act into law. Every business now needed to track employees' hours, wages, and the amount to be paid into the new Social Security fund. The government also needed thousands of new machines to put the system in place. IBM was the only company that had calculating and tabulating machines that were up to the challenge. It had a backlog of machines in warehouses, factories that had been kept up to capacity, the best sales and service force in the industry, and research and education programs that would stay ahead of needs. Revenues were $20.3 million in 1931, fell to $17.6 million in 1933, then soared to $45.3 million in 1940.[26]

As World War II drew near, the economy expanded dramatically and shifted toward wartime production. IBM expanded its manufacturing capacity, including building a huge new plant near Poughkeepsie in 1941 that happened to be adjacent to where Glenn Curtiss had landed for refueling in his Albany–to–New York City flight thirty-two years earlier. In addition to its production of tabulating equipment, IBM built machine guns, tank guns, rifles, gas masks, hand grenades, bomb sights, components for submarines, and other war materiel. IBM products were used to keep track of soldiers; in bomb surveys; and in tracking missing-in-action

---

25. "Trade Leaders See Gains," *New York Times*, April 2, 1931; "Predicts Expansion of Mass Production," *New York Times*, February 14, 1932.
26. Maney, *The Maverick and His Machine*, 134–136; Cortada, *Before the Computer*, 147.

personnel, prisoners, displaced persons, relief materials, and captured items. They did some of the calculations on the Manhattan Project that produced the atomic bomb. IBM cooperated with Harvard University in producing the massive "Automatic Sequence Controlled Calculator" (ASCC) in 1944, which the navy used for calculating firing trajectories and which was later used for complex calculations in several scientific and engineering disciplines. Watson was, however, enraged when Harvard claimed credit for its development (and named it the Harvard Mark I) and slighted IBM's role. He cut off cooperation and turned to Columbia University where IBM established a research lab (named for Watson) in 1945.[27]

Watson also prepared for life after the war, predicting that the economy would expand, returning IBM employees would have jobs, and production would increase. "The war is changing everything," he told a planning meeting of IBM executives in 1943. "Everybody who makes any progress in business is going to work along different lines than they have ever worked before. The people who do not change in time are going to be sitting on the curbstone waiting for the parade to come by."[28] He developed plans to recycle IBM machines returned by the government at the end of the war by modifying and reducing some of their capabilities and leasing them to businesses as start-up machines. From there, after a few years' use, businesses could be expected to upgrade to newer IBM equipment. He authorized new products, for example, electric typewriters and the "407 Accounting Machine," introduced right after the war, that worked faster and better than any of its predecessors and outperformed its competitors.

IBM engineers also produced the "Selective Sequence Electronic Calculator" (SSEC), a hybrid that was one technological step beyond the ASCC/Harvard Mark I and used both paper tape and vacuum tube circuits. Another monster-sized machine, it had 21,000 relays, 12,500 vacuum tubes, and could perform complicated mathematical calculations with unprecedented speed. It was said to be 250 times faster than ASCC/Mark I. Watson was so proud of it (and so desirous for all the world to see it) that he put it on display at IBM headquarters in New York City where pedestrians could watch it through the window.[29] Following the IBM press

27. IBM's ASCC Introduction, http://www-03.ibm.com/ibm/history/exhibits/markI/markI_intro.html.
28. Pugh, *Building IBM*, 118.
29. Selective Sequence Electronic Calculator, http://www-03.ibm.com/ibm/history/exhibits/701/701_coi59.html.

material closely, the *New York Times* reported: "The new machine, it was said, combines 'the speed of electronic circuits' with 'a memory capacity' and the necessary control to utilize this speed and capacity on 'the most complex problems of science in institutions of learning, in government, and industry.' . . . the new machine follows the pattern of a man's mind in performing sequences of complex calculations."[30]

IBM emerged from the war as the nation's leading data-processing company. Business was booming as the postwar economy expanded, reacting to pent-up demand for new products, and people purchased houses, cars, appliances, clothing, and other goods in record quantity. IBM's foreign business also increased. But competition was also rising, with expanding rivals such as Burroughs, Sperry Rand, and Honeywell challenging IBM for the postwar market. Tom Watson, seventy-one years old when the war ended, perpetuated the IBM strategies and culture he had built, favored slow and deliberate research and development even as rival companies were accelerating, and was skeptical about emerging technologies. His outsized ego, overconfidence in his own insights, and reluctance to change were becoming a liability for his company.

In considering a successor, nepotism trumped an objective search for the best future leader. Watson groomed his son, Thomas Watson Jr. (1914–1993), to succeed him as head of IBM. Watson junior had been a difficult child and an indifferent student who loved his father but constantly defied his authority. Brown University reluctantly admitted him as a favor to Watson senior. After graduation, he worked as a salesman for IBM and enlisted as a pilot in the Army Air Corps, 1940 to 1945. He considered becoming an airline pilot, but his commanding officer, who had observed the growth of his leadership skills, urged him to go back to IBM. He decided to give it a try, returning in 1946. With his father's support and the board's compliance, he was promoted to vice president six months later, to executive vice president in 1949, and president in 1952. Watson senior gradually relaxed his control, though he stayed on as chief executive officer with ultimate decision-making power until just before his death in 1956. Watson junior proved to be a capable leader. Senior and junior built postwar IBM but often seemed to be pulling in opposite directions, with the father clinging to the old ways and the son employing a more consultative leadership style, showing more wariness about upstart rivals, pushing for faster innovation, and exhibiting more concern

---

30. "Mechanical 'Brain' Is Given to Science," *New York Times*, January 28, 1948.

about public perception of IBM. They fought constantly, often openly in
IBM headquarters. "[D]ad and I got into big arguments practically every
month," Tom Watson Jr. recalled in his memoirs. "We'd reconcile and try
to cooperate, but pretty soon he'd second-guess me on a decision or I'd
express an opinion on something he thought was none of my business, and
we'd go at it again."[31]

In fact, the Watsons could not afford long personal fights because
IBM was in a race with its rivals for the next generation of machines.
The government was funding some of the competition to encourage
new designs rather than having to rely on just one company. The army
contracted with the University of Pennsylvania to develop a machine
to calculate artillery firing tables. The Electronic Numerical Integrator
and Calculator (ENIAC), completed in 1946, relied on vacuum tubes
and electronic circuits, a technological step up from electromechanical
relays like the ones in IBM's tabulating machines. The inventors, Pres-
per Eckert and John Mauchly, formed their own company and developed
the Universal Automatic Computer (UNIVAC) in 1949. But they ran
out of money and approached IBM to buy them out. In a meeting with
Watson senior, Mauchly, "a lanky character who liked to flout convention
. . . slumped down on the couch and put his feet up on the coffee table."
Watson, annoyed, kept the meeting short. IBM's lawyers had warned that
buying up the upstart company would open IBM to allegations of violating the antitrust laws. The inventors left in something of a huff. "This
guy Mauchly wears those loud socks," Watson told his son. "I wouldn't
want him in my business anyway."[32] The inventors went to Remington
Rand, which bought them out and began producing UNIVACS in quantity. Remington Rand scored a public relations coup in November 1952,
when a UNIVAC machine accurately projected a landslide for Dwight
Eisenhower in the presidential election that year.

In the meantime, IBM, in the unusual position of being behind its
rivals and wary of upstart companies, once again found a way to race to the
head of the industry. Watson senior gradually acknowledged the need for
new approaches; Watson junior, more technologically astute, spearheaded
change. Alarmed by UNIVAC, Watson senior ordered work accelerated
on a new machine, unveiled in late 1946 as the "603 Electronic Multiplier,"

31. Watson and Petre, *Father, Son & Co.*, 182.
32. Ibid., 135–136, 198; Maney, *The Maverick and His Machine*, 345.

which IBM calls "the first electronic calculator ever placed in production" and which could multiply large numbers faster than anything else on the market.[33] It was succeeded by faster machines in the late 1940s. IBM had more or less caught up with its rivals. But the UNIVAC prediction in the 1952 election spurred new activity. By now, Tom Watson Jr. was in charge of most operations. After a number of arguments with his father, he hired new, more innovative engineers for both the Endicott labs and the engineering and production facility at Poughkeepsie. The "IBM 701 Electronic Data Processing Machine," which debuted in April 1953, stored programs in an internal electronic memory and was in effect the transition from punched card machines to electronic computers. At a press conference to unveil the machine, Tom Watson Jr. called it "the most advanced, most flexible high-speed computer in the world," twenty-five times faster than the SSEC, which the company had launched in 1948.[34] UNIVAC had won the PR game temporarily with the 1952 election prediction, but the 701 turned out to be a better, more versatile machine and, coupled with IBM's superior sales and service force, soon outsold UNIVAC.

Tom Watson junior also set the Endicott engineers there to work on a smaller, simpler, sleeker machine, launched in 1953 as the "IBM 650 Magnetic Drum Data Processing Machine." Versatile and relatively inexpensive to lease, the 650 became the most popular computer of the 1950s. "Its ability to handle . . . bread-and-butter applications made the 650 hot," Tom Watson Jr. recalled. "While our giant, million-dollar 700 series machines got the publicity, the 650 became computing's Model T."[35] In the meantime, Remington Rand lost its focus on computers and its competitive edge, branching out into electric razors and other products. By the end of the 1950s, IBM was clearly ahead of all its rivals, sometimes derisively referred to in the popular press as "The Seven Dwarfs."

Time magazine ran a cover story on "Corporations: The Brain Builders" in March 1955 with a picture of Tom Watson Jr. and, behind him, a machine that had tape spools for eyes and mechanical arms pushing buttons on a console. It wasn't an actual IBM machine, but it conveyed the image of a powerful company that made machines that could think like

---

33. IBM 603 Electronic Multiplier, http://www-03.ibm.com/ibm/history/exhibits/vintage/vintage_4506VV2193.html.
34. IBM 701, http://www-03.ibm.com/ibm/history/exhibits/701/701_intro3.html; 701 Announced, http://www-03.ibm.com/ibm/history/exhibits/701/701_announced.html.
35. Watson and Petre, *Father, Son & Co.*, 244.

humans. "Clink, Clank, Think" ran the caption behind Watson's picture. The article was mostly about IBM, though others were noted as also producing equipment. It focused on the 702 Electronic Data Processing Machine, "a giant brain" that "can remember enough information to fill a 1,836-page Manhattan telephone book—any figure, word, chemical or mathematical symbol—and work the information at the rate of 7,200 unerring logical operations per second." "Our job is to make automatic a lot of things now done by slow and laborious human drudgery," Watson was quoted as saying. "[I]n the coming age of automation, unlimited areas for electronic machines will open up for IBM. . . . the entire horizon of factory automation is beginning to open up for electronics."[36]

The next year, 1956, saw the settlement of an antitrust suit brought by the federal government against IBM in 1952 that charged that IBM was restraining trade in violation of the antitrust laws. Watson junior privately acknowledged the strength of the federal case. "We knew that sooner or later the government would come after us. Our equipment was in the accounting departments of virtually every American company, and the government knew all about us because we were in every federal agency too . . . . [we] held about 90 percent of the market for punch-card machines."[37] The company and the government reached an agreement that forced IBM to sell as well as lease machines, accept restrictions on punch card production, license its patents under certain conditions, and accept other limitations. The Justice Department's order loosened IBM's grip on some parts of the industry. But Tom Watson Jr. realized that its impact would be limited: Punched-card work was on the wane by that time, to be replaced by up-and-coming electronic computers. IBM engineers were already hard at work on that technology.

The Legacy

Hailing Tom Watson Sr. on his eightieth birthday in 1954, a *New York Times* editorial noted that he had risen from humble beginnings in Painted Post to become "one of the most successful business executives" in U.S. history. He was always

---

36. "Corporations: The Brain Builders," *Time*, March 28, 1955, 89–96.
37. Watson and Petre, *Father, Son & Co.*, 218.

a man of simple, unaffected character, genial, approachable and eager to give any good cause a helping hand. New York knows him well for his interest in civic and charitable affairs and a patron of the arts. . . . His machines have freed man from drudgery, multiplied productivity, opened new vistas in science, enlarged the usefulness of man's mind.[38]

Watson senior stepped aside in 1956, made his son CEO, and died a few weeks later. In many ways a model corporate leader, his legacy also included staying too long and exhibiting a leadership style that was increasingly out of date in the fast-paced postwar world. Watson junior had had plenty of time to get ready but later described himself as "the most frightened man in America" when he assumed full responsibility.[39] He stayed in charge until 1971, when a heart attack forced him out. Watson streamlined the administrative structure, stepped up research and development, and invested $5 billion in developing a new breakthrough "System 360" in 1964, a state-of-the-art "family" of computers that used interchangeable software and could handle a full range of commercial and scientific applications ranging from small to large.

After Tom Watson Jr. retired in 1971, the next two CEOs let the company sag. IBM became cautious, bureaucratic, and distracted, for instance, entering an ill-advised foray into the copier business. Lou Gerstner, who became CEO in 1993, noted that "a company's initial culture is usually determined by its founder's mindset—that person's values, beliefs, preferences and also idiosyncrasies. It has been said that every institution is nothing but the extended shadow of one person. In IBM's case, that was Thomas J. Watson Sr." Gerstner revived and updated Watson's principles—excellence in everything the company does, superior customer service, respect for the individual—in making the company an innovative leader once again.[40]

In 2011, celebrating the hundredth anniversary of its predecessor, the Computing-Tabulating-Recording Company, IBM went searching for the roots of its success. "Nearly all the companies our grandparents admired have disappeared," noted an IBM centennial insert in the *Wall Street*

38. "Thomas J. Watson at 80," *New York Times*, February 17, 1954.
39. Watson and Petre, *Father, Son & Co.*, vii.
40. Louis V. Gerstner, *Who Says Elephants Can't Dance? Leading a Great Enterprise through Dramatic Change* (New York: Harper Business, 2002), 182.

Journal. But IBM endured and prospered because it stuck to the values of its founding president, adapting them to fit evolving business conditions. Tom Watson senior's "most enduring contribution to business was his intentional creation of something that would outlast him—a shared corporate culture." Watson set forth values about customer service, managing for the long term, making and developing markets rather than just entering them, taking risks and making investments, consistently meeting high standards, and building trust. The company affirmed a determination to stick with those principles as it entered its second century. Managing according to values in changing times "requires leaders to show up in defense of the future" every day.[41] Tom Watson senior might have said the same thing.

---

41. IBM insert in the *Wall Street Journal*, June 16, 2011, http://www.ibm.com/ibm100/common/images/junespecial/ibm_centennial.pdf.

11
April 15, 1947

Breaking the Color Line

Jackie Robinson was a model of courage, determination, resilience, and athletic skills. *Photo courtesy of National Baseball Hall of Fame and Museum Library, Cooperstown, New York.*

The Most Exciting Opening Day in Baseball History

*M*ore than twenty-six thousand fans crowded into Ebbets Field to see the Brooklyn Dodgers' 1947 opening game against the Boston Braves on April 15, 1947. The Dodgers and the Braves, longtime rivals, were both strong teams, about evenly matched, but the game itself was not the cause of the excitement in Brooklyn that cool spring day.

This was no ordinary opening day: For the first time in modern Major League Baseball, a black player, Jack Roosevelt "Jackie" Robinson, would be taking the field as part of the Dodger team. Public anticipation had been building since 1946 when Robinson had made his debut on the roster of a Dodger farm team, the Montreal Royals. This would be a historic day for a historic team in a historic setting. The Dodgers traced their history back to the "Brooklyn Grays," formed in 1883. As the team evolved, and professional baseball settled down to organization into two leagues, the National and the American, the team, part of the National League, had been officially named the Brooklyn Base Ball Club but called informally the Grooms, Superbas, and Robins. Brooklyn residents, whose borough was crisscrossed with trolley rapid transit lines, had been derisively called "trolley dodgers," and their team came to be called "Dodgers" until 1933, when, having become a term of affection, it became their official title. The team was less than outstanding in the 1930s, and one persistent fan yelled, "Yez bums, yez!" from behind the chicken wire back of home plate at just about every home game during the Depression. This name stuck, too, but in an affectionate way, with Brooklynites gradually taking to calling their team "Dem Bums." Attending Dodger games was an obsessive pastime in Brooklyn. Whites and blacks both enjoyed the game. But until this day, only whites put on the Dodger uniform and played the game.[1]

Ebbets Field, built in 1913 in a filled-in marshy area the locals had called Pigtown, was one of the smallest in the National League with a capacity of only thirty-two thousand. "When you had a box seat, you were practically playing the field," said longtime Dodger announcer Red Barber. Parking was limited to about seven hundred cars. But that didn't seem to matter much. About half the fans on any given day walked in off the streets from their homes nearby, and others came by bus, subway, and trolley. Branch Rickey, who moved from managing the St. Louis Cardinals to become the Dodgers' president and general manager in 1942, had grand plans to revitalize the team and raise it to contention for the National League pennant and even the World Series.[2]

Brooklyn itself was a crowded place, with over 2.6 million residents, and an economy undergoing change as wartime industries like

1. Glenn Stout, *The Dodgers: 120 Years of Dodger Baseball* (New York: Houghton Mifflin, 2004), 1–122.

2. Harvey Frommer, *New York City Baseball: The Last Golden Age, 1947–1957* (New York: Macmillan, 1980), 97–101.

the Brooklyn Navy Yard, which had employed seventy thousand people during the war, scaled back. Companies downsized or left because of an aging industrial infrastructure and cheaper labor costs elsewhere. Brooklyn's fifty breweries disappeared one at a time. The makeup of the population was beginning to change with the influx of black and Hispanic residents and the exodus of whites relocating to Queens, Long Island, New Jersey, and other places. Broadening automobile ownership after the war accelerated the outward migration to more open spaces. But Brooklyn was a noisy, vibrant, colorful place with a great deal of identity and pride. If it had been a city, it would have been the nation's fourth largest one. Many residents identified more intensely with Brooklyn than with New York City, of which it had been a part since 1898. "[I]t had lots of hallmarks of a city unto itself . . . a downtown of its own, with big department stores, lavish theaters, splashy restaurants, tall office buildings; it had a bunch of spiffy hotels with rooftop restaurants and grand ballrooms; it had belts of industry and commerce . . ."[3] Even the rest of New York City regarded Brooklyn as a separate, somewhat mysterious place, rough around the edges. Almost every Hollywood movie seemed to have a "typical" Brooklyn character, "a bare-armed, wisecracking, quasi-tough guy" named "Smitty" or "Frankie" who spoke in "the invented vernacular of Brooklynese" and loved "Dem Bums."[4]

Brooklyn, Ebbets Field, and the Dodgers each had glorious, intersecting histories. But on opening day in 1947, fans came to witness racial and social history being made. There had been integrated professional baseball up to the end of the nineteenth century, when a rising feeling of racial animosity and Jim Crow separatist regulations pushed the races apart. Segregation became the norm in the Southern part of the nation, where there were separate schools, beaches, and even restrooms for the two races. Talented blacks played in a parallel baseball system of Negro Leagues. The quality of play among the black teams was excellent. There was, however, a universally recognized but unwritten rule that blacks were not allowed in Major League Baseball, the teams in the National and American leagues. All of that began to change when Jackie Robinson came to bat. He failed to get a hit that day, but Brooklyn beat Boston 5 to 3, and the fabric of racial segregation in professional sports began to unravel.

---

3. Elliot Willensky, *When Brooklyn Was the World, 1920–1957* (New York: Harmony Press, 1986), 24–25.
4. Stout, *The Dodgers*, 123.

Getting Ready for Greatness

Jackie Robinson was born in rural Georgia in January 1919. His father walked out on the family six months later, and his mother moved the family to Pasadena, California, and kept them going through working as a domestic servant. Mallie Robinson taught Jackie and his older siblings to be proud of who they were but not to be confrontational. Jackie grew up knowing the burden of poverty and the sting of racism, including racial slurs, white standoffishness, and minor brushes with the law. But he became a determined competitor at playground games including soccer, baseball, football, and tennis. He excelled in sports at Pasadena Junior College and then went on to earn letters in baseball, football, basketball, and the long jump at UCLA. He also developed a temper and was inclined to challenge anyone who mouthed racial insults.

Financial pressures forced Robinson to leave the university without graduating, and he was drafted into the army in 1942. Assigned to a cavalry unit at Fort Riley, Kansas, he quickly became bored with tending to horses. He wanted to join the fort's baseball team, but it was whites-only. Recruited for the football team, where blacks were needed and welcome, he refused on principle because of the baseball team exclusion. Blacks were eligible to be officers even in the segregated army, but their applications to Officer Candidate School (OCS) were often rejected on the excuse that they lacked leadership ability. When that happened to Robinson, he appealed to black boxing champ Joe Lewis, who was also in the army at Fort Riley. With Lewis's support, Robinson and a few other blacks on base were admitted to OCS. The new second lieutenant was appointed "Morale Officer" for black troops at Fort Riley and listened to repeated complaints about the demeaning impact of segregation. One issue was long lines for blacks to enter the snack bar and base store, known as the PX, through a separate, blacks-only entrance, and few seats and poor service for them when they got in. Robinson kept pushing until accommodations for blacks improved.[5]

Robinson was transferred to a tank battalion at Fort Hood, Texas, and hoped to join the fighting in Europe. But on July 6, 1944, Robinson boarded an army bus with a civilian driver and sat down beside the wife of a fellow black officer. He knew both the woman and her husband and

---

5. Jackie Robinson and Alfred Duckett, *I Never Had It Made: The Autobiography of Jackie Robinson* (New York: Harper Perennial, 2003), 1–25.

just wanted to chat. The woman was light skinned. The army had just issued orders desegregating buses, but the order was not well known and inconsistently applied. The white driver, believing the woman was white, ordered him to move to the back of the bus. Robinson refused, presaging Rosa Parks's decision to stay put in her seat in a public bus in Montgomery, Alabama, eleven years later. He was ordered off the bus, taken into custody by military police, and, after arguing with an assistant provost marshal and insisting he had done nothing wrong, was charged with several infractions, including insubordination, drunkenness, and conduct unbecoming an officer. It was a weak, puffed-up set of charges, unworthy of the U.S. Army. Sensing he would be railroaded, he appealed to the NAACP, which asked the army for information on the case. Robinson's treatment began receiving press attention, and the army backed down, dropping several of the charges. At his court martial, Robinson testified to the insulting treatment and racial insults he had received. His commanding officer appeared as a character witness. After short deliberation, he was found not guilty on all counts. He later recalled: "[T]his was not a case involving a violation of the Articles of War or even military tradition, but simply a situation in which a few individuals sought to vent their bigotry on a Negro they considered 'uppity' because he had the audacity to exercise rights that belong to him as an American and a soldier." But he was through with the army, and vice versa. He applied for a medical discharge on the basis of an old sports injury to an ankle and was out of the service by November. Jackie Robinson knew he could excel at sports. Soon, he was playing outstanding baseball for the Kansas City Monarchs, a Negro League franchise.[6]

Opening the Door to History

Robinson was ready for a greater challenge. But it was Dodger general manager Branch Rickey who led and managed the process of getting him into Major League Baseball. A determined baseball visionary, Rickey was a bundle of contradictions. He cherished baseball traditions but introduced transformative innovations such as the Minor League farm system.

---

6. Jules Tygiel, "The Court Martial of Jackie Robinson," in Tygiel, ed., *The Jackie Robinson Reader: Perspectives on an American Hero* (New York: Dutton, 1997), 40–51; Carl T. Rowan with Jackie Robinson, *Wait till Next Year: The Life Story of Jackie Robinson* (New York: Random House, 1960), 82–83.

His pious faith earned him the nickname "the Mahatma," but his frugality and stinginess with salaries also earned the sobriquet "El Cheapo." He abhorred alcohol but constantly smoked cigars. He respected baseball's rules but determined to break the unwritten code barring blacks were from professional baseball teams. Rickey determined to be the first manager to break that "color line." He knew there were many capable black players whose talents were being underutilized in the Negro League. Rickey understood there was money to be made through integration: More black fans would attend, and attendance in general would go up as more talented players joined the teams and play became more exciting. He wasn't able to do it at the St. Louis Cardinals where he managed for many years; that team was too conservative on racial issues and its setting, in the South, where Jim Crow prevailed, made it impossible. But he believed he could do it in Brooklyn, a much more cosmopolitan area with relaxed and progressive views on race.[7]

One of Rickey's motives was a deep sense of social justice. As a young college baseball coach, he had been mortified when a black player on his team was denied a room at a South Bend, Indiana, hotel. Years later, he said: "I believe that racial extractions and color hues and forms of worship become secondary to what men can do. The denial of equality of opportunity to qualify for work to anyone, anywhere, any time, is understandable to me." He felt that segregation perpetuated prejudice and integration of sports teams undermined it. "You can't meet it with words. You can't take prejudice straight on. It must be done by proximity. Proximity! The player alongside you. No matter what the skin color or language. Win the game. Win all. Get the championship and the check that goes with it."[8] But his main motive was winning baseball games, which also meant a profit for him, his franchise, and his players. Black players had immense talent, which he determined to harness. Always a detailed planner—he wrote notes to himself on slips of paper, napkins, and coffee shop menus—Rickey did his homework, talked with managers of Negro League teams, and sent his own scouts to see the best players in action. Often cautious, Rickey told people he was considering starting up a new team in the Negro League, but he had something much more radical in mind, bringing a black player onto the Dodger roster. He needed to find an outstanding black player who would be assertive but not lash out in

7. Jimmy Breslin, *Branch Rickey* (New York: Viking, 2011), 1–55.
8. Ibid., 14, 28, 113.

response to the racially motivated jeers and attacks that were sure to come. "How could a man with a distinctive personality keep it untarnished with constant absorption of attacks calculated to destroy his self-respect?" he asked himself. "The trial candidate must never lose his sense of purpose nor lower his sights from the ultimate goal of making good off the field."[9]

Jackie Robinson was recommended by several trusted friends, including Rickey's chief scout. He was already well known because of his notable UCLA career, was making a good record in Kansas City, was a nondrinker, and had long been engaged and planned to marry and so had the added benefit that he would be a family man. Longtime commissioner of baseball Kenesaw Mountain Landis, a supporter of the segregated status quo, died in 1944 and was succeeded the next year by Albert "Happy" Chandler, a former Kentucky governor and U.S. senator who seemed more receptive to change on racial issues. New York State was not a perfect model of racial harmony by any means: A race riot in Harlem in 1943 resulted in several deaths and widespread property destruction. But New Yorkers' racial views were moderating and Brooklyn was a diverse and tolerant community. In March 1945, the New York State Legislature passed the Ives-Quinn Act banning employment discrimination on the basis of race, national origin, or religion and establishing a State Commission against Discrimination to enforce it. It was the nation's first state antidiscrimination law.[10] Branch Rickey, a staunch Republican, had encouraged the legislation through backchannel communications to state party leadership. Advocates for black equality cited the law in pressuring New York's baseball teams to begin hiring blacks. Rickey now had the force of New York State law behind him.

Rickey invited Robinson to an interview in Brooklyn on August 28, 1945, stunning him with the news that he was being interviewed for a position with the Dodgers rather than the new black team that Rickey was rumored to be organizing. Robinson was ecstatic. But Rickey lectured Robinson that he would have to be a model of unbending forbearance:

> We can't fight our way through this, Jackie. . . . There's virtually nobody on our side. No owners, no umpires, very few newspapermen. And I'm afraid many of the fans will be hostile. We're

9. Branch Rickey with Robert Riger, *The American Diamond: A Documentary of the Game of Baseball* (New York: Simon & Schuster, 1965), 45.

10. Richard Norton Smith, *Thomas E. Dewey and His Times* (New York: Simon & Schuster, 1982), 444–448.

in a tough position, Jackie. We can win only if we convince the world that I'm doing this because you're a great ballplayer, a fine gentleman. . . . But let me tell you it's going to take an awful lot of courage.

How would Robinson react, he asked, if pitchers threw beanballs at him, runners slid into him with spikes out, or hotel clerks turned him away with racial taunts? Robinson chafed under the questioning. "Mr. Rickey, do you want a ballplayer who's afraid to fight back?" "I want a ballplayer with guts enough not to fight back!" Rickey retorted. The two men struck a grand bargain: Robinson would get his chance to prove himself, but he would need to excel as a player and at the same time exercise almost superhuman restraint in the face of totally unjustified attacks. Rickey signed Robinson to play for the Montreal Royals, a Dodger farm team in the International League, with a signing bonus of $3,500 and a salary of $600 per month. If he made good there, he would move up to the Dodgers.[11]

Rickey arranged for a press conference in October 1945 to introduce Robinson. "Just be yourself," he counseled Robinson. "Simply say that you are going to do the best you can and let it go at that." Sportswriter Al Parsley reported in the *Montreal Herald* that the press was, if not hostile, at least "belligerently indifferent." Jimmy Powers, sports editor of *New York Daily News*, wrote, "Robinson will not make the grade in the big leagues this year or next . . . Robinson is a thousand-to-one shot."[12]

Jackie married his fiancée, Rachel Isum, in February 1946 in Los Angeles. Thereafter, Rachel was to be a constant supporter and advisor, encouraging him when things got rough, cheering him when he rose to the occasion and persevered. The newlyweds headed for spring training with the Royals in Florida. They were bumped off connecting airline flights in New Orleans and Pensacola and white people took their seats. They took a rickety bus to Daytona Beach and complied when the driver ordered them to sit in the back. Rickey knew local hotels would refuse to accommodate them and arranged for them to take a room in the home of a local black couple.[13] He arranged for Wendell Smith, a black sportswriter for

11. Breslin, *Branch Rickey*, 66; Rowan with Robinson, *Wait till Next Year*, 113–118.
12. Roger Kahn, *Beyond the Boys of Summer: The Very Best of Roger Kahn*, edited by Rob Miraldi (New York: McGraw-Hill, 2005), 262.
13. Rachel Robinson with Lee Daniels, *Jackie Robinson: An Intimate Portrait* (New York: Abrams, 1996), 46–52.

the *Pittsburgh Courier*, one of the men who had recommended Robinson, to travel to the same cities as Robinson to cover the games. Smith sometimes doubled as chauffeur and informal counselor when Robinson encountered particularly virulent racism. Robinson was forced to leave the Dodgers' pre-training camp at Sanford, near Daytona Beach, after a delegation of city officials told Rickey they would not allow blacks and whites on the same field. When the Royals traveled to Deland, Florida, for an exhibition game with Indianapolis, a local policeman bolted onto the field. "Get off the field right now or I'm putting you in jail. We ain't havin' [racial epithet] mix with white boys in this town." Robinson seethed but left quietly.[14]

The ordeals made Robinson stronger and prepared him for what lay ahead. The Robinsons moved into an apartment in Montreal, a cosmopolitan city where they felt comfortable. The Royals opened against the Jersey City Giants on April 17, 1946, before twenty-five thousand fans, many who had traveled via the Hudson tunnels to see Robinson, who put on a spectacular show with bunts, hits, and stolen bases, leading his team to a 14 to 1 victory. The rest of the season was a challenge but also a triumph. Opposing pitchers tried to hit him with beanballs. Opposing coaches and players insulted him with vile racial epithets. New York players were mostly tolerant or restrained. The Buffalo Bisons were hospitable to the Royals and their new player. But players on the Syracuse Chiefs taunted Robinson, and one player released a black cat onto the field as Robinson came to bat, yelling, "Hey, Jackie, there's your cousin!" Time was called as the umpire ordered the Syracuse players to stop harassing Robinson and the frightened cat was carried off the field. Robinson then hit a double and scored when the next hitter singled to center. "I guess my cousin's pretty happy now!" he shouted as he passed the Syracuse dugout.[15] Robinson's spirited, courageous, outstanding performance in game after game propelled the Royals to the 1946 Minor League championship.

Robinson exceeded Rickey's expectations; earned the respect of his team members and opposing teams; and won the gradual, sometimes begrudging, acknowledgment of sportswriters. Rickey was telling more and more people that he planned to move Robinson up. Jimmy Powers, sports editor for the *New York Daily News*, wrote over eighty columns

---

14. Jules Tygiel, *Baseball's Great Experiment: Jackie Robinson and His Legacy* (New York: Oxford University Press, 1983), 99–143.
15. Robinson and Duckett, *I Never Had It Made*, 49.

criticizing Rickey's proposed initiative in 1946, asserting that it would disrupt if not destroy the game.[16] Major League owners balked. In the summer of 1946, they issued a statement to the effect that radical elements were behind the push for integration and that blacks were not good enough to play Major League Baseball. In January 1947, they voted 15 to 1 (with only Rickey in opposition) against integration on the spurious justification that it would cripple the Negro teams. Rickey appealed to Commissioner Chandler, whose political skills and sense of fair play prevailed. "I'm going to meet my Maker some day and if he asks me why I didn't let [Robinson] play and I say it's because he's black, that might not be a satisfactory answer. So, bring him in!"[17]

In January, Rickey met with thirty black professionals and civic leaders in Brooklyn, with the sobering message that *if* Robinson moved up—the decision was not made yet, he insisted—gloating and celebration by the black community would provoke a backlash. "If any individual, group, or segment of Negro society uses the advancement of Jackie Robinson in baseball as a triumph of race over race, I will regret the day I ever signed him to a contract!"[18] Rickey moved spring 1947 Royals and Dodger training out of Florida to Cuba and Panama to prevent a repetition of the racial problems Robinson had encountered in 1946. Several Dodger players drafted a petition to the effect that they would not play on the same team as Robinson. Team manager Leo Durocher got wind of it and summoned the team to a tense meeting at one o'clock in the morning. "I hear some of you don't want to play with Robinson," said the irate Durocher. He continued,

> I'm the manager and I'm paid to win and I'd play with an elephant if he could win for me and this fellow Robinson is an elephant. You can't throw him out on the bases and you can't get him out at the plate. This fellow is a great player. He's gonna win pennants. He's gonna put money in your pockets and mine. . . . I don't want to see your petition! I don't want to hear anything about it![19]

The petition was scuttled.

16. Breslin, *Branch Rickey*, 93.
17. Stout, *The Dodgers*, 130.
18. Breslin, *Branch Rickey*, 98; Tygiel, *Baseball's Great Experiment*, 162.
19. Roger Kahn, *The Era, 1947–1957: When the Yankees, the Giants, and the Dodgers Ruled the World* (New York: Ticknor and Fields, 1993), 35–36.

Rickey announced Robinson's elevation from the Royals to the Dodgers on April 10, 1947. Many people in the stands five days later sported "I'm for Jackie" buttons. He went hitless and the historic, color-line breaking, precedent-setting debut was actually "quite uneventful," wrote a sportswriter for the *New York Times*. "I was nervous in the first play of my first game at Ebbets Field," the newest Dodger admitted. "But nothing has bothered me since," he added, setting a characteristically confident tone for the future.[20]

His first hit came in the second game of the season, against the New York Giants. His playing was not strong for the first couple of months. Opposing teams shouted insults; even Brooklyn fans sometimes booed. Ben Chapman, manager of the Philadelphia Phillies, was the worst offender. "Hey you, there, [racial epithet]! Yeah, you. You hear me. When did they let you out of the jungle?" "Hey, we don't need no [racial epithet] here." Robinson was stoic but later said it was the worse abuse he ever took, including as a kid in Pasadena and in the army. In May, Philadelphia's owner called Rickey to say his team wouldn't take the field if Robinson was there. He changed his mind after Rickey called his bluff and said Philadelphia would have to forfeit. Robinson's teammates came round to his defense during the game. When Chapman needled "Pee Wee" Reese, the captain of the team, about playing with a black, Reese jogged over to Robinson and put his arms around his shoulders in a gesture of solidarity and support. Baseball commissioner Chandler and the president of the National League, Ford Frick, called the Phillies' manager to protest Chapman's outrageous behavior. The widely read syndicated New York columnist Walter Winchell wrote that Chapman was a disgrace and should leave baseball. Chapman sent word to Robinson that he would like to make a fresh start. In a forgiving mood, Robinson agreed to pose with Chapman holding a bat between them. That way, Robinson explained, they would not actually have to shake hands. The tension is obvious in the photo, but Chapman's race baiting stopped. It had helped build support for Robinson among his teammates, fans, and the press.[21]

When Robinson was heckled by fans in Cincinnati during pregame practice, Reese again made a point of going over to Robinson, engaging him in conversation, and putting an arm around his shoulders in another very public gesture of support. The Chicago Cubs voted to go on strike

---

20. "Opening Day at Ebbets Field," *New York Times*, April 16, 1947.
21. Kahn, *The Era*, 47.

before the Dodgers and Robinson came there for their first home game; National League president Ford Frick quietly threatened them with being banned for life from baseball if they did. The St. Louis Cardinals, in a city where Jim Crow segregation was rigidly enforced, threatened the same thing, the press exposed it, and Frick issued a warning: "If you strike, you will be suspended from the league. . . . I do not care if half the league strikes. Those who do it will encounter swift retribution. . . . This is the United States of America and one citizen has as much right to play as another."[22] The strike threats evaporated.

Robinson's teammates got to know him as a person and support him more on the field. Press and fan hostility was gradually replaced by admiration and support for his playing skills. Rickey provided constant mentoring. "Be daring!" he counseled. Don't let your team and your fans down by taking the racists' bait. Hold your temper and respond by hitting the ball, stealing bases, and fielding. By midseason, Robinson's performance on the field had reached a new, higher level. His style was dramatic and entertaining, particularly bunting (and beating out throws to first base), dancing off base to distract the pitcher, and stealing bases (including occasionally home base, something very rare in the Major Leagues). He played in more games than any other Dodger, batted .297, led the league in stolen bases, and made amazing, dramatic defensive plays. Fans loved it. Sportswriters praised it. His spirited performances helped pilot Brooklyn to the National League pennant (but even Robinson's talent was not enough to defeat their cross-city rivals, the New York Yankees, in the 1947 World Series).[23]

Robinson's star had risen. He had spirit, he worked hard, and he was very good at the game. The Dodgers designated September 23, 1947, as "Jackie Robinson Day," and he received an interracial goodwill plaque, a television, cash gifts, and a new Cadillac ("No more riding on buses," said his wife Rachel). [24] Baseball's trade paper, *Sporting News*, designated him Major League Baseball's "Rookie of the Year." *Time* magazine made him its cover story in September. He had endured "the toughest first season any ballplayer has ever faced. He made good as a major leaguer and proved himself as a man." The story praised his skills. "He is not only jack rabbit fast but one thought and two steps ahead of every base runner in the

---

22. Tygiel, *Baseball's Great Experiment*, 186.
23. Frommer, *New York City Baseball*, 61–64.
24. Robinson with Daniels, *Jackie Robinson*, 80.

business. He beats out bunts, stretches singles into doubles. . . . He dances and prances off base, keeping the enemy's infield upset and off balance, and worrying the pitcher." Branch Rickey, "the smartest man in baseball," has changed the game by bringing Robinson into it.[25]

Defending Patriotism, Attacking Racism

Jackie Robinson's growing fame led him into discussions and debates in the public arena. The late 1940s were years of the onset of the cold war between the United States and the Soviet Union. After World War II ended, communist governments were established in Poland, Czechoslovakia, East Germany, China, and other nations. As the menace abroad grew, there was increased attention to the possible threat posed by communist influence at home. Paul Robeson, a well-known black singer and actor, drew attention for his statements praising communism and condemning racism. Robeson, who had also been an outstanding football player and a lawyer with a degree from Columbia Law School, fought for integration, including in the sport of baseball, and he congratulated Jackie Robinson when he joined the Dodgers. As his attacks on entrenched racism became more strident, and his praise of the Soviet Union for its tolerance more pronounced, he was barred from performing in many places and hounded by the press and government. In May 1947, for instance, a permit to give a concert in Albany was issued, then revoked after an outcry about his political views, then reinstated by the courts with a restriction that he could sing but not give a speech.[26] In a speech in Paris in April, 1949, Robeson told an audience, "It is unthinkable that American Negroes would go to war on behalf of those who have oppressed us for generations against the Soviet Union which in one generation has lifted our people to full human dignity." The comment was part of a long speech, but it was pulled out by the press and became the focus of public anger in the United States. The NAACP and other black leaders disavowed it. The House Committee on Un-American Activities (HUAC), which was investigating alleged communist influence at home, decided to investigate the issue of potential

25. "Rookie of the Year," *Time* magazine, September 22, 1947, http://www.time.com/time/subscriber/article/0,33009,798173,00.html.
26. "An Anniversary: Paul Robeson in Albany, May 9, 1947," http://www.albany.edu/history/robeson1947.html.

black disloyalty should the cold war turn into a hot one. The committee invited Jackie Robinson, one of the most prominent blacks in the nation, to testify on Robeson's assertion.[27]

Robinson knew his testimony would garner national attention. He needed to avoid pandering to the HUAC by denouncing a fellow black activist but also avoid condoning disloyalty to the nation. Branch Rickey and other colleagues helped him draft the speech. He turned out to be as effective in public speaking as he was in hitting curve balls and stealing bases. Robinson used the forum to make a masterful case against racism and to appeal to American ideals and patriotism.[28]

Self-effacing modesty. ". . . I am a professional ballplayer. . . . I don't pretend to be an expert on communism or any other kind of 'ism'" he told the committee. Professional athletes should avoid taking partisan stands that could divide their fans.

The HUAC itself is controversial. "[S]ome of the policies of this committee have become political issues," he gently reminded the congressmen. This was a reference to the committee's crusade against leftists while at the same time ignoring right-wing groups like the Ku Klux Klan.

Blacks face tough challenges, but they are not the only ones. "[Y]ou can put me down as an expert on being a colored American. . . . I know that life in these United States can be mighty tough for people who are a little different from the majority—in their skin color or the way they worship their God or the way they spell their names."

A start has been made toward integrating baseball, but the work needs to continue. Robinson shrewdly used the forum for a quick overview of integration in baseball. "[A] start has been made, and progress goes on, and Southern as well as Northern fans are showing that they like the way things are working."

Blacks are determined to make progress. "We're going to make progress in other American fields," Robinson insisted. Blacks naturally resent and will fight racial slurs and discrimination but "this has got absolutely nothing to do with what Communists may or may not be trying to do."

But blacks hate communism. "[T]he more a Negro hates communism because it opposes democracy, the more he is going to hate any other

27. Ronald A. Smith, "The Paul Robeson-Jackie Robinson Saga and a Political Collision," in Tygiel, ed., *The Jackie Robinson Reader: Perspectives on an American Hero* (New York: Dutton, 1997), 169–188.
28. "Text of Jackie Robinson's Statement to House," *New York Times*, July 19, 1949.

influence that kills off democracy in this country—and that goes for discrimination in the Army, and segregation of trains and buses, and job discrimination because of religious beliefs or color or place of birth."

Communists are not responsible for black dissatisfaction. Communists denounce racism, Robinson admitted, but blacks really don't pay much attention to them. "Negroes were stirred up long before there was a Communist party, and they'll stay stirred up long after the party has disappeared—unless Jim Crow has disappeared by then as well."

Robeson's statement is "silly." Robinson dealt with the burning issue of Robeson only briefly. Calling him a "famous ex-athlete and a great singer and actor," and adding two qualifiers—"if Mr. Robeson actually made" the statement and "he has a right to his personal views"—Robinson dismissed the statement by saying it sounded "silly" to him.

Blacks will fight for America. Moving quickly away from any more discussion of Robeson, Robinson assured the committee that blacks— "and Italians and Irish and Jews and Swedes and Slavs"—would work to keep their nation out of war but would "do their best to help their country win the war" if one came.

A masterful ending. Blacks and other Americans have too much invested in America to throw it away through disloyalty and the "siren song" of Communism. "But that doesn't mean that we're going to stop fighting race discrimination in this country until we've got it licked. . . . We can win our fight without the Communists and we don't want their help."

Jackie Robinson caught a plane back to New York and arrived in time for a night game against the Chicago Cubs. Robinson's eloquent congressional testimony was followed by an exciting demonstration of his baseball skills. In the sixth inning, he walked, stole second, advanced to third when the Cubs' catcher overthrew the second baseman, and then stole home. He tripled in the eighth inning to drive in the third Dodger run. The Dodgers won, 3 to 0.[79] Press commentary the next day was almost all favorable: Reporters emphasized (and some exaggerated) his refutation of Robeson and downplayed or summarized his other points. But the speech, read in its entirety, ranks as one of the most thoughtful public utterances on civil rights issues in the late 1940s.

Later, though, Robinson had second thoughts. He never said he regretted the speech but late in life admitted, "I have grown wiser and closer to painful truths about America's destructiveness." Robeson sacrificed

---

29. Kahn, *The Era*, 205.

himself and his career and "was sincerely trying to help his people."[30] Robeson's career was already in peril by the time Robinson gave his measured speech. A concert scheduled for Peekskill, New York, in August 1949 featuring Robeson and other entertainers had to be cancelled when a jeering, rock-throwing mob appeared at the site. It was held a month later with heavy police protection, but as the concert attendees drove away, they were confronted by angry protestors who threw rocks through car and bus windshields, pulled people from their cars, beat them, and yelled, "[G]o back to Russia, you [racial epithet]." Robeson was shadowed by the FBI, his passport was confiscated, entertainment bookings were scarce, and his civil rights militancy continued to make him the center of attention and controversy.[31]

A Decade of Exciting Baseball

Robinson played for the Dodgers from 1947 to 1956. There continued to be death threats, beanballs, and other harassment, but gradually his outstanding, spirited play, particularly consistently hitting and stealing bases, won over opposing players, fans, and sportswriters. Branch Rickey continued as a mentor and eased tensions by trading away Dodger players who showed continuing animosity toward Robinson. He became a model for younger players, including black players Roy Campanella and Elton Howard who followed him onto the Dodger roster. Jackie Robinson hats and jackets could be purchased at Macy's department store. He became a celebrity, spoke widely, was featured in a comic book series and played himself in a 1950 film about his life, *The Jackie Robinson Story*. He endorsed various commercial products, including Bond Bread, Borden's milk, and Old Gold cigarettes. The ads played on his handsome good looks and some also included his wife Rachel and son Jackie junior. But the ads, like the man, were pioneers. They were among the first commercial messages aimed at the mass market that featured a black man or a black family.[32] He helped the Dodgers rise to the pinnacle of baseball and win National League pennants in 1947, 1952, 1953, and 1956 and the World Series (over their archrivals, the Yankees) in 1955.

---

30. Jackie Robinson, *I Never Had It Made*, 85–86.
31. Paul Robeson Jr., *The Undiscovered Paul Robeson: Quest for Freedom, 1939–1976* (New York: Wiley, 2010), 173.
32. Arnold Rampersad, *Jackie Robinson: A Biography* (New York: Ballantine Books, 1998), 189.

Other teams slowly followed Rickey's pioneering example, starting with the Cleveland Indians and the St. Louis Browns later in 1947. The New York Giants hired their first black player in 1949. By 1954, twelve of the sixteen Major League teams had black players. The New York Yankees were still not among them. In a 1953 TV interview, Jackie Robinson accused the Yankees of racism and refused to apologize when the enraged Yankees demanded it. A black player recruited in 1954 did not work out and was quickly banished to a Yankee farm team. The Yankees finally hired their first black player, Elston Howard, in 1955.[33]

Jackie and Rachel tried to purchase homes in Westchester County, Long Island, and Connecticut, and each time they found a place they wanted, the house was taken off the market or sold to someone else. It was rank housing racial discrimination and they finally gave up. They bought a vacant lot near Stamford, Connecticut; built a home; and were gradually accepted by their initially resentful white neighbors. Jackie's base running still featured too-frequent collisions with opposing players and an impressive but dangerous method of sliding into base that knocked defenders off their feet and sent them flying. Robinson became more assertive as time passed, often arguing with umpires and implying that racism rather than his own mistakes were behind the calls against him. He was ejected from a 1954 game against Milwaukee for confronting the umpire. As he left, he swung his bat and it slipped (his version) or he threw it (critics' view) and hit three spectators in the stands. He later apologized and a lawsuit brought by an injured spectator was settled out of court. But he began to realize his patience was wearing thin and his determination to win at all costs becoming too strong. In another 1954 game, when an umpire called a ground-rule double on his teammate Duke Snider rather than a home run, which Robinson believed it was,

> I cleared out of the dugout. The Dodger bench jumped up too and I thought they were with me. Then I ran out to the field to argue. We needed the game and were trailing by three runs. After a minute of argument, I saw I was alone. No one had followed me out to protest. And the boos had begun. . . . I had to walk across the infield with the boos ringing in my ears.[34]

---

33. Kahn, *The Era*, 54–55.
34. Jackie Robinson, "Now I Know Why They Boo Me," *Look* (January–February 1955) in Tygiel, ed., *The Jackie Robinson Reader*, 193–202.

Robinson argued with Dodger manager Walter Alston and had little rapport with Walter O'Malley, who succeeded Rickey as team CEO in 1950.

Robinson was aging and too often his temper was getting the best of him. In 1956, he retired from baseball to become an executive at Chock full o'Nuts coffee company, just before O'Malley could carry out a decision to trade him to the New York Giants. "There shouldn't be any mystery about my reasons," he said in a farewell article in *Look* magazine. "I'm 38 years old, with a family to support. . . . At my age, a man doesn't have much future in baseball—and very little security." You start slipping, and "pretty soon they're moving you around like a used car. You have no control over what happens to you. I didn't want that."[35] Walter O'Malley did not care whether Robinson stayed or retired. Faced with static attendance at Dodger games, the space limitations of aging Ebbets Field, and limited parking capacity near the stadium, he asked the city to subsidize purchase of land to build a grand new enclosed stadium about a mile away. Robert Moses, New York City's powerful director of parks and transportation, and other city authorities balked at the investment of public funds. Moses suggested an alternative location, the city-owned site of the 1939 World's Fair in Flushing Meadows, Queens. O'Malley refused, insisting that the Brooklyn Dodgers would not become the Queens Dodgers. In 1957, he moved the Dodgers to a very receptive and welcoming Los Angeles. Brooklyn's star player had left in 1956 and now its team left town as well. Ebbets Field was soon torn down and replaced by an apartment complex. Something of the heart, character, and spirit of Brooklyn left with the Dodgers, never to return.[36]

Continuing to Make History

The final two decades of Jackie Robinson's life were played out off the field but in full view of the public. He collaborated with professional writers to produce a memoir, *Wait till Next Year*, in 1960; a history of the integration of baseball based on interviews with a number of players, *Baseball Has Done It*, in 1964; and an autobiography, *I Never Had It Made*, in 1972. Many of his activities after retiring from the Dodgers reflected the

35. Jackie Robinson, "Why I'm Quitting Baseball," *Look* (January 1957) in Tygiel, ed., *The Jackie Robinson Reader*, 214.
36. Henry D. Fetter, "Revising the Revisionists: Walter O'Malley, Robert Moses, and the End of the Brooklyn Dodgers," *New York History* 89 (Winter 2008), 54–74.

racial and political tensions of the era. Often, it felt a bit like the old days when he was trying to steal a base, got trapped between bases, and extricated himself only through quick thinking and agile footwork. Hailed as a black pioneer and hero, he was inclined now to be a speaker and supporter, someone who showed up at civil rights protest rallies rather than organized and led them. He criticized black apathy and acquiescence with the status quo but also counseled against militancy. He helped found and then served as board chairman for Freedom National Bank, a minority-owned commercial bank based in Harlem. He established the Jackie Robinson Construction Company to build low- and moderate-income housing units. He hailed the arrival of more black professional baseball players but criticized the fact that there were no black managers. He praised President Dwight Eisenhower's use of federal troops to enforce the desegregation of Little Rock High School in 1957, but when the president the next year urged blacks to exercise "patience and forbearance," Robinson protested. "I respectfully remind you that we have been the most patient of all people," he wrote the president. "We want to enjoy now the rights that we feel we are entitled to as Americans."[37]

He began working extensively with the NAACP, a progressive group that insisted on civil rights reform but eschewed black militancy and separatism. In his civil rights work, he went on speaking tours and supported fundraising rather than taking leadership positions. He focused on housing and employment issues. "When I quit [baseball], I went into the NAACP and the conservatives found me very hard to take. They were men of eighty. Their attitude was: don't rock the boat," he told baseball writer Roger Kahn. "Today [ca. 1970], militants find me hard to take. Their attitude is 'burn everything.'"[38]

Often, he struggled to find a middle course. He worked with Martin Luther King on racial issues but disagreed with King's opposition to the war in Vietnam. Condemning the burning of black churches in Alabama in 1962, he noted that living conditions of many Southern blacks were disgraceful. At the same time, he faulted Northern blacks for not taking more responsibility for improving the conditions of those in the South.[39]

---

37. Jackie Robinson to President Dwight D. Eisenhower, May 13, 1958, in Michael G. Long, ed., *First-Class Citizenship: The Civil Rights Letters of Jackie Robinson* (New York: Times Books, 2007), 56–57.
38. Roger Kahn, *The Boys of Summer* (New York: Harper, 1987), 406.
39. "Jackie Robinson Stresses Need for North to Aid South's Negroes," *New York Times*, September 26, 1962.

He supported blacks developing political leadership roles but accused black Harlem congressman Adam Clayton Powell of hiding behind a false defense of racism when he faced corruption charges in the 1960s. Black Muslim leader Malcolm X sneered that Robinson had been lifted to success by whites such as Rickey and condemned his accommodationist views. Robinson retorted that blacks needed to continue insisting on their rights, and that segregationists secretly liked Malcolm X because "you have played right into their hands" by supporting militant confrontation and undermining moderate black leadership.[40]

Robinson was never fully comfortable with either political party. He admired Senator Hubert Humphrey, an early champion of civil rights, but when Humphrey lost the 1960 Democratic presidential nomination to John F. Kennedy, Robinson felt Kennedy courted Southern segregationist politicians and was lukewarm on civil rights. In a move widely criticized by friends, he endorsed and campaigned for Republican Richard Nixon in 1960, only to be disillusioned when the Republican Party seemed to ignore black voters and Nixon showed little interest in civil rights issues. He believed that the party's 1964 presidential nominee, Senator Barry Goldwater, was too conservative and supported his opponent, Lyndon Johnson. Robinson admired New York Republican governor Nelson Rockefeller's progressive views and policies on race issues, the governor hired him as a special assistant for community affairs in 1966, and the two became friends. "I got together the so-called militants and offered to do what I could to communicate their beefs to the governor, to housing people, and to industry," Robinson recalled in his autobiography. He felt his work "did make a difference" but "not enough of a difference" because of "the neglect of blacks in the state of New York which had long preceded the Rockefeller administration."[41] But Robinson left the post after a couple of years, disillusioned with Rockefeller, whom he felt had deserted progressivism in an effort to appeal to conservative Republicans in his quest for the presidency. He supported his old hero Hubert Humphrey in 1968, only to see him defeated by Richard Nixon.

In his autobiography, written not long before his death, he reflected a sense of accomplishment alongside unfulfilled goals: ". . . I cannot, as an individual, rejoice in the good things I have been permitted to work for

40. Jackie Robinson and Malcolm X, "An Exchange of Letters" (1963), in Tygiel, ed., *The Jackie Robinson Reader*, 240.
41. Robinson and Duckett, *I Never Had It Made*, 208.

and learn while the humblest of my brothers is down in a deep hole hollering for help and not being heard." On the other hand, his goals seemed tempered and modest:

> I am not a fanatical integrationist. I don't think there is any particular magic in a white kid sitting next to a black kid in a classroom. I simply don't want all-black classrooms and all-black schools in a system where the best teachers and the best administrators go to the white school and the worst to the black. . . . I want the freedom to rise as high in my career as my ability indicates. I want to be free to follow the dictates of my own mind and conscience without being subject to the pressures of any man, black or white.[42]

Jackie Robinson died in 1972 of diabetes. Robinson personified dogged determination and uphill, against-the-odds struggle and triumph. "He comes to win," baseball veteran Leo Durocher put it simply. "He beats you." He exemplified energy and skill. "Adventure! Adventure! The man is all adventure," Branch Rickey insisted. "I only wish I could have signed him five years sooner."[43] He showed the potential of talent unleashed from the shackles of prejudice. "Robinson could hit and bunt and steal and run," said baseball writer Roger Kahn. "He had intimidation skills and he burned with a dark fire. He wanted passionately to win. He bore the burden of a pioneer and the weight made him stronger."[44] Robinson "combined militance with a sense of martyrdom and combined deference with defiance. . . . he reassured white authority but his very presence seemed to undermine it."[45] Like many other exceptional New Yorkers, Jackie Robinson was hard to categorize. He was a catalyst of change, sometimes inconsistent, sometimes accommodating, and sometimes defiant. His courage and ability helped alter the course of state and national history.

---

42. Ibid., 102.
43. Kahn, *The Boys of Summer*, 392.
44. Ibid., xix.
45. Gerald L. Early, *A Level Playing Field: African American Athletes and the Republic of Sports* (Boston: Harvard University Press, 2011), 180–181.

12
June 24, 1954

A New Enterprise for Moving around New York

Governor Thomas E. Dewey on a bulldozer at the ground-breaking for the New York State Thruway at Liverpool, July 1946. *Photo courtesy of New York State Archives.*

Opening New York's "New Erie Canal"

On June 24, 1954, Governor Thomas E. Dewey officially opened a 112-mile section of the New York State Thruway from Lowell, near Utica, to West Henrietta, near Rochester. Construction of the superhighway had begun back in 1946, three shorter segments had already been opened, and a few more would be dedicated by the end of 1955, when the road would be substantially finished. But this day of public opening was the most carefully scripted, highest-visibility public event. Dewey, a Republican first elected in 1942, was in his last year as governor, though he had not yet announced his intention to retire. The June 24 dedication ceremonies turned out to be the last major public event for one of New York's most effective but also highly partisan and controversial governors.

Dewey had earned a reputation for tough prosecution of organized crime figures as a federal prosecutor, special state prosecutor, and New York County district attorney before being elected governor. Energetic, determined, impatient with underlings, and contemptuous of Democrats, Tom Dewey pushed past obstacles and rolled over opposition. He forced his agenda, blending social progressivism with fiscal conservatism, through the compliant Republican-dominated legislature. He eliminated obsolete bureaus and cut waste in state agencies but supported mental health, education, and other social programs. Accused of being a mild New Dealer, he emphatically denied the charge and declared that people must show independence and do things for themselves. But "of course we are running a welfare state," and conservatives who wanted to roll back the state's security and welfare programs are "living in the middle ages." He signed the nation's first state antidiscrimination law in 1945 and initiated the State University of New York in 1948. Dewey's suits were well tailored, his speeches polished, and his insistence on the prerogatives and dignity of the governorship unrelenting. "Good government is not an abstraction," said the governor. "It is not a disembodied spirit fluttering vaguely around the gable of the Capitol at Albany. It is made up of a team of live, active, vigorous men and women doing vital tasks with energy and independence." Dewey "got joy out of attainment," recalled Herbert Brownell, a longtime friend and campaign manager.[1] June 24, 1954, was a pinnacle of triumph and attainment for Dewey.

The day's activities were carefully orchestrated by the Thruway Authority's robust public relations department. Publicity chief Robert Monahan worked closely with L. Judson Morehouse, executive director of the New York State Good Roads Association, a coalition of highway contractors, travelers, and others who had backed Dewey's vision for the grand highway. Morehouse organized an honorary Celebration Committee for the Thruway opening, chaired by the nation's foremost automobile executive, Alfred P. Sloan Jr., chairman of the board at General Motors. "Who can deny that, next to food, clothing and shelter, the motor vehicle in its various forms has first lien on the purchasing power of the American people?" asked Sloan in an article in the association's newsletter. Another celebration committee member, Harvey Firestone, CEO of the tire company that bore his name, stated that "America's future progress depends

---

1. Richard Norton Smith, *Thomas E. Dewey and His Times* (New York: Simon & Schuster, 1982), 349–350.

on better and safer highways." Governor Dewey, on the eve of the opening event, called it "the greatest superhighway ever built at the lowest cost and totally self-supporting."[2]

After a ribbon cutting and brief speech at Lowell at 10:00 a.m., the governor entered his state limousine and headed west, leading a cavalcade of over two hundred vehicles. As one event organizer noted, "[T]he cavalcade will underline the economic advantages offered by the super highway and dramatize how *everyone* in the state benefits as a result of transportation savings, etc." There were Chevrolets, Fords, and Plymouths, the sorts of cars that most citizens drove every day. Flashy cars included a Ford Skyliner convertible, an Oldsmobile Starfire Coupe, and a Pontiac Star Chief Catalina. Seven passenger buses and a Reo school bus constituted a modest nod to mass transit. Then came trucks belonging to New York businesses, including Genesee Beer, GLF (farm supplies), General Baking Company, and even a Babcock Baby Chick Pullman. There were dump trucks of the sort that had done so much of the hauling in the construction of the road. Bringing up the rear of the procession were ambulances and fire trucks, and finally, military vehicles, reminding people of the road's potential use for moving military forces and evacuating cities in the event of an enemy attack.[3]

The motorcade stopped at Syracuse for the first of two major public events. The local organizing committee had turned out hundreds of eager citizens to witness history in the making. Radio-TV announcer Ward Bond served as master of ceremonies for an hour-long celebration. An air force band played patriotic songs. "Milk maids" representing the Syracuse Milk Dealers' Association handed out free bottles of milk. The crowd cheered as Dewey's car came into view. "Miss Thruway," selected a few days earlier by the chamber of commerce and the *Syracuse Post Standard*, greeted the governor and his party. Dewey seemed to be in a combative rather than a celebratory mood. This opening is "a triumph over bitter opposition and character assassination," he said, referring to Democrats who had opposed the enterprise. Like DeWitt Clinton's political enemies who had derided

---

2. New York Good Roads Association, Press Release June 14, 1954, and *Roads* newsletter June 24, 1954; New York State Thruway Authority Records, Speeches and News Releases, 1946–1961, New York State Archives, Albany, New York.

3. "Instructions for Staging Vehicular Section of Thruway Cavalcade" and "Revised Fact Sheet about the Thruway Opening," by the Syracuse Opening Committee, New York State Thruway Authority Records, Public Relations Planning and Publications Files, 1950–1969, New York State Archives. Emphasis in original.

the Erie Canal as "Clinton's Gutter," these shortsighted politicians had called the Thruway "Dewey's Upstate Boulevard." Now everyone could see that it was "the greatest, most useful advance in highway transportation in the history of the world." It cost less per mile than any comparable highway in the nation and had "no frills or niceties," despite the claims of "reckless characters" who exaggerated its costs. The entire road, when finished, would be three times the length of the New Jersey Turnpike and one hundred miles longer than the Pennsylvania Turnpike. Safety would be paramount—no intersecting roads, only gentle hills, long sight distances. Already, shopping centers and factories (including a new GE plant close to the ceremony's location) were clustering near the highway. Land values in the Syracuse area near the new road had gone up 1,000 percent. "Everyone in the state is the beneficiary," exclaimed the governor.[4]

Dewey and his entourage moved west to Rochester for an evening banquet at a downtown hotel. Continuing his Erie Canal theme, the governor asserted that Tammany Hall politicians had opposed it just as their present-day counterparts, Democrats, had tried to forestall the Thruway. "What astonishes me about the business of government is how the centuries pass and the names and projects change, but politics remain the same," he told the assembled dignitaries. The canal had led to phenomenal growth for Rochester and the entire state, and "history is repeating itself right now" through new enterprises springing up, such a new TV assembly plant at nearby Batavia. "The Thruway has triumphed over every kind of political opposition, over inflation, war shortages and the obstacles of nature itself."[5] Dewey flipped an electric switch that turned on the lights and activated the toll booths along the route, opening the route to traffic.

By early July, over 8,500 cars were using the new section of the Thruway every day. The news coverage often reflected the ample publicity material distributed by the Thruway Authority's publicity office. The *New York Times* noted that 85 percent of New York's population lived within twenty miles of the route, it would move traffic out of towns and speed products to market, and would be a boon to local real estate and business development.[6] *Time* magazine called it the first section of what will be "the

---

4. "Text of an Address by Governor Thomas E. Dewey Prepared for Delivery at Syracuse. . . . June 24, 1954," New York State Thruway Authority Records, Speeches, and News Releases, 1946–1961, New York State Archives.
5. "Text of an Address by Governor Thomas E. Dewey Prepared for Delivery at Rochester. . . . June 24, 1954," New York State Thruway Authority Records, Speeches, and News Releases, 1946–1961, New York State Archives.
6. "New Main Street for New York," *New York Times*, June 20, 1954; and "Thruway to Officially Open Today," *New York Times*, June 24, 1954.

longest, best-planned, and most remarkable toll road in America." Even the rest and dining areas were closely regulated: "Sample rules: a cup of coffee will mean exactly seven ounces and will costs 10 cents; a frankfurter must weigh at least one-ninth of a pound and be served with a choice of relish and mustard; authorized repair garages must provide 'comfortable accommodations' for stranded drivers while mechanics tinker with their cars." There was even a stream full of trout running down the center of the dividing median near Manchester! Like the Erie Canal, the new road was expected to drastically lower transportation costs, and its tolls would bring largesse into the state treasury.[7]

Carl Carmer, a well-known popular historian, added historical perspective in an article entitled "In the Path of the Pioneers." The Thruway followed the water-level route along the Hudson and Mohawk rivers, the same route that Indian trails, turnpikes, railroads, and previous major highways followed for centuries. The impact of the opening of the Erie Canal in 1825 had been "immediate and almost incredible." Now the Thruway was operating in "the historic route that built the Empire State." History suggested it would raise New York to new levels of greatness.[8]

Vision of a New Superhighway

Politicians in Albany had begun talking about a new highway from Buffalo to Albany to New York City as early as the 1930s. New York already had Route 5 running from Albany to Ripley on the Pennsylvania state line, completed in the 1920s; U.S. Route 20, running from Boston across Massachusetts and New York to the Pacific Coast and incorporating a number of old east-west turnpikes; and U.S. routes 9 and 9W, on the east and west sides of the Hudson respectively, running from Albany to the outskirts of New York City. But all of these roads ran through cities and villages, intersected other routes, and were known all too often for their congestion, potholes, and accidents. The number of cars kept increasing. By 1939, about 130 million people were driving in the United States; there were more than 31 million cars, trucks, and buses on the road; and people traveled about 285 billion miles. The overcrowded, outdated highways contrasted with the vision for the future presented in General Motors' highly publicized "Futurama" exhibit at the 1939 New York World's Fair.

---

7. "Highways: The Concrete Canal," *Time*, July 5, 1954.
8. Carl Carmer, "In the Path of the Pioneers," *New York Times*, June 25, 1954.

It showed cities and the countryside of the future connected by broad, multilane expressways where cars moved smoothly and swiftly to their destinations.[9] Robert Moses, using expansive powers as state parks commissioner and manager of New York City urban planning and redevelopment efforts, had by 1939 built the Southern State, Northern State, Wantagh, and Cross Island parkways on Long Island. Moses's roads anticipated the Thruway and other superhighways: four-lanes, limited access, grade separations at crossroads, medians, and parks and woods along the sides, all geared to produce a pleasant, quick, and safe driving experience. The cross-state Pennsylvania Turnpike, opened in 1940, showed what determined state effort could do, and also the potential for new roads to lure businesses, tourists, and other travelers from New York to its neighbor to the south. Across the sea, Germany's Autobahn was proving its value in speedy movement of Adolf Hitler's military forces.[10]

In 1942, Governor Herbert Lehman appointed a postwar planning commission to propose public works projects that could be implemented quickly after the war ended and help keep the economy from sliding into a slump when wartime production ended. The commission recommended a new New York City–to–Buffalo road. Manhattan assemblyman Abbot Low Moffat, chairman of the Assembly Ways and Means Committee, weary of years of stop-and-go driving to and from Albany on Route 9, pushed through authorizing legislation in 1942. The road would be costly, but the legislation did not specify any new revenue source. Geography dictated that it must be built on the west side of the Hudson, but the legislation did not specify how it would be connected with New York City. Tom Dewey, taking office in January 1943, began wrestling with implementation issues. They could be postponed for a while—construction would have to be delayed until the war ended—but then they would have to be addressed.

From a Rocky Start to a Solid Foundation

Dewey realized that New York's future growth and prosperity depended on good roads. In 1945, he initiated a multiyear, multi-million-dollar

---

9. Tom Lewis, *Divided Highways: Building the Interstate Highways, Transforming American Life* (New York: Viking, 1997), 38–45.

10. Michael R. Fein, *Paving the Way: New York Road Building and the American State, 1880–1956* (Lawrence: University Press of Kansas, 2008), 115–122.

construction project with a goal of building a network of state highways designed to connect communities, serve an ever-expanding suburbia, integrate markets, and develop industry. He appointed Bertram D. Tallamy, a seasoned veteran of highway, water, and sewer construction in the Buffalo region, as Commissioner of Public Works, increased the size of the department, toned up its professionalism, and pushed through laws increasing its authority to set standards for county, town, and village projects as a condition of state aid.[11] A comprehensive 1949 report on the state of New York's highways gave him even more ammunition. "[T]he state highway system is in critical condition. . . . People want more elbow room and they are pushing out along or adjacent to good highways. The American way of life is irrevocably geared to the motor vehicle." The future would include "more people, more cars, more traffic." Construction of the new Thruway would save millions of dollars that otherwise would need to be spent on upgrading existing highways that it would parallel.[12]

Dewey's support for the Thruway coincided with his vision of Republican-style activist, government: Promote economic growth, minimize economic regulations, and fund public works projects on a pay-as-you go basis.[13] The booming wartime economy had produced a handsome surplus in the state treasury that even the fiscally cautious Dewey assumed would continue. He ordered the beginning of construction of the Thruway at three points: Silver Creek near Buffalo, Liverpool just west of Syracuse, and Saugerties in the mid-Hudson Valley. Starting in three geographically dispersed places increased the chances for continued funding from the legislature. The cost estimate was $202 million (the final cost would actually be more than three times that amount). The governor traveled to Liverpool to break ground on July 11, 1946. "Its pavement and bridges will be built to carry, with ease and efficiency, the heaviest commercial vehicles and the family car," he declared. "It will provide a great new artery to connect the agricultural and recreational regions of the state with urban areas." New York's future greatness would be assured by having a modern highway transportation system "just as the Erie Canal brought new prosperity to the state a century ago." After heaving the first symbolic shovelful of dirt,

---

11. Ibid., 180–194.
12. New York State Department of Public Works and U.S. Department of Commerce, Bureau of Public Roads, *Cooperative Highway Needs Study* (Albany: 1949), 16, 137, 158, copy in New York State Thruway Records, Public Relations Planning and Publication Files, 1950–1969.
13. Fein, *Paving the Way*, 197–198.

the governor climbed on a bulldozer and began the grading work. Dewey and the bulldozer were a symbolic pair: Anything standing in the way of the project was going to be shoved aside.[14]

The state had a $500 million postwar surplus, said the governor, so there would be no need for bonds or tolls. Commissioner Bertram Tallamy's Department of Public Works (DPW) began an intensive publicity campaign, with news releases and press briefings. The majority of New York's population and "the bulk of its industrial and commercial enterprises" were located in the Thruway corridor, and "motorists bogged down in some of the heaviest traffic found anywhere" would soon be getting relief. "The entire route will be devoid of obstacles to the easy flow of traffic. Intersections at grade will be non-existent. No traffic lights will blink along its course." Factories and shopping malls would be built along the road, property values would rise, and homeowners' property taxes decline. [15]

The euphoria did not last long. Dewey, running for reelection as governor in 1946, faced a formidable opponent, U.S. Senator James M. Mead. He called the state surplus a Dewey "slush fund" and said it should be used to aid returning veterans and build houses and mental hospitals. The Thruway was a "postponable luxury boulevard. . . . It takes men, money, and materials away from housing." Democratic campaign themes included: "Forget about highways and let's have houses!" and "Hospital beds rather than road beds!" The combative Dewey called his opponents ignorant, their allegations "fantastic and cruel." New York has the resources to meet public needs for housing, hospitals, and highways simultaneously. "We must build highways fit for the future of the State or bear the blame for thousands of injured and maimed and dead" on existing overcrowded roads.[16] Public confidence in Dewey's ability to advance a broad agenda through careful management of state fiscal resources carried the day. Dewey overwhelmed Mead, and the Republicans kept their comfortable legislative majorities.

But the road ahead turned out to be a bumpy one. Dewey's wartime surplus melted away as the state adjusted to a postwar economy. State

---

14. "Work on Thruway Started by Dewey," *New York Times*, July 12, 1946.
15. Fein, *Paving the Way*, 184; "Highway of the Future," *Christian Science Monitor*, August 30, 1946; "Thruway Near Reality," *New York Times* July 7, 1946.
16. "Mead Criticizes Dewey on Schools," *New York Times*, October 13, 1946; "Dewey Is Accused of Dodging Issues," *New York Times*, October 17, 1946; and "Foes Twist Facts, Dewey Declares," *New York Times*, October 23, 1946.

highway construction costs for roads other than the Thruway turned out to be much higher than expected. Federal restrictions and rationing linked to Marshall Plan aid in rebuilding war-ravaged Europe created steel shortages. Postwar inflation ate up highway construction dollars. By the fall of 1949, three years after Dewey broke ground for the grand new version of the Erie Canal, only forty-eight miles had been completed. A barrage of criticism began to rise. "Our neighboring states are rapidly expanding their highway systems, an action which may lead to the ultimate diversion of industry as well as tourist travel from New York State," said a September 1949 grumbling resolution of the New York State Automobile Dealers Association. A month later, State DPW chief Tallamy released a new estimate of total projected Thruway construction costs: $400 million, double the estimate of a few years earlier. Dewey's retort to critics—"you can't pick highways out of a Sears-Roebuck catalog!"—and his repeated insistence that the Thruway was essential to New York's future did not quiet the skeptics.[17]

By early 1950, Dewey faced four problems: paying for the Thruway, managing the construction project (already proving too much for the DPW, swamped with other state road projects and supervising highway aid to local governments), meeting Democratic opposition, and connecting to New York City. By the end of the year, he had addressed them all.

In February 1950, the governor proposed an entirely new approach to funding, construction, and operation. A new Thruway Authority would be created to construct and operate the road. It would be empowered to issue up to $400 million in bonds. The bonds would be retired, and the road maintained, from the fees for special licenses for Thruway users. (Building toll booths was initially rejected as impractical because the booths would cause traffic backups.) Critics, some of whom had lambasted Dewey for the slow pace of construction, now lined up to criticize his new plan. The president of the Automobile Club of New York said the proposal was "little more than a shakedown of the motorist." The president of the Motor Carriers Association, representing the trucking industry, declared, "[W]e believe the use of state highways should be free. We oppose the establishment of any more commissions ... because we already have enough governmental commissions which seem to be accountable

---

17. Fein, *Paving the Way*, 148–149; "Speed-Up of Work on Thruway Urged," *New York Times*, September 14, 1949; and "First Thruway Link," *New York Times*, October 9, 1949.

to no one." The chairman of the state Democratic committee reminded people of Dewey's promise at the Liverpool groundbreaking, "[W]e will pay as we go without plunging the state into a debt to be paid by our grandchildren."[18]

Dewey, as usual undaunted by critics, appointed a committee to flesh out his new vision and develop a proposal. As the committee worked, the canny governor built support in two key areas, Westchester County and New York City. State DPW chief Tallamy hammered out a two-part agreement with Westchester County executive Herbert C. Gerlach. One, the road would cross the Hudson near Tarrytown and run through the county to the Major Deegan Expressway at the New York City line. The exact crossing point and route would be worked out through discussion between state and county officials. Two, the state would begin construction of the New England Thruway, linking New Rochelle to Connecticut, long a Westchester priority.[19]

In early March, New York City Democratic mayor William O'Dwyer endorsed the governor's Thruway proposal. Dewey had committed to help speed construction of expressways in New York City to be financed in part by state and federal funds. The mayor's endorsement undercut state Democratic Party plans to thwart the Thruway; most of the party members came from New York City. It was a shrewd political coup for the governor. Asked whether it would put him in conflict with Democrats who opposed it, O'Dwyer said: "I wouldn't know anything about that. I'm a city manager." Dewey professed surprise at the allegations of political maneuvering. The Thruway would mean safe travel and, he continued, "I can't see anything political in saving lives."[20]

Dewey sent his proposal to the legislature on March 10. The new Thruway Authority would build the rest of the road, including determining the exact route through Rockland and Westchester counties and the Hudson River crossing point. It would be authorized to issue up to $500 million in bonds, which would have state credit behind them, ensuring investor confidence and a low interest rate. That would require amending

18. "Authority Planned to Push Thruway," New York Times, February 14, 1950; "Thruway License Held Shakedown," New York Times, February 15, 1950; "Fitzpatrick Asks Halt on Thruway," New York Times, February 20, 1950; and "State Democrats Try to Bar State Works," New York Times, February 21, 1950.
19. "Thruway to Cross Westchester; Compact Is Reached at Albany," New York Times, March 3, 1950.
20. "O'Dwyer Endorses Plan on Thruway," New York Times, March 7, 1950.

the state constitution, which would necessitate another vote of approval by the next annual session of the legislature and approval by the voters at the polls. Dewey called the Thruway "the most important physical development ever undertaken in the State of New York." It would be "self-supporting and self-liquidating, . . . it will not cost the state one red cent." In fact it would free up state funds for other highway construction as well as for building schools and hospitals.[21]

Democratic opponents fumed that the proposal was rushed, designed to mask Dewey's mismanagement of the postwar budget surplus and give him a boost in an election year. But the opposition was divided because of O'Dwyer's support, and the bill sailed through the Republican-dominated legislature. The governor signed it in a public ceremony on March 21 where he emphasized it would lower transportation costs and keep New York competitive in industry and commerce. Dewey immediately made appointments to the new three-person Thruway Authority: Bertram Tallamy, the DPW chief who had helped spearhead Thruway plans, was named chairman; R. Burdell Bixby, Republican strategist who had been serving as secretary to the governor; and David J. Martin, a New York City real estate developer and political ally of Mayor O'Dwyer.

Politics and Geography

The new Authority got down to work. The law gave it broad authority to condemn land and push forward with construction. The new commissioners proved to be politically astute and excellent spokesmen for the enterprise. Chairman Tallamy spoke frequently at meetings of chambers of commerce, newspaper editors, and other influential groups. He emphasized several themes: The road was self-financing through bonds that would be retired from the fees from user licenses; it would aid commerce, speed shipments from farm to market, and reduce transportation costs; boost vacation travel; reduce accidents; and lower auto insurance costs.[22] The Authority hired dozens of new engineers, set high professional

---

21. Press Release, March 8, 1950, in New York State Thruway Authority Records, Speeches, and News Releases, 1946–1961, New York State Archives; "Governor Defends Thruway Fee Plan," *New York Times*, March 10, 1950.
22. Bertram Tallamy speech to Annual Convention of Town Highway Superintendents, September 21, 1950; Tallamy, "Thruway Ends and Means," *New York Professional Engineer*, December 1950, in New York State Thruway Authority Records, Public Relations Planning and Publications Files, 1950–1969, New York State Archives.

standards, and established a highly effective media office. News releases and reports emphasized that the Thruway would relieve traffic congestion, lower transportation costs, and perhaps best of all, "it will be paid for by the user." Its promotional work was unprecedented in state government. The Thruway Authority was "a heavily capitalized public corporation with a powerful public relations machine," notes highway historian Michael Fein.[23]

Dewey sought a third term in the fall of 1950. Democrats nominated New York City congressman Walter A. Lynch, who proved to be a lackluster candidate. The Democrats accused Dewey of arrogance, overspending on highways, and neglecting other needs such as the mentally ill. Dewey was called "a little Stalin" running "a politburo" in Albany. The Thruway was a "hastily conceived and inadequately planned highway" that would be "shoved down the throats of the taxpayers in those communities through which it will pass." Dewey called the Democrats "a crew of wreckers" and "boss-ridden puppets." He scoffed at their claims of overspending on the Thruway and other projects. "Democrats running on an economy platform?" sneered the governor. "Now I've seen everything except sunrise at seven o'clock at night." But, taking no chances, he campaigned vigorously. He spoke via statewide TV, a pioneering move. He stood outside in the biting wind to shake hands with guards reporting to work at Dannemora state prison. Usually stiff and proper, he unlimbered and spent forty-five minutes in a fireman's hat on the running board of a fire engine in Malone. He won with a majority of over a half million votes.[24]

Dewey resumed the campaign for the Thruway in his annual message to the legislature in January 1951: "We have a desperate need for a new express highway to speed motor vehicle emergency equipment and the products of an expanded economy in our state." In February the legislature approved state backing for Thruway bonds. The Authority's publicity office went into high gear to assure voter approval of the required constitutional amendment in the fall. "Construction is under way throughout the state," said a rosy report in the summer, with seventy miles under construction, and engineers and contractors at work in twenty-one counties.

23. "THRUWAY BENEFITS," Undated, ca. May 1950, New York State Thruway Authority Records, Public Relations Planning and Publications Files, 1950–1969, New York State Archives; Fein, *Paving the Way*, 51.
24. Smith, *Dewey*, 565–573.

Construction would provide employment for about eighteen thousand men for four years. Production of materials, supplies, and equipment used in construction would give employment to another twenty thousand workers. Approval by the people would permit borrowing at low rates, accelerating construction and leading to lower construction costs and in turn lower cost to users. The finished road would boost the state's economy.[25] New York City mayor Vincent R. Impellitteri, O'Dwyer's successor, endorsed it. Robert Moses, New York's construction coordinator, called the Thruway an "integral and indispensable part" of the metropolitan transportation program.[26] In November the state's voters approved the constitutional amendment by a 4 to 1 margin.

The Authority issued new bonds early in 1952 at the low rate of 1.1 percent because of state backing. Feeling vindicated, governor Dewey told the press that "it is doubtful if any other authority was ever able to float a loan on such favorable terms."[27] By the next spring, contracts for construction of the rest of the road were in effect. Work accelerated. Bertram Tallamy and his colleagues shifted their advocacy message, noting that land values were rising wherever the Thruway advanced and that businesses and shopping centers were beginning construction along the route. There were a few policy shifts, including a decision to build toll booths and charge on a per-trip basis, in addition to issuing special Thruway access licenses.

As mile after mile of concrete was poured, Dewey and Tallamy continued their public relations push to sustain public support for the Thruway, even as cost estimates rose. Speaking to the New York State Society of Newspaper Editors in February 1954, Tallamy made the usual case about "the greatest project of its kind ever undertaken" to build "the longest, safest, and most beneficial highway in the world." He urged them to avoid "muddy thinking and fuzzy writing" about escalating costs. Cost to secure right of way and move dirt were greater than expected, and steel shortages had driven up costs for bridges and guardrails. Despite "the devastating effect of inflation," construction costs "have kept pace with, or a little ahead of, the price of pork chops, automobiles, newsprint,

25. New York State Thruway Authority, *An Interim Report on the New York State Thruway*, Summer 1951, 22, in New York State Thruway Authority Records, Public Relations Planning and Publications Files, 1950–1969, New York State Archives.
26. "Moses Urges Vote for Thruway Issue," *New York Times*, October 15, 1951.
27. "Thruway Borrows $60,000,000 at 1.1%," *New York Times*, April 1, 1952.

or six-room houses."[28] Dewey condemned Democrats for trying to score political points by criticizing "the greatest development of the twentieth century" for New York. "If you don't build, you die in this modern civilization." In fact, the Thruway would not be enough. The governor boldly proposed four more superhighways: from Albany to the Canadian border (now called I-87 or the Northway), Binghamton to the St. Lawrence River (I-81), the Southern Tier Expressway, and the Long Island Expressway. All would be constructed after he left office.[29]

Crossing the Hudson

Construction accelerated but so also did controversy in Rockland and Westchester counties. Governor Dewey had made a decision that the road would run south from Albany on the west side of the Hudson River, but instead of continuing to the New Jersey border, as originally planned, it would cross the Hudson between Rockland County and Westchester County and connect with the Major Deegan Expressway at the New York City line. A separate section would be built later connecting it to New Jersey. But where to cross? Crossing toward the north meant more of the road would be in Westchester County, where settlement was relatively denser and land values more expensive than in Rockland. But crossing south of the Village of Nyack in Rockland County would put the bridge in an area where the law reserved bridge-building authority to the Port Authority of New York (now the Port Authority of New York and New Jersey). In May 1950 the Authority proposed to build its own cross-Hudson bridge and connect with the Thruway. That would siphon traffic—and tolls—away from the proposed Thruway Authority bridge, and Dewey vetoed it.[30] Tallamy and the Thruway Authority engineers found just the right crossing point in Rockland County near Nyack on the west shore, where there was an opening in the hills and relatively gentle slopes down to the river, to near Tarrytown in Westchester County on the east bank. But it happened to be where the Hudson was at its widest. Tallamy

28. Bertram D. Tallamy, "The Thruway Moves Ahead," February 1, 1954, in New York State Thruway Authority Records, Public Relations Planning and Publications Files, 1950–1969, New York State Archives.
29. Fein, *Paving the Way*, 221–222; *New York Times*, February 10, 1954.
30. "Port Body Gives in on Thruway Span," *New York Times*, May 12, 1950.

was at first unspecific as to where the road would run and the river would be crossed. But by mid-1950, rumors began to circulate about the bridge's probable location and local opposition began to build at both ends over the disruption the new road and bridge would cause.

The patient, diplomatic Tallamy spent a good deal of time in Rockland and Westchester counties over the next couple of years. His engineers settled on a specific route and crossing point, but he wanted to win over local residents and adjust the route to meet local objections. Nyack was particularly important. Merchants worried that shoppers would cross the bridge and spend their money in Tarrytown or White Plains. An avalanche of angry telegrams and letters made their way to Albany. The Rockland County supervisors passed a resolution asserting that the bridge might cause an ice blockage in the river and opposing the selected crossing point, though they did not offer alternatives. The mayor of Grand View said his community was "the beauty spot of the Hudson, which should not be destroyed by a bridge." The Nyack school board complained that the road and the bridge would remove taxable structures and cut into its tax base. Old buildings in the potential route were suddenly referred to as "historic" structures. A former army colonel and former air force colonel living in Nyack issued a joint statement that the bridge would be "a saboteur's dream and a bomber's delight" in the event of war.[31]

Chairman Tallamy countered that the road would boost land values, assessments, and therefore taxes flowing into the coffers of the Nyack school board and other local governments. It would bring shoppers into Nyack and reduce traffic by keeping people who were just passing through off the village's streets. He made some adjustments to the route and added another access/exit route to mollify local merchants. The Army Core of Engineers, whose approval was required before the bridge could be built, ordered some minor changes to avoid possible ice buildup. But Tallamy, like his boss the governor, insisted that the public interest must prevail. "Local conditions cannot be accepted as governing in the choice of the Thruway route," he told a meeting of concerned citizens in Nyack.[32] A court ruled against the Nyack school board's suit to force the state to pay

---

31. "Residents Oppose Tappan Zee Bridge," *New York Times*, May 1, 1950; "Ice Jams Are Feared," *New York Times*, December 20, 1959; "Opinion Is Divided on Thruway Plan," *New York Times*, December 23, 1950; and "Thruway Span Seen Bomb Target," *New York Times*, January 25, 1951.
32. "Thruway Chairman Defends Plan to Span Hudson at Widest Point," *New York Times*, December 22, 1950.

compensation for lost taxes. Opposition gradually diminished to what the Rockland County commissioner of public works called "this ugly, creeping thing, which has been burrowing its way from Buffalo." State plans to shift the Ramapo River to make way for the road would have covered up three Village of Suffern reserve wells. The village dispatched armed police to chase away the state surveyors. "We represent the State of New York," protested one of the engineers. "I don't care whom you represent!" responded a village trustee, John Petrone, who had driven to the scene to help evict the state employees. "Get out of here! Governor Dewey is not the king of New York State yet!" The surveyors retreated, the state proposed a sluiceway to carry the river over the wells and not disturb them, the village concurred, and the confrontation abated.[33]

The situation in Westchester County across the Hudson from Rockland was also complicated. Westchester had more suburban development and was growing faster than Rockland. Many of its residents were commuters, shopping centers were springing up, and it was already a land of highways. There were seven north-south parkways by 1930. As noted earlier, Westchester County executive Herbert Gerlach endorsed the road and secured state commitment to other highway construction in the county in return. But as the probable route became known, anxiety and protests mounted, particularly in and around Tarrytown. The bridge would take houses and land, land values would decrease, and the village would lose 10 percent of its total real estate tax base, declared Mayor Charles S. Haines in September, 1950.[34] Citizens organized protest meetings. The ever-statesmanlike Bertram Tallamy visited to calm fears and make adjustments to the route, particularly in Yonkers, the only city in the county. Westchester County officials expressed satisfaction that the adjustments would result in minimal property damage. Tallamy sweetened the deal by offering to rebuild part of the Cross County Parkway and carefully negotiating the route of the Cross Westchester Expressway between the State Thruway and the New England Thruway.[35] Speaking at Rye in Westchester County in May 1953, Tallamy asserted that the new road would draw shoppers

33. "Foes of Thruway Fewer in Number," *New York Times*, August 23, 1953; "Suffern to Fight Plan of Thruway," *New York Times*, October 31, 1953.
34. "Protests on Thruway," *New York Times*, September 13, 1950; Fein, *Paving the Way*, 115.
35. "Thruway Aligned in Westchester," *New York Times*, January 23, 1951; "Thruway Revises Westchester Plan," *New York Times*, January 12, 1952; "Controversial Westchester Route Linking Thruways Set," *New York Times*, May 12, 1954.

from elsewhere, including across the Hudson (a message he did not repeat in speeches across the river in Rockland County). "Our whole pattern of community life is geared to the motor vehicle," and Westchester would benefit in many ways from the new road.[36] As the construction continued, General Foods moved its world headquarters to a point in Westchester near the route; Allstate Insurance opened a new regional headquarters; and the $30 million Cross County Center, touted as the world's largest shopping center, opened just off the road in Yonkers. The tax base went up.

Construction on the cross-Hudson bridge began in 1952. The bridge, just over sixteen thousand feet in length, required extraordinary design because of its length and because bedrock needed to support it at the center was far below the surface of the river. A new technology, developed and tested in World War II, was employed. Right after the allies stormed the beaches at Normandy on D-Day, they towed in huge, buoyant concrete caissons called Phoenixes and anchored them in the seabed to make harbors for war materiel shipped in from England behind the invading troops. The Phoenixes, like the invasion itself, had been developed in secret, and they proved their worth. One of their designers, Emil Praeger, went to work for Madigan Hyland Engineers, a New York firm, after the war. Madigan Hyland had close ties to Robert Moses, which helped them get New York City contracts. The floating concrete caisson technology was used in rebuilding Pier 57, a city-owned structure that reached out into the Hudson River at 15th Street, after a destructive fire in 1947. Madigan Hyland got the contract to be the chief consulting engineers for the construction of the Thruway. Jack Madigan and Emil Praeger sold Dewey and Tallamy on the use of buoyant concrete caissons for the Tappan Zee Bridge. Eight of the concrete boxes were constructed at Haverstraw, floated down the river, sunk to the water line, and anchored to the bedrock more than two hundred feet below. Dewey called it "D-Day technology" that would save millions of dollars in construction costs. Newspapers said the caissons would be like "soft pillows" and that motorists would "literally drive on air."[37]

---

36. Bertram Tallamy, "The Thruway and Westchester County," May 19, 1953 in New York State Thruway Authority Records, Public Relations Planning and Publications Files, 1950–1969, New York State Archives.
37. Donald L. Wolf, Crossing the Hudson: Historic Bridges and Tunnels of the River (New Brunswick: Rutgers University Press, 2010), 177–195.

Politics and Progress

Tom Dewey, his vision for the grand highway a reality and his contempt for Democrats in full view, looked like a candidate for reelection at the June 24, 1954, opening events. But early in September, he bowed out. Four gubernatorial campaigns (three successful), twelve years of hard work as governor, and two unsuccessful presidential campaigns (1944 and 1948) had left him weary. He looked forward to a postgubernatorial career as a New York City corporate lawyer and senior statesman of the Republican Party. He presided at two more Thruway section openings in the fall, Rochester to Buffalo and Utica to Newburgh, almost completing the road. The high-energy Thruway news media office continued its use of hyperbole and superlatives in portraying the accomplishments. The second opening made the Thruway longer than any other expressway or tollway in the nation with costs per mile substantially below comparable roads such as the New Jersey Turnpike and the Massachusetts Turnpike. In addition to the benefits to the traveling public, "the Thruway . . . present[ed] countless new vantage points for enjoying the scenic beauty of the Mohawk and Hudson valleys." Dewey beamed at the official openings but could not refrain from calling the road's critics "the stupidest, most ignorant partisan bunch of opponents I ever saw in any legislature."[38]

The Republicans nominated U.S. senator Irving M. Ives, a moderate with a solid if undistinguished record, for governor. The Democratic nominee was former diplomat, businessman, and millionaire Averell Harriman. But much of the campaign was about the Dewey record, and Dewey campaigned energetically for Ives, sometimes crowding him out of the limelight and becoming a handy surrogate target for the Democrats. Republicans portrayed Harriman as an out-of-touch rich man with a shady past, including bribing a judge and cutting a business deal with Adolf Hitler in wartime Poland. He was "unfit for the office" and "seeking the best job $40 million can buy," Governor Dewey told a campaign crowd. "A smile and a promise are a very empty substitute for performance." Ives painted Harriman as the puppet of New York City Democrats. Harriman called Republicans "cramped, narrow, joyless, and above

38. "Fact Capsule for Opening Newburgh-Westmoreland Section," October 26, 1954, in New York State Thruway Authority Records, Public Relations Planning and Publications Files, 1950–1969, New York State Archives; "More of Thruway Opened by Dewey," *New York Times*, October 27, 1954.

all, fearful." Dewey had used state programs for political benefit. Work on the Thruway had been rushed, including expensive overtime payments, "so the governor can snip some ribbons." Quick-drying cement that would have to be replaced was used to meet the fall opening deadlines, said Harriman. Harriman effectively refuted the smears on his business record. One of the nastiest campaigns in state history ended in one of the closest results, with Harriman elected by slightly over eleven thousand votes out of five million cast.[39]

By the time Harriman took office in January 1955, the Thruway was nearly finished. He proved to be a tone-deaf politician and faced stubborn opposition from Republicans who still held the majority in the legislature. He soon discovered that the budget surplus that Dewey had left was in fact encumbered by commitments already made. Instead of expanding state programs as he had planned, the hapless governor was forced to order cutbacks. When the legislature passed a bill to name the Thruway for Dewey, Harriman vetoed it on the grounds that naming a highway for an individual was unprecedented. Harriman's act looked petty and petulant (the road was officially named for Dewey in 1964). In another sour note, in the fall voters rejected a proposal for road construction bonds other than the Thruway. The Harriman administration had not made a strong case, and voters were angry that the state gasoline tax was being diverted to other purposes. A scaled-down proposal that included a requirement for most gas tax receipts to be dedicated to highway work passed the next year, but the governor's disinterest in highway policy was apparent.[40]

On December 15, 1955, Harriman journeyed through a snowstorm to Suffern to dedicate and open the cross-Hudson span, now called the Tappan Zee Bridge. It was an official holiday in Nyack and Tarrytown, schools were closed, high school bands played, and there were large public turnouts for the festivities. The recent history of local opposition and obstruction was all but forgotten. Always adept at working for positive press coverage, the Thruway Authority hosted a dinner the night before for media representatives at the nearby swank Bear Mountain Inn.

---

39. Rudy Abramson, *Spanning the Century: The Life of W. Averell Harriman, 1891–1986* (New York: William Morrow and Company, 1992), 504–511; "Governor Assails Issues Foes Raise," *New York Times*, September 23, 1954; "Harriman Assails Foes on Jobless," *New York Times*, September 26, 1954; "Dewey Defends Record on Jobs," *New York Times*, October 15, 1954; *New York Times*, October 25, 1954; "Harriman Assails 'Scheme' by Dewey," *New York Times*, October 31, 1954.

40. Fein, *Paving the Way*, 225–227.

Press materials called the bridge "the largest of its kind in the world," well worth the $60 million it had cost. About 70 percent of the weight was supported by "buoyant underwater caissons," the largest of which was half the size of a city block, weighed fifteen thousand tons, and whose use had saved "many millions of dollars." The new bridge required 14,610 tons of reinforcing steel, 59,250 tons of structural steel, 153,900 cubic yards of concrete, and its roadway encompassed 27 acres of pavement. The nearly completed Thruway had cost $1,340,000 per mile, less than comparable superhighways in other states. A new Ford assembly plant close to the bridge symbolized the boost the road and bridge would give the local economy. [41]

The governor arrived late, delayed by the snow, at the head of a four hundred–vehicle cavalcade. Sixteen women pickets from the villages of Sparkhill, Grand View, and Piermont confronted him with "SAVE OUR VILLAGES" signs. They wanted to protest the proposed route of the connection from the Thruway to the New Jersey state line. Harriman went over to them, received their letter of concern, and invited them to join him in the official ribbon cutting. His remarks were brief and perfunctory. As soon as Mrs. Harriman cut the ceremonial ribbon, air force jets roared overhead, the USS Rizzi fired a seventeen-gun salute, and a Yonkers ferry, the Weehawk, sent up a geyser of water. Drivers in the official motorcade piled into their vehicles, paid a $.50 toll, and hurried across the bridge. Tom Dewey, who may not have been invited, said that pressing business kept him from attending. He sent a congratulatory telegram, calling the Thruway "our high road to the future."[42] Harriman spoke briefly at a celebratory luncheon in Tarrytown. His lack of engagement and enthusiasm at the Tappan Zee dedication was indicative of his tenure as governor. He was defeated for reelection by Nelson Rockefeller, a progressive Republican, in 1958.

The new Thruway was hailed in the press as an unqualified success: a safe, high-speed road running along New York's mainline, reducing travel time and transportation costs, spurring economic and commercial growth,

41. "Thruway Fact Sheet" and "Official Program, Thruway Celebration," December 1955, in New York State Thruway Authority Records, Public Relations Planning and Publications Files, 1950–1969, New York State Archives.
42. "Thruway Opened with Dedication of Last Toll Link," *New York Times*, December 16, 1955; Thomas Dewey telegram to B. D. Tallamy, December 15, 1955, in New York State Thruway Authority Records, Public Relations Planning and Publications Files, 1950–1969, New York State Archives.

and pushing up land values. Lowell Thomas, famed author, news commentator, world traveler, and a personal friend of Tom Dewey, wrote a short laudatory book, *The New York Thruway Story*, in 1955. Much of the book was based on press releases and other materials furnished by the always-helpful Thruway press office. A driver pulling onto the new road would have "driving conditions unparalleled anywhere in the world. For the entire length of the run he never has to stop for a traffic light or an intersection. He never has to slow down for a dangerous curve or a steep hill." Efficient management had held costs down. Thomas cited new factories, shopping centers, resorts, and motels springing up along the new road. "The Thruway runs through two glorious river valleys which bestow upon it vistas of mountain peaks and deep-soil farm land, of rushing water and quiet forest glades" and has "historical buildings, museums, parks and monuments" all along the route.[43] The new road was "the key to New York State," said a 1956 feature article in *National Geographic*. "Drums of history echo on every mile. . . . the Thruway adds to the wealth and well-being of the Empire State—and the Nation as a whole."[44]

In 1956, at the initiative of President Dwight Eisenhower, Congress authorized $25 billion for construction of the Interstate Highway System. New York was considered a model for the national effort, and the Thruway's master statesman, Bertram Tallamy, was appointed federal highway administrator to oversee the massive nationwide effort. The Thruway proved to be a financial success, but the tolls remained to help offset operating expenses and upgrades long after the road's original costs had been recouped. Over the next few years, the Niagara Thruway provided access to Niagara Falls, the Berkshire Connector was added from the Thruway to the Massachusetts Turnpike, and the Garden State Parkway Connector linked the road with the parkway in New Jersey. Years later, the Thruway Authority was assigned maintenance responsibility for the Cross Westchester Expressway and the New England Thruway on the eastern side of Westchester County.

Dewey's grand vision was mostly a success. But in retrospect, it had significant limitations. It centered on automobile and truck transportation and disregarded mass transit. To Dewey, Tallamy, and the other road planners of the 1950s, mass transit outside the state's biggest cities meant a few

---

43. Lowell Thomas, *The New York Thruway Story* (Buffalo: Henry Stewart, 1955).
44. Matt C. McDade, "New York's New Main Street," *National Geographic* (November 1956), 570, 618.

Greyhounds and other buses. The Thruway hastened the demise of state railroads, including the mighty New York Central, whose tracks the road more or less paralleled most of the way from New York City to Buffalo. It accelerated the decline of the Barge Canal, successor to the Erie, which had already lost most of its traffic to railroads and highways. In an ironic historic reversal, the canal system, hailed by Tom Dewey as the model for the Thruway, was turned over to the Thruway for operation in 1992.

The Thruway was integrated into the national interstate system, but by the late 1960s the entire concept of parkways came under question and even attack. Roads like the Thruway took congestion off city streets, but they also took business and commerce and made it easy for people to relocate out of urban areas. The arterials that connected cities to the interstates often cut through poor neighborhoods or helped divide cities along racial lines. They were accused of contributing to "white flight" from the cities to the suburbs, now easily and quickly accessible. Massive housing developments and sprawling shopping malls came to be regarded as a blight rather than a benefit. The overreliance on automobiles contributed to air pollution and other environmental problems. "The soaring roadway over the city, the highway along the waterfront—once the dream of engineers, planners, and right-minded citizens—we now regard as a curse upon civic life," wrote transportation historian Tom Lewis. "The highways show our grace and vision, but they also reveal, at times, our impetuousness and shortsightedness."[45] Building the Thruway required a high degree of political leadership and constituted a good example of New York's history of continual striving. But it also demonstrates that, with the passage of time and the application of historical perspective, what seemed like an enlightened public achievement at the time can also have limitations and unintended consequences.

---

45. Lewis, *Divided Highways*, 292–294; Fein, *Paving the Way*, 234.

13
April 22, 1964

The World's Fair Opens in New York

The Unisphere and the New York State Pavilion, shown in this 2006 photo, symbolized the World's Fair's global theme but also New York's leadership.

A Tempestuous Beginning

The New York World's Fair opened twice, on April 22, 1964, and April 21, 1965, each time for a six-month's season to take advantage of New York City's agreeable spring, summer, and early fall weather. The fair's themes, "Peace through Understanding" and "Man's Achievement on a Shrinking Globe in an Expanding Universe," were symbolized by a twelve-story high spherical steel model of the earth called the "Unisphere," with three large orbit rings around it, representing the first two astronauts to circle the globe in space and the first active telecommunications satellite. The fair's site, city-owned property in Flushing Meadows, Queens, was the same location as an earlier world's fair, held 1939 to 1940. Deciding on a site in the city for the new fair was easy: Much of the needed infrastructure—water, sewer, and lighting—was already in place, the transportation network providing access was superb, and there were no other viable sites in the city.

The people who proposed the fair were New York City business leaders who had enjoyed the earlier fair as young people, wanted their children to have a similar memorable experience, and saw it as a way to boost the city's public tourism and economy. They persuaded New York City mayor Robert Wagner, who also had fond memories of visiting the earlier fair, that a new fair would be a good way to commemorate the establishment of the English colony of New York in 1664. More importantly, it would bring in millions of tourists, generate lots of business, and help cement the city's world-class status as a cultural and entertainment leader. Wagner prevailed on the state legislature to create a World's Fair Corporation in 1960. New York easily beat a few other U.S. cities that were also interested in hosting a fair and secured federal endorsement the same year.[1]

World's fairs, or expositions as they were sometimes called, began with the spectacular Crystal Palace Exposition in London in 1851. After that, they became something of the rage in Europe and the United States, which hosted ten extravaganzas, in Atlanta, Buffalo, St. Louis, Seattle, San Francisco, and other cities over the next century. Fairs built on various themes and served various purposes: demonstrating international understanding, exhibiting national culture and might, celebrating industrial production and consumerism, educating visitors about science and history, and promoting patriotism and national unity.[2] The 1939–1940 New York World's Fair built on the theme of "The World of Tomorrow" and introduced such marvels as air conditioning, television, and nylon stockings. The 1964–1965 fair, despite its official themes of peace and global understanding, was much more a celebration of affluence, consumer capitalism, scientific achievements, and the glories of American culture and technology. *Time* magazine's cover story on the first year's opening, entitled "The World of Already," noted that "the 1964 fair displays not what might be done in the future, but rather what has already been done. The 1939 fair was a promise. The 1964 fair is a boast."[3] It also presented a sanitized, almost conflict-free world. There were no exhibits depicting inequality, injustice, or pressing social problems.

1. Lawrence R. Samuel, *The End of the Innocence: The 1964–1965 New York World's Fair* (Syracuse: Syracuse University Press, 2007), 3–9.
2. Robert W. Rydell, John E. Findling and Kimberly Pelle, *Fair America: World's Fairs in the United States* (Washington: Smithsonian Institution, 2000), 1–13.
3. "Fairs: The World of Already," *Time*, June 5, 1964.

The fair opened a few months after the assassination of President John F. Kennedy in November 1963, an event that had shocked the nation but not undermined its optimism and confidence. Early 1964, compared to what was coming, was a period of complacency and quiet, essentially an extension of the placid, affluent 1950s. Historian Jon Margolis calls it "the last innocent year" before an extended period of crisis and tumult that witnessed the burgeoning of the civil rights movement, the push for women's rights, the campaign against poverty, and mounting protests against the war in Vietnam.[4]

Work was still incomplete on some of the pavilions on opening day, April 22, 1964. A cold rain fell much of the day—"grim, November-like weather," a press report called it—inauspicious, drenching the opening parade. President Lyndon Johnson officially opened the fair with a speech that predicted an era of peace and the end of poverty and discrimination. Johnson, who had become president when Kennedy was assassinated, hoped to be elected in his own right in the fall and was pushing a civil rights bill through Congress. But the day produced portents of things to come. Civil rights demonstrators, disputing Johnson's sincerity and angry over the fair's alleged failure to hire blacks and minorities, interrupted his speech with chants of "Jim Crow Must Go!" and "Freedom Now!" They held up placards that said, "A World's Fair Is a Luxury but a Fair World Is a Necessity." Clearly annoyed, the president at one point paused and said, "[W]e do not try to disguise our imperfections or cover up our failures. No other nation in history has done so much to correct its flaws." Mayor Robert Wagner told the crowd that "miracles have been performed" to get the magnificent fair ready in time. "Indeed, the fair as a whole is a kind of miracle." Governor Nelson Rockefeller put in a plug for the New York State pavilion. Other dignitaries dwelled on the fair's themes of peace and understanding. But the day of celebration had already turned into something of a spectacle. Civil rights pickets and demonstrators appeared at several places on the fairgrounds later in the day, and a group blocked the entrance to the New York State Pavilion. James Farmer, national director of the Congress of Racial Equality (CORE), declared his goal was to publicize "the melancholy contrast between the idealized world of the Fair and the real world of brutality, prejudice, and violence in which the American negro is forced to live." The next day, Johnson called

---

4. Jon Margolis, *The Last Innocent Year: America in 1964—The Beginning of the "Sixties"* (New York: William Morrow and Company, 1999), viii.

the protestors "rude," New York senator Jacob Javits apologized for their disrespect, and the mayor called the protest an "ill chosen action." The grand fair was off to a sour start, launching a two-year run that would entertain and educate nearly fifty-two million visitors but also generate a good deal of controversy.[5]

A Brooding Presence over the Fair

The successes of the fair—and the problems that beleaguered it—were both largely due to the president of the World's Fair Corporation, Robert Moses (1888–1981). In an extraordinary career that began in the 1920s, Moses had served as state parks commissioner, the city's parks commissioner, coordinator of city road and arterial construction and slum clearance, and head of the Triborough Bridge and Tunnel Authority. In some years, he had held city and state positions simultaneously, giving him vast power. An article in the *New York Times* just before the fair opened, entitled "Builder of the Fair," summarized his accomplishments: "Jones Beach, the Robert Moses Niagara Power Plant (the largest hydroelectric facility in the Western world), the Verrazano-Narrows Bridge, 10 other bridges, two tunnels, 75 state parks, 481 miles of highway, 660 playgrounds, 21,000 acres of city parkland, 100,000 units of public and private housing." Moses had been a natural choice for fair CEO, favored by Mayor Wagner, Governor Rockefeller, and leaders of New York's banking and business community whose support—and in the case of bankers, investment dollars—were essential to the fair's success. For a builder of such great accomplishments, developing and managing a fair that would occupy only 660 acres and last only two years was expected to be easy. In fact, it was meant to be something of a valedictory for Moses, a glide path to retirement. City and state authorities had arranged (and required) that he resign all of his other posts except the Triborough position and devote his time to the fair. The *Times* article went on to explain that Moses, impatient, assertive, and skilled at wielding power, had commented to one group years earlier, "I did not come here with an alabaster box of precious ointment to soothe your tender skins." When the Triborough Bridge, one of his signature accomplishments, was completed, a ferry service between Manhattan and

---

5. "Stall-In, Leaders Picket at Fair in Test of Police," *New York Times*, April 19, 1964; "Rain Soaks Crowd," *New York Times*, April 23, 1964; Samuel, *The End of the Innocence*, 32–36.

Queens was supposed to cease operations. When it did not, Moses had ordered one of his derrick barges into the slip while the ferryboat was out to destroy its landing dock. "Act first and argue in court later," was one of his operating principles.[6]

Moses liked to repeat that "you can't make an omelet without breaking eggs" and "those who can, build. Those who can't, criticize." As fair director, Moses would prove to be utterly self-assured, imperious, close to dictatorial. Moses's single-minded determination and energy got the fair organized and made it mostly a success. But his heavy-handed style dominated the enterprise. "There loomed before [the fair] the figure of its creator, dominating the scene, muting its gaiety, casting a dark shadow across its brightness, a figure not inviting but hostile, a figure of arrogance and controversy and rage," says Robert Caro, his critical biographer.[7] Four of Moses's traits wound up limiting his effectiveness. One, his autocratic management style was outdated by the 1960s. Two, the fair itself was actually a secondary priority for him. Moses had been the city's parks commissioner during the 1939–1940 fair, had helped develop the site, and had wanted it to become the centerpiece of a string of public parks in Queens after it closed. Lack of funds prevented that, but Moses was determined to use this new fair—*his* fair—to leave a legacy of a spectacular chain of parks. Three, his many years of urban renewal by bulldozing slums and using the power of eminent domain to run over community opposition to build highways, parks, and beaches had earned him an army of critics. To them, Moses seemed indifferent to the public interest. He was out of touch with the new generation of urban planners who saw city neighborhoods not as slums to be cleared but as "complex, delicate organisms full of precious street life, small businesses, vital ethnic and generational relationships and intricate family patterns."[8] Fourth, Moses waged a war with the press, which for years had been critical of his work. Even for a powerful figure like Moses, battling the media, much of it based in New York City, would be a no-win proposition. When the fair encountered budget and other problems, Moses got the blame. When it garnered praise, the press tended to look past Moses and credit individual exhibitors and pavilions.

---

6. "Builder of the Fair: Robert Moses," *New York Times*, April 22, 1964.
7. Robert A. Caro, *The Power Broker: Robert Moses and the Fall of New York* (New York: Vintage, 1975), 1102.
8. Morris Dickstein, "From the Thirties to the Sixties: The New York World's Fair in Its Own Time," in Queens Museum, ed., *Remembering the Future: The New York World's Fair from 1939 to 1964* (New York: Rizzoli, 1989), 32.

Robert Moses took charge of fair planning after being appointed its director early in 1960. He filled out the fair's executive staff with people who had worked with him before, had proven their loyalty, and who were unlikely to question his decisions. He issued contracts for fair security, publicity, insurance, and janitorial and maintenance services without full competitive bidding, which he once referred to as a waste of time. He decided right away that the fair corporation would not build pavilions, as its predecessor had in 1939, but instead would lease out sites and let exhibitors build as they wished. That would maximize revenues, ensuring a post-fair surplus for parks development. It would also set the stage for razing them after the fair closed, making way for the parks Moses envisioned. He dismissed criticisms that the approach would result in a scattered hodge-podge of styles. "You mean you're going to tell General Motors what kind of building to put up?" he asked. By international agreement, world's fairs needed the sanction of the Bureau of International Expositions in Paris. The BIE had sanctioned a fair in Seattle in 1962, and its rules forbade more than one fair in a nation in a single decade. Fairs could not have a duration of more than six months. They could not charge foreign governments for exhibition space. Moses's plans contravened all three of these requirements, but BIE officials signaled there might be room for negotiation and compromise. "We don't take this B.I.E. business very seriously," Moses told reporters in 1962, later referring to "that bunch of clowns in Paris." The affronted international fair commissioners forbade membership participation, which meant that Britain, France, most other European nations, Canada, and Australia turned down Moses's invitations to lease space and build pavilions. The Soviet Union also declined, based mostly on cold-war antipathy toward the United States. Moses enlisted nations of lesser renown and compensated in other ways, such as securing materials for an exhibit on Winston Churchill in the fair's second year, but the international character of the "World's Fair" was muted.[9] It was predominantly an American event.

Drawing on an analysis of attendance at past fairs and buoyed by his own rosy promises that this would be the greatest fair in history, Moses predicted an attendance of seventy million people, which proved to be about eighteen million more than actually attended. He secured a $24 million appropriation from the city for upgrades to the streets and utility

---

9. Samuel, *The End of the Innocence*, 9–12; "The City: So Long at the Fair," *Time* 79 (March 9, 1962), 82–83.

systems and sold bonds to New York banks, confidently promising to pay it all back and have money left over to build parks. Moses decided there would be no midway, which he associated with freak shows, bawdy dancing, gambling, and other forms of vice or at least poor taste. An "Amusement Area" with tasteful entertainment would have to suffice. The leading band would be one of Moses's favorites, Guy Lombardo and his Royal Canadians, who would hold forth at the Tiparillo Band Pavilion. Lombardo said his band played "the sweetest music this side of heaven," and it was smooth, harmonic, and slow, unlikely to be confused with "rock 'n roll," which was becoming popular with the younger set. Moses invited the Vatican and several major religious groups to lease space and build worship sites. He hired Pinkerton guards to keep things in order. He dismissed critics who said he was a kill-joy, tamping down the fun and frolic that drew people to fairs, and something of a scrooge, demanding too much money for his leases. The press is skilled at "planting suspicion, poisoning minds, rousing the mob spirit, quoting out of context," he said. He called media critics of his fair policies "dyspeptics, grouches, grumblers, hit-and-run writers."[10]

A few days before the fair opened, Moses shrugged off reports that there might be civil rights demonstrations or other problems on opening day. "I don't like jittery people around me," he said. What about reports that he had vetoed a plan for an exhibition of avant-garde modern art? "I don't dictate art here," he insisted, but it has to be in "good taste." A friend had a painting done by a monkey, he continued. "My friend likes monkey paintings. I don't and I think there are too many monkey paintings around and the left-wingers are in love with them." What about criticisms of lack of an architectural theme at the fair? "Architects and designers can afford to take a chance on a building that is only up for two years. If it works, fine; if it doesn't, you know it was a lousy idea. A fair like this is a great place to experiment." How about dancing shows in the amusement area? "They'll be in good taste and they'll be amusing," Moses beamed. "I've personally looked over the costumes, every one of them. Everyone will have a good time and the public will not be offended in any way."[11]

He explained that the fair was a high-toned way "to distinguish mere change from genuine progress," to promote peace and "reconcile differences by simple, friendly human contacts." The fair would include

---

10. Caro, *The Power Broker*, 1097–1101.
11. "A Relaxed Moses Expounds on Fair," *New York Times*, April 11, 1964.

religious pavilions and no "over-the-line vulgarity just short of censorship and police intervention." Critics had generated "futile controversy and name calling." Besides, the ultimate goal was "a fine park. . . . reminiscent of the Fair and adapted to the needs and pleasures of coming generations."[12] The fair received mostly positive reviews from the people who attended in the summer and fall of 1964. It was fun, colorful, educational, entertaining, a joyous experience. A *Saturday Evening Post* feature article called it "a gaudy paradise . . . an all but overwhelming combination of commerce and technology, imagination and sheer excitement."[13] But there were also rough spots. Civil rights picketing and leafleting continued through the spring and summer. Some of the exhibits did not open until summer. Fair attendance was less than expected. Exhibitors who were paying high premiums to lease space began to complain to Moses when crowds were smaller than he had predicted; when he turned a deaf ear, they went to the news media. Attendance at the subdued Amusement Area was low, and by summer, some of the entertainment acts were closing. Moses resisted pleas for reduced fees for students to boost attendance. New York City comptroller Abraham Beame asserted that any profits from the fair should go to support education rather than Moses's park scheme. Some media critics liked the variety of random architectural styles, but others panned it and blamed Moses for allowing architectural anarchy. *New York Times* architectural critic Ada Louise Huxtable called the fair "disconnected, grotesque, lacking any unity of concept or style" but grudgingly admitted that "those accidental juxtapositions and cockeyed contrasts. . . give it its particular attraction and charm."[14]

Some visitors faulted the fair for not exciting the imagination. John Skow, a contributing writer to the *Saturday Evening Post*, spent a wearying and uninspiring day at the fair in May. It was "vast, colorful clutter" but lacking an inspiring "leap of mind" or central themes. "The audience leaves, vaguely puzzled" at the end of the day.[15]

Seemingly happiest when battling critics, Moses reminded a newswriter in May, "I've never been given a job on a popularity basis." In June, he lambasted New York bankers and the businesses for their faint-hearted

---

12. Robert Moses, "Why a Fair? And Why This Fair?" *New York Times*, April 19, 1964.
13. "The Great Fair," *Saturday Evening Post*, 237 (May 23, 1964), 27.
14. Ada Louise Huxtable, "Architecture: Chaos of Good, Bad, Joyful," *New York Times*, April 22, 1964.
15. John Skow, "Who Needs the World's Fair?" *Saturday Evening Post* 237 (May 23, 1964), 12, 14.

support of the fair. He invited business leaders to a meeting to provide advice on the fair's management, then cancelled the meeting when the press got wind of it. The first season closed in October, with attendance—and income—well below predicted levels. Moses blamed "ants . . . gremlins and leprechauns" in the press for their "gratuitous sophisticated nastiness" in exaggerating high prices at the fair, harping on complaints by exhibitors, emphasizing problems with transportation and hotel accommodations, and scaring people away with reports on racial unrest in the city that summer. Their "lack of pride and loyalty" to New York City was shameful, the president of the fair declared.[16]

Over the winter, Moses and his staff solicited new exhibitors and relaxed entertainment rules to allow discotheques and "go-go dancers," but they had to be suitably clad. Mayor Wagner, in a promotional article just before the second year's opening, reminded everyone that the fair had generated a great deal of tourism and boosted the city's economy. "The fair is back in all its colors, soaring architecture, exciting exhibits," he said. "It is a carnival and a campus, a road that leads back to the beginning of man and a path that charts his future. It is a babble of tongues, and an accent that is uniquely American. . . . an echo of New York—an international showcase with a hometown flavor."[17] Opening day, April 21, was warm and sunny, with bands, a parade, and fireworks. Vice President Hubert Humphrey, a popular politician with a sunny disposition that seemed to match the balmy day, told a cheering crowd—protestors had threatened disruption but had not shown up—that "this fair is one of the great achievements of our country." Not wanting to provoke any response from the crowd other than applause, the vice president confined the rest of his speech to political bromides, then set out on a brisk walking tour of the fair, surrounded by secret service guards, newsmen trailing along behind. Moses called the fair "an intellectual picnic." The opening day crowd was 158,000, more than three times the previous year's opening crowd. Year Two of the fair was off to a glorious start.[18]

16. Bill Davidson, "The Old S.O.B. Does it Again," *Saturday Evening Post* 237 (May 23, 1964), 36–41; "Moses Accepts Citation with a Few Harsh Words," *New York Times*, June 4, 1964; "Moses Says Press Harmed the Fair," *New York Times*, October 16, 1964.
17. Robert F. Wagner, "A New Yorker Goes to the Fair," *New York Times*, April 18, 1965.
18. "Humphrey Stars as Show Reopens," *New York Times*, April 22, 1965; "Moses Calls Fair 'Intellectual Picnic,' Lashes at Critics," *New York Times*, May 5, 1965; Samuel, *The End of the Innocence*, 73–75.

The ebullient feeling did not last long. Attendance dropped off, bobbed back up in the fall, but finished below 1964 levels. Moses worked with exhibitors and the city's Convention and Visitor's Bureau on promotional advertising but fired the fair's PR firm, cutting publicity. He raised admission fees against the advice of his own staff and his many media critics, who advocated lowering them. He rebuffed exhibitors who were losing money and begging for a reduction in their lease rents. He railed against reports by "mud throwers" in the news who reported on the fair's problems. He accused weathermen of discouraging attendance by reporting "a 20% chance of precipitation" rather than "80% chance of fair weather."[19] He refused to open the fair's financial accounting books even to its finance advisory committee, leading to the resignations of several leading bankers—including David Rockefeller, president of Chase Manhattan Bank—and rumors that the fair was headed for insolvency. George Moore, the chair of the committee, beseeched Moses to get the fair's financial house in order, leading to a confrontation:

> Moore: Bob, we've found bills of six and seven figures that weren't booked. We just can't continue to operate without reliable information.
>
> Moses: George, your figures are wrong. You don't know what you're talking about.
>
> Moore: Bob, I've been in the banking business all my life and it there's one thing I know it's a column of figures.[20]

Sensing a potential scandal, media reports harped on Moses's mismanagement rather than the fair's glorious attractions.[21] New York City comptroller Abe Beame audited the fair's accounts and issued a scathing report that criticized poor planning, noncompetitive contracts, and wasted funds and concluded "controls necessary for good management were lacking."[22] The fair wound up in the red, unable to pay back the funds the city had fronted for infrastructure construction, and defaulting on 60 percent of its bonds.[23]

19. "Moses Seeks Aid of Weathermen," *New York Times*, May 19, 1965.
20. Samuel, *The End of the Innocence*, 20.
21. Murray Kempton, "Foul-Up at the Fair," *New Republic* (February 20, 1965), 13–14.
22. "World's Fair Mismanaged, Beame Charges in Report," *New York Times*, September 1, 1965; "Fair Audit Calls Management Lax," *New York Times*, December 22, 1965.
23. Samuel, *The End of the Innocence*, 85–86.

Robert Moses had sequestered funds to clean up the site and convert it to a park and drew on additional funds from the Triborough Bridge and Tunnel Authority, which he still headed, to complete the work. Contemptuous of his critics, he wrote his own valedictory in the form of a twenty-page pamphlet, *The Saga of Flushing Meadow*, published by the Authority in the spring of 1966. In his rendition, the Flushing Meadow area, at first bucolic countryside, had been degraded into an ash and refuse dump with "rats big enough to wear saddles" through the indifference of city officials. Novelist F. Scott Fitzgerald had called it "the valley of ashes" in his popular 1925 novel *The Great Gatsby*. The first glimmer of hope for a new future was the Grand Central Parkway, built by Moses in the 1930s through "this wasteland in which were buried 30 years of the offscourings, tin cans, cast-off baby carriages, and umbrellas . . ." Then came the proposal for the first world's fair, which Moses insisted he had to "sell" to Mayor Fiorello LaGuardia. The fair left behind highways, bridges, water lines, and other public improvements, many of them constructed under Moses's direction as city parks commissioner. The second world's fair added more improvements. The fair was a stunning success, educating and entertaining millions, bringing New York billions in business and garnering international recognition. Of course, it also provided a platform for grumblers and critics, he explained. Some investors had lost money. "True, we are having a few disgruntled noteholders, none of them *in extremis*, who have learned that a fair is not a business in the ordinary sense." There were not sufficient funds to build a chain of parks as he had hoped. One would have to suffice. But the proposed Flushing Meadows Park, planned and shaped by Moses, would be a lasting legacy, "on the scene of a notorious ash dump, one of the very great municipal parks of our nation."[24]

New York at the Fair

New York's political and business leaders used the fair to highlight the state's preeminence and leadership. Like much of the rest of the fair, New York pavilions were immodest celebrations of accomplishments rather than previews of the future. Four of them—New York State, New York City, IBM, and Eastman Kodak—are particularly notable.

---

24. Robert Moses, *The Saga of Flushing Meadow* (New York: New York Triborough Bridge and Tunnel Authority, 1966), http://www.nywf64.com/saga01.shtml; *New York Times*, April 11, 1966.

The variety and glory of New York State. Governor Nelson Rockefeller established the goal for the New York pavilion: Present the state's grandeur, scenic beauty, and cultural achievements in a way that made the pavilion stand out. Rockefeller personally selected the design architect, Philip Johnson, who had designed the new state theater at Lincoln Center and worked on other projects where the Rockefeller family had an interest. Johnson was known for his innovative, elegant, but also tasteful and practical design; he lived in a glass house of his own design, and, as he put it, "I like to be buttoned on to tradition. . . . to improve it, twist it, and mold it." He set out to create "an unengaged free space as an example of the greatness of New York rather than a warehouse full of material."[25]

His New York State Pavilion had three features. The first consisted of three domed observation towers, the tallest at 226 feet constituting the highest point on the fairgrounds, one way of meeting the governor's mandate of showing New York's superiority. A beaming Rockefeller suggested at the dedication that people arriving at the fair start here; you could see the entire fairgrounds and plan your day. The second element, called the "Tent of Tomorrow," was covered by the largest cable suspension roof in the world and supported on tall concrete piers. The main floor of the Tent of Tomorrow was a large-scale version of a Texaco oil company road map of the state, 130 feet by 166 feet—"over half the size of a football field," said a Texaco ad—showing all its major highways, streams, lakes, and mountains. Despite its official name, the Tent of Tomorrow was really meant to demonstrate New York's magnitude today; fairgoers could walk over the 567 interlocked colorful terrazzo tiles from Montauk to Buffalo. Around the map were displayed an exhibit by the State Power Authority (formerly headed by Robert Moses), a fine arts gallery, and space for other activities such as fashion shows and performances by school and community groups, and "a conservation area, a rose garden, exhibits from regional museums and the state's smaller industries." On some days, state legislators were available in the mezzanine to explain their work and receive citizen suggestions for new laws.[26]

Next to the tent was the "Theaterama," a large, cylindrical movie theater with a 360-degree screen that gave the visitor a spectacular film tour of

25. Ada Louise Huxtable, "He Adds Elegance to Modern Architecture," *New York Times*, May 24, 1964; "Back on the Map: Revisiting the New York State Fair Pavilion at the 1964/65 World's Fair," http://www.conlab.org/acl/thereallybigmap.
26. "New York State," in *Official Guide: New York World's Fair*, 1964, http://www.nywf64.com/newyor01.html.

the state, highlighting prominent scenic, industrial, cultural, and entertainment sites. The exterior of the building was decorated with "pop art" by ten contemporary artists, commissioned by Philip Johnson. The *Official Guide* referred to "such unlikely subjects as an auto wreck, the Statute of Liberty, and a comic-strip redhead."[27] All the "pop art" was innovative but subdued, in good taste, uncontroversial. The only exception was a mural at the entrance by Andy Warhol consisting of giant mug shots of the FBI's thirteen "Most Wanted" criminals. Right before opening day, it was covered over after Governor Rockefeller expressed his displeasure and the artist received death threats from one of the "most wanted." Warhol quickly offered a substitute, a giant painting of Robert Moses. But it looked too much like some of the men in the thirteen "most wanted." Moses was not amused and said no.[28]

The historical development and built environment of New York City. The New York City Pavilion was cosponsored by the City Parks Department (which Robert Moses had headed for many years) and the Triborough Bridge and Tunnel Authority (of which he was still chair). The building had a history of its own: Originally built for the first world's fair, it had served as temporary headquarters for the new United Nations from 1946 to 1950. It presented the only exhibit to reflect the original idea of the fair, the three hundredth anniversary of New York. Art, artifacts, sculptures, and photographs from thirty-four of the city's museums, libraries, botanical gardens, and zoos traced the history of the city from 1664 to the recent past. A Triborough theater showed a film about the city's bridges and tunnels. The highlight of the pavilion, however, was the "Panorama of the City of New York," said to be the world's largest three-dimensional model. It featured miniatures of almost every one of the city's 835,000 buildings, and all of its streets, bridges, parks, ferry terminals, and airports. Most New York City residents could spot their own apartment or office building, perhaps with the help of field glasses that could be rented on site. Visitors could take a "helicopter" ride a few feet above the miniature city, listening to a recorded narrative on the city's history and contemporary features by famed broadcaster and world traveler Lowell Thomas.[29] The "Panorama" and the Triborough film, with their messages about the

---

27. Ibid.
28. Samuel, *The End of the Innocence*, 135–136.
29. "New York City," in *Official Guide: New York World's Fair*, 1964. http://www.nywf64.com/newyorcit01.shtml; Samuel, *The End of the Innocence*, 136–137.

unequalled New York City built environment were, of course, reminders of the accomplishments of New York's greatest builder, Robert Moses.

Information processing made understandable. IBM, with headquarters in New York City and manufacturing plants in Endicott and Poughkeepsie, had one of the fair's most popular pavilions. Thomas Watson Jr., IBM president, wanted to rival the company's presence his father, and predecessor as president, had arranged for the 1939–1940 fair. The shell of IBM's pavilion resembled the moveable type ball on the company's "Selectric" typewriters. The company introduced its breakthrough System 360, a state-of-the-art "family" of computers, in 1964. Its pavilion had computers on display but not for fairgoers to try out. IBM was trying instead to convince people that it was the leader in making futuristic technology practical and easy to use. The experience at the IBM Pavilion began with an audience of five hundred seated on steeply tiered seats at ground level. When the program was about to begin, this "people wall" was lifted over fifty feet by hydraulic rams into the pavilion's central theater. A film, "The Information Machine," shown on fifteen slide and movie projectors, explained that computers were not really all that mysterious; essentially, they worked like the human mind to solve problems. On the little stages in adjacent areas, mechanical figures acted out vignettes four minutes long about such topics as computer logic and information handling systems. In one mini-play, *The Case of the Elusive Train,* the renowned fictional detective Sherlock Holmes, in a dialog with his assistant Dr. Watson, solves the mystery of the disappearance of the "Glasgow Express" and identifies the train hijackers. He uses a series of "yes/no" and "true/false" questions. "In explaining the solution to the amazed Watson, the great detective points out that he used the same simple logic that is used in programming a computer," the IBM exhibit booklet explained. "Programmers must tell a computer in great detail exactly how the machine should process information logically."[30]

In another area, visitors could write any date after 1851 on a card that was then fed into the experimental scanner of an IBM data processing system. The system included a capsule summary of a news story from every day of the *New York Times,* which began publishing that year. The computer printed the news summary for the day out on a souvenir card. In

---

30. *IBM Pavilion Guide,* 1964, http://www.nywf64.com/IBM03.shtml; *New York World's Fair Pavilion,* http://www-03.ibm.com/ibm/history/exhibits/vintage/vintage_4506VV 2085.html.

another demonstration, an IBM employee typed Russian sentences into a computer, and a printer a few feet away translated them and printed them back out in English. The fair's organizers designated July 8, 1964, as "IBM Day," reprising similar events at the 1939–1940 fair. Former president Dwight D. Eisenhower spoke, saluting IBM as a great American company and praising Thomas Watson Jr. for his visionary leadership. But Ike confessed that he hadn't "the slightest idea of how a computer works."[31]

Photography taken to a new level. Eastman Kodak, headquartered in Rochester, at that time the world's leading purveyor of cameras and film, built a striking pavilion made mostly of concrete cast to look like natural stone. It resembled a "futuristic moonscape" and won an award from the Concrete Industry Board of New York for innovative design.[32] Around the top on the outside were displayed five photographic prints, thirty by thirty-six feet, which Kodak said were the world's largest and which changed periodically. Inside, visitors could watch a film entitled "The Searching Eye," providing a child's-eye view of common and unusual wonders of the world. It used time-lapse photography, underwater and aerial scenes, close-in and far-out photos, and "stop action." It was one of the fair's outstanding media productions. "For sheer visual excitement, boldly inventive imagination, and technical virtuosity, it has rarely been equaled," said a *New York Times* reviewer.[33] Exhibits explained the history of photography—the pioneering work of the company's founder, George Eastman, naturally got lots of coverage—and demonstrated the use of photography in all phases of modern life, including education and commerce. Visitors could bring in their own cameras for instruction in how to get the best shots and to experiment on a number of staged backgrounds. Technicians were available to make free minor camera adjustments and repairs. The pavilion helped boost sales of Kodak's inexpensive, easy-to-load "Instamatic" cameras, introduced in 1963.

The New York government and business pavilions had different fates after the fair closed. IBM and Kodak employees carted their equipment back to Endicott and Rochester, respectively, and their pavilions were razed. The New York City Pavilion was converted into the Queens Museum of Art; it still houses the "Panorama of the City of New York."

---

31. "Eisenhower Ovation at Fair," *New York Times*, July 9, 1964.
32. "Kodak Pavilion at the Fair Wins Concrete Group Award," *New York Times*, August 23, 1964.
33. Jacob Deschin, "Kodak at Fair," *New York Times*, April 19, 1964.

The New York State Pavilion was handed over to the city, which used it for a roller skating rink for a while. But maintenance costs exceeded what the city was willing to spend, the roof deteriorated and leaked, and water ruined the spectacular New York State map. The building, derelict and abandoned, still stands in what is now Flushing Meadows-Corona Park.

Fun and Enlightenment at the Fair

Fairs blend entertainment, education, popular culture, color, sounds, spectacle, and crowds. They succeed by evoking a sense of the unusual, the unexpected, the marvelous, and the wonderful. The New York City world's fair—for all of its controversies and assertions of self-promotion by government and corporations—enlightened, entertained, and was just a plain good time for millions of people. Some examples of what people recalled as the most interesting and memorable follow.[34]

The Pietà. The Vatican had its own pavilion at the fair and agreed to have Michelangelo's famous statue, the *Pietà*, brought over from the Vatican where it had been installed in 1499. It depicts the body of Jesus on the lap of his mother Mary after the Crucifixion. It was protected by armed guards and bullet-proof glass. Visitors rode past it on a slow-moving conveyor. The statue was bathed in blue light and Gregorian chants played over loudspeakers. Many fairgoers found the experience deeply moving and spiritual.

To Be Alive! The Johnson's Wax Pavilion presented an eighteen-minute film *To Be Alive!*, hailed as the fair's best media show. Photographed in Africa, Italy, and the United States, it was designed to show how children in various parts of the world mature into adulthood. It began with a sped-up sequence of New York masses rushing to work, hundreds of people jamming the sidewalks, cars and buses moving in a blur. Then it suddenly slowed, showing a boy staring through a prism that changes the face of the city, another boy in a jungle learning the rhythm of a drum, and other young people in various parts of the world. A narrator, speaking in the first person, described his life from childhood to manhood. The central theme was that "there can be great joy in simply being alive!"[35]

---

34. The source for this section is Samuel, *The End of the Innocence*, and the other sources cited in notes 35–39.
35. Johnson's Wax, *Golden Rondell—Pavilion Guide*, 1964, http://www.nywf64.com/johwax04.shtml.

Transportation's future? GM's *Futurama* at the 1939–1940 world's fair had projected a future of cars running on expressways connecting cities and vibrant suburbs. The vision had helped inspire two decades of super-highways, including the New York State Thruway. GM's *Futurama II* was more scattered, speculative, and fanciful. Sitting in contour seats equipped with speakers, visitors were moved past animated scenes, including, in the words of the official program:

> In a trip to the moon, visitors see a weird landscape of craters and spaceships.
>
> An underwater scene shows the ocean floor being tapped for oil and vacationers relaxing at a resort beneath the surface.
>
> Tomorrow's city is shown with midtown airports, high-speed bus-trains, super skyscrapers, moving sidewalks and underground freight conveyor belts.[36]

Most visitors liked it, but few got excited. Some complained that they had no interest in exploring Antarctica or living under the sea. The city of the future, which concluded the ride, struck some people as a nightmare of congestion dominated by layers of highways.[37]

Disney magic. Several exhibits included features designed and installed by the Disney Company. Disney's "It's a Small World" ride at the Pepsi-Cola Pavilion was a particular crowd favorite, "taking visitors along a global boat ride past such icons as the Eiffel Tower, a Dutch windmill, and the Taj Mahal, while 350 doll-sized animatronic figures winked, blinked, and sang of world peace."[38] Disney's fascinating mechanical Abraham Lincoln in the Illinois Pavilion recited excerpts from his most famous speeches, blinking and gesturing with lifelike movements.

U.S. government's patriotic presence. In the Federal Pavilion, visitors could view *Voyage to America,* the story of immigration, and then take *The American Journey,* a tunnel ride that combined still photographs, film, music, and narration to present American history since 1492. NASA and the Department of Defense sponsored the United States Space Park where you could touch Aurora 7, the spaceship that had carried astronaut Scott

---

36. General Motors Pavilion, *Official Guide: New York World's Fair,* 1965, http://www.nywf64.com/gm01.shtml.

37. Dickstein, "From the Thirties to the Sixties," in Queens Museum, ed., *Remembering the Future,* 31.

38. Samuel, *The End of the Innocence,* 110.

Carpenter into orbit in 1962, and see a model of the Apollo rocket that would carry men to the moon in a few years. For the more serious-minded visitor, there was the "Challenges to Greatness" area that included exhibits describing in a general way some of the issues facing the nation. But they were designed not to upset fairgoers. "The exhibits are not intended necessarily to indicate solutions to our problems," the official description cautioned, "but to direct your attention to them."[39]

Food at the fair. Most visitors found the food acceptable, sometimes too expensive, and not memorable, with one exception: "Belgian" waffles. They were larger and lighter than regular waffles, had deep pockets in a grid pattern, and were topped with fruit (usually strawberries) and confectioners' sugar or whipped cream. Originally sold by a vendor in the "Belgian Village," they soon became so popular that you could get them all over the fair. They were the perfect snacks for fair visitors on the go.

The Fair and Its President Revisited

For a generation after the fair closed, most historians ignored it, called it unimaginative in comparison to the 1939–1940 New York fair, or dismissed it as an escapist celebration of complacency and affluence. But that began to change in the twenty-first century as historians carried out more research and put the fair into historical context. They pointed out, for instance, that attendance at the fair was lower than predicted, but, at nearly fifty-two million people, it exceeded all previous fairs and was the equivalent of over a quarter of the U.S. population in 1960. It didn't preview any stunning scientific breakthroughs, but it did showcase outstanding elements of American and foreign culture. Measured in terms of enjoyment and happy memories, it warrants high grades. In terms of promoting New York City and boosting its economy, it also merits praise. The fair's evaluation as a modest success was best reflected in Lawrence Samuel's 2007 book, *The End of the Innocence.* He concludes,

> [T]here were really two fairs in Queens in 1964 and 1965, or at least two constructions of its past. The first is steeped in its official memory, the business enterprise that lost money, overcharged exhibitors, offended the intellectual and aesthetic elite. The other

---

39. *United States Pavilion—Pavilion Guide*, 1964, http://www.nywf64.com/unista08.shtml.

can be found in its popular memory—the experience that most visitors found thoroughly enjoyable, if not enthralling, that sparked imaginations and reshaped people's vision of the world.[40]

The fair didn't leave a legacy of Moses's planned string of parks, but it did leave a large, outstanding public park with many amenities, now called Flushing Meadows-Corona Park, used by thousands of people every year.[41]

Robert Moses had floated the idea of naming it "Robert Moses Park" but found little support. He lost his last significant hold on power in 1968 when the Triborough Bridge and Tunnel Authority was merged into the new Metropolitan Transportation Authority. Moses was offered the position of "consultant," which gave him an office and a secretary but no real power, and he faded from public view. To explain his philosophy and work, he published *Public Works: A Dangerous Trade* in 1970.[42] It was mostly a compilation of letters, articles, editorials, and press releases, adding little to what the public already knew and revealing almost nothing about his deeper motivations and reflections. Moses soon encountered an extraordinary critical biographer who altered his public image. *Newsday* reporter Robert A. Caro's 1,200 page 1974 biography, *The Power Broker: Robert Moses and the Fall of New York*, a magnificent piece of research and writing, won a Pulitzer Prize for biography. Caro portrayed Moses as a "master builder" whose early works, for example, state parks and Long Island expressways, were mostly beneficial. But his later work, including arterials in New York City, public housing, and the fair, were too expensive, ran up public debt, destroyed neighborhoods, and were administered by a polarizing figure with too much power who was given to ruthlessly running over opposition. The book was published at a time of severe fiscal crisis and near bankruptcy for New York City, partly attributable, critics said, to Moses's overbuilding in the prior three decades.

Moses would not go quietly. He accused Caro of listening only to his enemies and ignoring his impact for the public good. The book "is full of mistakes, unsupported charges, nasty, baseless personalities and random haymakers . . . dirt and misinformation . . . stink bombs," he said in a

---

40. Samuel, *The End of the Innocence*, 198–199. Samuel also summarized his views in "The End of America's Innocence," *New York Archives* (Summer 2011), 28–31.
41. Marc H. Miller, "Something for Everyone: Robert Moses and the Fair," in Queens Museum, ed., *Remembering the Future*, 45–72.
42. Robert Moses, *Public Works: A Dangerous Trade* (New York: McGraw-Hill, 1970).

public letter to Caro when the book was published. Moses was unapologetic: "I raise my stein to the builder who can remove ghettos without removing people as I hail the chef who can make omelets without breaking eggs." The essential trait of leadership was not being a visionary or defining a clear mission, the great builder insisted. Instead, it was inspiring people and expecting them to reciprocate with unwavering support. "It is personal loyalty, not loyalty to abstract principles, but unshakable, never-failing loyalty which gives support in the clinches."[43] The public letter was vintage Moses, going on the offensive, conceding nothing. But the negative image spun by Caro's lengthy best-selling book stuck.

Historians' views of Moses gradually evolved. In 1993, urban historian Joel Schwartz questioned the concept of Moses as a "master builder" who imposed his own vision on New York's urban landscape and instead portrayed him as part of a liberal consensus about the need for urban renewal. After realizing belatedly that slum clearance and highway building had accelerated division of New York City along income and racial lines, his erstwhile supporters, and then historians like Caro, blamed Moses for the consequences.[44] In 2007, Moses was at least partially rescued, reevaluated, and elevated to a new, more respectable status. Columbia University urban historian Kenneth Jackson contended that Moses gave New York "the wherewithal to adjust to the demands of the modern world" and that for the most part his highways, public housing projects, and other construction projects were built economically, had structural integrity and durability, and were still in service. Moses might be haughty and impatient, but he got things done, a virtue from the perspective of the early twenty-first century when government often seemed slow and bound up with red tape. Moses might cut corners with budgets and move funds around in a way that skirted the law, but he was personally honest. "A dedicated public servant in the best sense of that term," Jackson concluded.[45]

Robert Moses was in many ways a typical New York leader—confident, proactive, determined, pragmatic—but too often, particularly

---

43. Robert Moses, "Comment on a New Yorker Profile and Biography," August 26, 1974, http://www.bridgeandtunnelclub.com/detritus/moses/index.htm.
44. Joel Schwartz, *The New York Approach: Robert Moses, Urban Liberals, and Redevelopment of the Inner City* (Columbus: Ohio State University Press, 1993).
45. Kenneth T. Jackson, "Robert Moses and the Rise of New York: The Power Broker in Perspective," in Hilary Ballon and Kenneth T. Jackson, eds., *Robert Moses and the Modern City: The Transformation of New York* (New York: W.W. Norton, 2007), 70; Michael Powell, "A Tale of Two Cities," *New York Times*, May 6, 2007.

toward the end of his career, his negative traits overshadowed the good ones. The world's fair was a typical New York enterprise: big, bold, colorful, audacious, proud, exuding energy. "The prophets and early croakers of doom as usual were wrong," Moses asserted when the fair closed for a final time in October 1965.[46] It was at least a measured success: it entertained and inspired people. In the fall of 1964, Consolidated Edison, the electric company in New York City, sponsored a contest for junior high school and high school students to define what the fair signified. Winners got medallions and cash awards presented by Robert Moses and the president of Con Ed. The winning essay said that although the fair's theme was "Peace through Understanding," its real basis is "peace through people." To another student, the central theme was "the magnificent things men can create when they work together." Another saw it as a showcase of "our expanding scientific knowledge" and speculated: "[W]ho knows how many potential giants of the arts or sciences" it may inspire?[47]

The fair was "a gigantic and kaleidoscopic extravaganza," said a *New York Times* editorial on closing day: "[I]ntangible things—the sights and sounds and artistry and magic—will linger in memory. . . . We shall miss the fair. It may have ended up in the red, but all of those who did come out to view it over the last two years are a little richer for the experience."[48] That seems like a fitting closing for a signature New York venture.

---

46. "End of Fair—Results Appraised," *New York Times*, October 17, 1965.
47. "Jersey Girl Wins $5,000 for Essay on Fair's 'Vitality,'" *New York Times*, November 16, 1964; Samuel, *The End of the Innocence*, 60.
48. "Farewell to the Fair," *New York Times*, October 17, 1965.

14

August 2, 1978

Environmental Crisis and Citizen Activism

Lois Gibbs, president of the Love Canal Homeowners Association, discusses the Love Canal health crisis with Governor Hugh Carey in 1978. *Photo Courtesy of SUNY Buffalo Archives.*

A Crisis in the Making

New York State commissioner of health Robert Whalen delivered a stunning announcement at an Albany press conference on August 2, 1978: A landfill in Niagara Falls known as Love Canal had been a dumping site for toxic chemicals over many years and was being designated a major public health hazard. There is "a great and eminent peril to the health of the general public residing at or near the site," said Dr. Whalen.

It constitutes a public nuisance and an extremely serious threat and danger to the health, safety and welfare of those using it, living near it, or exposed to the conditions emanating from it, consisting, among other things, of chemical wastes lying exposed

281

on the surface in numerous places and pervasive, pernicious and obnoxious chemical vapors and fumes affecting both the ambient air and the homes of certain residents living near such sites.

The evidence was alarming, including a "significant excess" of miscarriages and birth defects over the previous few years. The commissioner recommended that pregnant women and families with children under two years old living in houses adjacent to the southern end of the landfill leave their homes immediately and that an elementary school on the site be closed. People should stop eating vegetables from gardens near the site. The same day, Governor Hugh Carey announced the appointment of a task force headed by Commissioner of Transportation William Hennessy to recommend what the state should do next.[1]

It turned out to be the beginning of one of New York State's greatest public health crises. But what did Whalen really mean? How serious was the menace: bad smells in the air or poison that would harm or kill people? Why should pregnant women and children under two evacuate and other women, men, and older children stay? The announcement caused consternation in the Love Canal neighborhood in Niagara Falls. "When this announcement was made, there was not one state representative or health person at the Love Canal area to respond to questions," noted Lois Gibbs, who lived near the site, had attended the press conference, and was about to emerge as the leading Love Canal citizen activist. "There was no one to tell us where affected people should go, what the order meant, or who would pay for the move. People were literally standing in the streets by the hundreds not knowing what to do, mothers with babies in their arms, old people and children crying, and absolutely panicked."[2] It was like blowing the trumpet as a call to battle but not ordering the charge. State policy in apparent disarray, vacillating between alarm and seeming indifference, was to be all too common as the crisis unfolded.

Like most crises, this one had long historical roots. Niagara Falls had long been a mecca for newlyweds, tourists, and others who were thrilled at the renowned beauty of the spectacular falls. But the city also had a gritty industrial side. "It is at once a city of wondrous natural endowments, yet also a workmare for the moguls of energy and industry, beaten often and

---

1. "Health Chief Calls Waste Site a 'Peril,'" *New York Times*, August 3, 1978.
2. Lois Gibbs, "The Need for Effective Governmental Response to Hazardous Waste Sites," *Journal of Public Health Policy* 2 (March 1981), 45.

with a hard hand," wrote Michael Brown, a *Niagara Gazette* reporter who helped expose the health peril at Love Canal.[3] The falls had the capacity to generate plentiful, cheap hydroelectric power for industry. The city's location on the New York Central Railroad and near New York's famed Erie Canal made for quick, cheap transportation of raw materials and manufactured goods and easy access to major markets. Over the years, Niagara Falls attracted more than its share of dreamers and promotional schemers. In 1893, Niagara Falls developer William T. Love proposed a model city of two hundred thousand people with factories, parks, and other amenities in the village of LaSalle, adjacent to the city of Niagara Falls. It would be powered by inexpensive electricity generated by a navigable canal to be excavated between the upper and lower levels of the Niagara River. Love, a tireless promoter, built support within the local business, press, and political communities. He even had a song composed, "The Model City," to the tune of "Yankee Doodle":

> Every body's come to town
> Those left we all do pity
> For we'll have a jolly time
> At Love's new Model City.
>
> If you get there before I do
> Tell 'em I'm a comin' too
> To see the things so wondrous true
> At Love's new Model City.
>
> They're building now a great big ditch
> Through dirt and rock so gritty
> They say 'twill make all very rich
> Who live in Model City.[4]

Love, politically well-connected, arranged to address a joint session of the legislature in May 1893 to promote his visionary scheme. Lawmakers

---

3. Michael H. Brown, *Laying Waste: The Poisoning of America by Toxic Chemicals* (New York: Washington Square, 1979), 1.

4. New York State Department of Health, *Love Canal: Public Health Time Bomb—A Special Report to the Governor and the Legislature* (Albany: New York State Department of Health, September 1978), 3, http://www.health.ny.gov/environmental/investigations/love_canal/lctimbmb.pdf.

quickly approved a bill establishing the Modeltown Development Corporation with sweeping powers to condemn land and divert water from the upper Niagara River, even to the point of turning off Niagara Falls, for Love's canal. It would be "the most appealing and beautiful town site in existence . . . the new manufacturing center of America," Love beamed to Albany reporters. The developer met with Governor Roswell Flower, a sober-minded Democrat who was skeptical about Love's overblown rhetoric and the bill's grant of unprecedented power. Modeltown would demonstrate what an entrepreneurial New Yorker could do to enhance the Empire State's growth and prosperity, Love explained. Soon the governor could visit Modeltown to be cheered by its happy residents as he dedicated productive factories powered by clean electricity generated by the canal. Flower signed the bill. Love went to work with great fanfare, buying land, laying out streets, constructing several homes and a factory, and digging the first segment of the canal. But the economy soon dropped into a depression and Love's funding evaporated. Congress passed a law restricting private infringement on Niagara Falls. Advances in electricity generation and transmission technology made it less advantageous for industry to locate next to sources of electrical power. Modeltown failed, a model only of overhyped development schemes. By the turn of the century, the sole remaining feature was a short segment of Love's proposed canal, sixty feet wide and thirty feet deep. The City of Niagara Falls annexed LaSalle in 1927, bringing the canal segment within its boundaries.[5]

Elon Hooker, a Rochester native with engineering degrees from the University of Rochester and Cornell, a shrewd early twentieth-century business entrepreneur, saw some of the same advantages at Niagara Falls that had attracted Love: lots of water, cheap electricity, superb transportation, and friendly, probusiness local governments. Niagara Falls had another advantage for Hooker and others who were leading development of the chemical industry: relative proximity to the salt mining facilities in the Syracuse area. Salt was essential to the manufacture of chlorine, caustic soda, bleach, disinfectants, paper, and soap. Hooker founded the Hooker Electrochemical Company in Niagara Falls in 1906. The company grew

5. "A Model Industrial City," *New York Times*, May 31, 1893; "Celebration at Niagara Falls," *New York Times*, August 1, 1894; Patrick McGreevy, "Imagining the Future at Niagara Falls," *Annals of the Association of American Geographers* 77 (March 1987), 48–62; Ginger Strand, *Inventing Niagara: Beauty, Power and Lies* (New York: Simon & Schuster, 2009), 241–243.

slowly until World War I gave it and other American electrochemical companies a dramatic boost by cutting off supplies from Europe. By the end of the war, Hooker Chemical had expanded into synthetic dyes, perfumes, and medications made from coal tar. In World War II, it expanded again to make more chemicals and plastics, a key ingredient for synthetic rubber, and unspecified ingredients for the secret Manhattan Project that produced the atomic bomb. In 1945, its Niagara Falls plant was manufacturing over a hundred products, including "many chlorinated organic compounds made from benzene and toluene, insecticides . . . plasticizers, acid chlorides and many others."[6] After the war, it expanded rapidly in plastics and chemicals. It built two other plants in Niagara Falls and others elsewhere in the country. The Niagara region became a center for the chemical industry. By 1970, there were nine major chemical-producing companies in Niagara County, employing nearly 5,300 people. The chemical industry produced toxic wastes that were often discharged into waterways—the mighty Niagara River was sometimes used for flushing away toxins—or buried in the ground, usually outside of heavily populated areas. Lois Gibbs later recalled that on many days there was a vague "chemical smell" in the air in Niagara Falls. But nobody complained. It "smelled like a good economy" because of the jobs the chemical industry supported.[7]

Hooker Chemical operated a number of dumps in and around Niagara Falls. As they were to remind everyone repeatedly after the Love Canal crisis hit, state and federal regulations were loose, essentially requiring only that the chemical wastes be covered up so as not to attract vermin and flies. All of Hooker's disposal sites met that very low standard. Environmental awareness was dawning slowly. New York State had restricted, but not prohibited, discharge of toxic wastes into streams in the Water Pollution Control Act of 1949. Rachel Carson's 1962 book *Silent Spring* had connected the death of birds to the insecticide DDT, but the toxic effect of chemical waste in landfills was just beginning to get attention. New Yorkers celebrated "Earth Day," April 22, 1970, the beginning of a national movement to restore a healthy, clean, sustainable environment,

---

6. R. Lindley Murray, "Hooker Electrochemical Company: Progress and Prospects," *The Analysts Journal* (June 1957), 38–44; Robert Emmet Hernan, *This Borrowed Earth: Lessons from the Fifteen Worst Environmental Disasters around the World* (New York: Palgrave Macmillan 2012), 61–63.

7. Lois Gibbs, *30 Years after Love Canal*, March 8, 2010, http://www.youtube.com/watch?v=1xOnHtWYRs.

but state oversight of landfills was light. Barry Commoner's 1971 book *The Closing Circle* had explained "everything must go somewhere" and that "throwing away" manmade materials can damage the environment. But companies like Hooker provided jobs, paid taxes, and made chemical-based materials that benefited people everywhere. Waste was an inevitable by-product. "This ain't no chocolate factory," a former Hooker employee remarked in 1979.[8]

Most of Love's abandoned mini-canal was filled in, but the remainder, a sixteen-acre rectangle, owned by the Niagara Power and Development Company by the 1930s, was located conveniently near Hooker's main Niagara Falls factory. Hooker secured the power company's permission to dump chemical refuse there, bought the site in 1942, drained out the water, lined the sides with clay, and accelerated dumping. Some of the material was sealed in fifty-five-gallon steel drums; some was dumped directly into the pit. The City of Niagara Falls used the site to dump municipal waste until 1948. Local residents recalled seeing U.S. Army trucks at the site during World War II, but the Department of Defense later denied dumping anything there. Hooker dumped about twenty-two thousand tons of material comprising more than eighty types of chemicals including benzene, chloroform, lindane, tolune, trichloroethene, and carbon tetrachloride. Some of these chemicals were known to cause anemia, liver damage, and breathing and respiratory problems; others were known or suspected carcinogens; one, dioxin, present in small quantities, was among the deadliest toxins on earth. The dumpsite was full by 1953 and Hooker covered it with dirt. Grass and other vegetation began to slowly grow on top, giving it an almost parklike appearance. Local people called it Love Canal, though Love was long gone and it was really an abortive canal segment rather than a real canal.

In the meantime, Niagara Falls was booming in the early 1950s, in part because of the local chemical industry. The city needed land to build a new elementary school in the LaSalle section and attempted to buy the site from Hooker. The company at first demurred, citing health concerns, but the Board of Education pressed, threatening to take the land under the power of eminent domain. Hooker was presented with a chance to get rid of a liability and at the same time play the role of good corporate citizen. In April 1953, it sold the land to the city for a dollar. Hooker's

---

8. "Study at Hooker Plant Found '75 Emissions Dangerous to Health," *New York Times*, April 17, 1979.

attorneys inserted a provision in the deed that the city acknowledged that the site contained buried "waste products resulting from the manufacture of chemicals by the grantor at its plant in the City of Niagara Falls," the school "assumes all risk and liability incident to the use thereof," and that "no claim, suit, action or demand of any nature whatsoever" shall be made against the company. School officials later claimed Hooker had verbally minimized the health risk; Hooker asserted that the school had been insistent on taking the land and had been adequately warned. The contractor excavating for the school's foundation soon hit drums of chemical waste. The school board casually shifted the site about a hundred feet north and the construction resumed. The school opened in 1955. The school district sold much of the land along the site to private developers who built new homes for the growing population. By the late 1950s, there were about two hundred homes clustered around the site or within a couple of blocks of it, and hundreds more nearby. The city housing authority constructed a low-income housing project. A solid working-class neighborhood had grown up along the abandoned canal. People moving into the new homes had no idea that they were adjacent to a chemical landfill.

Dimensions of the Threat

Over the years, the clay cover on the canal began to crack and chemicals oozed to the surface. They broke through the soil on the sides and began to seep into basements. They surfaced on the school playground. Early in 1976, two reporters for the *Niagara Gazette*, alerted by residents that something was wrong, tested several sump-pumps in the basements of homes near the site and found toxic chemicals in them. In 1977/1978, another reporter for the paper, Michael Brown, carried out an informal door-to-door survey and discovered that many of the residents had severe health problems, women had suffered multiple miscarriages, and children were born with severe birth defects. As complaints rose and press reports insisted there was a serious health problem, the city pushed back. The mayor began grumbling that the newspaper would alarm people, scare away tourists, bring down real estate prices, and alienate Hooker Chemical.[9]

9. Levine, *Love Canal*, 14–21.

Brown kept up the reports. His stories were graphic and shocking. One morning in 1974, he reported, Tim and Karen Schroeder had looked out the back window of their home that bordered the Love Canal site to see that their backyard fiberglass pool had risen two feet above the ground. The pool had been pushed out of the ground by "'chemical water'—rancid liquids of yellow and orchid and blue." They tried to fill in the hole, but soon the toxic liquid was surfacing in their yard and seeping into their basement. Karen Schroeder gave birth to a daughter with severe birth defects.[10] By the spring of 1978, city and county health officials, hoping for evidence to disprove the growing chorus of complaints about the site, asked the State Health Department to conduct tests. The local congressman, John LaFalce, got the federal Environmental Protection Agency to begin its own investigation. Regional EPA administrator Eckardt C. Beck, visiting that spring, and later recalled what he saw: "Corroding waste-disposal drums could be seen breaking up through the grounds of backyards. Trees and gardens were turning black and dying. . . . Puddles of noxious substances were pointed out to me by the residents. . . . Everywhere the air had a faint, choking smell. Children returned from play with burns on their hands and faces.[11] In the summer of 1978, Donald McNeil, an investigative reporter for the *New York Times*, came to town and began to file stories with headlines like "Upstate Waste Site May Endanger Lives: Abandoned Dump in Niagara Falls Leaks Possible Carcinogens."[12]

Local citizen activists also began demanding action. Lois Gibbs, who owned a home along with her husband a couple of blocks from the site, did not set out to become the leader of the advocacy. She hailed from Grand Island, a few miles up the Niagara River, and her husband Harry was a chemical worker at the local Goodyear Tire plant. "In 1974, I moved into Love Canal with my husband and my one year old child and bought the American dream," she recalled in an interview years later. "I had the picket fence. I had the swing set. I had the mortgage. I had two cars. . . . It was literally the American dream . . ."[13] She became concerned when her son Michael came down with seizures and was diagnosed with epilepsy and

---

10. Michael H. Brown, "Love Canal and the Poisoning of America," *Atlantic Monthly* (December 1979), 33–47.
11. Eckardt C. Beck, "The Love Canal Tragedy," *EPA Journal* (January 1979), http://www2. epa.gov/aboutepa/love-canal-tragedy 13.
12. "Upstate Waste Site May Endanger Lives," *New York Times*, August 2, 1978.
13. Philip Shabecoff, *A Fierce Green Fire: The American Environmental Movement* (New York: Island Press, 2003), 27.

a urinary tract infection. She read Mike Brown's articles in the *Niagara Gazette*, learning that the chemicals in her neighborhood, and beneath her son's school, could cause blood diseases, leukemia, and various nervous reactions. She asked her brother-in-law, a professor of biochemistry at State University of New York at Buffalo, to help her interpret the technical terminology and recommend more sources for her to read. Concluding that the air in her son's school was contaminated and hurting his health, she demanded that he be transferred. The superintendent refused; if he did it for Lois Gibbs, he would have to do it for every other parent who made the request. She surveyed neighbors and found multiple health problems among people living near the canal. She began circulating a petition to close the school. She attended meetings organized by state and county health officials and was increasingly dissatisfied with their admissions that there was a problem but they could not say how serious it was or what should be done. Lois Gibbs concluded that the officials were evading the issue, dissembling, or simply did not know what to do.

Determined to get more answers, on August 1, 1978, Gibbs, her husband Harry, and her neighbor Debbie Cerrillo, whose daughter had severe birth defects, drove to Albany in the Gibbs family's 1972 Oldsmobile for what they had been told would be a meeting with Health Commissioner Whalen the next day. It was a hot three-hundred-mile journey on a low budget, none of the three had ever been to Albany before, and they had trouble finding a motel they could afford. The next day, August 2, they were stunned when Whalen strode into the auditorium for the meeting, which had attracted about fifty people from Niagara Falls, and made his bombshell announcement. They had come to talk, get information, and offer advice. Now they felt like window dressing at an event contrived to make it look like there had been consultation with the Love Canal residents before Whalen's speech to the press. To Gibbs and her neighbors in attendance at the meeting, Whalen had unmasked a threat to their very lives but not offered any real help. Gibbs shouted at Whalen, "You're murdering us!" Cerrillo, hearing that only pregnant women and children under two were being recommended for evacuation, got up and demanded: "What about my two-and-a-half year old? She's out of luck, right?"[14] Whalen, sensing the anger of the crowd, called a break and left

---

14. Hernan, *This Borrowed Earth*, 73–75; Lois Marie Gibbs, *Love Canal: My Story* (Albany: State University of New York Press, 1982), 26–29.

the meeting. He did not return after the break. His assistants had few answers. Gibbs and her neighbors, angry, frightened, and disillusioned, headed back to Niagara Falls.[15]

Lurching toward Resolution

Lois Gibbs addressed an apprehensive group of Love Canal neighbors when she returned home that night, reassuring them of state interest but cautioning against expecting too much. The next day, state health officials and Tom Frey, Governor Hugh Carey's chief of state operations, met with residents who demanded to know what the evidence really showed. Frey equivocated and said more survey and data-gathering work would be needed. People in attendance shouted, "We want out!" and "Where's Carey?" The next day, people from the community assembled again, formed the Love Canal Homeowners Association, and elected the well-informed, outspoken Gibbs as president. They established four goals: Get anyone who wanted to leave evacuated; keep up property values; get the canal fixed properly; and conduct air, soil, and water sampling throughout the whole area to determine how far the contamination had really spread.[16]

Gibbs possessed extraordinary energy, tenacity, and determination. She was about to begin developing communication, leadership, and political skills on the fly and change the course of environmental history. The new association became the rallying point for Love Canal activism and Gibbs its leader and spokesperson. But there was a good deal of diversity of opinion. Many leaders in the movement were, like Gibbs, working-class mothers and they emphasized concerns about the health of families, particularly children. Some men living in the affected region were mostly worried about real estate values and advocated a tax or mortgage boycott to force action. Others, though, thought the protest would lead to a reduction in chemical industry jobs and resented their wives spending time on protest instead of adhering to the traditional roles of taking care of their families and homes. Residents of the housing project near the site, mostly blacks, were renters and felt their concerns were overshadowed by those of white homeowners. They sought help from the NAACP and for a while organized their own, separate protest organization. Another group,

---

15. Levine, *Love Canal*, 30–35.
16. Gibbs, *Love Canal: My Story*, 38–40.

the Ecumenical Task Force, a mostly middle-class group that included members from elsewhere in Niagara Falls and beyond its borders, made Love Canal a part of broader environmental activism. Part of Gibbs's leadership challenge was to listen, negotiate, accommodate everyone's views insofar as possible, and keep all these groups pulling together.[17]

On August 5, the *New York Times* ran an editorial entitled "Time Bomb in Love Canal." "[C]areless, virtually unregulated waste-disposal practices" caused the crisis, and there were many other dump sites in New York and across the nation that were also leaking poison.[18] Love Canal had evolved from a crude ditch filled with castoff chemicals to a lead story on the evening national news. Two days later, Governor Carey visited the site. The state would buy homes bordering the canal, he announced. His response to a question seemed to indicate the state would buy other homes if they were shown to be contaminated. A few days later, state health officials explained that what the governor had *really* meant was that the state would relocate people beyond the homes that backed up to the canal *only* if they could show that they had health disorders directly connected with materials in the Love Canal. That set off more angry outbursts to the news media. Carey hedged again a few days later with the statement, "Where there's a medical diagnosis that there can be impairment to an individual's health, we will tend to that person."[19] The changing signals from Albany looked like waffling.

To clarify things, the state task force designated Ring 1 homes, the ones that backed up to the canal. Ring 2 covered the next block. The "outer ring" with potential but, the state said, very unlikely, contamination covered a much broader area, from 93rd Street to 102nd Street, ten blocks. The state would purchase Ring 1 homes and pay for people's relocation. Those homes would be demolished as part of a containment plan that the governor's Love Canal task force was developing. The task force developed a plan to cap the landfill with plastic and more soil and dig trenches and ditches to siphon off the liquid chemicals and pipe them to a specially constructed treatment station. People in Ring 2 would be evacuated if they could demonstrate a peril to their health. People in the outer ring were apparently on their own. That included Lois Gibbs and dozens of others.

---

17. Elizabeth D. Blum, *Love Canal Revisited: Race, Class and Gender in Environmental Activism* (Lawrence: University Press of Kansas, 2008), 1–119.
18. *New York Times*, August 5, 1978.
19. Levine, *Love Canal*, 56.

Gibbs and her allies demanded more and faster action. She proved to be a superb organizer, brought dozens of members into the new association, and held press conferences attended by the growing army of reporters who had converged on Niagara Falls. She arranged for them to talk mostly with women, mothers like herself who could point to the menace to home and family. She asserted that the state was being evasive and moving too slowly. She arranged for TV crews to interview residents, tour their homes' basements, and visit spots where they could film chemicals percolating out of the ground. She cooperated with the renters to help make sure their concerns were addressed. Gibbs badgered officials of the state Love Canal task force, which set up shop in the school that had quickly closed after Whalen's August 2 announcement, for answers. When they seemed less than forthcoming, which was often, she called officials in Albany. "The people on site can't make any decisions, so why waste time? I'll talk to the people with some power."[20] She raised money through voluntary contributions and began the sale of T-shirts with the logo "Love Canal: Another Product of Hooker Chemical." Capping and drainage work began in the fall after the homeowners association had insisted on building in extensive safety features such as suppressing airborne noxious fumes. The state began buying up homes, and crews flattened them and the school and buried the debris under the new cap. There was a mild stench in the air, and residents were only partially reassured when a Health Department official told them, "[I]t will smell like Hooker but it won't hurt you." Bonnie Snyder watched as her house was demolished. "It was very hard to leave my home," she told the *New York Times'* Don McNeil. "My doctor said it was like I was mourning for my house. When I got my last furniture out, I felt like I'd buried someone. But I had to leave for Bethany's sake" (her two-year-old daughter).[21]

One of the issues, of course, was money. Carey had help New York City avoid bankruptcy a few years earlier, and the state budget was still very tight. The more generous the governor's commitment to buy contaminated homes and relocate residents, the more the state would have to come up with the funds from its environmental and Health Department budgets or through a special legislative appropriation. Carey, running for reelection in 1978, wanted to be seen as a compassionate leader but not

---

20. Ibid., 78.
21. Gibbs, *Love Canal: My Story*, 59; Levine, *Love Canal*, 41–58; "Emptied Niagara Neighborhood Now Looks Like a Disaster Area," *New York Times*, November 22, 1978.

labeled as a spendthrift. There had been rumors of army dumping on the site, denied by DOD, but that, plus the magnitude of the work to be done, led to assertions in the media that the federal government should take some of the responsibility. Carey prevailed on President Jimmy Carter to declare Love Canal a federal disaster area, which he did on August 7, making the cleanup eligible for federal funds. Hopes rose: Federal resources were practically boundless.

But hopes dropped again when officials of the Federal Disaster Assistance Administration (FDAA) hedged. This was the first time that emergency funds would have been used for something other than a natural disaster. The FDAA would need to make up new regulations, and the state would have to meet their requirements. Lois Gibbs joined a delegation of state officials and local residents who traveled to Washington later in August for difficult and inconclusive negotiations with federal disaster program managers. Gibbs returned disillusioned and frustrated, as she had from Albany earlier in the month. "They made decisions, or tried to and tried not to. I was the window dressing. I learned how fast politicians can say one thing and then turn right around and do another." After a few months of negotiation the FDAA agreed to partially reimburse the state for "remedial construction," the cost of demolishing houses that had to be torn down in order to put in the ditches and drains for the cleanup plan. That could be stretched to cover most of the houses in Ring 1. Federal dollars began to flow, though it was more like a slow trickle than the flood of money that state officials and Love Canal residents had hoped for.[22]

While the politicians continued their blend of support and posturing, the state Health Department issued a long report in September, dramatically entitled *Love Canal: Public Health Time Bomb*. It listed the toxic chemicals and noted menacingly that "virtually all of man's physiologic systems can be pathologically influenced by exposure to chemicals" identified at the site. It endorsed the governor's evacuation plan and the containment and cleanup plan put forth by the task force. It concluded with a recommendation for more study, something almost every government report recommended, to the frustration of residents.[23]

The report was meant to show that the state had stepped up to its responsibilities for the health of its citizens who were Love Canal victims. But to those people, it seemed evasive, open-ended, and inconclusive.

22. Levine, *Love Canal*, 58–69.
23. New York State Department of Health, *Love Canal: Public Health Time Bomb*.

How toxic were the chemicals? How broad an area should be evacuated? "The state's words meant nothing," Gibbs recalled. "Every single day we had to go out and fight."[24] Residents were skeptical when the state resumed its health surveys in the fall. All told, residents completed about 2,700 questionnaires, some long, confusing, and complicated, and provided about 4,300 blood samples. The volume of blood samples overwhelmed the capacity of the Department of Health lab in Albany to analyze them, causing delays. Results were sent not to individuals but to family doctors who often wanted no part of the work or were reluctant to deliver news that might be used in lawsuits against Hooker. Doctors often charged people for an office visit just to interpret the results, adding to the residents' resentment of the whole thing, and even then in many cases the results were inconclusive. It seemed like a lot of data collection, analysis, and reporting for no particular purpose. Even the most expert medical professionals could not state with certainty the effects of exposure to a certain mix of toxic chemicals in a school or in someone's basement. People wanted straight answers and help; health officials responded with scientific information that was technically complex and difficult or impossible to interpret. "We deal with physical facts, not with social and political matters," one state health official explained.[25]

By late fall 1978, people beyond the governor's designated evacuation area began to apply for the state Health Department to evacuate them and buy their homes, submitting documentation of health problems, including Health Department surveys, to prove their case. The reviews in Albany took a long time. The department granted a few but rejected most with the explanation that they had not proven their case. One woman with a very high reading of chemical contamination in her basement asked a state health official what to do: Two people in the house had asthma, two others had epilepsy. "Just throw the laundry in and come right back up," he advised. "Don't spend any time down there." Gibbs escalated her attacks and demands for the state to expand the evacuation/house purchase area. She called the "child abuse hotline" in Albany and demanded that Commissioner Whalen be arrested for child abuse. She and some neighbors went on the *Phil Donahue Show*, a nationally syndicated television talk program, to plead their case. Representatives of the renters' association stepped up their pleas. When President Carter flew into Buffalo for a

24. Gibbs, *Love Canal: My Story*, 57–58.
25. Levine, *Love Canal*, 24, 35, 72–87.

campaign rally for Governor Carey in early November, Love Canal community residents showed up and picketed with signs faulting both the governor and the president for inaction. By that point, they had perfected the art of the slogan with signs with such messages as "Victim of Love Canal" and "Give Me Liberty. I've Already Got Death." Debbie Cerrillo, the activist who had accompanied Gibbs to Albany back in August, got close to Carter and tried to tell him about Love Canal. He shook her hand and smiled but all he said was, "I'll pray for you."[26]

By the end of 1978, Gibbs and her allies had emerged as full-fledged, well-organized community citizen activists, particularly adept at getting media coverage. Media coverage helped mobilize support in this and other environmental issues because people are likely to assume that the more attention the media pay to an issue, the more important it is. It motivates elected officials to overcome reluctance to address an issue in part because they fear the consequences of negative publicity.[27] Gibbs honed several messages: We are blameless victims, we need help, the government has an obligation to help us, procrastination can kill us. One homeowner told a reporter, "We've lost all of our options. Can't rent, can't sell, can't walk away from it." Gibbs kept her coalition together despite accusations that she was a publicity hound, cared only about her own home in the "outer ring," was not pressing the state enough, or would drive the chemical industry out of Niagara Falls. She appealed to the residents of the housing project near the canal who resented that homeowners were getting buyouts while they were just being displaced and included their concerns in discussions with the state. "We're a family," she repeatedly said. "We can have our fights but we stick together against our enemies. Remember, we have to work together to get out of this mess."[28] She and her allies organized lots of public demonstrations. Gibbs arranged for a visit by high-profile actor and environmental advocate Jane Fonda. She sent empty baby caskets to Governor Carey's office, alerting the media when they arrived to emphasize that the governor's limited evacuation was harming children. Love Canal activists staged a "die-in" at an annual meeting of Hooker Chemical stockholders. In a letter to the *New York Times*, Gibbs acknowledged the state's evacuation of many families but

---

26. Gibbs, *Love Canal: My Story*, 68–79.
27. Judith A. Layzer, *The Environmental Case: Translating Values into Policy*, 2nd edition (New York: CQ Press, 2005), 52.
28. Levine, *Love Canal*, 194–195.

asserted that those who remained in the neighborhood are faced with "the choice of staying and risking illness or abandoning their homes and going bankrupt." What should they tell their children when they ask, "Mommy, why do we have to live here with the chemicals?"[29]

Dr. David Axelrod succeeded Robert Whalen as health commissioner in January 1979. He was more politically astute and diplomatic than Whalen and made several trips to Niagara Falls to meet with residents. People living near the site were evacuated during the containment work, but they had to return to their homes when it was completed. Axelrod ordered evacuation of families with pregnant women and children under the age of two beyond the original evacuation area when traces of dioxin, a deadly chemical, were discovered in the site early in 1979. But once a child reached age two, the families were supposed to move back into their homes. He was willing to consider extending the evacuation zone, but said he lacked proof that the contamination had spread more broadly. The state's policies were hard to explain and even harder to understand. Love Canal residents burned effigies of Carey and Axelrod.[30]

Axelrod wanted more data, and Gibbs came up with a new approach. Old stream beds and ditches, remembered by old-time residents and visible on old maps and photos, washed the chemicals longer distances into damp, swampy areas some distance from the canal. She called these drainage conduits "swales," a term that actually meant something slightly different, small valleys. Gibbs drew the swales on a map. She ignored the state health data and instead took out her own health-survey notebook, compiled by walking around the neighborhood a couple of years earlier and supplemented by what residents had told her subsequently. She plotted disease groups using different symbols for each group: "[C]entral-nervous-system problems, including hyperactivity; migraines and epilepsy; birth defects and miscarriages; and respiratory disorders. Suddenly a pattern emerged!" The illnesses clustered along the old swales, proving the chemicals had flowed well beyond what the state admitted, past Rings 1 and 2 into the outer ring. The *Niagara Gazette* published her sketch. The "swale theory" became the source of public debate. A health official scoffed that it was useless "housewife data." Gibbs then enlisted the help of Dr. Beverly Paigen, a cancer researcher at Roswell Memorial Institute in

29. Lois Gibbs, "At Love Canal, People Still Wait for Solutions," *New York Times*, August 9, 1979; Thomas Fletcher, "Neighborhood Change at Love Canal: Containment, Evacuation, and Resettlement," *Land Use Policy* 19 (2002), 311–323.
30. Gibbs, *Love Canal: My Story*, 99.

Buffalo who had become an informal pro bono advisor to the Love Canal Neighborhood Association. Paigen carried out a survey that essentially confirmed Gibbs's swale theory. Health Department officials denounced both Gibbs's and Paigen's work as scientifically incorrect.[31]

The desultory back-and-forth continued as 1979 ended and 1980 began. Individuals living beyond the designated evacuation area continued submitting documentation about health problems. A scientific journal reported that many people seemed to be suffering from "a vague assortment of psychophysiological problems such as depression, irritability, dizziness, nausea, weakness, fatigue, insomnia, and numbness in extremities."[32] In May 1980, a federal Environmental Protection Agency study, intended to be confidential, was leaked to the *New York Times*. It reported that a sizeable percentage of the people in a sample survey were suffering from "supernumerary acentric chromosomes," which sounded particularly menacing. Love Canal activists used the report to renew their demand for wider state evacuations. Governor Carey shot back, "[A]nyone can ring the fire alarm. It takes a lot of money to send the fire engines out. We've sent them out; we know what it costs." "He is trying to get off the hook," Gibbs responded. "Carey sounds just like Hooker."[33]

Carey saw an opportunity: Use the report to renew pressure on the federal government to pay for relocation of residents who were panicked by the new EPA study. "Permanent relocation away from the contaminated area is the only reasonable way to deal with the trauma being experienced by area residents and to reduce the threat of a major health catastrophe," said the governor. The new federal report "indicates [they] have extraordinary exposure to cancer, birth defects, and crippling and possibly killing diseases. . . . People have been told that they cannot live in these homes and they must be relocated elsewhere."[34] Carey had executed a neat political pivot, turning attention away from state reports and state action (except for reminding everyone that the state had already spent $40 million) and directing it toward President Carter.

---

31. Levine, *Love Canal*, 87–112; Michael Brown, "A Toxic Ghost Town," *New York Times*, July 1, 1989.
32. Constance Holden, "Love Canal Residents under Stress," *Science* 208 (June 13, 1980), 1243.
33. "Damage to Chromosomes Found in Love Canal Tests," *New York Times*, May 17, 1980; "Carey Criticizes Facets of Study on Love Canal," *New York Times*, May 19, 1980.
34. *Niagara Gazette*, May 24, 1980, http://library.buffalo.edu/specialcollections/lovecanal/documents/clippings/5-24-80a1.html.

On May 19, 1980, the Love Canal Homeowners Association invited two EPA officials who happened to be visiting the area to come to the association's offices to meet with residents to discuss the EPA study. Once they were inside, Gibbs and her colleagues refused to let them leave. They gave the federal officials homemade sandwiches and cookies as they listened to citizens' complaints and talked with news reporters, who were allowed into the building to broadcast the event. An angry crowd had gathered outside. Someone outlined the letters "EPA" with gasoline on the grass nearby and set it on fire. "We're not holding them hostage," Gibbs told reporters. "We're protecting them because the crowd outside will tear them apart." She called federal EPA officials in Washington and Congressman LaFalce, who promised to speak with President Carter. In the evening, FBI agents, U.S. marshals from Buffalo, and Niagara Falls police entered the building without resistance and escorted the EPA officials out through the crowd. No kidnapping or hostage-taking charges were ever filed. Love Canal people demanded answers and action from Washington "or this will look like a Sesame Street picnic!" Gibbs told reporters as the federal officials were driven away.[35]

Carey's demand and Gibbs's direct action shifted the focus to Carter. Running for reelection, he was well behind his challenger, California governor Ronald Reagan, and needed New York's electoral votes. On May 21, he announced that the EPA would provide funding to relocate up to seven hundred Love Canal residents for a year, on a matching basis with New York funds. On October 1, he flew into Niagara Falls to sign the legislation authorizing the promised funds and also funds to clean up another waste site in the region. In an acknowledgment of Lois Gibbs's role, he invited her to join him on the stage for the signing of the bill.[36] (Carter won Niagara County but lost the state and the election to Ronald Reagan.)

Carter's signature freed federal funds and federal and state authorities soon worked out evacuation and purchase of homes in what had been called Ring 2 and the Outer Ring and would in the future be called the "second evacuation area." The federal funding was adjusted and, with the addition of state funds, the evacuation and purchases were permanent. About eight hundred families were eventually evacuated and reimbursed

---

35. Gibbs, *Love Canal: My Story*, 145–158.
36. Pierre Berton, *Niagara: A History of the Falls* (Albany: State University of New York Press, 2009), 329–330; "Carter Signs Cleanup Bill on Upstate Toxic Wastes," *New York Times*, October 2, 1980; Gibbs, *Love Canal: My Story*, 165–166.

for their homes by the government. Residents in the low-income complex received limited assistance with relocation expenses. The Love Canal neighborhood was soon something of a barren landscape: houses along the canal demolished and buried, those further out boarded up, fences with signs warning people that this was a hazardous area.

The Crisis Reverberates

But that was not the end of the story. The federal and state governments both sued Hooker Chemical, asserting that the company knew, or should have known, that its actions would harm public health even though they were legal at the time they were committed. The cases dragged on for years. In 1994, Hooker, by then a subsidiary of Occidental Petroleum Corporation, agreed to pay New York State $98 million. The next year, it agreed to pay the federal government $129 million to the settle that case. EPA administrator Carol M. Browner said, "[T]he Love Canal settlement underscores this Administration's firm commitment to ensuring that polluters—not the American people—pick up the tab for cleaning up toxic waste dumps." Occidental also took over responsibility for the treatment facility that was still treating runoff chemicals.[37] Hooker settled lawsuits brought by individual residents of the area for undisclosed amounts of money. Love Canal also resulted in stronger state and federal regulations of dump sites. It also led indirectly to the Comprehensive Environmental Response, Compensation, and Liability Act of 1980, establishing what came to be called the Superfund for cleanup of sites contaminated with hazardous substances

In June 1980, Governor Carey commissioned a blue ribbon panel chaired by Dr. Lewis Thomas, the highly respected chancellor of the Memorial Sloan-Kettering Cancer Center in New York City, to critique previous studies. Thomas's report, issued in October of 1980, said Paigen's study "cannot be taken seriously" and is "literally impossible to interpret." The EPA chromosome study was dismissed as "inadequate." Lack of coordination between state and federal authorities had fueled rather than resolved public anxiety. The report reached a startling conclusion: "There has been no demonstration of acute health effects linked to hazardous

---

37. "Occidental to Pay $129 Million in Love Canal Settlement," December 21, 1995, http://www.justice.gov/opa/pr/Pre_96/December95/638.txt.html.

wastes at the Love Canal site." The day after the report, however, Dr. Thomas acknowledged that there were "environmental problems" that made the area "a highly unpleasant place in which to live and work" and that therefore the evacuations were justified.[38] A state Health Department report the next year asserted that there had been "early involvement of area residents in [Love Canal] task force decision making"; emphasized the wisdom and timeliness of the governor's evacuation policy; and stated that there had been "no apparent excess in any form of cancer," no excess of birth defects, and only a slight to moderate excess of miscarriages.[39] Follow-up health studies over several years were inconclusive or seemed to show only slightly elevated incidences of health problems in former Love Canal residents. "The scientific study of Love Canal looks more like a prize fight than a search for truth," says Allan Mazur, a Syracuse University professor who has analyzed all the studies and reports. "Scientific" data and reports were often intended to support particular points of view and policies, place blame, or avoid it.[40]

By 1990, after a good deal of cleanup work, the EPA certified the outermost areas as habitable, and the Love Canal Area Revitalization Agency, the government agency that owned the abandoned homes, began selling them. The homes sold well below the cost of other Niagara Falls houses, and there were plenty of buyers. "Owning a home is the American dream," said one new homeowner, who had been attracted by the bargain prices. Others thought the threat had been exaggerated in the first place. "This area has been tested and tested and tested," said one new homeowner. "This is the most tested piece of real estate in the United States."[41]

Lois Gibbs disagreed. Skeptical of government's assessment of health risk, she denounced the decision to let people move back as a ploy to get poor and middle-class people to assume unacceptable risk. In 1981, her marriage over partly as a result of the stress attendant on all of her

38. "Carey Panel Discounts Two Studies on Love Canal Health Problems," *New York Times*, October 11, 1980; "Love Canal Skeptic Favors Relocations," *New York Times*, October 12, 1980.
39. New York State Department of Health, *Love Canal: A Special Report to the Governor and Legislature* (Albany: New York State Department of Health, April 1981), http://www.health.ny.gov/environmental/investigations/love_canal/lcreport.htm.
40. Allan Mazur, *A Hazardous Inquiry: The* Rashomon *Effect at Love Canal* (Boston: Harvard University Press, 1998), 192.
41. "Despite Toxic History, Residents Return to Love Canal," August 7, 1998, http://www.cnn.com/US/9808/07/love.canal.

Love Canal work, she had moved to Arlington, Virginia, and soon remarried. She was hailed as "Mother of the Superfund." The actress Marsha Mason played Gibbs in a fictionalized, made-for-TV movie about Love Canal. Gibbs went on to found the Citizens Clearinghouse for Hazardous Wastes, which evolved into the Center for Health, Environment, and Justice, to serve as a clearinghouse for information about the health effects of toxic chemicals. She published an account of her Love Canal work, authored a book entitled *Dying from Dioxin*, and wrote and lectured widely on the issue of children's vulnerability to environmental toxins. She achieved national prominence in the environmental justice field.[42]

In 1998, Gibbs wrote that the crisis at Love Canal "demonstrated how ordinary citizens can gain power to win their struggle if they are organized. . . . this movement consists of home-makers, farmers, blue-collar workers, ranchers—urban, suburban, rural and low-income people—and communities of color.[43] Years later, she reflected that "one key lesson from Love Canal is that a blue collar community with next to no resources was able to win its fight for justice and open the eyes of the nation and the world to the serious problems of environmental chemicals and their effects on public health."[44] Over the years, Gibbs noted, "the thing we learned, and we learned it by the seat of our pants, is that these issues are not scientific issues. They're not legal issues. They're political issues."[45] The whole Love Canal story demonstrated the interplay of industrial history, environmental issues, and politics. That sort of complexity has been common in New York since its first days as a state.

42. "About Lois," http://chej.org/about/our-story/about-lois.
43. Lois Marie Gibbs, *Love Canal: The Story Continues* (Gabriola Island, BC: New Society, 1998), 1–2.
44. Lois Gibbs, "35 Years of Progress since Love Canal," February 2, 2013, http://chej.org/2013/02/35-years-of-progress-since-love-canal.
45. Shabecoff, *A Fierce Green Fire*, 236.

15

September 11, 2001

New York's Resilience

New York City firefighters on 9/11 displayed the resilience that characterized their agency throughout its history. *Photo courtesy of the Fire Department of the City of New York.*

On September 11, 2001, terrorists hijacked four commercial airliners and flew two of them into the Twin Towers of the World Trade Center (WTC) in New York City. The resulting explosions and fires led to the collapse of both towers, with a loss of 2,752 victims, including 343 New York City firefighters. The work of the Fire Department of the City of New York (FDNY) is at the heart of the story in this chapter. The story of Thomas Von Essen, commissioner of the department on 9/11, related later in this chapter, reveals much about the operations of the department. The career of battalion chief Joseph Pfeifer after 9/11, also discussed here, provides insights into the department's resiliency after the attack.

The WTC included five other buildings, all destroyed or substantially damaged when the towers collapsed. At its dedication in April 1973, Governor Nelson Rockefeller said the center would reaffirm New York's "accustomed place as the major capital of world commerce."[1] By 2001, the

---

1. "Governors Dedicate World Trade Center Here," *New York Times*, April 5, 1973.

Twin Towers, each 110 stories high, were home to 430 banking, finance, insurance, import/export, bond trading, and transportation companies from twenty-eight nations as well as several trade and professional associations. On an average day, about 50,000 people worked there and 140,000 people rode the elevators to visit offices, dine in restaurants (including the famed Windows on the World at the top of the North Tower), or take in the breathtaking view from the observation deck at the top of the South Tower. The Twin Towers were a symbol of New York City's proud and assertive leadership in American finance and commerce. Terrorists had detonated a truck bomb in a public parking area beneath the North Tower in February 1993. They killed six people and injured a thousand but failed in their goal of toppling the North Tower into the South Tower. FDNY's heroic work in extinguishing fires started by the bomb and rescuing survivors enhanced its reputation for being able to overpower any disaster.

FDNY traced its origins to 1648 when Dutch authorities in New Amsterdam adopted an ordinance levying fines for dirty chimneys and establishing a "fire watch" to stand guard at night. An organization known as the "Prowlers" was formed and equipped with leather buckets, hooks, and ladders to fight fires. An all-volunteer fire department was organized after the Revolution and served until superseded in 1865 by a paid department. Mandates for fire sprinklers and increased inspections followed the Triangle Fire of 1911, and the size of the department increased as the city grew in the twentieth century. In the mid-1960s, New York City was swept by crime, racial unrest, drugs, and riots. Protestors burned buildings; landlords sometimes torched their own buildings to collect insurance. The city's poorest neighborhoods sustained the most damage. In some cases, firefighters were pelted with rocks and bottles as they fought fires. Veteran New York firefighters called these "the war years."[2]

The number of fires began to decline in the mid-1970s. Thomas Von Essen, who joined the department in 1970 and became commissioner in 1996, began his career in the Bronx, scene of many of the worse fires. It was grueling, sometimes frightening work, but, he recalled years later, you always had the satisfaction of beating the enemy, destructive fires. Von Essen joined the Uniformed Firefighters Association, the union of

2. Terry Golway, *So Others Might Live: A History of New York's Bravest—The FDNY from 1700 to the Present* (New York: Basic Books, 2002), 11–300; Dennis Smith, *Report from Engine No. 82* (New York: Saturday New York Press, 1972), 1–50; Thomas Von Essen, *Strong of Heart: Life and Death in the Fire Department of New York* (New York: Regan Books, 2002), 75–78, 86.

frontline firefighters. He excelled at rough union politics (where meetings sometimes featured shouting matches and shoving episodes), was noted as a tough but fair negotiator, and was elected president in 1993. His union endorsed Republican Rudolph Giuliani for mayor in 1993, the only municipal union to do so. He developed a good working relationship with the mayor, even accompanying him to Yankees' baseball games. Tight budgets made salary increases rare, but Von Essen was able to avoid layoffs, preserve health benefits, and restore to full strength crews that had been reduced under previous mayors. He supported and implemented Giuliani's controversial plan to merge Emergency Medical Services (the city's ambulance corps) into the fire department. Defending a 1995 contract, Von Essen said that critics were wrong in "bemoaning an alleged lack of givebacks by the unions" and instead should applaud "the collective efforts of the mayor and the unions to cope with the fiscal crisis."[3]

Giuliani, impressed by Von Essen's diplomacy and leadership, appointed him as commissioner in 1996. A union chief who had never risen above the rank of firefighter or served as a Fire Department officer was suddenly elevated to lead the department. Frontline firefighters rejoiced at the recognition of one of their own; skeptics saw it as a reward for being conciliatory toward the mayor. Over the next few years, Von Essen strengthened fire regulations, upgraded equipment, built a new training academy, improved training, and created five new squads to fight major fires. In his memoirs, though, he recalled being accused of "pigheadedness, micromanaging, and vindictiveness—not *completely* unfairly."[4] The diplomacy that had been evident when Von Essen was union president gave way to an arbitrary management style. He and police commissioner Howard Safir both dragged their feet in implementing a protocol from the mayor to establish unified incident commands at major disasters. Von Essen made little progress in hiring more women and minorities but resented criticism for not having done more. He purchased new, digital hand-held radios for firefighters in 2001 but had to order their withdrawal after complaints from the union he formerly headed that they did not work reliably.[5] He reorganized the department's management and

---

3. Von Essen, *Strong of Heart*, 75–78, 86–122; Thomas Von Essen, "New York City Unions Cooperate in Crisis," *New York Times*, July 12, 1995.

4. Von Essen, *Strong of Heart*, 4.

5. "Fire Officials Admit Procedural Lapse in Putting New Radios into Service," *New York Times*, April 11, 2001.

supervisory structures, rotated battalion chiefs around the city to broaden their experience, and instituted measures to hold commanders accountable for subordinates' performance. Those unsettling changes led to a confrontation with the officers' union, which voted a resolution of "no confidence" in the commissioner in March 2001. The largely symbolic but very public rebuke shook department morale and jarred the public's perception of FDNY's near invincibility.[6]

FDNY's effectiveness, however, seemed to be unhampered. By 2001, the number of annual fire deaths and injuries were at a fifty-year low. The department was distinguished by three traits. One was a sense of camaraderie and bonding. David Halberstam, Pulitzer Prize–winning author, wrote a history of one of the fire stations that responded on 9/11. Firefighters have "the sense of doing something of value." A firehouse "is like a vast, extended family," and firefighters "share terrifying risks; their loyalties to one another, by the demands and dangers they face, must be instinctive and absolute."[7] Selfless dedication was a second defining trait. Firefighters "reported for work early because they loved their jobs and each other. . . . they were prepared to risk injury and death to save a stranger."[8] Striking a balance between officers giving direction and individual firefighters taking initiative was a third characteristic. On-site officers were carefully trained to observe, make decisions, and commit resources. But, as a veteran firefighter put it, "[U]nless there's a firefighter at the nozzle on the end of that hose, crouched beneath the scorching, one-thousand-degree smoke rolling out of that doorway, there's no way that fire gets knocked down. That firefighter is our primary asset."[9]

Disaster and Confusion

FDNY was strong and well prepared, but the 9/11 attack overwhelmed its capacities. "The firefighters arriving at the towers faced a situation that spun wildly and rapidly out of their control, in a way we had never

6. "60 Fire Chiefs Join to Protest Commissioner," *New York Times*, March 7, 2001; "Commissioner of Fire Department Loses Support of Officers," *New York Times*, March 9, 2001; Von Essen, *Strong of Heart*, 163–182.
7. David Halberstam, *Firehouse* (New York: Hyperion, 2002), 7–8, 32, 158.
8. Golway, *So Others Might Live*, 328.
9. John Salka, *First In, Last Out: Leadership Lessons from the New York Fire Department* (New York: Portfolio, 2004), 16, 24–25.

anticipated," Von Essen recalled. "Firefighters are accustomed to bringing order and control. In this case, that was impossible."[10] Mayor Rudolph Giuliani came to the scene and established an overall command post a few blocks north of the towers. Von Essen, the chief of department, and other top officers arrived on the scene, established their command post in the North Tower, quickly concluded that the fires could not be extinguished, and began dispatching firefighters to rescue civilians. But they had to move the post up the street after the South Tower collapsed and the North Tower was weakened. Radio communication was deficient in the towers. The police developed their own command center, and communication between the fire and police departments was sporadic. Police and fire department radios were incompatible. Fire officers did not hear dispatches about the extent of damage from a police helicopter hovering above the towers. Chain of command was unclear after the chief of the department and the deputy chief were killed when the North Tower collapsed.

A month after the attack, Von Essen initiated an oral history project to interview firefighters and emergency medical technicians who had been on scene that day. The interviews would be kept confidential and used only for future planning, the commissioner assured them. The firefighters and emergency medical technicians poured forth fresh, vivid recollections. There were many stories of bravery and selfless acts in evacuating people from the towers. But there were also many stories of lack of information, disrupted chain of command, absence of clear orders, fear, and confusion.[11]

Coordination and communication were serious problems. The fire department's hand-held "handy talkies" did not work well in the buildings. Commanders lost contact with firefighters ascending the towers to rescue people, and many firefighters did not hear the order to evacuate the North Tower before it collapsed. "We had very little communication via handy talkie" as the rescue efforts proceeded, Assistant Chief Joseph Callan recalled. "[W]e had very little control or contact, communication wise, with the units that were on the upper floors." Lieutenant Warren Smith arrived at the North Tower and was ordered to go up a stairway. "No specific orders or anything like that, just go up, see what you can

---

10. Von Essen, *Strong of Heart*, 279.
11. The rest of this section draws on Bruce W. Dearstyne, "The FDNY on 9/11: Information and Decision Making in Crisis," *Government Information Quarterly* 24 (2007), 29–46. The oral histories are available at http://www.nytimes.com/packages/html/nyregion/20050812_WTC_GRAPHIC/met_WTC_histories_01.html.

do, basically . . ." Battalion Chief Richard Picciotto, arriving at the North Tower, "rushed into the lobby. I see the commander, a chief higher than me, he's going insane. He's overloaded. So there's companies waiting to be—you know, what do we need? What do we need?" Picciotto noted the confused state of affairs but decided to act. He took his men up the stairs and began rescuing people but then decided to order an evacuation based on his own reading of the situation and in the absence of information or authorization from higher authorities. His decision was made too late, and he and others were trapped for more than four hours when the tower collapsed, a harrowing experience he later described in a book. Chief Albert Turi recalled quickly realizing "that there is no possible way that we could extinguish this fire. . . . and that it should strictly be an evacuation procedure and to get as many people out of the building as quickly as we can. I remember being extremely concerned that we would have a lot of our people up in the building and a third aircraft would then strike it."

Many interviewees remembered having difficulty just understanding what was happening and processing information. Approaching the North Tower, Captain David Loper recalled "just being overwhelmed, trying to figure out what we were going do to when we got there. I just couldn't figure it out. Every time you size up a situation, you can come up with some kind of a plan, but I couldn't on [sic] this particular case." Zachary Goldfarb, an EMS division chief, rushed to the scene and took refuge in an ambulance as the first tower collapsed, then emerged to treat injured people. His explained:

> I have to tell you that I'm not sure what happened or where the command post was at this point. I didn't know—see, this situation was like war in that, you know, you've heard the expression the five [fog] of war. Too much stuff happened sometimes too quickly for you to sort it all out and make logical decisions based on what's real. . . . You try and make the best decisions with the information that you have, which is flawed, and you kind of go from there because you have no alternative.

Investigation and Blame

After the attacks, the department turned to the sad responsibility of recovery and funerals for dead colleagues. Tales of heroism emerged: firefighters rushing up the stairs of the doomed buildings to usher people out to safety, sometimes losing their own lives as a result. An estimated twenty-five thousand people evacuated the buildings to safety, making the casualty figure much lower than expected. New York's firefighters were elevated in the media to iconic status, selfless heroes. "New York's firefighters became a symbol of defiance in the face of terror, an inspiration in a world that has become immensely more frightening and complicated," wrote historian Terry Golway in his laudatory history of the department, published in 2002.[12] People all over the country sported FDNY hats, T-shirts, and pins.

Saluting that spirit of resilience led to acknowledging the accomplishments and glossing over the command and communications problems that had contributed to at least some of the firefighters' deaths. Von Essen, in his memoirs published in 2002, admitted that "radio contact was sporadic at best" and "confusion reigned" but asserted that determined, well-trained firefighters saved thousands of lives. Officers and firefighters on the scene had to make "dozens of snap decisions under enormous pressure with limited knowledge" of the situation. Rudolph Giuliani, whose term of mayor concluded at the end of 2001, published a book on leadership in 2002, which included a dramatic account of his own leadership on 9/11 and praised the fire and police departments. "New Yorkers are particularly adept at rallying in a crisis," he wrote. "Perhaps because of the city's size and complexity, it sometimes takes a really big event before New Yorkers realize how strong they are. The bigger the challenge, the more they rise to the occasion which actually makes it easier to lead." Both the police and fire departments were well prepared and responded well to a disastrous attack that could not have been anticipated.[13]

Before long, though, a crescendo of doubt and dissent began to build. The first flash point came in October 2001. Von Essen, interviewed on the TV news show *60 Minutes*, was asked about department morale. "The guys love what they do," he responded. "I told anyone who's got a problem to suck it up and move on." That ill-considered comment upset firefighters who were still mourning their fallen comrades. They booed the commissioner at a commemorative event for their fallen comrades at Madison Square Garden later that month. In November, Giuliani and Von Essen cut back on the number of firefighters digging through rubble at

---

12. Golway, *So Others Might Live*, 342.
13. Von Essen, *Strong of Heart*, 277–279; Rudolph Giuliani, *Leadership* (New York: Hyperion, 2002), 368.

the site. There was no chance of finding more survivors. But firefighters, who still wanted to "bring our brothers home" by searching for remains, denounced the decision as callous. The department just wanted to save on overtime pay, some said. Firefighters protesting the decision skirmished with police who tried to bar them from the site. One police officer was hurt. Giuliani sided with the police but temporarily authorized a boost in the number of firefighters on the site, with better supervision. Firefighters condemned their commissioner for trailing along with the mayor to too many media events and appearing on television rather than being at the site himself. In November, with Giuliani's term almost completed, a crestfallen Von Essen resigned.[14]

In early 2002, *New York Times* investigative reporters Jim Dwyer and Kevin Flynn obtained some of the oral histories that the department had promised would be kept confidential. The reporters noted only that the transcripts had been "made available" and did not identify who provided them. The *Times* reporters quoted selectively to document confusion, poor communications, lack of clear orders, and faulty radios. Companies arrived but did not report to any staging area. The command structure was so fractured that more firefighters were still arriving on the scene more than an hour after the collapse. "So there we were. We were in the middle of West Street, a few thousand guys waiting for orders," said Lieutenant Robert Larocco. "It really wasn't happening in a concerted effort. Perhaps there were small splinter groups of guys getting orders to do things." The *Times* also acquired police radio tapes with recordings from the helicopters overhead. In a helicopter hovering above the North Tower, a police observer said, "[I]t looks like it's glowing red . . . its [collapse] inevitable. I don't think this has too much longer to go." But firefighters did not get that message. Lieutenant Warren Smith, deciding on his own to evacuate the North Tower, ran into colleagues on their way up. "There definitely were firefighters that we were picking up on the way down that had no knowledge" of the evacuation order. [15] The *Times* joined several survivors' families in petitioning for a release of all the oral histories under

14. "Split in Ranks: Commissioner Hears the Boos of Firefighters," *New York Times*, October 24, 2001; "Firefighters in Angry Scuffle with Police at Trade Center," *New York Times*, November 3, 2001; "Fire Commissioner to Leave Proud, if Sad and Bewildered," *New York Times*, November 9, 2001; Von Essen, *Strong of Heart*, 262–272.
15. "Before the Towers Fell, Fire Dept. Fought Chaos," *New York Times*, January 30, 2002; "9/11 in Firefighters' Words," *New York Times*, January 31, 2002; "9/11 Exposed Deadly Flaws in Rescue Plan," *New York Times*, July 7, 2002.

New York's Freedom of Information law. The department resisted, citing promises of confidentiality and the sensitivity of the information, leading to more assertions of a cover-up of its management problems. The histories were finally released under court order in August 2005, and the *Times* made them available online.[16]

Hastily compiled books published in 2002 with interviews of firefighters and survivors of the collapse presented additional evidence of uncertainty and disorder.[17] Perhaps most damaging to the department was a memoir by Battalion Commander Richard Picciotto, who survived the collapse of the North Tower, where he had been leading a rescue squad. The book was a thrilling tale of heroism. But Picciotto cast himself as a defender of firefighters, "constantly standing up for my men, rallying against this or that piece of unfair treatment or foolishness" by the department's leadership. He railed against "bean counters in the administration" who had limited the number of supervisors, compromised on training, and sent firefighters out with faulty radios and other substandard equipment. "[T]he tighter we are on money matters, the harder it is for firefighters to do their jobs and for the true leaders—not the brass upstairs, but the guys on the line—to truly lead."[18] By the summer of 2002, there was widespread public debate over FDNY administration's alleged cutting corners and taking risks with firefighters' safety. The mother of a firefighter killed at the WTC said she had lost faith in "the competence of the city of New York" because of the "gross incompetence of leadership, lack of communication, rivalry, lack of technology, and absence of command and control" that had been revealed by press reports and books.[19]

Michael Bloomberg, a wealthy business magnate who had made a fortune as an entrepreneur assembling and selling business information, was elected mayor in November 2001. An independent who had switched party affiliation earlier in the year from the Democratic to Republican

16. *New York Times*, August 13, 2005. *Times* reporters Jim Dwyer and Kevin Flynn published *102 Minutes: The Unforgettable Story of the Fight to Survive inside the Twin Towers* (New York: Times Books, 2005) based in part on the oral histories.

17. Dennis Smith, *Report from Ground Zero* (New York: Viking, 2002); Dean E. Murphy, *September 11: An Oral History* (New York: Doubleday, 2002); Mitchell Fink and Lois Mathias, *Never Forget: An Oral History of September 11, 2001* (New York: William Morrow, 2002).

18. Richard Picciotto with Daniel Paisner, *Last Man Down: A Firefighter's Story of Survival and Escape from the World Trade Center* (New York: Berkley Books, 2002), 32, 71–72, 241–242.

19. Sally Regenhard, Letter to the Editor, *New York Times*, July 10, 2002.

Party, the new mayor promised businesslike, efficient government. He was eager to put to rest the quarrels of the Von Essen years and the nagging questions about the department's performance and the police and fire departments' lack of cooperation on 9/11. The mayor appointed Nicholas Scoppetta, a seasoned administrator who had overhauled the city's child welfare system, as commissioner of the department. He had a reputation for fairness, decisiveness, and getting things done. Determined that the city should learn from, but not dwell on, the past, Bloomberg hired McKinsey & Company, a highly regarded New York–based consulting firm, to study both the police and fire departments. McKinsey did the report mostly pro bono, charging the city only for out-of-pocket expenses.

Scoppetta made internal documents and the department's oral histories available to McKinsey's analysts, who also interviewed dozens of firefighters and officers directly. Their report on FDNY, released in July 2002, was immediately made public. It began by acknowledging that the attack was "unparalleled in nature and magnitude. . . . Never before had such buildings been so severely damaged by explosion and fire that they collapsed to the ground." It acknowledged the bravery and heroism of firefighters. But it described communications and command weaknesses and lapses in detail. Too many firefighters and EMS personnel converged on the scene (some without having been officially dispatched there). At times it was not clear who was in charge. Officers lost track of which groups of firefighters were in which locations. Radios malfunctioned and information was spotty. FDNY command was in disarray particularly after the collapse of the first tower. "We just set up a command post to try to manage what we could physically see in front of us," said one division chief. "After the collapse there was a natural flow [of firefighters] toward chiefs, but we didn't know where the command post was supposed to be," said another commander. Coordination between the fire and police departments was "minimal," the report said.[20]

The report certainly revealed departmental shortcomings on 9/11. But in line with Bloomberg and Scoppetta's direction, the report emphasized the future rather than the past: Its official title was *Increasing FDNY's Preparedness*. The report advanced broad recommendations for increased operational preparedness, including an Incident Command System to ensure fire and police coordination at major disasters, a recommendation

---

20. McKinsey & Company, *Increasing FDNY's Preparedness*, 2002, http://www.nyc.gov/html/fdny/html/mck_report/toc.html.

also advanced in a McKinsey's companion report on the police department. It recommended improved planning and management, stronger communications and technology capabilities, and enhancement of the department's system of member and family support services.

The release of the report touched off another round of public debate. The report missed the point that both the police and fire departments had responded well, said ex-mayor Giuliani in an interview. Some firefighters who died knew the risk they were facing but, like ships' captains who are expected to go down with their sinking vessels, chose to continue rescuing people rather than heeding calls to evacuate. "You have to understand the nature of a firefighter. It's like the nature of a Navy captain." Moreover, "[T]hey [McKinsey & Company] don't know most of the things that happened," said Giuliani. "Maybe if they read the book [Giuliani's recently published work *Leadership*, described previously] they will get a sense of the facts they missed in doing the report."[21] "Its mindset before 9/11 was self-confidence," said Charles Jennings, a professor of fire science at John Jay College. "[I]t's kind of discouraging to go through this and see issues raised that most people watching the department were already aware of." What is really needed is "a cultural change."[22]

Building the New FDNY

The McKinsey report led to redefinition of FDNY's mission in the post-9/11 era, substantial reorganization, new strategies and tactics, and a cultural change along the lines that Professor Jennings and other objective observers endorsed. FDNY proved to be a leading example of a resilient New York institution. Holding a press conference right after its release, Mayor Bloomberg announced that he would immediately move to implement most of its recommendations. For the fire department, technical upgrades, such as new radios and better communications technology in high-rise buildings, would come right away. He also ordered better cooperation between the police and fire departments. "Interagency competition may be unavoidable and even healthy to some extent, but it can never

---

21. "Giuliani Says City Was Prepared on 9/11," *New York Times*, September 29, 2002.
22. "One Year Later: World Trade Center Tragedy Prompts Reassessment of Responses," *EHS Today*, October 24, 2002, http://ehstoday.com/fire_emergencyresponse/ehs_imp_12311.

impair our ability to respond to emergencies," he insisted. "The stakes are just too high." Scoppetta and police commissioner Raymond Kelly had already begun conversations looking toward more cooperation, radio communications problems would be fixed, and a fire department representative would begin riding in police helicopters surveying fires from the air.[23] In public pronouncements, Scoppetta acknowledged "the sheer and unprecedented magnitude of the event" but said the department was not at all defensive. It was planning for how it could "improve and better prepare itself for the multitude of challenges inherent in another catastrophic emergency." The department quickly began to decentralize its command structure, streamline dispatching, improve staging, field-test new radios, and improve evacuation procedures for high-rises.[24]

The department went ahead with a major reorganization, adding more chiefs at the middle-management level. It strengthened training. It began consulting with the U.S. Military Academy at West Point and the Naval War College for advice on strengthening its chain of command and fighting terrorist attacks. It drew on the U.S. Forest Service, which had long experience with coordinated responses to forest fires, on how to develop an effective incident command. It established a task force headed by R. James Woolsey, former director of the CIA, to assess and strengthen technical readiness, including communications. The universe of potential dangers and emergencies facing New Yorkers had changed and increased dramatically, Scoppetta kept emphasizing, so the department needed to change in a commensurate way. For the first time in its history, the department developed a strategic plan similar in format to what model businesses used, embodying many of McKinsey's recommendations. It set forth six "key goal areas" and twenty "priority objectives." Under the goal of "Improve Emergency Response Operations," the department committed to develop its Incident Command System; automate and streamline mobilization plans; strengthen its "Special Operations Team," which would respond to major disasters; and develop plans for addressing catastrophic threats such as weapons of mass destruction. The next year it issued a "First Year Scorecard" indicating the status of each objective and highlighting "Key Accomplishments." Strategic planning became an integral part of the way the department conducted its business after that, paralleled by annual

---

23. "Mayor Promises Better Response to Catastrophes," *New York Times*, August 20, 2002.
24. Nicholas Scoppetta, "WTC: Analysis of FDNY's Response and Proposed Reforms/Changes," *Fire Engineering* (October 2002), 91–94.

reports that indicated accomplishments but also identified shortfalls and improvement opportunities. It represented a sea change for an agency that had been accustomed to setting up ad hoc command sites, improvising at the site of disasters, and counting on the courage of its firefighters to overcome any obstacle.[25]

A major advance came with the establishment of a state-of-the-art operations center in 2006. It enabled top-level commanders to monitor fire and emergency medical activity throughout the city, supervise daily responses, and manage large-scale disasters. Chiefs no longer rushed to the scene of major fires and other disasters. Instead, they could now monitor operations of fire engine companies and ladder companies, access real-time reports from on-site commanders, and track fire vehicles and ambulances. They could access feeds from police department helicopters, traffic cameras, and news media. The center also provided digital versions of floor and building plans for major buildings and access to databases, maps, photos, and other information from city, state, and federal agencies. The center solved a major 9/11 problem, lack of information. It also made coordination with the police department much easier.[26]

There were disputes and setbacks along the way. In the event of another terrorist attack, or the deployment of hazardous materials such as poison gas, should the police or fire department take charge of the response? Federal guidelines issued in 2003 required a command protocol as a condition of receiving federal Homeland Security funding. Tired of the interagency bickering and unwilling to lose federal dollars, Mayor Bloomberg in May 2004 announced tentative adoption of a "Citywide Incident Management System." It designated police as the lead agency in an event involving "actual or suspected crime or terrorism." It was widely seen as a triumph for Kelly and a defeat for Scoppetta.[27]

The work of the federal 9/11 commission investigating the terrorist attacks also impacted the city's approach to its emergency services. The

25. Fire Department of the City of New York, *Strategic Plan, January 1, 2004–2005*, http://www.nyc.gov/html/fdny/pdf/pr/2004/strategic_plan/strategic_plan_whole.pdf; and *Strategic Plan 2004–2005, First Year Scorecard*, http://www.nyc.gov/html/fdny/pdf/pr/2005/strategic_plan/first_year_scorecard.pdf.

26. "Nerve Center," *Fire Chief* (June 2009), 46–53; Darrell K. Taft, "Never Again: Today's FDNY Is Stronger and Better Prepared," *Eweek*, September 6, 2011, http://www.eweek.com/c/a/Government-IT/FDNY-Fortifies-Communications-IT-Systems-in-a-Post911-World-690496.

27. "City Agencies Argue on Coordinated Response to Disasters," *New York Times*, May 15, 2004.

commission held its first hearings in the city on March 31 and April 1, 2003. Bloomberg was uncooperative, contending that reviewing New York City's response was beyond the commission's purview and refusing to release documents until threatened with U.S. Justice Department litigation. His testimony was petulant, complaining about inadequate federal funding for the city's anti-terror work.

The commission returned on May 18–19, 2004, after staff had drafted a report critical of the city's response, particularly lack of communications. The commission's cochairs recalled later feeling that fire and police department bravery had been "mythologized" and deeper flaws glossed over. The first day staff presented an oral report, including video shot on 9/11 and narrative interpretation from Peter Hayden and Joseph Pfeifer, who were among the onsite commanders that day. Commission member John F. Lehman said, "I think the command and control and communications of this city's public service is a scandal" and its disaster-response plans "not worthy of the Boy Scouts, let alone this great city." Bloomberg's just-issued Incident Command System protocol "simply puts in concrete a clearly dysfunctional system." That comment was "outrageous," said former commissioner Von Essen in his testimony. New York's tabloid newspapers, the *Daily News* and the *Post*, cried insult and demanded an apology to the city. The next day, former mayor Giuliani began by asserting that "our enemy is not each other" but the terrorists. He testified that the attack was unprecedented, the response well coordinated, demonstrating that New Yorkers "handle big things brilliantly." People in the audience interrupted, shouting that they should ask about radios and cooperation. Mayor Bloomberg condemned "armchair quarterbacks" who exaggerate police-fire rivalry, asserting that the two departments worked well together in emergencies. New York is the safest city in the nation, he told them. He returned to the issue of federal aid: New York State received $5.47 per capita in Homeland Security grants compared to Nebraska, which got $14.33, and Wyoming, which received $38.31. The hearings had mostly stirred up old issues but also kept the pressure on city government to strengthen its capacity. The commission's final report, issued in July, acknowledged heroism, described the communications and coordination problems, but also noted the city's progress.[28]

---

28. "Panel Criticizes New York Action in Sept. 11 Attack," *New York Times*, May 19, 2004; "Giuliani Presents Tough Defense to Sept. 11 Panel," *New York Times*, May 20, 2004; Thomas H. Kean and Lee H. Hamilton, *Without Precedent: The Inside Story of the 9/11*

The debate over leadership at disasters resumed early in 2005. In April, Bloomberg signed an executive order formally mandating the adoption of the Incident Command System that he had initially issued the previous year. Scoppetta concurred, but Peter Hayden, chief of the department and a hero of 9/11, publically resisted. The City Council held hearings where Hayden, using "startlingly frank language," suggested Bloomberg's order represented a power grab by the police department. Bloomberg was unmoved. "Look, we are going to have everybody working together to protect the people of the City of New York. And anybody who doesn't feel that they can do that . . . can't work here." Hayden gave in and effectively implemented the protocol.[29] Hayden quietly retired the next year and was replaced by Salvatore Cassano, a thirty-six-year veteran of the department who had been serving as chief of operations since September 2001. Cassano, politically adept, got on well with the mayor, fire commissioner, and the police. Rivalry continued, but the two departments worked well together.

A Resilient New Yorker

The progress and changes in the department can be traced by following the career of Joseph W. Pfeifer. A battalion chief on 9/11, he responded to a report of a gas leak near the WTC early in the morning. A French filmmaking crew happened to be there that day, making a documentary on the experiences of a probationary firefighter under Pfeifer's command. One of the filmmakers was with Pfeifer when the first plane hit, captured it on film, and trailed after Pfeifer as he raced to the North Tower and called in an alarm. Pfeifer dispatched the first firefighters who arrived on scene to evacuation work in the towers. His brother Kevin, a firefighter from another battalion, passed him, went up the stairs with his group, and was later killed in the collapse. Soon higher-level officers took over command.

Commission (New York: Alfred A. Knopf, 2006), 46–55, 212–231; National Commission on Terrorist Attacks Upon the United States, "Emergency Response: Staff Statement No. 13," "Eleventh Public Hearing," May 18–19, 2004, and *The 9/11 Commission Report*, 278–323, http://govinfo.library.unt.edu/911.

29. "Mayor Says It's Best to Let Police Control Terror Scenes," *New York Times*, April 23, 2005; "Disaster Plan Is Deeply Flawed, Council Is Told," *New York Times*, May 10, 2005; *Emergency Response: Citywide Incident Management System*, http://www.nyc.gov/html/oem/html/about/about_cims.shtml.

Following their orders, Pfeifer called for rescuers in the North Tower to evacuate but realized the radios were not working. He barely escaped before the tower collapsed, then returned to aid in the recovery efforts. He gave his oral history to the department, was featured in a documentary film on 9/11 that drew on the French filmmakers' footage, was interviewed for some of the histories published in 2002, and testified before the 9/11 Commission at the May 2004 hearing in New York City.

Joseph Pfeifer did not just go back to what he had been doing. He personified the department's—and the city's—spirit of resilience and moving forward in response to a disaster. He recognized that the department needed to change its way of thinking and strengthen its capacity to respond to terrorist attacks. He helped overhaul management practices, identified new policy and budget priorities, and created new partnerships to supplement the department's existing strengths. Through hard work and a lot of study, he became the department's expert on homeland security. Pfeifer already had a bachelor's degree from Cathedral College and a master's in theology from the Immaculate Conception Seminary. In the next decade, he achieved a master's in public administration from the Kennedy School of Government at Harvard and a master's in security services from the Naval Postgraduate School. He became a fellow and visiting lecturer at the Kennedy School, a fellow at the Combating Terrorism Center at West Point, and a visiting instructor at the Naval Postgraduate School. He gave presentations at Harvard, Columbia, the Wharton School at the University of Pennsylvania, and abroad. Continuing full time at the department through it all, with occasional leaves, he organized and headed the department's Center for Terrorism and Disaster Preparedness in 2006.

Pfeifer's ideas, expressed in articles, book chapters, and lectures, exemplify the sorts of new approaches that came to permeate the department. For instance: To meet the terrorist threat, you need "real-time information provided directly to decision-makers." This requires finding new ways to share information within, and between, agencies. "The objective of this approach is to blend technology with social interaction to understand threats and mitigate their effects." Terrorist attacks are unpredictable and, as they unfold, they can push organizations beyond their normal capabilities. To anticipate this, you need to build in "command resilience": core competencies, situational awareness, flexible decision-making, and innovation. "Command resiliency is achieved by overcoming organizational bias and integrating organizational preparedness and operational adaptability into a synergistic response network." In a dangerous crisis, emergency responders naturally tend to "turn to their own"—firefighters pair up with other firefighters, police join together in small groups. In a complex situation, leaders need to make sure that people do just the opposite—embrace the other group or groups so that everyone's strengths are united. Pfeifer developed what he called the "5 C" concept—command and control, connect, collaborate, and coordinate—which became a precept of FDNY leadership training.[30]

Mayor Bloomberg had given the police the responsibility for leading in case of terrorist attacks, but the fire department developed its own terrorism and disaster preparedness strategy. The first plan, in 2007, set forth strategies of organizational adaptability, training to respond to crises such as hazardous materials, information sharing networks, and on-site evaluation and collaboration, all the tenets that Pfeifer was explaining in his speeches and his writings. The department's second plan, released in December 2011, took into account recent terrorist activity, including "mobile attackers striking targets through an innovative weapons mix of firearms, explosives and fire." The 2007 plan said department commanders would "provide direction and vision"; the 2011 plan changed that to "refine the vision, based on experience." The earlier plan had a goal to "understand a complex threat," but the latter one redefined that to "adapt to anticipate a changing threat environment." The 2007 plan noted "trends toward centrally controlled terrorist organizations," but four years later, the emphasis was on "concern over domestically radicalized terrorists, 'lone wolves,' and terror networks."[31] The plans are very good examples of using planning to keep institutions changing and adaptive.

---

30. These examples are from Joseph W. Pfeifer, "Network Fusion: Information and Intelligence Sharing for a Networked World," *Homeland Security Affairs* 8 (October 2012), 1–19; Joseph W. Pfeifer, *Command Resiliency: An Adaptive Response Strategy for Complex Incidents*, Thesis, Naval Postgraduate School, 2005, http://www.dtic.mil/cgi-bin/GetTRDoc?AD=ADA439581; Michael Useem, "Leading on 9/11 and Beyond: New York City Fire Department's Joseph Pfeifer," interview, September 8, 2011, *Knowledge@Wharton*, http://knowledge.wharton.upenn.edu/article.cfm?articleid=2839; and Joseph W. Pfeifer, "Adapting to Novelty: Recognizing the Need for Innovation and Leadership," *WNYF* 72 (2012), http://www.hks.harvard.edu/var/ezp_site/storage/fckeditor/file/pdfs/centers-programs/programs/crisis-leadership/Pfeifer_2012-1%20wnyf_Adapting%20to%20Novelty.pdf.
31. Fire Department, City of New York, *Terrorism and Disaster Preparedness Strategy* (April 2007), http://www.nyc.gov/html/fdny/pdf/events/2007/tdps/terrorism%20strategy_complete.pdf; Fire Department, City of New York, *Counterterrorism and Risk Management Strategy* (December 2011), http://www.nyc.gov/html/fdny/pdf/publications/FDNY_ct_strategy_2011_12.pdf.

FDNY, 9/11, and New York's Spirit

The fire department evolved and strengthened its capacities after 9/11, just as the City of New York did. There were some rough patches: disputes with the mayor over closing a few firehouses and resistance to increasing the number of women and minority firefighters until the courts intervened and forced action. But overall, it was a story of resilience and adaptation. The department cooperated with the police on several major incidents including a blackout in August 2003, an airplane emergency landing in the Hudson River in January 2009, and a car bomb in Times Square in May 2010. Firefighters were trained for the new, more complex responsibilities that 9/11 and its aftermath had thrust on their department. Response times decreased—four minutes and two seconds for structural fires in 2011— indicating how precisely the department tracked and reported on critical measures. The year 2012 set an all-time record for the fewest fire fatalities in the city's history.[32]

Working with the University of Pennsylvania's Wharton School of Business, FDNY's Fire Academy developed its leadership and teamwork training to the point where corporations turned to it to learn how to organize and manage teams. In 2010, it began offering "Team Challenge" workshops. "The challenge takes members from a variety of businesses . . . such as finance, engineering, law, and systems development—and puts them into real firefighting scenarios to improve business skills." A Google executive explained why that company contracted with FDNY for training: "To innovate, we encourage a team of people to come together and consider a variety of perspectives to design new solutions." In one training session, participants ran up four flights of stairs and then lowered each other by rope off the edge of the building to learn trust. They crawled through a dark, winding tunnel. "It taught us how to adapt to a new situation and build confidence to perform under pressure in stressful and isolating environments," said one participant. In a fire simulation, a team entered a building "while fire began to crawl up the wall and then over their heads." The team leader—"the nozzle man"—directed the hose to extinguish the flames, while the rest of the team supported his efforts.

32. "Mayor Bloomberg and Fire Commissioner Cassano Announce 2012 Sets All-Time Record for Fewest Fire Fatalities in New York City History," January 2, 2013, http://www.nyc.gov/portal/site/nycgov/menuitem.b270a4a1d51bb3017bce0ed101c789a0/index.jsp?doc_name=/html/om/html/2013a/events_01.html.

FDNY—criticized for lax administration on 9/11—was now showing corporate executives how to manage teams in crises.[33]

In October 2001, Mayor Giuliani worked with BBDO, one of the city's leading advertising agencies, to create six short TV spots to highlight New York's buoyancy and encourage shoppers and tourists to resume visits to the city. They were titled "The New York Miracle." The idea was that well-known New Yorkers excel at unexpected things, demonstrating the can-do spirit of their city. In one segment, a graceful ice skater at Rockefeller Center turns out to be the actor Woody Allen, who deadpans at the end that it is the first time he has ever put on skates. Retired New York Yankees' catcher Yogi Berra conducts the New York Philharmonic orchestra. A gentleman seen from a distance running the bases at Yankee Stadium makes it to home base and is revealed to be former secretary of state Henry Kissinger. At the end of each segment, Mayor Giuliani appeared, imploring viewers: "The New York miracle! Be part of it!"[34]

September 11, 2001, tested but did not break New York's spirit. It shocked one of its key institutions, the fire department, but that agency came back stronger than ever. In his testimony before the 9/11 Commission in May 2004, Mayor Michael Bloomberg reminded the audience of his city's greatness and its spirit in recovering from the attack:

> To people around the world, New York City embodies what makes this nation great. That's a function of our status as the world's financial capital, driven not only by Wall Street but [also] our international prominence in such fields as broadcasting, the arts, entertainment and medicine. Such is New York's importance that to a great extent, as goes its economy, so goes the country's. If Wall Street is destroyed, Main Street will suffer. Beyond that, New York embraces the intellectual and religious freedom and cultural diversity that makes us truly the world's second home. We are a magnet for the talented and ambitious from every corner of the globe. In short, we embody the strengths of America's

---

33. Gregory Pfeifer, "Fight Fire with Learning," *Chief Learning Officer* (September 2012), 56–57, 62; Gregory Pfeifer and Preston Cline, "Firefighters for a Day," *Wharton Leadership,* http://wlp.wharton.upenn.edu/LeadershipDigest/training-with-the-fdny.cfm.

34. Anthony Vagnoni, "Making the 'New York Miracle' Commercials: The Story of How the Campaign Came Together," *Advertising Age* (November 26, 2001), http://adage.com/print/33290.

freedom, and that makes us an inevitable target of those who hate our nation and what we stand for.[35]

The mayor had captured New York City's importance and also something of its spirit and the spirit of the state: strong, proud, defiant, resilient.

---

35. National Commission on Terrorist Attacks Upon the United States, "Eleventh Public Hearing," May 19, 2004, 68–69, http://govinfo.library.unt.edu/911/archive/hearing11/9-11Commission_Hearing_2004-05-18.htm.

BIBLIOGRAPHY

This bibliography lists the major sources for the book. Additional sources, for example, articles from journals and online websites, are listed in the footnotes of each chapter. Many of the published sources are available online, particularly from Google Books, http://books.google.com/?PH PSESSID=f8fdae66572b24ab8fc567c25fbccdcc, and Archive.Org, http://archive.org/index.php.

General Sources

Eisenstadt, Peter, editor-in-chief. *The Encyclopedia of New York State.* Syracuse: Syracuse University Press, 2005.

Ellis, David M., James A. Frost, Harold Syrett, and Harry J. Carman. *A History of New York State.* Ithaca: Cornell University Press, 1967.

Flick, Alexander C., ed. *History of the State of New York.* 10 vols. New York: Columbia University Press, 1933–1938.

Jackson, Kenneth T., ed. *The Encyclopedia of New York City.* 2nd edition. New Haven: Yale University Press, 2010.

Klein, Milton M., ed. *The Empire State: A History of New York.* Ithaca: Cornell University Press, 2001.

New York History (journal published by the New York State Historical Association)

New York Times

Introduction

Carmer, Carl. *Dark Trees to the Wind.* New York: William Sloane Associates, 1949.

Cuomo, Mario. *The New York Idea: An Experiment in Democracy.* New York: Crown, 1994.

Ellis, David M. *New York: State and City.* Ithaca: Cornell University Press, 1979.

Gould, David. *Forces: Three Themes in the Lives of New Yorkers.* Albany: New York State Museum, 1977.

Jackson, Kenneth T., and David S. Dunbar, eds. *Empire City: New York through the Centuries.* New York: Columbia University Press, 2002.

Klein, Milton M., ed. *New York: The Centennial Years, 1676–1976.* Port Washington: Kenikat Press, 1976.

Shaw, Ronald E. *Erie Water West: A History of the Erie Canal, 1792–1854.* Lexington: University of Kentucky Press, 1966.

Chapter 1. April 22, 1777: New York Begins

Adams, William Howard. *Gouverneur Morris: An Independent Life.* New Haven: Yale University Press, 2003.

Becker, Carl. *The History of Political Parties in the Province of New York, 1760–1776.* Madison: University of Wisconsin Press, 1909.

Brandt, Clare. *An American Aristocracy: The Livingstons.* New York: Doubleday, 1986.

Brookhiser, Richard. *Gentleman Revolutionary: Gouverneur Morris: The Rake Who Wrote the Constitution.* New York: Free Press, 2003.

Chernow, Ron. *Alexander Hamilton.* New York: Penguin Press, 2004.

Countryman, Edward. *A People in Revolution: The American Revolution and Political Society in New York, 1760–1790.* Baltimore: Johns Hopkins University Press, 1981.

Dangerfield, George. *Chancellor Robert R. Livingston of New York, 1746–1813.* New York: Harcourt Brace, 1960.

Dougherty, J. Hampton. *Constitutional History of the State of New York.* 2nd edition. New York: Neale, 1915.

Flick, Alexander. *The American Revolution in New York: Its Political, Social and Economic Significance.* New York: Ira Friedman, 1967.

Galie, Peter J. *Ordered Liberty: A Constitutional History of New York.* New York: Fordham University Press, 1996.

Gerlach, Don R. *Philip Schuyler and the American Revolution in New York, 1733–1777*. Lincoln: University of Nebraska Press, 1964.

Gerlach, Don R. *Proud Patriot: Philip Schuyler and the War of Independence, 1775–1783*. Syracuse: Syracuse University Press, 1987.

Johnson, Herbert A. *John Jay: Colonial Lawyer*. New York: Garland, 1989.

Johnston, Henry P., ed. *The Correspondence and Public Papers of John Jay*, I, 1763–1781. New York: Putnam, 1891.

Kaminski, John P. *George Clinton: Yeoman Politician of the New Republic*. Madison: Madison House, 1993.

Kirschke, James J. *Gouverneur Morris: Author, Statesman, and Man of the World*. New York: St. Martin's Press, 2005.

Lincoln, Charles Z., ed. *Messages from the Governors*, II, 1777–1822. Albany: J. B. Lyon, 1909.

Mason, Bernard. *The Road to Independence: The Revolutionary Movement in New York, 1773–1777*. Lexington: University of Kentucky Press, 1966.

Miller, Melanie R. *An Incautious Man: The Life of Gouverneur Morris*. Wilmington, DE: ISI Books, 2008.

Morris, Richard B. *John Jay, the Nation and the Court*. Boston: Boston University Press, 1967.

Morris, Richard B., ed. *John Jay: The Making of a Revolutionary*. New York: Harper & Row, 1975.

The Papers of John Jay. http://www.columbia.edu/cu/lweb/digital/jay.

Pell, John, II. G., ed. *Essays on the Genesis of the Empire State*. Albany: New York State American Revolution Bicentennial Commission, 1979.

Polf, William A. *1777: The Political Revolution and New York's First Constitution*. Pamphlet. Albany: New York State American Revolution Bicentennial Commission, 1977.

Schechter, Stephen L., ed. *The Reluctant Pillar: New York and the Adoption of the Federal Constitution*. Albany: New York State Commission on the Bicentennial of the United States Constitution, 1987.

Schechter, Stephen L., and Richard B. Bernstein, eds. *New York and the Union*. Albany: New York State Commission on the Bicentennial of the United States Constitution, 1990.

Stahr, Walter. *John Jay: Founding Father*. New York: Hambledon and London, 2005.

Wood, Gordon S. *The Creation of the American Republic, 1776–1787*. Chapel Hill: University of North Carolina Press, 1969.

Young, Alfred. *Democratic Republicans of New York: The Origins, 1763–1797*. Chapel Hill: University of North Carolina Press, 1967.

Historic Site
Senate House State Historic Site. Kingston, New York.

Chapter 2. February 4, 1826: Fiction Trumps History

Anderson, Fred. *Crucible of War: The Seven Years' War and the Fate of Empire in British North America, 1754–1766*. New York: Vintage Books, 2000.

Barr, Daniel P. *Unconquered: The Iroquois League at War in Colonial America*. New York: Praeger, 2006.

Berleth, Richard. *Bloody Mohawk: The French and Indian War and American Revolution on New York's Frontier*. Hensonville, NY: Black Dome Press, 2009.

Conn, Peter. *Literature in America: An Illustrated History*. New York: Cambridge University Press, 1989.

Cooper, James Fenimore. *The Last of the Mohicans*. New York: Penguin Books, 1986.

Cooper, Susan Fenimore. *Pages and Pictures from the Writings of James Fenimore Cooper with Notes*. New York: W. A. Townsend, 1861.

Dekker, George P., and John P. McWilliams, eds. *Fenimore Cooper: The Critical Heritage*. Boston: Routledge & Kegan Paul, 1973.

Franklin, Wayne. *James Fenimore Cooper: The Early Years*. New Haven: Yale University Press, 2007.

Hauptman, Laurence M. *Conspiracy of Interests: Iroquois Dispossession and the Rise of New York State*. Syracuse: Syracuse University Press, 2001.

Jennings, Francis. *Empire of Fortune: Crowns, Colonies and Tribes in the Seven Years' War in America*. New York: Norton, 1988.

King, Thomas. *The Inconvenient Indian: A Curious Account of Native Peoples in North America*. Minneapolis: University of Minnesota Press, 2013.

Long, Robert Emmet. *James Fenimore Cooper*. New York: Continuum, 1990.

Marcus, Greil, and Werner Sollors, eds. *The New Literary History of America*. Cambridge: Belknap Press of Harvard University Press, 2009.

McWilliams, John. *The Last of the Mohicans: Civil Savagery and Savage Civility*. New York: Twayne, 1995.

Peck, H. Daniel, ed. *New Essays on the Last of the Mohicans*. New York: Cambridge University Press, 1992.

Ringe, Donald. *James Fenimore Cooper*. Boston: Twayne, 1962.

Steele, Ian K. *Betrayals: Fort William Henry and the "Massacre."* New York: Oxford University Press, 1990.

Taylor, Alan. *William Cooper's Town: Power and Persuasion on the Frontier of the Early American Republic*. New York: Random House, 1995.

Online Source
James Fenimore Cooper Society, http://external.oneonta.edu/cooper.

Movie
The Last of the Mohicans, 1992, Dir. Michael Mann.

Chapter 3. July 4, 1839: The Farmers' Rebellion

Christman, Henry. *Tin Horns and Calico: The Thrilling Unsung Story of an American Revolt against Serfdom*. New York: Henry Holt, 1945.

Deloria, Philip J. *Playing Indian*. New Haven: Yale University Press, 1998.

Ellis, David W. *Landlords and Farmers in the Hudson-Mohawk Region, 1790–1850*. Ithaca: Cornell University Press, 1946.

Huston, Reeve. *Land and Freedom: Rural Society, Popular Protest, and Party Politics in Antebellum New York*. New York: Oxford University Press, 2000.

Mayham, Albert Champlin. *The Anti-Rent War on Blenheim Hill: An Episode of the 1840s*. Stamford, NY: Stonecraft Industries, 2006; reprint of original, published in 1906.

McCurdy, Charles. *The Anti-Rent Era in New York Law and Politics, 1839–1865*. Chapel Hill: University of North Carolina Press, 2001.

Summerhill, Thomas. *Harvest of Dissent: Agrarianism in Nineteenth-Century New York*. Urbana: University of Illinois Press, 2005.

Chapter 4. July 20, 1848: A Demand for Equal Rights

Barry, Kathleen. *Susan B. Anthony: A Biography of a Singular Feminist*. New York: New York University Press, 1988

Basch, Norma. *In the Eyes of the Law: Women, Marriage and Property in Nineteenth-Century New York*. Ithaca: Cornell University Press, 1992.

Colman, Penny. *Elizabeth Cady Stanton and Susan B. Anthony: A Friendship That Changed the World*. New York: Henry Holt, 2011.

Cott, Nancy F. *No Small Courage: A History of Women in the United States*. New York: Oxford University Press, 2000.

Du Bois, Ellen Carol. *Feminism and Suffrage: The Emergence of an Independent Women's Movement in America, 1848–1869*. Ithaca: Cornell University Press, 1978.Du Bois, Ellen Carol. *Woman Suffrage and Women's Rights*. New York: New York University Press, 1998.

Du Bois, Ellen Carol. *Elizabeth Cady Stanton: Feminist as Thinker*. New York: New York University Press, 2007.

Ginsberg, Lori D. *Untidy Origins: A Story of Woman's Rights in Antebellum New York*. Chapel Hill: University of North Carolina Press, 2005.

Ginsberg, Lori D. *Elizabeth Cady Stanton: An American Life*. New York: Hill and Wang, 2009.

Gordon, Ann D., ed. *The Selected Papers of Elizabeth Cady Stanton and Susan B. Anthony*. 5 vols. New Brunswick: Rutgers University Press, 1997–2009.

Griffith, Elisabeth. *In Her Own Right: The Life of Elizabeth Cady Stanton*. New York: Oxford University Press, 1984.

McMillen, Sally G. *Seneca Falls and the Origins of the Women's Rights Movement*. New York: Oxford University Press, 2008.

Stanton, Elizabeth Cady. *Eighty Years and More: Reminiscences, 1815–1897*. Published in 1898. Boston: Northeastern University Press, 1993; rpt.

Stanton, Elizabeth Cady, Susan B. Anthony, Matilda Joslyn Gage, and Ida Husted Harper, eds. *History of Woman Suffrage*. 6 vols., various publishers, 1881–1922.

Stanton, Elizabeth Cady. *The Woman's Bible. Part I. Comments on Genesis, Exodus, Leviticus, Numbers and Deuteronomy* (1895). *Part II. Comments on the Old and New Testaments from Joshua to Revelation* (1898). New York: European, 1895 and 1898.

Stanton, Theodore, and Harriot Stanton Blatch, eds. *Elizabeth Cady Stanton as Revealed in Her Letters, Diary and Reminiscences*. 2 vols. New York: Harper and Bros., 1922.

Ward, Geoffrey C. *Not for Ourselves Alone: The Story of Elizabeth Cady Stanton and Susan B. Anthony*. New York: Alfred A. Knopf, 1999.

Weatherford, Doris. *A History of the American Suffrage Movement.* Santa Barbara: ABC-CLIO, 1998.

Wellman, Judith. *The Road to Seneca Falls: Elizabeth Cady Stanton and the First Woman's Rights Convention.* Urbana: University of Chicago Press, 2004.

Wheeler, Marjorie Sprull, ed. *One Woman, One Vote: Rediscovering the Woman Suffrage Movement.* New York: New Sage Press, 1995.

Online Sources

Elizabeth Cady Stanton Trust, http://www.elizabethcadystanton.org.

Iowa State University, Archive of Women's Political Communication, http://www.womenspeecharchive.org.

National Parks Service Women's Rights National Historical Park. http://www.nps.gov/wori/index.htm.

Rutgers University, The Elizabeth Cady Stanton and Susan B. Anthony Papers Project, http://ecssba.rutgers.edu/docs/documents.html.

Susan B. Anthony Center for Women's Leadership, http://www.rochester.edu/sba/about.html.

Susan B. Anthony Museum and House, http://susanbanthonyhouse.org/about-us/mission.php.

"Votes for Women": Selections from the National American Woman Suffrage Association Collection, 1848–1921, http://memory.loc.gov/ammem/naw/nawshome.html.

Historic Site

Women's Rights National Historical Park, Seneca Falls, New York.

Movie

Not for Ourselves Alone: The Story of Elizabeth Cady Stanton and Susan B. Anthony, a film by Ken Burns and Paul Barnes, 1999, http://www.pbs.org/stantonanthony.

Chapter 5. October 1, 1851: Striking a Blow for Freedom

Barkun, Michael. *Crucible of the Millennium: The Burned-Over District of New York State in the 1840s.* Syracuse: Syracuse University Press, 1981.

Bordewich, Fergus M. *Bound for Canaan: The Epic Story of the Underground Railroad, America's First Civil Rights Movement.* New York: Armistad, 2006.

Cross, Whitney R. *The Burned-Over District: The Social and Intellectual History of Enthusiastic Religion in Western New York, 1800–1850*. Ithaca: Cornell University Press, 1950; rpt. 1981.

Dann, Norman K. *Practical Dreamer: Gerrit Smith and the Crusade for Social Reform*. Hamilton, NY: Log Cabin Books, 2009.

Faulkner, Carol. *Lucretia Mott's Heresy: Abolition and Women's Rights in Nineteenth-Century America*. Philadelphia: University of Pennsylvania Press, 2011.

Harlow, Ralph Volney. *Gerrit Smith: Philanthropist and Reformer*. New York: Henry Holt, 1939; rpt. Russell and Russell, 1972.

Johnson, Paul E. *A Shopkeeper's Millennium: Society and Revivals in Rochester, New York, 1815–1837*. New York: Hill and Wang, 2004.

Loguen, Jermain Wesley, and Elymas Payson Rogers. *The Rev. J. W. Loguen, as a Slave and as a Freeman*. Syracuse: J. G. K. Truair, 1859.

May, Samuel J. *Some Recollections of Our Antislavery Conflict*. Boston: Fields, Osgood, 1869.

McFeely, William S. *Frederick Douglass*. New York: Norton, 1991.

McManus, Edgar J. *A History of Negro Slavery in New York*. Syracuse: Syracuse University Press, 1970.

Pease, Jane H. *They Who Would Be Free: Blacks' Search for Freedom, 1830–1861*. New York: Athenaeum, 1974.

Sernett, Milton C. *North Star Country: Upstate New York and the Crusade for African American Freedom*. Syracuse: Syracuse University Press, 2002.

Sorin, Gerald. *The New York Abolitionists: A Case Study of Political Radicalism*. Westport, CT: Greenwood Press, 1970.

Sperry, Earl R. *The Jerry Rescue*. Syracuse: Onondaga Historical Society, 1924.

Stauffer, Jon. *The Black Hearts of Men: Radical Abolitionists and the Transformation of Race*. Cambridge: Harvard University Press, 2002.

Strong, Douglas M. *Perfectionist Politics: Abolitionism and the Religious Tensions of American Democracy*. Syracuse: Syracuse University Press, 1987.

Tyler, Alice Felt. *Freedom's Ferment: Phases of American Social History to 1860*. New York: Harper, 1966.

Wellman, Judith. *Grassroots Reform in the Burned-Over District of Upstate New York: Religion, Abolition, and Democracy*. New York: Garland, 2000.

Yacavone, Donald. *Samuel Joseph May and the Dilemmas of the Liberal Persuasion, 1797–1871*. Philadelphia: Temple University Press, 1991.

Online Sources

Samuel J. May Antislavery Collection (Cornell University), http://digital. library.cornell.edu/m/mayantislavery.

National Abolition Hall of Fame and Museum (Peterboro, NY), http:// www.abolitionhof.org/home.

Chapter 6. March 30, 1899: Pollution and Politics

Boyle, Robert. *The Hudson River: A Natural and Unnatural History.* New York: Norton, 1979.

Brinkley, Douglas. *The Wilderness Warrior: Theodore Roosevelt and the Crusade for America.* New York: Harper Collins, 2009.

Chessman, G. Wallace. *Governor Theodore Roosevelt: The Albany Apprenticeship, 1898–1900.* Cambridge: Harvard University Press, 1965.

Duffy, John. *A History of Public Health in New York City.* 2 vols. New York: Russell Sage Foundation, 1968–1974.

Fox, William F. *History of the Lumber Industry in the State of New York.* Harrison, NY: Harbor Hill Books, 1976.

Graham, Frank, Jr. *The Adirondack Park: A Political History.* Syracuse: Syracuse University Press, 1978.

Grondahl, Paul. *"I Rose Like a Rocket": The Political Education of Theodore Roosevelt.* New York: Free Press, 2004.

Hays, Samuel P. *Conservation and the Gospel of Efficiency: The Progressive Conservation Movement, 1890–1920.* Cambridge: Harvard University Press, 1959.

Hazen, Allen. *Clean Water and How to Get It.* Rev. ed. New York: John Wiley & Sons, 1914.

Henshaw, Robert E. *Environmental History of the Hudson River.* Albany: State University of New York Press, 2011.

Hoornbeek, John A. *Water Pollution Policies and the American States: Runaway Bureaucracies or Congressional Control?* Albany: State University of New York Press, 2012.

Kranz, Marvin W. Pioneering in Conservation: A History of the Conservation Movement in New York State, 1865–1903. PhD dissertation, Syracuse University, 1961.

Lewis, Tom. *The Hudson: A History.* New Haven: Yale University Press, 2005.

Martin, Roscoe C. *Water for New York: A Study in State Administration of Water Resources* Syracuse: Syracuse University Press, 1960.

Melosi, Martin V., ed. *Pollution and Reform in American Cities, 1870–1930*. Austin: University of Texas Press, 1980.

Melosi, Martin V. *The Sanitary City: Environmental Services in Urban America from Colonial Times to the Present*. Abridged ed. Pittsburgh: University of Pittsburgh Press, 2008.

Melosi, Martin V. *Precious Commodity: Providing Water for America's Cities*. Pittsburgh: University of Pittsburgh Press, 2011.

Morris, Edmund. *The Rise of Theodore Roosevelt*. New York: The Modern Library 1979.

Morton, Roscoe H. *Water for New York: A Study in State Administration*. Syracuse: Syracuse University Press, 1960.

Murphy, Earl F. *Water Purity: A Study in Legal Control of Natural Resources*. Madison: University of Wisconsin Press, 1961.

New York State Board of Health. *Annual Report*, 1890–1900.

New York State Conservation Commission. *Annual Report*, 1911–1927.

New York State Conservation Commission. *Report on the Pollution of Streams*, 1923.

New York State Department of Health. *Annual Report*, 1901–1925.

New York State Fisheries, Game, and Forest Commission. *Annual Report*, 1895–1899.

New York State Forest, Fish and Game Commission. *Annual Report*, 1900–1911.

New York State. *Public Papers of the Governor*, 1899–1923.

Ravenel, Mazyck, ed. *A Half Century of Public Health: Jubilee Historical Volume of the American Public Health Association*. New York: American Public Health Association, 1921.

Sedgwick, William T. *Principles of Sanitary Science and the Public Health*. New York: Macmillan, 1902; rpt. 1905.

Stradling, David. *The Nature of New York: An Environmental History of the Empire State*. Ithaca: Cornell University Press, 2010.

Tarr, Joel A. *Retrospective Assessment of Wastewater Technology in the United States, 1800–1972*. Report to the National Science Foundation, October 1977. NTIS Accession no. PB275884.

Terrie, Philip G. *Contested Terrain: A New History of Nature and People in the Adirondacks*. Blue Mountain Lake: Adirondack Museum and Syracuse University Press, 1997.

Ward, Henry B. *Stream Pollution in New York State*. Albany: Conservation Commission, 1919.

Weidner, Charles A. *Water for a City: A History of New York City's Problem from the Beginning to the Delaware River System.* New Brunswick: Rutgers University Press, 1974.

Wesser, Robert F. *Charles Evans Hughes: Politics and Reform in New York, 1905–1910.* Ithaca: Cornell University Press, 1967.

Whipple, George C. *The Value of Pure Water.* New York: John Wiley & Sons, 1907.

Whipple, Gurth. *A History of a Half a Century of the Management of the Natural Resources in the Empire State, 1885–1935.* Albany: J. B. Lyon, 1935.

Chapter 7. April 15, 1903: Intervening for the Children

Bass, Herbert. *"I Am a Democrat": The Political Career of David Bennett Hill.* Syracuse: Syracuse University Press, 1961.

Blumberg, Dorothy. *Florence Kelley: The Making of a Social Pioneer.* New York: A. M. Kelley, 1966.

Chessman, G. Wallace. *Governor Theodore Roosevelt: The Albany Apprenticeship, 1898–1900.* Boston: Harvard University Press, 1965.

Davis, Allen F. *Spearheads for Reform: The Social Settlements and the Progressive Movement, 1890–1941.* New York: Oxford University Press, 1967.

Fairchild, Frederick R. *The Factory Legislation of the State of New York. Publications of the American Economic Association.* 3rd series, vol. 7, no. 4. New York: Macmillan, 1905.

Felt, Jeremy P. *Hostages of Fortune: Child Labor Reform in New York State.* Syracuse: Syracuse University Press, 1965.

Hindman, Hugh. *Child Labor: An American History.* Armonk, NY: M. E. Sharpe, 2002.

Hurwitz, Howard. *Theodore Roosevelt and Labor in New York State, 1880–1900.* Studies in History, Economics, and Public Law, no. 500. New York: AMS, 1968.

Kelley, Florence. *The Autobiography of Florence Kelley: Notes of Sixty Years.* Edited and with an introduction by Kathryn Kish Sklar. Chicago: Charles H. Kerr, 1986.

Lubove, Roy. *The Progressives and the Slums: Tenement House Reform in New York City, 1870–1917.* Pittsburgh: University of Pittsburgh Press, 1962.

Morris, Edmund. *The Rise of Theodore Roosevelt*. New York: Random House, 2010.

Nasaw, David. *Children of the City: At Work and Play*. New York: Oxford University Press, 1985.

New York Child Labor Legacy Project. *From Forge to Fast Food: A History of Child Labor in New York State: Vol. II, Civil War to the Present*. Albany: New York State Education Department, n.d.

Orleck, Annelise. *Common Sense and a Little Fire: Women and Working-Class Politics in the United States, 1900–1965*. Chapel Hill: University of North Carolina Press, 1995.

Scheuer, Jeffrey. *Legacy of Light: University Settlement's First Century*. New York: University Settlement, 1985.

Schneider, David M., and Albert Deutch. *The History of Public Welfare in New York State, 1867–1940*. Chicago: Patterson Smith, 1941.

Siegel, Beatrice. *Lillian Wald of Henry Street*. New York: Macmillan 1983.

Sklar, Kathryn Kish. *Florence Kelley and the Nation's Work: The Rise of Women's Political Culture, 1830–1900*. New Haven and London: Yale University Press, 1995.

Sklar, Kathryn Kish, and Beverly Wilson Palmer. *The Selected Letters of Florence Kelley, 1869–1931*. Urbana: University of Illinois Press, 2009.

Trattmer, Walter I. *Crusade for the Children: A History of the National Child Labor Committee and of Child Labor Reform in America*. Chicago: Quadrangle Books, 1970.

Online Sources

Children's Aid Society, http://www.childrensaidsociety.org/about/history/history-firsts.

Henry Street Settlement—Our History, http://www.henrystreet.org/about/history.

National Consumers League History, http://www.nclnet.org/about-ncl/history.

New York Society for the Prevention of Cruelty to Children, http://www.nyspcc.org/nyspcc/history.

The Social Welfare History Project, http://www.socialwelfarehistory.com.

Chapter 8. May 29, 1910: First in the Air

Brady, Tim, ed. *The American Aviation Experience: A History*. Carbondale: Southern Illinois University Press, 2000.

Crouch, Tom. *The Bishop's Boys: Life of Wilbur and Orville Wright.* New York: W.W. Norton, 1989.

Curtiss, Glenn, and Augustus Post. *The Curtiss Aviation Book.* New York: Frederick A. Stokes, 1912.

Eltscher, Louis R., and Edward M. Young. *Curtiss-Wright: Greatness and Decline.* New York: Twayne, 1998.

Gray, Charlotte. *Reluctant Genius: Alexander Graham Bell and the Passion for Invention.* New York: Arcade, 2006.

Grossnick, Roy A., and William J. Armstrong. *United States Naval Aviation 1910–1995.* 4th ed. Washington, DC: Naval Historical Center, Department of the Navy, 1997.Hallion, Richard P. *Taking Flight: Inventing the Aerial Age from Antiquity through the First World War.* New York: Oxford University Press, 2003.

Jakab, Peter L. *Visions of a Flying Machine: The Wright Brothers and the Process of Invention.* Washington: Smithsonian Institution Press, 1990.

Roseberry, Cecil R. *Glenn Curtiss: Pioneer of Flight.* Syracuse: Syracuse University Press, 1991.

Shulman, Seth. *Unlocking the Sky: Glenn Hammond Curtiss and the Race to Invent the Airplane.* New York: Harper Collins, 2002.

Smith, Richard K. *First Across! The U.S. Navy's Transatlantic Flight of 1919.* Annapolis: Naval Institute Press, 1986.

Trimble, William F. *Hero of the Air: Glenn Curtiss and the Birth of Naval Aviation.* Annapolis: Naval Institute Press, 2011.

Online Sources

Centennial of Naval Aviation, 1911–2011, http://www.public.navy.mil/airfor/centennial/Pages/welcome.aspx.

Glenn H. Curtiss Museum, http://www.glennhcurtissmuseum.org.

Naval History and Heritage Command, http://www.history.navy.mil.

U.S. Centennial of Flight Commission, *Centennial of Flight,* http://www.centennialofflight.gov/index.cfm.

Wright Brothers Aeroplane Company (virtual museum), http://www.wright-brothers.org/General/Museum_Entrance/Museum_Entrance.htm.

Museum

Glenn H. Curtiss Museum, Hammondsport, New York.

Chapter 9. March 25 and 29, 1911: Fires Change History

Downey, Kirsten. *The Woman behind the New Deal: The Life of Frances Perkins, FDR's Secretary of Labor and His Moral Conscience.* New York: Doubleday, 2009.

Golway, Terry. *So Others Might Live: A History of New York's Bravest—the FDNY From 1700 to the Present.* New York: Basic Books, 2002.

Greenwald, Richard A. *The Triangle Fire, the Protocols of Peace, and Industrial Democracy in Progressive Era New York.* Philadelphia: Temple University Press, 2005.

Huthmacher, J. Joseph. *Senator Robert F. Wagner and the Rise of Urban Liberalism.* New York: Atheneum, 1968.

Martin, George. *Madam Secretary: Frances Perkins.* New York: Houghton Mifflin, 1976.

Mercer, Paul, and Vicki Weiss. *The New York State Capitol and the Great Fire of 1911.* Charleston: Arcadia, 2011.

Orleck, Annelise. *Common Sense and a Little Fire: Women and Working-Class Politics in the United States, 1900–1961.* Chapel Hill: University of North Carolina Press, 1995.

Perkins, Frances. *The Roosevelt I Knew.* New York: Viking Press, 1946.

Roseberry, Cecil R. *Capitol Story.* Albany: State of New York, 1964.

Smith, Alfred E. *Up to Now: An Autobiography.* Garden City: Garden City Publishing, 1929.

Stein, Leon. *The Triangle Fire.* Ithaca: Cornell University Press, 1962.

Von Drehle, David. *Triangle: The Fire That Changed America.* New York: Grove Press, 2004.

Ward, Geoffrey C. *A First-Class Temperament: The Emergence of Franklin Roosevelt.* New York: Harper & Row, 1989.

Wesser, Robert F. *A Response to Progressivism: The Democratic Party and New York Politics, 1902–1918.* New York: New York University Press, 1986.

Online Sources

Cornell University, *Remembering the 1911 Triangle Fire*, http://www.ilr.cornell.edu/trianglefire/legacy/index.html.

Harvard University Open Collections Program, *Women Working 1800–1930*, http://ocp.hul.harvard.edu/ww/nysfic.html.

Remembering the Triangle Fire Coalition, *Triangle Fire Open Archive.*, http://rememberthetrianglefire.org/open-archive.

U.S. Department of Labor/Occupational Safety and Health Administration, *The Triangle Shirtwaist Factory Fire*, http://www.osha.gov/oas/trianglefactoryfire.html.

Chapter 10. February 14, 1924: Leading into the Information Age

Austrian, Geoffrey D. *Herman Hollerith: Forgotten Giant of Information Processing.* New York: Columbia University Press, 1982.

Beniger, James R. *The Control Revolution: Technological and Economic Origins of the Information Society.* Boston: Harvard University Press, 1986.

Buchholz, Todd G. *New Ideas from Dead CEOs: Lasting Lessons from the Corner Office.* New York: Harper Collins, 2007.

Campbell-Kelly, Martin, and William Aspray. *Computer: A History of the Information Machine.* New York: Basic Books, 2004.

Carlisle, Rodney. *Scientific American Inventions and Discoveries.* New York: Wiley, 2004.

Chandler, Alfred D., Jr. *Inventing the Electronic Century: The Epic Story of the Consumer Electronics and Computer Industries.* New York: Free Press, 2001.

Cortada, James W. *Before the Computer: IBM, NCR, Burroughs, Remington Rand, and the Industry They Created, 1865–1956.* Princeton: Princeton University Press, 1993.

Cortada, James W. *The Digital Hand Volume II: How Computers Changed the Work of American Financial, Telecommunications, Media, and Entertainment Industries.* Oxford: Oxford University Press, 2006.

Flint, Charles Ranlett. *Memories of an Active Life: Men, and Ships, and Sealing Wax.* New York: G. P. Putnam's Sons, 1923.

Gerstner, Louis V. *Who Says Elephants Can't Dance? Leading a Great Enterprise through Dramatic Change.* New York: Harper Business, 2002.

Groner, Alex. *The American Heritage History of American Business and Industry.* New York: American Heritage, 1972.

Inglis, William. *George F. Johnson and His Industrial Democracy.* New York: Huntington Press, 1935.

Maney, Kevin. *The Maverick and His Machine: Thomas Watson, Sr. and the Making of IBM.* New York: Wiley, 2004.

Pugh, Emerson W. *Building IBM: Shaping an Industry and Its Technology* (History of Computing). Boston: MIT Press, 2009.

Smith, Gerald R. *The Valley of Opportunity: A Pictorial History of the Greater Binghamton Area.* Norfolk: Donning, 1988.

Smith, Gerald R. *Partners All: A History of Broome County, New York.* Norfolk: Donning, 2006.

Sobel, Robert. *The Great Boom, 1950–2000: How a Generation of Americans Created the World's Most Prosperous Society.* New York: St. Martin's Press, 2000.

Sobel, Robert. *Thomas Watson, Sr.: IBM and the Computer Revolution.* Washington, DC: Beard Books, 2000.

Watson, Thomas J. *As a Man Thinks . . . : The Man and His Philosophy of Life as Expressed in His Editorials.* New York: IBM, 1954.

Watson, Thomas J., Jr., and Peter Petre. *Father, Son & Co.: My Life at IBM and Beyond.* New York: Bantam, 2000.

Watson, Thomas, Jr. *A Business and Its Beliefs.* New York: McGraw Hill, 2003.

Yates, JoAnne. *Control through Communication: The Rise of System in American Management.* Baltimore: Johns Hopkins University Press, 1993.

Yates, JoAnne. *Structuring the Information Age: Life Insurance and Technology in the Twentieth Century.* Studies in Industry and Society. Baltimore: Johns Hopkins University Press, 2006.

Zahavi, Gerald. *Workers, Managers, and Welfare Capitalism: The Shoemakers and Tanners of Endicott Johnson, 1890–1950.* Champaign: University of Illinois Press, 1988.

Online Sources

The Bundy Museum of History and Art (Binghamton), http://www.bundymuseum.org/site3.

Columbia University Computing History, http://www.columbia.edu/cu/computinghistory./

Early Office Museum, http://www.officemuseum.com.

IBM Archives, http://www-03.ibm.com/ibm/history/using/index.html.

Chapter 11. April 15, 1947: Breaking the Color Line

Breslin, Jimmy. *Branch Rickey.* New York: Viking, 2011.

Early, Gerald L. *A Level Playing Field: African American Athletes and the Republic of Sports.* Boston: Harvard University Press, 2011.

Frommer, Harvey. *New York City Baseball: The Last Golden Age, 1947–1957*. New York: Macmillan, 1980.

Kahn, Roger. *The Boys of Summer*. New York: Harper, 1987.

Kahn, Roger. *The Era, 1947–1957: When the Yankees, the Giants, and the Dodgers Ruled the World*. New York: Ticknor and Fields, 1993.

Kahn, Roger. *Beyond the Boys of Summer: The Very Best of Roger Kahn*. Edited by Rob Miraldi. New York: McGraw-Hill, 2005.

Long, Michael G., ed., *First-Class Citizenship: The Civil Rights Letters of Jackie Robinson*. New York: Times Books, 2007.

Lowenfish, Lee. *Branch Rickey: Baseball's Ferocious Gentleman*. Lincoln: University of Nebraska Press, 2007.

Mann, Arthur. *Branch Rickey: American in Action*. Cambridge, MA: Riverside Press, 1957.

Rampersad, Arnold. *Jackie Robinson: A Biography*. New York: Ballantine Books, 1998.

Rickey, Branch, with Robert Riger. *The American Diamond: A Documentary of the Game of Baseball*. New York: Simon & Schuster, 1965.

Robeson, Paul, Jr. *The Undiscovered Paul Robeson: Quest for Freedom, 1939–1976*. New York: Wiley, 2010.

Robinson, Jackie. *Baseball Has Done It*. Philadelphia: Lippincott, 1964.

Robinson, Jackie, and Alfred Duckett. *I Never Had It Made: The Autobiography of Jackie Robinson*. New York: Harper Perennial, 2003.

Robinson, Rachel, with Lee Daniels. *Jackie Robinson: An Intimate Portrait*. New York: Abrams, 1996.

Rowan, Carl T., with Jackie Robinson. *Wait till Next Year: The Life Story of Jackie Robinson*. New York: Random House, 1960.

Stout, Glenn. *The Dodgers: 120 Years of Dodger Baseball*. New York: Houghton Mifflin, 2004.

Tygiel, Jules. *Baseball's Great Experiment: Jackie Robinson and His Legacy*. New York: Oxford University Press, 1983.

Tygiel, Jules, ed. *The Jackie Robinson Reader: Perspectives on an American Hero*. New York: Dutton, 1997.

Willensky, Elliot. *When Brooklyn Was the World, 1920–1957*. New York: Harmony Press, 1986.

Online Sources

Jackie Robinson Day: April 15, http://mlb.mlb.com/mlb/events/jrd.

Jackie Robinson: I Am 42, http://mlb.mlb.com/iam42/index.jsp.

Movies
The Jackie Robinson Story, 1950, Dir. Alfred E. Green.
42, 2013, Dir. Brian Helgeland.

Chapter 12. June 24, 1954: A New Enterprise for Moving around New York

Abramson, Rudy. *Spanning the Century: The Life of W. Averell Harriman, 1891–1986*. New York: William Morrow, 1992.
Caro, Robert A. *The Power Broker: Robert Moses and the Fall of New York*. New York: Vintage Books, 1975.
Fein, Michael R. *Paving the Way: New York Road Building and the American State, 1880–1956*. Lawrence: University Press of Kansas, 2008.
Lewis, Tom. *Divided Highways: Building the Interstate Highways, Transforming American Life*. New York: Viking, 1997.
New York State Department of Public Works and U.S. Department of Commerce, Bureau of Public Roads. *Cooperative Highway Needs Study*. Albany: New York State Department of Public Works, 1949.
Smith, Richard Norton. *Thomas E. Dewey and His Times*. New York: Simon & Schuster, 1982.
Thomas, Lowell. *The New York Thruway Story*. Buffalo: Henry Stewart, 1955.

Archival Records
New York State Thruway Records, New York State Archives, Cultural Education Center, Albany
Speeches and News Releases, 1946–1961.
Public Relations Planning and Publication Files, 1950–1969.

Chapter 13. April 22, 1964: The World's Fair Opens in New York

Balon, Hillary, and Kenneth T. Jackson, eds. *Robert Moses and the Modern City: The Transformation of New York*. New York: W. W. Norton, 2007.
Bender, Thomas. *The Unfinished City: New York and the Metropolitan Idea*. New York: New Press, 2002.
Caro, Robert A. *The Power Broker: Robert Moses and the Fall of New York*. New York: Vintage, 1975.

Cotter, Bill, and Bill Young. *The 1964–1965 New York World's Fair.* Charleston: Arcadia, 2004.

Gelernter, David. *1939: The Lost World of the Fair.* New York: The Free Press, 1995.

Lewis, Hillary, and Stephen Fox. *The Architecture of Philip Johnson.* New York: Bullfinch Press, 2002.

Margolis, Jon. *The Last Innocent Year: America in 1964—The Beginning of the "Sixties."* New York: William Morrow, 1999.

Moses, Robert. *Public Works: A Dangerous Trade.* New York: McGraw-Hill, 1970.

Nicholson, Bruce. *Hi, Ho, Come to the Fair: Tales of the New York World's Fair of 1964–1965.* Huntington Beach: Pelagian Press, 1989.

Official Guide: New York World's Fair, 1964–1965. New York: Time-Life Books, 1964.

Queens Museum, ed. *Remembering the Future: The New York World's Fair from 1939 to 1964.* New York: Rizzoli, 1989.

Rydell, Robert W., John Findley, and Kimberly Pelle. *Fair America: World's Fairs in the United States.* Washington: Smithsonian Institution, 2000.

Samuel, Lawrence R. *The End of the Innocence: The 1964–1965 New York World's Fair.* Syracuse: Syracuse University Press, 2007.

Schultz, Franz. *Philip Johnson: Life and Work.* New York: Alfred A. Knopf, 1994.

Schwartz, Joel. *The New York Approach: Robert Moses, Urban Liberals, and Redevelopment of the Inner City.* Columbus: Ohio State University Press, 1993.

Singh, Susan. *Complexities in Conservation of a Temporary Post-War Structure: The Case of Philip Johnson's New York State Pavilion at the New York World's Fair.* Philadelphia: University of Pennsylvania Graduate Program in Historic Preservation, 2004.

Online Sources

Flushing Meadows-Corona Park World's Fair Association, http://www.theparkwatchdog.org/

The New York World's Fair, http://www.nywf64.com.

New York 1964 World's Fair, http://www.westland.net/ny64fair.

The Pavilion: Philip Johnson's New York State Pavilion Design. http://www.conlab.org/acl/thereallybigmap/exhibit/design.html.

Robert Moses and the Modern City, http://www.learn.columbia.edu/moses.

Reviving the New York State Pavilion, http://www.newyorkstatepavilion. org/revivenewyorkstate.pdf.

Chapter 14. August 2, 1978: Environmental Crisis and Citizen Activism

Berton, Pierre. *Niagara: A History of the Falls.* Albany: State University of New York Press, 2009.

Blum, Elizabeth D. *Love Canal Revisited: Race, Class and Gender in Environmental Activism.* Lawrence: University Press of Kansas, 2008.

Brown, Michael H. *Laying Waste: The Poisoning of America by Toxic Chemicals.* New York: Washington Square, 1981.

Davies, Kate. *The Rise of the U.S. Environmental Health Movement.* Lanham, MD: Rowman & Littlefield, 2013.

Fletcher, Thomas. *From Love Canal to Environmental Justice: The Politics of Hazardous Waste on the Canada-U.S. Border.* Peterborough, ON: Broadview Press, 2003.

Gibbs, Lois Marie. *Love Canal: My Story.* Albany: State University of New York Press, 1981.

Gibbs, Lois Marie. *Dying from Dioxin: A Citizen's Guide to Reclaiming Our Health and Rebuilding Democracy.* Boston: South End Press, 1995.

Gibbs, Lois Marie. *Love Canal: The Story Continues.* Gabriola Island, BC: New Society, 1998.

Gibbs, Lois Marie. *Love Canal and the Birth of the Environmental Health Movement.* Washington, DC: Island Press, 2011.

Hernan, Robert E. *This Borrowed Earth: Lessons from the Fifteen Worst Environmental Disasters around the World.* New York: Palgrave Macmillan 2012.

Layzer, Judith A. *The Environmental Case: Translating Values into Policy.* 2nd edition. New York: CQ Press, 2005.

Levine, Adeline G. *Love Canal: Science, Politics, and People.* Lexington, MA: Lexington Books, 1982.

Mazur, Allan. *A Hazardous Inquiry: The* Rashomon *Effect at Love Canal.* Boston: Harvard University Press, 1998.

New York State Department of Health. *Love Canal: Public Health Time Bomb—A Special Report to the Governor and the Legislature.*

Albany: New York State Department of Health, September 1978. http://www.health.ny.gov/environmental/investigations/love_canal/lctimbmb.pdf.

New York State Department of Health. *Love Canal: A Special Report to the Governor and Legislature.* Albany: New York State Department of Health, 1981, http://www.health.ny.gov/environmental/investigations/love_canal/lcreport.htm.New York State Department of Health. *Love Canal Emergency Declaration Area—Decision on Habitability.* Albany: New York State Department of Health, 1988, http://www.health.ny.gov/environmental/investigations/love_canal/lcdec88.pdf

Reed, Jennifer. *Love Canal.* Philadelphia: Chelsea House, 1982.

Shabecoff, Philip. *A Fierce Green Fire: The American Environmental Movement.* Washington, DC: Island Press, 2003.

Strand, Ginger. *Inventing Niagara: Beauty, Power and Lies.* New York: Simon & Schuster, 2009.

Thomas, Robert E. *Salt & Water, Power & People: A Short History of Hooker Electrochemical Company.* Niagara Falls: Hooker Chemical Company, 1955.

Vig, Norman J., and Michael E. Kraft. *Environmental Policy: New Directions for the Twenty-First Century.* 8th ed. New York: CQ Press, 2012.

Online Sources

Boston University School of Public Health, *Lessons from Love Canal: A Public Health Resource,* http://www.bu.edu/lovecanal/main.html.

Lois Gibbs, *Love Canal,* http://turbulence.org/Works.superfund/video.html.

Love Canal Collection, SUNY Buffalo Archives, http://library.buffalo.edu/specialcollections/lovecanal.

New York State Department of Health, Love Canal Follow-Up Health Study, http://www.health.ny.gov/environmental/investigations/love_canal.

United States Environmental Protection Agency, Love Canal—Press Releases and Articles, http://www.epa.gov/history/topics/lovecanal.

Movies

ABC News, *The Killing Ground,* 1979.

Lois Gibbs: The Love Canal Story, 1982, Dir. Glenn Jordan.

Chapter 15. September 11, 2001: New York's Resilience

Dwyer, Jim, and Kevin Flynn. *102 Minutes: The Untold Story of the Fight to Survive Inside the Twin Towers*. 2nd ed. New York: Times Books, 2011.

Fink, Mitchell, and Lois Mathias. *Never Forget: An Oral History of September 11, 2001*. New York: William Morrow, 2002.

Golway, Terry. *So Others Might Live: A History of New York's Bravest— The FDNY from 1700 to the Present*. New York: Basic Books, 2002.

Giuliani, Rudolph W. *Leadership*. New York: Hyperion, 2002.

Halberstam, David. *Firehouse*. New York: Hyperion, 2002.

Kean, Thomas H., and Lee H. Hamilton, *Without Precedent: The Inside Story of the 9/11 Commission*. New York: Alfred A. Knopf, 2006.

Luft, Benjamin. *We're Not Leaving: 9/11 Responders Tell Their Stories of Courage, Sacrifice and Renewal*. New York: Greenpoint Press, 2011.

Merrill, Will G. *9/11 Ordinary People: Extraordinary Heroes: NYC—The First Battle in the War against Terror!* New York: Create Space, 2011.

Murphy, Dean E. *September 11: An Oral History*. New York: Doubleday, 2002.

Picciotto, Richard, with Daniel Paisner. *Last Man Down: A Firefighter's Story of Survival and Escape from the World Trade Center*. New York: Berkley Books, 2002.

Salka, John. *First In, Last Out: Leadership Lessons from the New York Fire Department*. New York: Portfolio, 2004.

Smith, Dennis. *Report from Ground Zero*. New York: Viking, 2002.

Von Essen, Thomas, with Matt Murray. *Strong of Heart: Life and Death in the Fire Department of New York*. New York: Regan Books, 2002.

Online Sources

New York Times, The September 11 Records, August 12, 2005, http://graphics8.nytimes.com/packages/html/nyregion/20050812_WTC_GRAPHIC/met_WTC_histories_full_01.html

9/11 Commission, http://www.9-11commission.gov/report/index.htm.

Center for History and the New Media and American Social History Project/Center for Media and Learning, *The September 11 Digital Archive*, http://911digitalarchive.org/index.php.

Long Island World Trade Center Program, *Remembering 9-11: An Oral History of Responders to the WTC Attack*, http://www.911

respondersremember.org/index.php?option=com_content&view=art
icle&id=86&Itemid=1.

New York City Fire Department, http://www.nyc.gov/html/fdny/html/
home2.shtml.

New York City Fire Museum, http://www.nycfiremuseum.org.

The Unofficial Home Page of FDNY, http://www.nyfd.com.

About the Author

Dr. Bruce W. Dearstyne holds a BA in history from Hartwick College and a PhD in history from Syracuse University. He has taught New York State history at the University at Albany, State University of New York; State University of New York at Potsdam; and Russell Sage College. He is the author of *Railroads and Railroad Regulation in New York State, 1903–1913* (1986) and coauthor of *New York: Yesterday, Today, and Tomorrow* (1990). He has also written dozens of articles on history, archives, libraries, and related topics. He served on the staff of the Office of State History, 1973 to 1976, and was a program director at the State Archives, 1976 to 1997. Dearstyne was an associate professor at the College of Information Studies, University of Maryland, 1997 to 2000; a professor, 2000 to 2005; and he continues to serve there as an adjunct professor. He also directed the university's joint HiLS (History/Library Science) graduate program, 1997 to 2005. He was the guest editor and writer of two articles in a special issue of the journal *The Public Historian*, August 2011, "Strengthening the Management of State History: Issues, Perspectives and Insights from New York." He also published more than forty articles on New York State history in the Sunday "Perspective" section of the Albany *Times Union*, 2009 to 2014.

INDEX

Note: Italics indicate illustrations

New York State Pavilion (*continued*)
270–271; Nelson Rockefeller
dedication speech, 261–262, 270–271
New York State Senate, 10–13, 19, 181,
188
New York State Teachers' Association,
73
New York State Thruway: Authority,
254–258; connectors 257; cost, 256;
Dewey, Thomas E., *237*, 237–247,
250–258; economic growth and, 240,
242–243, 256; financing of, 244–249,
255–257; geography, 247–250;
highway politics and, 254–258;
history of, 237–241; Interstate
Highway System incorporation,
257–258; opening ceremonies, *237*,
237, 239–240; politics of, 242–247;
road-building, 243–250; Tallamy,
Bertram, 243–247, 249–254, 256–
257; Tappan Zee Bridge, 250–256;
vision, 241–242
The New York Thruway Story
(Thomas), 257, 271
New York World's Fair (1939–40),
204, 259–260, 263–264, 272–273,
275–276
New York World's Fair (1964–65):
architectural policy, 265–270;
attendance, 264–267, 276; Civil
Rights demonstrations, 261–262,
265; finances, 265, 268; history of,
259–262; impact, 276–279; Moses,
Robert, 262–269, 271–273, 277–279;
New York State Pavilion, *259*, 261,
269–270, 274; pavilions, 270–276;
planning, 262–269; promotion of,
267–269, 274, 276; scientific and
technological innovations, 260–261,
266, 272
New York Yankees, 226, 230–231, 305,
321
Newman, Pauline, 133, 182
Niagara Falls, 281–283, 285–290, 292–
296, 298. *See also* Love Canal

Niagara Power and Development
Company, 286
9/11 attacks. *See* Fire Department,
City of New York (FDNY); World
Trade Center
Nyack: New York State Thruway and,
250–251, 255

O'Gorman, James A., 189
O'Malley, Walter, 232
Odell, Benjamin B., 115, 131, 144–145,
147–148
Oswego, 2, 28, 30, 90; water supply,
124
Outlook, 127, 144, 180

Paigen, Beverly, 296–297, 299
Palisades Interstate Park, 111
Paltsits, Victor Hugo, 189–191
Parkman, Francis, 38
Peck, Charles, 137
Perkins, Frances, 174, 188, 192–193;
factory laws and, 143, 180–184
Pershing, John J., 170
Peterboro, 66, 95, 107
Pfeifer, Joseph, 303, 316–319
Phillips, Wendell, 78–79
Picciotto, Richard, 308, 311
The Pioneers (Cooper), 24
Platt, Thomas Collier, 111, 139,
144–145
Pollution: identifying, 112–114;
Mohansic State Hospital Project,
125–129; NYS Conservation
Commission, 114, 121–122, 129–
130; politics and, 109–112, 129–130;
public health policy, 114–122;
Rochester Sewage Disposal Project,
117, 122–125. *See also* Love Canal;
Water pollution; sewage discharge,
116, 122–125
Porter, Eugene, 117, 126
*Power Broker: Robert Moses and
the Fall of New York (Caro)*, 263,
277–278

3 1170 00987 9044